Nietzsche's Enlightenment

Nietzsche's Enlightenment

The Free-Spirit Trilogy of the Middle Period

PAUL FRANCO

The University of Chicago Press
Chicago and London

Paul Franco is professor of government at Bowdoin College and the author of *Michael Oakeshott: An Introduction, Hegel's Philosophy of Freedom,* and *The Political Philosophy of Michael Oakeshott.*

The University of Chicago Press, Chicago 60637
The University of Chicago Press, Ltd., London
© 2011 by Paul Franco
All rights reserved. Published 2011.
Printed in the United States of America

20 19 18 17 16 15 14 13 12 11   1 2 3 4 5

ISBN-13: 978-0-226-25981-9 (cloth)
ISBN-10: 0-226-25981-1 (cloth)

Library of Congress Cataloging-in-Publication Data

Franco, Paul, 1956–
  Nietzsche's enlightenment : the free-spirit trilogy of the middle period /
Paul Franco.
       p.   cm.
  Includes bibliographical references and index.
  ISBN-13: 978-0-226-25981-9 (hardcover : alk. paper)
  ISBN-10: 0-226-25981-1 (hardcover : alk. paper) 1. Nietzsche, Friedrich
  Wilhelm, 1844–1900. 2. Nietzsche, Friedrich Wilhelm, 1844–1900.
  Menschliches, allzumenschliches. 3. Nietzsche, Friedrich Wilhelm, 1844–
  1900. Morgenröthe. 4. Nietzsche, Friedrich Wilhelm, 1844–1990. Fröhliche
  Wissenschaft. 5. Ethics. 6. Philosophy.   I. Title.
  B3317.F69 2011
  193—dc22

                                                        2010049973

For Joe

CONTENTS

On the back cover of the 1882 edition of *The Gay Science*, Nietzsche wrote: "This book marks the conclusion of a series of writings by FRIEDRICH NIETZSCHE whose common goal is to erect *a new image and ideal of the free spirit*." He then went on to list the three books that belong to this series: *Human, All too Human* (along with its two supplements, *Mixed Opinions and Aphorisms* and *The Wanderer and His Shadow*), *Daybreak: Thoughts on the Prejudices of Morality*, and *The Gay Science*. This comment clearly indicates that Nietzsche thought of these books as belonging together and as being unified by a common theme; it perhaps even justifies my referring to them as a "trilogy." At any rate, it is these three books from Nietzsche's so-called middle period that I subject to careful examination in this study.

Why study Nietzsche's middle works, which are so much less well known than the great works of Nietzsche's maturity—*Zarathustra, Beyond Good and Evil,* and the *Genealogy of Morals*—and even to some extent his earlier works—*The Birth of Tragedy* and *Untimely Meditations*? I suppose the obvious reason is precisely that they are less well known, especially *Human, All too Human* and *Daybreak*. This is not to say that references to various aphorisms in these works do not abound in the secondary literature; but there has been relatively little systematic study of these works apart from how they either anticipate or do not anticipate Nietzsche's later doctrines. A signal exception to this general pattern is Ruth Abbey's pioneering study, *Nietzsche's Middle Period*, which traces a number of individual themes—morality, psychology, vanity, pity, women, and the relations between the sexes—throughout the middle works.[1] Also noteworthy are various scholarly efforts to examine these works for what they have to say about the influence of other writers on Nietzsche—for example, the French moralists, certain neo-Kantian

7

philosophers, and a host of Darwinian historians of morality—and Nietzsche's critical engagement with them.[2]

It is not merely the desire to plug a scholarly hole, however, that motivates my study of Nietzsche's middle works. More important, these works disclose a Nietzsche who is different from the popular image of him and even from the Nietzsche described in much of the secondary literature: a rational Nietzsche, a Nietzsche who is a friend of the Enlightenment and of science, a Nietzsche who preaches modesty and moderation instead of passionate excess and Dionysian frenzy.[3] It is this appealing image of the thinker found in the middle works that partly accounts for the recent scholarly attention paid to them, not only in Abbey's book but also in the discussions of various analytic writers who are especially attracted to the idea of a Nietzsche who embraces reason and science.[4]

It is not, of course, enough to characterize Nietzsche's middle period in terms of an undifferentiated commitment to reason, science, the Enlightenment, or even more misleadingly "positivism," for with respect to each of these notions Nietzsche imparts his own distinctive meaning. In order to uncover and flesh out that meaning, it is necessary to go through each of the individual works that comprise the free-spirit trilogy and subject it to careful analysis. Before embarking on that task, I provide a biographical prologue that sketches Nietzsche's early attachment to and eventual disillusionment with the romantic theory of culture that he took from his reading of Schopenhauer and his formative friendship with Wagner. According to this theory, Socratic rationalism and Enlightenment science had led to the fragmentation and spiritual impoverishment of modern culture, and only art and myth could restore it to wholeness. The Bayreuth Festival of 1876 was in many ways the consummate expression of this romantic theory of culture, and Nietzsche's horrified flight from the festival marked the beginning of his career as a free spirit.

The problem of modern culture provides the focus of my analysis of *Human, All too Human* in chapter 1. In this first work of the free-spirit trilogy, Nietzsche repudiates his early Wagner- and Schopenhauer-influenced romanticism and aligns himself for the first time with the "manly" scientific spirit of the Enlightenment. What distinguishes this sudden turn to science from any simple positivism, however, is that it remains embedded in the concern with cultural unity and wholeness that had been the pervasive preoccupation of Nietzsche's earlier writings. But whereas in those earlier writings Nietzsche looked to art and myth to resolve the aimlessness and fragmentation of modern culture, in *Human, All too Human* he explores the possibility of erecting a genuine culture on knowledge. The knowledge-seeking free spirit replaces the artist-priest as the linchpin of cultural renewal.

As much as it departs from his earlier outlook, *Human, All too Human* remains a transitional work, born of Nietzsche's struggle against Wagner's romantic theory of culture. This accounts for some of the book's peculiar features—its hostility to violent passion, for example, and its un-Dionysian emphasis on repose, moderation, and contemplation. The second work of Nietzsche's free-spirit trilogy, *Daybreak*, on the other hand, marks a complete breakthrough. In this work, which I take up in chapter 2, morality moves to the center of Nietzsche's critical attention. Though he had dealt with morality in *Human, All too Human*, his analysis there was embedded in his larger critique of romanticism, focusing on the way morality falsely blackens the world and thereby gives rise to the intoxicating remedies provided by religion and art. In *Daybreak*, he shifts his critical attention away from romanticism to the Darwinian utilitarianism of his friend Paul Rée and especially Herbert Spencer. Such utilitarianism, he argues, not only fails to grasp the irrational origins of morality, it also threatens to reduce humanity to bland mediocrity or sand, "small, soft, round, unending sand" (*D* 174). This shift in critical focus is also reflected in Nietzsche's new conception of the very activity that defines his ideal of the free spirit. Whereas in *Human, All too Human* he emphasized the role of knowledge in calming or moderating the passions, in *Daybreak* he speaks of the free-spirited quest for knowledge as itself a passion.

In the third work of the free-spirit trilogy, *The Gay Science*, which I examine in chapter 3, Nietzsche provides his deepest reflections on science and the possibility of making knowledge a life-enhancing instead of a life-desolating power. This task of "incorporating" knowledge—as Nietzsche now refers to it—involves a new appreciation of art and its role in preventing science from becoming mired in morality and asceticism. It is by joining with art and adopting its good will toward appearance that science ultimately becomes "gay" or "joyful" (*fröhliche*). Such a union of art and science is at the heart of what is known as Nietzsche's perspectivism, and it raises all the paradoxes and problems that are associated with the latter doctrine. While my analysis of *The Gay Science* does not necessarily resolve all these paradoxes and problems, it does aim to show that Nietzsche's claim that our knowledge relates only to a constructed, simplified, and even falsified world does not deprive us of the ability to make meaningful distinctions between better and worse, or more and less honest, interpretations.

The 1882 edition of *The Gay Science* famously concludes with the announcement of Nietzsche's most enigmatic doctrine, the eternal recurrence.

The placement of this announcement inevitably raises the question of the relationship between the rational or scientific Nietzsche of the middle works and the more familiar, prophetic Nietzsche of the later ones, the Nietzsche who not only teaches the eternal recurrence but also proclaims the *Übermensch*, the will to power, the revaluation of all values, and, most ominously, "great politics." Here the comment on the back cover of *The Gay Science* once again becomes relevant, for it points not only to the unity of the middle works but also to the fact that a period in Nietzsche's philosophical development—the period devoted to the ideal of the free-spirited quest for knowledge—has come to an end. Does this imply that Nietzsche abandons his commitment to reason, science, and moderation in his later works? Does it suggest that this commitment was merely an aberration, an anomaly, perhaps a reaction to his youthful flirtation with Wagnerian romanticism, as some scholars have claimed?[5] Finally, did Nietzsche have good reasons for leaving his ideal of the knowledge-seeking free spirit behind and advancing to a different, perhaps more coherent or compelling, certainly more controversial, ideal? And if so, why ultimately should we care about the middle works?

To answer these questions, I undertake in chapter 4 a synoptic analysis of Nietzsche's later works with a view to determining what has changed in his outlook and, so far as is possible, why. Without anticipating the whole of my argument, let me state preliminarily my main conclusions on the questions just posed. I do not think that the skeptical, rationalistic position Nietzsche adopts in his middle works is either inconsistent or anomalous with respect to his later outlook. The commitment to reason, intellectual honesty, and science—in a word, freedom of spirit—remains absolutely vital to Nietzsche's mature philosophy. This is not to say, however, that Nietzsche's position does not develop in significant ways as he moves from the middle to the later works. I will argue that his mature philosophy addresses certain difficulties connected with the original free-spirit ideal—again, in a word, its asceticism—and that it in no way marks a dogmatic hardening or narrowing of his philosophical outlook, as Abbey and other scholars sympathetic to the middle works have maintained.[6] Indeed, the modification effected by the later works actually begins in the middle period itself and is epitomized by the phrase that Nietzsche used as the title for the third and final work from that period: *fröhliche Wissenschaft*, gay science.

Returning to the middle works, the interpretation of which constitutes the bulk of this study and also its most important contribution, let me say a little more about the methodological principles that govern my approach. As is clear from the outline above, I devote one chapter to each of the three works from the middle period, treating each work as much as possible as a coherent whole and not merely as a collection of monadic aphorisms. Even at this late date, the interpretation of Nietzsche's writings often suffers from inattention to the context of and interrelationships between the aphorisms that make up his books—"*Gedanken-Kette*," or "chains of thought," he tellingly refers to them (*SB* 6:223; *KSA* 11:37 [5])—and from the refusal to treat his books *as* books or integral wholes. This is surprising, given how careful and self-conscious a writer Nietzsche was. In what follows, I have taken to heart the advice he gives to readers of his books in the Preface to *Daybreak*:

> I just as much as my book, are friends of the *lento*. It is not for nothing that I have been a philologist, perhaps I am one still, that is to say, a teacher of slow reading:—in the end I also write slowly. Nowadays it is not only my habit, it is also to my taste—a malicious taste, perhaps?—no longer to write anything which does not reduce to despair every sort of man who is "in a hurry." For philology is that venerable art which demands of its votaries one thing above all: to go aside, to take time, to become still, to become slow. . . . But for precisely this reason it is more necessary than ever today . . . in the midst of an age of "work," that is to say, of hurry, of indecent and perspiring haste, which wants to "get everything done" at once, including every old or new book:—this art does not so easily get anything done, it teaches to read *well*, that is to say, to read slowly, deeply, looking cautiously before and aft, with reservations, with doors left open, with delicate eyes and fingers. . . . My patient friends, this book desires for itself only perfect readers and philologists: *learn* to read me well!— (*D* Preface 5)

The methodological determination to read Nietzsche's books as integral or coherent wholes and not merely as collections of isolated fragments is not, of course, uncontroversial. A whole school of interpretation, French and deconstructionist, has dedicated itself to showing the impossibility of such "totalistic" readings of Nietzsche's aphoristic texts. Sarah Kofman speaks for this school when she writes that the aphoristic form in Nietzsche "destroys the traditional categories of the book as a closed totality containing a definitive meaning, the author's; in such a way it deconstructs the idea of the author as master of the meaning of the work and immortalizing himself through it. The aphorism, by its discontinuous character, disseminates meaning and appeals to the pluralism of interpretations and their renewal: only movement is immortal."[7] Without denying that the attention paid to style and literary form in Nietzsche's texts by writers like Kofman, Deleuze, Derrida, and Blondel can often be illuminating, their exaggerated claims against any sort of inherent meaning in texts and on behalf of the endless play of perspectives lead to a kind of interpretive nihilism that makes it impossible for us to learn anything from Nietzsche, much less be changed by him. As I hope to show concretely in what follows, it is perfectly possible to be attentive to the peculiar and polysemous form of Nietzsche's writing without succumbing to the bow-unbending "hypothesis that the totality of Nietzsche's text, in some monstrous way, might well be of the type 'I have forgotten my umbrella.'"[8]

Because there are genuine difficulties involved in deciphering the highly aphoristic works of the middle period, I have drawn liberally from Nietzsche's notebooks, or *Nachlass*, to help "fix" his meaning. This, of course, stirs up an ancient controversy over the use of such unpublished material. The controversy has mainly swirled around the notes collected in *The Will to Power* and the use made of them by interpreters such as Heidegger. My own use of the notes from the *Nachlass*, however, has nothing to do with Heidegger's claim that they contain Nietzsche's authentic philosophy. Rather, it is connected in the first place with the very writerly qualities to which I have just alluded. Precisely because Nietzsche is such a consummate and self-conscious writer, he seeks to surprise, perplex, and provoke his reader. This often leads to the concealment of his meaning, which the notes from the *Nachlass* help to mitigate. In addition, the notes provide crucial evidence about what Nietzsche is reading at any given time and with whom he is engaging. Finally, for any study that is concerned with tracing the development of Nietzsche's thought, as this one is, the notes shed important light on when certain ideas arise or shifts in Nietzsche's thinking take place. None of this suggests that the notes can take the place of a careful reading of the published texts or serve as anything more than a supplement or aid to such a reading.

After subjecting Nietzsche's middle works to the careful, "philological" reading outlined above, one thing becomes quite clear: these works are not nearly as unified or univocal as Nietzsche's comment on the back of *The Gay Science* suggests. Nietzsche's thought undergoes tremendous development over the course of the middle period, from his repudiation of Wagner, Schopenhauer, and romanticism in *Human, All too Human* to his questioning of the ascetic aspects of the free-spirited quest for knowledge in *The Gay Science*. Indeed, what makes the middle works so fascinating is that they allow us to observe Nietzsche working through the implications of his rejection of romanticism and his adoption of scientific skepticism up to the point where he arrives at his mature philosophical position. It is during the middle period that Nietzsche truly becomes Nietzsche. All of this means that we must remain attentive to the subtle differences and shifts of emphasis between the individual works that belong to the middle period. By doing so, we may hope to get a better handle on why Nietzsche ends up philosophically where he does.[9]

As usual, I have accrued many debts over the course of writing this book. The Earhart Foundation, Bowdoin College, and the Fletcher Family Fund generously provided grants to support the research and writing of the book. More generally, Bowdoin has provided me with the ideal environment in which to grow as a scholar and teacher. My colleagues in the government department and the college as a whole have been wonderfully stimulating and helpful. The students in my Nietzsche seminars have been amazingly generous with their insights and, more important, their questions. Three students who did excellent honors projects on Nietzsche with me deserve special thanks: Matt Polazzo, Mark Hendrickson, and Ben Stern. I also want to thank my editor at Chicago, John Tryneski, for his energetic support of the book. And I want to thank the anonymous reviewers of the manuscript for their incredibly helpful comments and suggestions. Finally, I want to dedicate this book to my brother Joe, early roommate and oldest friend, who has borne some heavy responsibilities this past year with wisdom and grace.

ABBREVIATIONS

References to Nietzsche's works appear with the following abbreviations. I have generally relied on the English translations by either Walter Kaufmann or R. J. Hollingdale, though in a number of instances I have modified the translations slightly. For Nietzsche's notebooks and correspondence, I have generally used my own translations of the German text in the *Kritische Studienausgabe*. References are to aphorism or section number, unless otherwise noted.

A   *The Antichrist* (with *Twilight of the Idols*). Translated by R. J. Hollingdale. Harmondsworth: Penguin, 1968.

AOM   *Assorted Opinions and Maxims* (in *Human, All too Human*). Translated by R. J. Hollingdale. Cambridge: Cambridge University Press, 1986.

BGE   *Beyond Good and Evil*. Translated by Walter Kaufmann. New York: Vintage, 1966.

BT   *The Birth of Tragedy*. Translated by Walter Kaufmann. New York: Vintage, 1967.

D   *Daybreak: Thoughts on the Prejudices of Morality*. Translated by R. J. Hollingdale. Cambridge: Cambridge University Press, 1997.

DS   "David Strauss: The Confessor and the Writer" (in *Untimely Meditations*). Translated by R. J. Hollingdale. Cambridge: Cambridge University Press, 1983.

EH   *Ecce Homo* (with *On the Genealogy of Morals*). Translated by Walter Kaufmann. New York: Vintage, 1967.

GM   *On the Genealogy of Morals* (with *Ecce Homo*). Translated by Walter Kaufmann and R. J. Hollingdale. New York: Vintage, 1967.

GS   *The Gay Science*. Translated by Walter Kaufmann. New York: Vintage, 1974.

HH   *Human, All too Human.* Translated by R. J. Hollingdale. Cambridge: Cambridge University Press, 1986.

KSA   *Sämtliche Werke: Kritische Studienausgabe in 15 Bänden.* Edited by Giorgio Colli and Mazzino Montinari. Berlin: Walter de Gruyter, 1980. *Nachlass* cited by volume, notebook, and note number in brackets.

RWB   "Richard Wagner in Bayreuth" (in *Untimely Meditations*). Translated by R. J. Hollingdale. Cambridge: Cambridge University Press, 1983.

SB   *Sämtliche Briefe: Kritische Studienausgabe.* Edited by Giorgio Colli and Mazzino Montinari. Berlin: Walter de Gruyter, 1986. Cited by volume and page number.

SE   "Schopenhauer as Educator" (in *Untimely Meditations*). Translated by R. J. Hollingdale. Cambridge: Cambridge University Press, 1983.

TI   *Twilight of the Idols* (with *The Antichrist*). Translated by R. J. Hollingdale. Harmondsworth: Penguin, 1968.

UDH   "On the Uses and Disadvantages of History for Life" (in *Untimely Meditations*). Translated by R. J. Hollingdale. Cambridge: Cambridge University Press, 1983.

UM   *Untimely Meditations.* Translated by R. J. Hollingdale. Cambridge: Cambridge University Press, 1983.

WP   *The Will to Power.* Translated by Walter Kaufmann. New York: Vintage, 1968.

WS   *The Wanderer and His Shadow* (in *Human, All too Human*). Translated by R. J. Hollingdale. Cambridge: Cambridge University Press, 1986.

Z   *Thus Spoke Zarathustra.* Translated by Walter Kaufmann. Harmondsworth: Penguin, 1966.

Birth of a Free Spirit

Grinning from behind my first period is the face of Jesuitism: I mean the conscious holding on to illusion and the forcible incorporation of that illusion as the basis of culture.

—Nietzsche, Note from the fall of 1883 (*KSA* 10:16 [23])

In August 1876, ill and disillusioned with the events surrounding the first Bayreuth Festival, Friedrich Nietzsche fled to the resort of Klingenbrunn in the Bohemian Forest and began to write the notes that eventually formed the first part of *Human, All too Human*. This book would mark Nietzsche's decisive break with his earlier philosophy and with the two figures who exercised the greatest influence on it, Arthur Schopenhauer and Richard Wagner. In *Ecce Homo*, Nietzsche called the book "the monument of a crisis" (*EH* 3.HH.1). The break with Wagner that lay at the heart of this crisis had, of course, been brewing for some years prior to the writing of *Human, All too Human*, going back at least as far as 1874. Nietzsche's notebooks from that year already contain numerous critical observations on Wagner as an actor whose art is primarily concerned with producing striking effects. And in August 1874, Nietzsche deliberately provoked the Master by leaving the score of Brahms's *Triumphlied* prominently displayed on the piano at Wahnfried. But it was only with the publication of *Human, All too Human* in 1878 that the cord was definitively cut and Nietzsche declared his independence from Wagner, Schopenhauerian pessimism, and all forms of romanticism in one fell swoop.[1]

What had brought Nietzsche to this critical turning point? To answer this question, it is necessary to unravel his complicated relationship to Wagner and Schopenhauer in the years leading up to the Bayreuth Festival of 1876. Nietzsche's relationship to Wagner was, of course, as he himself frequently acknowledged, the most important relationship of his life. In *Ecce Homo*, he recalls his visits as a young professor to the Wagners' home at Tribschen between 1869 and 1872 as "the first deep breath of my life," and he refers to Wagner as "the great benefactor of my life" (*EH* 3.HH.5–6). It was during his conversations with Wagner at Tribschen that Nietzsche's ideas for *The Birth of Tragedy* (published in 1872) first took shape, and it was to Wagner that Nietzsche ultimately dedicated his first book. Nietzsche was also deeply involved in the planning and promotion of the Bayreuth Festival. He was one among the small circle of friends present at the laying of the foundation stone in May 1872, and his essay "Richard Wagner in Bayreuth," which appeared in July 1876, was considered to be one of the most eloquent testaments of the cultural significance of the festival. Long after he had broken with him, Nietzsche could still write of Wagner that, "everything considered, [he] has so far been the only one, or at least the first, who has had some sense of what I'm up to" (*SB* 7:205).[2]

There were many common interests that brought Nietzsche and Wagner together in the early 1870s—music, Schopenhauer's pessimistic philosophy, the Greeks—but the unifying thread running through these interests was a shared preoccupation with the problem of contemporary German culture. In Wagner's case, this was what the Bayreuth Festival was all about. Against the individualism, materialism, and unheroic secularity of the age, the performance of the Ring Cycle at the festival was meant to unify German culture by reanimating its mythical underpinnings and restoring to life a sense of sacred awe. As the sea of faith receded in the nineteenth century—a condition Nietzsche would later theorize under the rubric of "nihilism"—art needed to step in and take over the cultural role that religion used to play. Wagner explicitly endorses this understanding of the religious function of art in his 1880 essay "Religion and Art": "One might say that where religion becomes artificial, it is reserved for art to save the spirit of religion by recognizing the figurative value of mythic symbols which the former would have us believe in their literal sense, and revealing their deep and hidden truth through an ideal presentation."[3]

Nietzsche makes a similar diagnosis of "the fundamental malady of modern culture" in *The Birth of Tragedy*. He, too, sees the loss of religion and myth, the "tremendous secularization" of the modern age, as destructive of cultural wholeness and vitality. "[W]ithout myth," he writes, "every culture loses the healthy natural power of its creativity: only a horizon defined by myths completes and unifies a whole cultural movement." More distinctively, he attributes the destruction of religious myth to Socratism, science, and especially the modern historical sense. Because of its "tremendous historical need," modern culture "has no fixed and sacred primordial site but is doomed to exhaust all possibilities and to nourish itself wretchedly on all other cultures." Only through art, specifically music, can religious myth be rejuvenated and modern culture restored to health. This is what happened in ancient Greece as a result of Dionysian music, and Nietzsche believes it can happen again in modern Germany through the influence of Wagnerian music (*BT* 10, 18, 23).

Nietzsche's privileging of art and religion over science in *The Birth of Tragedy* was, of course, influenced not only by Wagner but by the thinker they both revered: Schopenhauer. In *The World as Will and Representation* (1819/1844), Schopenhauer had shown how scientific knowledge, governed by the principle of sufficient reason, can only grasp the phenomenal world of appearances and does not reach to the world in itself, the world of the groundless will. In *The Birth of Tragedy*, Nietzsche credits Schopenhauer, along with Kant, with taking the momentous step of using science to reveal the limits of science. Kant and Schopenhauer, he writes, "have contrived . . . to use the paraphernalia of science itself to point out the limits and the relativity of knowledge generally, and thus to deny decisively the claim of science to universal validity and universal aims." This critique of scientific knowledge ultimately leads to "tragic resignation and the destitute need for art"; it paves the way for a "tragic culture" in which "wisdom takes the place of science as the highest end." Nietzsche sums up this movement from the self-critique of science to art in the figure of "the Socrates who practices music" (*BT* 15, 18).

Schopenhauer provided Nietzsche and Wagner, however, not merely with a negative critique of the pretensions of science; he also supplied them with a positive justification of the claims of art and religion to superior truth. Again in *The World as Will and Representation*, Schopenhauer argued that, insofar as scientific knowledge is subject to the principle of sufficient reason, grasping objects in relation to space, time, and causality, it remains the servant of the will. It is only in aesthetic contemplation that "knowledge tears itself free from the service of the will" and achieves genuine objectivity. It is only in art, "the work of genius," that "we lose ourselves entirely in the object" and become a "pure, will-less subject of knowledge."[4] For Wagner's and Nietzsche's purposes, it was of the utmost significance that, among the various forms of art, Schopenhauer attributed the highest degree of aesthetic objectivity to tragedy, which describes the "unspeakable pain, the wretchedness and misery of mankind" and thus attains "complete knowledge of the real nature of the world," and to music, which, transcending the limits of language, provides "a copy of the will itself" and expresses the "inner being, the in-itself of the world."[5]

An even more complete emancipation from servitude to the will can be found in religion, according to Schopenhauer. For here the will is silenced not merely for a few moments, as in aesthetic experience, "but forever, indeed completely extinguished." In the life of the saint, the human being "attains to the state of voluntary renunciation, resignation, true composure, and complete will-lessness." Examples of the denial of the will to live, which Schopenhauer identifies with "holiness," are to be found in the world's great religions, including Christianity and especially Hinduism and Buddhism.[6] Schopenhauer went on to elaborate on the crucial role of religion in human existence in his chapter "On Man's Need for Metaphysics" in *The World as Will and Representation*. The need for metaphysics, he argued there, arises from the natural wonder human beings feel as they confront death, finiteness, and the vanity of all effort. For the few who are able to devote themselves to thinking, this metaphysical need is satisfied through philosophy. But for the vast majority of human beings, this need is satisfied through religion, which presents the truth about the world in itself in allegorical form. Religion provides the ordinary human being with "consolation in the deep sorrows of life" and lifts him "above himself and above existence in time."[7]

There are, of course, other aspects to Schopenhauer's influence on *The Birth of Tragedy* besides his critique of science and defense of the superior claims of art and religion. His pessimistic understanding of existence as consisting primarily of pain and suffering is obviously of central importance to Nietzsche's interpretation of Greek tragedy. But for understanding the reversal in Nietzsche's philosophical outlook signaled by his flight from Bayreuth in 1876, it is Schopenhauer's view of the metaphysical significance of art and religion versus scientific knowledge that is most crucial. It is this view, which he shared with Wagner, that Nietzsche was to decisively reject in *Human, All too Human*.[8] The process by which this came about in the mid-1870s is what needs to be examined next.

In the writings immediately following *The Birth of Tragedy*—the unpublished *Philosophy in the Tragic Age of the Greeks* and the first two *Untimely Meditations*—Nietzsche's preoccupation with the problem of culture and his view that art rather than science contains the solution are still very much in evidence. In these writings, as well as in the unpublished notes contemporaneous with them, Nietzsche attributes the fragmentation of modern culture to the growth of the "immoderate, indiscriminate drive for knowledge," and he calls on art to restore cultural unity and wholeness (*KSA* 7:19 [21]). Sometimes he calls on religion as well to combat the disintegrating effects of science, but more often than not he sees art as taking "the place of disappearing myth" and supplying cultural unity "while religions die out" (*KSA* 7:19 [17, 23, 34]; 29 [203, 221]).[9] The negative conclusion that is drawn in all of these writings is that it is "impossible to erect a culture upon knowledge": "Our salvation does not lie in *knowing*, but in *creating!*" (*KSA* 7:19 [105, 125]).[10]

The most destructive form that science and the indiscriminate knowledge-drive take in the present age is history. Modern scientific history, which Nietzsche characterizes as "the science of universal becoming," breaks down the horizons that give unity and coherence to any healthy culture. By cramming ourselves with "the customs, arts, philosophies, religions, [and] discoveries of others," we become "walking encyclopedias" with a certain knowledge *about* culture but utterly incapable of embodying the living unity that marks a genuine culture (UDH 4). Nietzsche develops this critique of the modern historical sense in his second *Untimely Meditation*, "On the Uses and Disadvantages History for Life" (1874). There he calls on various forms of mythical and life-enhancing history to counteract the "deadly truths" (UDH 9) and barbarizing effects of modern scientific history. He also calls on "the eternalizing powers of art and religion" to prevent modern humanity from drowning in the sea of becoming upon which scientific history launches it (UDH 10).

What is somewhat new in these writings from 1872–73, especially in the unpublished notes, is the increased emphasis on the role of philosophy in restraining the indiscriminate drive for knowledge and thus in contributing to the goal of cultural unity. In a way, Nietzsche here elaborates on the theme of the "Socrates who plays music" from *The Birth of Tragedy*. Once again, he refers to the momentous critique of scientific knowledge by Kant and Schopenhauer, a critique that made room for religion and art. Even more, however, he invokes the pre-Platonic philosophers, who had an especially keen understanding of the role of philosophy as a "brake shoe" on the limitless drive for knowledge. In one note, he alludes to the "philosopher of tragic knowledge," who "controls the unleashed drive for knowledge" and thus "returns to art its rights." And in another, he claims that the "task of the philosopher" is "to consciously combat all the temporalizing elements—and thereby to support the unconscious task of art," through which "a people achieves the unity of all its characteristics" (*KSA* 7:19 [12, 17, 27, 34, 35]). Nietzsche is clear, however, that in this effort to restore cultural unity the role of philosophy is always secondary, while that of art is primary: "Philosophy cannot create a culture, but it can pave the way for one, or sustain one, or moderate one. . . . Culture can always only issue from the centralizing significance of an art form or a work of art" (*KSA* 7:23 [14]; 28 [2]).

Up to the end of 1873 and the writing of "On the Uses and Disadvantages of History for Life," then, Nietzsche's view on the renewal of culture on the basis of art rather than scientific knowledge remains fairly constant. The hint of something new, however, begins to appear in the notebooks of 1874, which contain numerous critical remarks on Wagner. Nietzsche repeatedly characterizes Wagner here as an "actor" who is primarily concerned with producing powerful effects. An age that has grown torpid and insensitive "requires extremely crude and powerful measures. The magnificent, intoxicating, confusing, the grandiose, the horrible, noisy, ugly, enraptured, nervous"—all of this Wagner supplies in his music and art. He is totally lacking in restraint and moderation, and he is also tyrannical, with the "tyrant's sensibility for the *colossal*" (*KSA* 7:32 [10, 15, 16, 20, 32, 34, 57]).

One of the most interesting comments Nietzsche makes about Wagner in these notebooks is that, in his drive to produce intoxicating effects, Wagner ends up having very little genuine moral effect on his audience: "There is something in Wagner's art that resembles flight from this world; it negates the world, it does not transfigure it. That is why it has no direct moral effect, but only indirectly a quietistic one. . . . Improvement of the real no longer is the goal, but rather destruction of or delusion about the real." Nietzsche goes on to link this escapist aspect of Wagner's art to Schopenhauer's philosophy:

> [I]n an age like the present one, [art] saps away part of the strength of dying religion. Hence the alliance between Wagner and Schopenhauer. . . . Here the Schopenhauerian "will to life" receives its artistic expression: this dull drive without purpose, this ecstasy, this despair, this tone of suffering and desire, this accentuation of love and ardor. Rarely a cheerful ray of sunshine, but many magic tricks that give artificial light.

Nietzsche's serious doubts about his former mentors become even more apparent in the conclusion of the note, when he asks "whether [Wagner's] art and Schopenhauerian philosophy are actually capable of improving a human being" (*KSA* 7:32 [44]).

It is perhaps surprising that at the very moment Nietzsche was asking this question, he was also engaged in writing the third of his *Untimely Meditations*, "Schopenhauer as Educator." But it would be a mistake to see this essay as a blanket endorsement of Schopenhauer's philosophy. Writing to his friend Paul Deussen in 1877, Nietzsche comments that "already when I wrote my essay on Sch[openhauer], I no longer held fast to any of the dogmatic points. I still believe now, as I did then, that it is of the highest importance . . . to go through Schopenhauer and use him as an educator. I only do not believe any longer he should educate to Schopenhauerian philosophy" (*SB* 5:265).[11] Even accounting for a certain amount of rewriting of his own history, it is clear from the text of "Schopenhauer as Educator" that Nietzsche is more interested in Schopenhauer as a heroic example of radical honesty and truthfulness than in his metaphysical doctrines of the will and resignation. In contrast to the Rousseauan and Goethean images of man, the "Schopenhauerian man voluntarily takes upon himself the suffering involved in being truthful." Insofar as such truthfulness involves the denial and destruction of all that currently passes for truth, the Schopenhauerian man seems "more like Mephistopheles than Faust." Despising his own happiness, he resolves "to destroy all that is becoming, to bring to light all that is false in things. He too wants to know everything, but not in the way the Goethean man does . . . [who] takes delight in the multiplicity of things; he is himself the first sacrifice to himself" (SE 4).

Like the critical remarks on Wagner from the 1874 notebooks, the emphasis on heroic truthfulness in the Schopenhauer essay seems to signal a fundamental shift in Nietzsche's assessment of the respective ranks of art and knowledge in relation to the problem of culture. That the problem of culture remains of central concern to Nietzsche in this essay is clear from the passage in which he characterizes our culture as one in which "haste and hurry [are] universal," the "waters of religion are ebbing away," and the sciences are "pursued without any restraint and in a spirit of blindest *laissez faire*," and he concludes that we "live in the age of atoms, of atomistic chaos" (SE 4). It is true that he echoes Wagner and Schopenhauer somewhat by claiming that the solution to the problem of modern culture lies in the "procreation of genius," that is to say, the "production of the philosopher, the artist, and the saint" (SE 3, 5). But the emphasis in the essay falls predominantly on the philosopher, and specifically on the philosopher understood as the ruthlessly honest destroyer of all comforting illusions and false beliefs. This is a far cry from the recommendation to indulge in self-conscious myths and life-enhancing illusions in the previous *Untimely Meditation* on history, and it looks forward to the conception of the free spirit that Nietzsche described to Louise Ott in September 1876: someone "who wants nothing more than to lose some comforting belief on a daily basis" (*SB* 5:185–86).

In 1875, Nietzsche did not publish anything, but his notebooks are full of notes for two projected *Untimely Meditations*: one on the Greeks and how scholars have misunderstood them, entitled "We Philologists"; the other on "Richard Wagner in Bayreuth." With respect to the former, Nietzsche emphasizes the terrible, evil, and violent features of the Greeks, which he believes have been ignored by classical scholars, all of whom—with the exception of Jacob Burckhardt—study the Greeks from the standpoint of "historical optimism" (*KSA* 8:5 [58]). This is consistent with the view Nietzsche took in *The Birth of Tragedy*, though here he puts even greater emphasis on the immorality of the Greeks, their "delight in deception, revenge, envy, slander, [and] lewdness": "The wisdom of their institutions lies in the lack of a distinction between good and evil, black and white. . . . This is the root of all liberality amongst the ancients; one seeks a tremendous discharge of the natural forces, not destruction and denial" (*KSA* 8:5 [146]). For all of that, Nietzsche still has not completely left Wagner and Schopenhauer behind, and he continues to state his aspirations for cultural renewal in terms that very much recall *The Birth of Tragedy*: "I wish to combine Schopenhauer, Wagner, and early Hellenism: that would provide a glimpse of a splendid culture" (*KSA* 8:6 [14]).

Mixed in with these more familiar observations, however, are ones that reflect the new emphasis on radical truthfulness found in "Schopenhauer as Educator." In one note, for example, Nietzsche writes: "I dream of a fellowship of men who are unconditional, know no indulgence, and want to be called 'destroyers': they hold the standard of their criticism to everything and sacrifice themselves to truth. The evil and the false must be brought to light!" (*KSA* 8:5 [30]). The clearest statement of Nietzsche's new ideal of truthfulness and the quest for knowledge, however, appears in a letter from December 1875 to his old friend Carl von Gersdorff. Here Nietzsche writes: "In my opinion, the *will to knowledge* may remain as the ultimate region of the will to live, as a region between willing and ceasing to will: a bit of purgatory . . . and a bit of Nirvana, as long as the soul thereby approaches a state of pure contemplation." He goes on to report that he is training himself "to get rid of the habit of *haste* in willing to know," and that he hopes thereby to achieve a "state of health in which the soul has retained only one impulse—the will to knowledge—and has become free of all other impulses and desires." Nietzsche's celebration of the will to knowledge in this letter is still framed in terms of Schopenhauer's contemplative ideal, and this will continue to be the case in his early free-spirit writings. Indeed, Nietzsche goes on to speak in this letter of "the constant joy of having found in Schopenhauer and Wagner educators" (*SB* 5:128–29). He is letting go of his former allegiances only very reluctantly.

Throughout 1875, Nietzsche was occupied with writing his fourth *Untimely Meditation*, "Richard Wagner in Bayreuth." The essay finally appeared on the eve of the Bayreuth Festival, in July 1876. Nietzsche clearly struggled in writing this essay, and the reason why is not hard to fathom. As we have seen, the notebooks from 1874 and to a lesser extent 1875 reveal a growing unease on Nietzsche's part toward Wagner and his art. Part of this unease stemmed from Nietzsche's new emphasis on truthfulness and the will to knowledge rather than art as the solution to the problem of modern culture. And yet the express charge of the Wagner essay was to pay homage to Wagner and to celebrate the cultural significance of Bayreuth. The challenge Nietzsche faced was how to be just to both sides of his deeply ambivalent feelings toward Wagner. That he was not altogether satisfied with his solution to this problem is evident in a later note, where he comments that his sketch of the Schopenhauerian man, "the destroying genius against all becoming," drove him "to skepticism against all honored, esteemed, and till then holy geniuses (including the Greeks, Schopenhauer, and Wagner) . . . The writing on Bayreuth was a pause, a sinking back, a rest-taking" (*KSA* 8:27 [34, 80]).

Contrary to what some interpreters have suggested, the essay is not an implicit critique of Wagner. It is a genuine homage, and one that should have pleased Wagner, and apparently did.[12] In order to accomplish this, though, Nietzsche took the things for which he had earlier criticized Wagner in his notebooks and made them into obstacles that Wagner either overcame or courageously opposed. Thus, as he did in his notebooks, Nietzsche acknowledges in his essay that Wagner's nature was characterized by a tremendous craving for power and desire to have influence over others. But now he claims that Wagner overcame this desire in the final, Schopenhauerian stage of his career: "The desire for supreme power, the inheritance of earlier years is wholly translated into artistic creativity; now he speaks through his art only to himself and no longer to a 'public' or folk." No longer did Wagner seek to influence the masses through gigantic effects; rather, he "renounced the idea of power . . . he was no longer concerned with aesthetic enthusiasms or the jubilation of excited masses, indeed he was filled with wrath to see his art fed so indiscriminately into the gaping maw of insatiable boredom and thirst for distraction" (RWB 8).

One of the most serious criticisms Nietzsche made of Wagner in his notebooks was that Wagner's art did not really try to reform or improve the world but merely to provide an escape from it through intoxication or delusion. In "Richard Wagner in Bayreuth," on the other hand, Nietzsche claims just the opposite; that Wagner's art is preeminently concerned with reform of the world and with the transformation of morality, politics, education, and society. In this regard, it is at odds with the corrupt art of the day, which seeks either amusement, distraction, intoxication, "artificially engendered excitement," or "stupefaction or delirium." Bayreuth is the culmination of the practical effort to reform and transfigure modern culture: "To us, Bayreuth signifies the morning consecration on the day of battle. We could not be done a greater injustice than if it were assumed we were concerned only with art" (RWB 4–5).

In many ways, Nietzsche's later comment in *Ecce Homo* that the "essay *Wagner in Bayreuth* is a vision of my future" is not altogether off the mark (*EH* 3.UM.3). The essay certainly provides an idealized portrait of Wagner, and it is on the basis of the real Wagner's divergence from this ideal that Nietzsche will soon criticize him. When Nietzsche arrived in Bayreuth at the end of July 1876, the discrepancy between the ideal of Bayreuth and the reality was immediately and crushingly apparent. In his Wagner essay, he had described the spectator at Bayreuth as something "worth seeing": "[A]ll those who attend the Bayreuth Festival will be felt to be untimely men: their home is not in this age but elsewhere" (RWB 1). Alas, the well-heeled bourgeoisie who attended the festival turned out to be all too much of the age. Nietzsche's describes his disappointment in a later note: "My mistake was that I came to Bayreuth with an ideal: therefore I had to experience the bitterest disillusionment. The profusion of hateful, deformed, over-spiced individuals repelled me violently" (*KSA* 8:30 [1]).

But it was more than just the vulgar reality of Bayreuth that repelled Nietzsche. In some ways, it was the ideal of Bayreuth itself, the ideal of a culture restored to wholeness through the self-conscious mythologizing of art, the ideal of Nietzsche's youth that had been nourished by his educators Wagner and Schopenhauer. This aspect of his disillusionment at Bayreuth Nietzsche described incisively in a letter to Mathilde Maier in July 1878: "That metaphysical befogging of all that is true and simple, the pitting of reason *against* reason, which sees every particular as a marvel and an absurdity; this matched by a baroque art of overexcitement and glorified extravagance—I mean the art of Wagner; both these things finally made me more ill" (*SB* 5:337–38). Up until 1874 and the essay on Schopenhauer, Nietzsche had pitted "reason against reason." Like Kant and Schopenhauer, he had used "the paraphernalia of science . . . to point out the limits and relativity of knowledge" and the need for the redemptive deed of art. This was the meaning of the "Socrates who plays music" (*BT* 15, 18). In the Schopenhauer essay and the notebooks of 1874–76, as we have seen, Nietzsche was already beginning to move away from his youthful aesthetic-cultural ideal and replacing it with one that took much more seriously reason, truthfulness, and knowledge. The disillusioning experience of Bayreuth finalized the break.

This brings us back to where we began: with Nietzsche's flight from Bayreuth to the village of Klingenbrunn in the Bohemian Forest. He eventually returned to Bayreuth and attended two series of performances of the *Ring* cycle. Two months later, having obtained a sabbatical from the University of Basel, he traveled to Sorrento, Italy, where his motherly friend Malwida von Meysenbug had set up a "cloister for free spirits" for Nietzsche, his friend Paul Rée, and his student Albert Brenner. As Nietzsche worked on what would eventually turn out to be *Human, All too Human*—at this point, he still thought of it as a fifth *Untimely Meditation*, retitled "The Free Spirit" from "The Plowshare"—Rée finished up his own book on *The Origin of the Moral Sensations*. Coincidentally, the Wagners happened to visit Sorrento at the end of October and spent a fair amount of time with Nietzsche. Cosima's diaries do not indicate that anything was amiss in these social interactions—apart from Nietzsche's poor health and her disapproval of "the Israelite" Rée—but Elisabeth Nietzsche has left behind a melodramatic account of a final conversation between Wagner and her brother, in which she claims the former spoke in pious tones about *Parsifal* and the latter remained stonily silent.[13] However that may be, after Wagner left Sorrento on 7 November 1876, Nietzsche was never to see him again.

From this point on, Nietzsche's rejection of both Wagner and Schopenhauer becomes ever more explicit. This is particularly true of Schopenhauer. In December 1876, Nietzsche wrote to Cosima Wagner that he had "almost suddenly become aware of a difference with Schopenhauer's teaching that has been slowly growing within me. I am not on his side on almost all general propositions" (*SB* 5:210). Six months later, he cautioned the musician Carl Fuchs about "the dangerous after-effects of Wagner" and about using Schopenhauerian metaphysical terms, for "I think I *know* that his metaphysics are all wrong and that all writings which bear their stamp will be one day unintelligible" (*SB* 5:262). The notebooks from this period tell a similarly critical story. Nietzsche dismisses Schopenhauer's notion of the "metaphysical need," and he denies that religion expresses the truth of things in allegorical form (*KSA* 8:19 [85, 100]; 23 [19]). He rejects Schopenhauer's distinction between appearances and the thing in itself and claims that Schopenhauer's notion of the "will to life" is bourgeois in nature: "It is not true that one wants existence at any price" (*KSA* 8:23 [12, 125]). Finally, in a note that reflects his newfound affinity with the Enlightenment, Nietzsche asserts that Schopenhauer and Wagner belong to the "counter-Enlightenment" (*KSA* 8:22 [17]).

What more than anything else links Schopenhauer and Wagner to the counter-Enlightenment, in Nietzsche's mind, is their effort to preserve the spirit of religion in philosophy and art. As we have seen, Wagner explicitly endorsed this understanding of the religious function of art and believed that his mythic music-dramas would replace religion as the source of cultural unity and wholeness in Germany. Of course, the ultimate expression of Wagner's hieratic conception of art was *Parsifal*, the work in which Wagner, as Nietzsche later put it, "sank down helpless and shattered before the Christian cross" (*HH* 2.Preface.3). When Nietzsche received his copy of *Parsifal* from Wagner in January 1878, he immediately wrote to Reinhart von Seydlitz that "it is all too Christian, time-bound, limited; sheer fantastic psychology; no flesh and much too much blood" (*SB* 5:300). Three months later, *Human, All too Human* appeared, and Nietzsche had a copy sent to Wagner. He later telescoped this exchange of books into one "miraculously meaningful coincidence," claiming that he received his copy of *Parsifal* at exactly the moment he sent *Human, All too Human*: "This crossing of the two books—I felt as if I heard an ominous sound—as if two swords had crossed" (*EH* 3.HH.5). While not literally true, this statement nicely captures what was at stake—philosophically, culturally, and biographically—in the first work of Nietzsche's free-spirit trilogy.

ONE

Human, All too Human and the Problem of Culture

Immediately upon opening *Human, All too Human*, the break that it consti-tutes with Nietzsche's earlier writings announces itself at the level of style. Gone is the labored effort to imitate the conventions of the scholarly trea-tise or the literary essay. Instead, we find numbered paragraphs of varying lengths, each with its own title and discrete argument. In the scholarly lit-erature, these paragraphs have conventionally been referred to as "apho-risms," and even Nietzsche refers to them as such, using the German words *Aphorismus* and *Sentenz*. But from the outset, it is clear that Nietzsche's apho-risms are very different from the brief, polished maxims of the French mor-alists La Rochefoucauld, Chamfort, and Vauvenargues, or the witty jottings of G. C. Lichtenberg, whom Nietzsche considered to be one of the masters of German prose (*WS* 109). While some of the aphorisms of *Human, All too Human* have the epigrammatic character found in these other writers—in the chapters on "Man and Society," "Woman and Child," and "Man Alone With Himself," for example—most consist of longer paragraphs designed to carry the weight of philosophically substantive discussions.[1]

What prompted this change in Nietzsche's style? Throughout the 1870s, he read constantly and with deep admiration the French moralists men-tioned above, along with Montaigne and Pascal.[2] But what seems to have brought home to him the possibilities of the aphorism for contemporary philosophical purposes was the use made of this literary form by his friend Paul Rée in his 1875 *Psychological Observations*. Both Rée and Nietzsche were attracted by the cool, detached, and scientific character of the aphorism, es-pecially as it was employed by the French moralists. For Nietzsche, the cold clarity of the aphorism took on special significance in his struggle against the cloudy enchantments of romanticism.[3] At one point, he even compares the great French moralists—Montaigne, La Rochefoucauld, La Bruyère, Fontenelle, Vauvenargues, and Chamfort—to his beloved Greeks. The Greeks, he claims, would have admired the "clarity and delicate precision" of these French writers, whereas they would have been filled with repugnance by the "obscurity and exaggeration" of Goethe's and Schopenhauer's styles. The former, Nietzsche sardonically comments, "liked to embrace the clouds more than he should have," and the latter "almost always wanders among images of things instead of things themselves" (WS 214).

It was not only the cold, precise, anti-romantic character of the aphorism that appealed to Nietzsche. He also recognized that its fragmentary nature could be very effective in conveying philosophical ideas. The incompleteness of an aphorism forces the reader to fill in what is left unsaid and thereby to think along with the philosophical writer. Nietzsche explains: the "incomplete presentation of an idea, of a whole philosophy, is sometimes more effective than its exhaustive realization: more is left for the beholder to do, he is impelled to continue working on that which appears so strongly etched before him in light and shadow, to think it through to the end" (HH 178). He makes a similar point in a note from the winter of 1876–77, adding that the maxim (Sentenz) not only makes the qualified reader work harder to understand an author but also keeps the unqualified reader from understanding what is being said: "therefore one can express questionable things harmlessly in maxims" (KSA 8:20 [3]). This esoteric function motivates Nietzsche's use of the aphorism throughout his career. As he puts it in a later remark: one of the reasons for his brevity is that, "being an immoralist, one has to take steps against corrupting innocents" (GS 381).[4]

As I pointed out in the preface with respect to the French deconstructionist reading of Nietzsche, however, one must guard against misinterpreting Nietzsche's aphoristic style in Human, All too Human, or in the middle works in general, as an effort to avoid any sort of systematic coherence, unity, or consistency.[5] Even Walter Kaufmann, who otherwise grasps that Nietzsche's aphorisms amount to more than "a glittering mosaic of independent monads," an "anarchy of atoms" belonging to no system or whole,[6] can fall into this misinterpretation with respect to the middle works. Of Human, All too Human he writes, for example, that Nietzsche proceeds "quite unsystematically and consider[s] each problem on its own merits without a theory to prove or an ax to grind."[7] But Nietzsche makes clear that by writing in fragments he does not mean to deny that they belong to a whole or that his insights are not profoundly interconnected. In an aphorism entitled "Against the Shortsighted," he writes: "Do you think this work must be fragmentary because I give it to you (and have to give it to you) in fragments?" (AOM

128). Against Kaufmann, but even more against the deconstructionist readings of Nietzsche by commentators like Deleuze, Derrida, and Kofman,
I argue in this chapter that the aphorisms that comprise *Human, All too
Human* are not simply isolated or disconnected insights and that Nietzsche
ultimately does have a theory to prove and even an ax to grind, albeit a very
complicated one.

One obvious way in which the aphorisms of *Human, All too Human* begin to lose the appearance of being isolated monads is that they are organized into thematic chapters, with metaphysics being treated in the first,
morality in the second, religion in the third, art in the fourth, culture in
the fifth, and so forth. The two "supplements" to *Human, All too Human*
that Nietzsche wrote—*Assorted Opinions and Maxims* (published in 1879)
and *The Wanderer and His Shadow* (published in 1880)—were not divided
into chapters as the original book was, but the aphorisms that comprised
them were again organized thematically and arranged in exactly the same
order as the original.[8] Still, though these chapter divisions supply a certain
organization to the book, they do not really provide a key to how the book
is to be read as a whole. The chapters stand alongside one another without
any clear indication as to how they are to be integrated into a single, coherent argument.[9]

In the absence of such an indication, most commentators end up pick-
ing out the parts of *Human, All too Human* that interest them and leaving
the rest alone. The aspect of the book that has received the most attention
is Nietzsche's investigation into the origin and nature of morality, since this
is the aspect that points most directly to his later genealogy of morals.[10] I,
too, take up this crucial aspect of the argument of *Human, All too Human* at
some length below. Nevertheless, the motivation for Nietzsche's investigation of morality remains mysterious unless it is placed in the context of
his dominant concern at the time with the problem of culture. Nietzsche
announces this theme in an important aphorism toward the beginning of
the book, disclosing at the same time the death of God that precipitates the
problem of culture:

> Since the belief has ceased that a God broadly directs the destinies of the
> world and . . . is leading mankind gloriously upward, man has to set himself
> ecumenical goals embracing the whole earth. . . . [I]f mankind is not to de-
> stroy itself through such conscious universal rule, it must first of all attain to
> a hitherto altogether unprecedented *knowledge of the preconditions of culture*
> as a scientific standard for ecumenical goals. Herein lies the tremendous task
> facing the great spirits of the coming century. (*HH* 25)

One of my main purposes in this chapter is to demonstrate that the theme of culture represents not merely an overlooked aspect of *Human, All too Human* but the key to the book as a whole and the axis around which all of the other reflections contained it in it—on metaphysics, morality, religion, and art—revolve.[11]

As I have already shown in the prologue, the problem of culture had been the pervasive preoccupation of Nietzsche's writings prior to *Human, All too Human*. There Nietzsche attributed the fragmentation of modern culture to the "immoderate, indiscriminate drive for knowledge" (*KSA* 7:19 [21]), especially as it was evinced in historical scholarship; and he called on art, myth, and sometimes even religion to restore cultural unity and wholeness. The negative conclusion that Nietzsche drew throughout these early writings, at least up to "Schopenhauer as Educator," was that it is "impossible to erect a culture upon knowledge" (*KSA* 7:19 [105]).

It is precisely this conclusion that Nietzsche rejects in *Human, All too Human*, arguing instead that the "higher culture" of the future will be based on knowledge and science rather than on religion, art, or metaphysical philosophy. The weakness of Nietzsche's earlier theory of culture—the weakness, in many ways, of romanticism in general—lay in its inability to provide the unity and wholeness it desperately sought. In the first *Untimely Meditation* on David Strauss, Nietzsche defined culture as "above all, unity of style in all the expressions of the life of a people" (DS 1). By this standard, however, Nietzsche's early theory of culture fails egregiously, requiring as it does the suppression of important aspects of the modern spirit and involving itself in the paradoxes of self-conscious deception and myth-making. *Human, All too Human*, on the other hand, by grounding culture on knowledge and reconciling it with the modern scientific spirit, makes a more plausible effort to achieve the cultural unity and wholeness that eluded the earlier theory. It is an effort to overcome the deadly "dialectic of Enlightenment" and reconcile science and culture, knowledge and life.[12]

The primary locus of Nietzsche's reflections on culture in *Human, All too Human* is the chapter entitled "Marks of Higher and Lower Culture," which is literally the central chapter (the fifth of nine) of the book. Interestingly, in one of Nietzsche's early plans for the book, he placed the chapter on "The Philosophy of Culture" first (*KSA* 8:25 [3]). The positive conception of culture defended in this chapter rests on a critique of the false notion of culture that Nietzsche finds dominant in nineteenth-century Europe. In the first instance, this involves a critique of romantic, Wagnerian art, which Nietzsche takes up in the fourth chapter of *Human, All too Human*. But the Wagnerian romantic-artistic cultural project is itself a derivative phenomenon resting on religious (Christian), moral, and ultimately metaphysical (Schopenhauerian) assumptions. Accordingly, these are subjected to critical analysis in the first three chapters of the book. It is to the deepest substratum of Nietzsche's critical excavation of the problem of modern culture—metaphysics—that we turn first.

The Errors of Metaphysics

The first chapter of *Human, All too Human* is entitled "Of First and Last Things" and deals with what Nietzsche regards as the fundamental errors of metaphysics. Though his critique of these errors has wide-ranging implications for the whole of the philosophical tradition, it is clear that the primary target is Schopenhauer's metaphysics. In the Preface to the *Genealogy of Morals*, Nietzsche claims that it was to Schopenhauer that *Human, All too Human*, "the passion and the concealed contradiction of that book, addressed itself as if to a contemporary (—for that book too was a 'polemic')" (*GM* Preface 5). Though Nietzsche refers specifically to Schopenhauer's moral teaching about pity in this passage, the first chapter of *Human, All too Human* indicates that his polemic extends at least equally to Schopenhauer's metaphysics.

The chapter begins with three important aphorisms devoted to philosophical method. In the first, Nietzsche asks the question: "[H]ow can something originate in its opposite, for example rationality in irrationality, the sentient in the dead, logic in unlogic, disinterested contemplation in covetous desire, living for others in egoism, truth in error?" (*HH* 1). This, of course, is exactly the question with which he begins his later account of "the prejudices of the philosophers" in *Beyond Good and Evil*, where he claims that the fundamental faith of metaphysical philosophy is the "faith in opposite values" (*BGE* 2). He makes a similar claim in *Human, All too Human*, arguing that metaphysical philosophy is characterized by its denial of the human, all too human origin of our highest values and by its assumption that "the more highly valued thing [has] a miraculous source in the very kernel and being of the 'thing in itself.'" Historical philosophy, on the other hand, whose method Nietzsche deploys throughout *Human, All too Human*, denies that any such opposites exist in human experience, holding instead that "the most glorious colors" in our moral, religious, and aesthetic conceptions "are derived from base, indeed despised materials" (*HH* 1; see also *WS* 67).[13]

Nietzsche elaborates on this historical approach to philosophy in the second aphorism. The common failing of all philosophers, he argues, is that they take human beings as they currently exist and assume that they are "eternal facts" embodying a fixed and constant nature. "Lack of historical sense is the family failing of all philosophers." What these philosophers fail to realize, according to Nietzsche, is that human beings and everything about them have *become*. This fact is easy to overlook if one's attention is confined to the last four thousand years of history, during which mankind "has not altered very much." The most fundamental changes in human nature took place prior to this period. Echoing English social theorist Walter Bagehot, whom he read in 1874, Nietzsche states that "everything *essential* in the development of mankind took place in primeval times" (*HH* 2).[14]

Before developing his specific criticisms of various metaphysical errors, Nietzsche devotes one final aphorism to the distinction between his new, historical approach to philosophical questions and the old, metaphysical approach. Given my focus in this chapter, it is noteworthy that this aphorism makes a connection between Nietzsche's new, historical approach to philosophy and the overarching question of culture. He writes: "It is the mark of a higher culture to value the little unpretentious truths which have been discovered by means of rigorous method more highly than the errors handed down by metaphysical and artistic ages and men, which blind us and make us happy." While the latter are no doubt "fair, splendid, intoxicating, perhaps indeed enrapturing," they nevertheless belong to a "lower culture." Here Nietzsche discloses the philosophy of history that frames the entire argument of *Human, All too Human*. Human history consists in the movement from a lower culture occupied with "spinning out forms and symbols" to a higher culture marked by a "manly," scientific spirit. In the latter, cultural energy is no longer spent on constructing sublime edifices; rather, "our arts themselves grow ever more intellectual, our senses more spiritual" (*HH* 3).

Since he refers to the "scientific spirit" in this aphorism, it is perhaps not amiss to say a little more about what exactly Nietzsche means by "science" in *Human, All too Human*—and, indeed, throughout the middle period. That he invokes the scientific *spirit* rather than science simply is in many ways characteristic of his understanding of this activity. Science is less about the products of inquiry than it is about the process of relentless and radical questioning of everything that presents itself as certain knowledge. As he puts it in another aphorism: "[T]he scientific spirit rests upon an insight into the methods [of science], and if these were lost all the other products of science together would not suffice to prevent a restoration of superstition and folly." Many people can learn the "facts of science," but this does not mean that they possess the "instinctive mistrust" that is the hallmark of the "spirit of science" (*HH* 635). The emphasis on method and mistrust in this aphorism remains a key feature of Nietzsche's understanding of science throughout his career,[15] and it receives vivid expression in the quote from Descartes' *Discourse on Method* that he chose as the motto for the 1878 edition of *Human, All too Human*.[16]

The aphorism from which I just quoted is one in a series of aphorisms at the end of *Human, All too Human* to which Nietzsche gives the collective title "Of Conviction and Justice" (*HH* 629–37). These aphorisms also shed important light on Nietzsche's conception of science, demonstrating that the "man of convictions is not the man of scientific thought" (*HH* 630). Insofar as a conviction (*Überzeugung*) rests on the belief that one possesses absolute truth on some matter, it is the very antithesis of the skepticism, doubt, and mistrust that drives the scientific spirit.[17] For this reason, Nietzsche states that "convictions are more dangerous enemies of truth than lies" (*HH* 483).[18] The scientific spirit is characterized more by the "pathos of seeking truth" than by the "pathos of *possessing* truth" (*HH* 633), and Nietzsche poignantly evokes this pathos in the final aphorism of *Human, All too Human* with the figure of the "wanderer," a figure that recurs throughout the middle works as the emblem of the free spirit (*HH* 638).

Let us now turn to the specific metaphysical doctrines that Nietzsche rejects in the first chapter of *Human, All too Human*. In connection with the lack of historical sense exhibited by philosophers, he highlights their tendency to see "'instincts' in man as he now is and assume that these belong to the unalterable facts of mankind" (*HH* 2). It is hard not to think of Schopenhauer and his doctrine of the "metaphysical need" here. For Schopenhauer, as we have seen, this need arises from the wonder that all human beings experience in the face of death, finiteness, and the ultimate fruitlessness of all effort; and it is satisfied by either religion or philosophy, which "lift man above himself and above existence in time" and provide consolation for the unavoidable sorrows of life.[19] Nietzsche, however, repeatedly denies the universality of this metaphysical need. In aphorism 26, he refers to Schopenhauer's doctrine of the "metaphysical need" (which he puts in quotation marks) as unscientific; and in the following aphorism, he states that "the needs which religion has satisfied and philosophy is now supposed to satisfy are not immutable; they can be *weakened* and *exterminated*" (*HH* 27). Later in the book, he again criticizes Schopenhauer for insufficiently weaning himself from religion and uncritically appealing to the metaphysical need religion aims to satisfy: "Scientific philosophy has to be very much on its guard against smuggling in errors on the basis of this need—an acquired and consequently also a transient need" (*HH* 131).[20]

In addition to the notion of a permanent metaphysical need, Nietzsche also rejects the notion of a "metaphysical world," a world independent of human thought and experience. He grants that some such world may exist: given that "we behold all things through the human head," we are perhaps entitled to ask what of the world would remain if we cut that head off. But the answer to such a question is of absolutely no practical value. In a manner reminiscent of Hegel's critique of the Kantian thing in itself, Nietzsche claims that the possibility of a metaphysical world in itself is of purely theoretical interest; "one can do absolutely nothing with it, not to speak of letting happiness, salvation, and life depend on the gossamer of such a possibility." Even if one could establish the existence of such a metaphysical world, the most one could say of it is that it is "an inaccessible, incomprehensible being-other," and this knowledge would again be of no practical value or interest (*HH* 9).

Nietzsche goes on to distinguish his skeptical position on the metaphysical world from two other influential views in an aphorism entitled "Appearance and Thing in Itself." The first view holds that it is possible to infer the nature of the thing in itself from the world of appearance, the latter being envisaged as "a painting that has been unrolled once and for all and unchangeably depicts the same scene" (*HH* 16). In a draft of this aphorism in his notebooks, Nietzsche ascribes this view to Schopenhauer (*KSA* 8:23 [125]). Against it, "more rigorous logicians" have argued that between the unconditioned thing in itself and the world of appearance there is absolutely no connection; "what appears in appearance is precisely *not* the thing in itself" (*HH* 16). This latter view belongs to the neo-Kantian philosopher Afrikan Spir, whose 1873 book *Denken und Wirklichkeit* (*Thought and Reality*) Nietzsche had studied carefully in the years leading up to the publication of *Human, All too Human*. In that book, Spir argues that our concepts obtain truth only in a world of self-identical being, a kind of Parmenidean One; they cannot be applied to the empirical world of becoming without falsifying that world. The gap between the true, metaphysical world and the apparent world can never be bridged.[21]

Though Nietzsche's position on the relationship between appearance and the thing in itself would seem to have more in common with Spir's view than with Schopenhauer's, he ends up rejecting both because they treat the apparent world as something fixed and finished and fail to grasp its radical historicity: "Both parties . . . overlook the possibility that this painting—that which we humans call life and experience—has gradually *become*, is indeed still fully in the process of *becoming*, and should thus not be regarded as a fixed object on the basis of which a conclusion as to the nature of its originator (the sufficient reason) may be either drawn or pronounced undrawable." It is on this evolving apparent world and its human, all too human determinants that Nietzsche wants us to fasten our attention. Nothing is to be gained by viewing it in relation to the unknowable thing in itself or metaphysical world. In terms of his later account of "How the 'True World' became a Fable" in *Twilight of the Idols*, Nietzsche already seems to have gone a long way toward abolishing the true or metaphysical world.[22] This becomes evident in the remarkable passage in which he elaborates on the evolving character of the apparent world:

> Because we have for millennia made moral, aesthetic, religious demands on the world, looked upon it with blind desire, passion, or fear, and abandoned ourselves to the bad habits of illogical thinking, this world has gradually *become* so marvelously variegated, frightful, meaningful, soulful, it has acquired color—but we have been the colorists: it is the human intellect that has made appearance appear and transported its erroneous basic conceptions into things. (*HH* 16)

This passage is significant not only for its vaporization of the metaphysical world but for its suggestion that our beliefs about the empirical world are false. Here we encounter Nietzsche's paradoxical "error theory" of judgment, which seems to raise so many philosophical difficulties.[23] Interestingly, Spir was influential in supplying Nietzsche with arguments for the erroneous character of the empirical world. But whereas Spir, like Parmenides, sought to bring out the incompatibility between thought and empirical experience in order to demonstrate that the former applied only to a world of self-identical being, Nietzsche, like Heraclitus, denies that we have access to such a world of pure being and instead shows that thought is part and parcel of the world of becoming. Thus, in an aphorism entitled "Fundamental Questions of Metaphysics," Nietzsche quotes Spir—here referred to as "a distinguished logician"—to the effect that the "primary law of the knowing subject" is that the true object of its thought can only be a self-identical and unchanging "substance," but he goes on to say that this law is itself something that has "evolved: one day it will be shown how gradually, in the lower organisms, this tendency comes into being: how the purblind mole's eyes of this organization at first never see anything but the same thing." It is only much later, after our eyes have been "educated in the highest scientificality," that we are able to emancipate ourselves from this primitive "belief that there are *identical* things" (*HH* 18).

Nietzsche dwells at some length on the false judgments characteristic of primitive humanity. Drawing on contemporary English anthropologists like Sir John Lubbock, he argues that dreams give us a valuable insight into how the primitive mind worked.[24] The same sort of erroneous inferences, arbitrary associations, and capricious connections that we experience in dreams characterized the mental operations of primitive humanity while awake: "in sleep and dreams we repeat once again the curriculum of earlier mankind" (HH 12). This is especially the case with primitive humanity's understanding of cause and effect. Just as in dreams we fabricate all sorts of causes to account for the sensations our bodies experience while asleep—for example, we dream we are lost in the desert to account for our thirst—so primitive humanity posited all sorts of imaginative causes for the sensations they experienced while awake. Here, again, dreams "take us back again to remote stages of human culture and provide us with a means of understanding them better" (HH 13).

But Nietzsche is not simply concerned to show that the erroneous manner of thinking characteristic of primitive humanity survives only in our dreams and has nothing to do with our daytime rationality. Insofar as our rationality rests on language, it too partakes of primeval error. For language carves up the world in a variety of ways, positing identities (and differences) that do not correspond to anything real in that world.[25] Primitive man, of course, believed that language actually describes the real world as it is. More recently, though, this belief in the direct correspondence between language and world has come to be doubted. Happily, Nietzsche tells us, this more recent insight has come too late to reverse the evolution of reason, which actually depends on the primitive belief that language corresponds to the real world. And he adds: "Logic too depends on presuppositions with which nothing in the real world corresponds, for example on the presupposition that there are identical things, that the same thing is identical at different times," and so forth (HH 11; see also 18 and 19).

Nietzsche thus highlights the erroneousness of the world of appearance in a variety of ways. But he does so not because he wishes to condemn the apparent world or somehow escape from it. The latter is neither possible nor desirable. The "errors and fantasies" woven into the fabric of the world of appearance and "inherited now by us as the accumulated treasure of the past" should be regarded as precisely that—"as treasure: for the value of our humanity depends upon it" (HH 16). With this statement, Nietzsche distinguishes his own "Enlightenment Project" from that of positivist thinkers who aim merely at the negative goal of showing that all metaphysics is an error. Once we have overcome metaphysics, he argues, it is then necessary to "take a few steps back" and grasp the historical justification of our metaphysical ideas and how they have contributed to the enhancement of mankind. Without such a "retrograde step," we will "deprive [ourselves] of the best that mankind has produced . . . for one may well want to look out over the top rung of the ladder, but one ought not to want to stand on it" (*HH* 20).[26]

Here Nietzsche's discussion of metaphysics returns to the question of culture, and the question arises: If error is inescapable, what role remains for the scientific spirit that serves as the distinguishing mark of "higher culture"? Science cannot simply dissolve the errors and illusions upon which civilization is built, but neither can it regard these errors and illusions in the same uncritical way that primitive humanity did. This is a dilemma that will crop up at several crucial points in Nietzsche's argument in *Human, All too Human*. Here he tries to find a middle path out of it by suggesting that science, whose labors will culminate in a complete "history of the genesis of thought," somehow stands above the errors and illusions of the apparent world without denying their necessity and importance (*HH* 16; see also *KSA* 8:23 [125]).

What, then, will postmetaphysical, scientific culture look like? Nietzsche anticipates that skepticism regarding metaphysical things will eventually become general among humanity, depriving human beings of the motivation to create works that outlast their paltry lifetimes: "[T]he attention of the individual is too firmly fixed on his own brief span of life and receives no stronger impulse to work at the construction of enduring institutions intended to last for centuries." Tocqueville recognizes a similar danger arising from skeptical, democratic ages.[27] Nietzsche, however, asks whether science can provide the sort of faith necessary to motivate enduring efforts and create enduring institutions in the future and answers in the affirmative: "[T]he sum of unimpeachable truths" produced by science "can in time become so great (in the dietetics of health, for example) that on the basis of them one may resolve to embark on 'everlasting' works." It is necessary to get farther away from "the slow-breathing repose of metaphysical ages," however, before science can begin to have this salutary effect (*HH* 22).

Nietzsche goes on to elaborate on this scientific or Enlightenment project. He predicts that the coming postmetaphysical age will be preceded by a period of unprecedented empirical research in which various philosophies of life, customs, cultures, and moralities are placed side by side, compared with one another, and ultimately judged favorable or unfavorable to the higher culture of the future (*HH* 23). Based on this research, humanity will be able *consciously* to evolve a new culture, "whereas formerly it did so unconsciously and fortuitously." Nietzsche insists that progress *is* possible—though not necessarily inevitable—but in order to bring it about we must abandon the romantic longing for "self-contained original national cultures" and aspire to more ecumenical goals (*HH* 24). It is in this context that the passage quoted at the beginning of this chapter appears, announcing the "tremendous task facing the great spirits of the coming century": namely, the acquisition of an "unprecedented *knowledge of the preconditions of culture* as a scientific standard for ecumenical goals" (*HH* 25).

Once again, however, Nietzsche expresses doubts about the feasibility of such a conscious culture based on scientific knowledge. He reminds us that it "is *error* that has made mankind so profound, tender, inventive," and that "it is the world as idea (error) that is so full of significance, profound, marvelous, and bearing in its womb all happiness and unhappiness" (*HH* 29). The illogical is necessary to mankind, as is injustice and the erroneous valuation of life (*HH* 31–33). Given that this is so, Nietzsche asks, "Will our philosophy not thus become a tragedy? Will truth not become inimical to life, to the better man?" In the "Uses and Disadvantages of History for Life," he had answered this question in the affirmative, pointing to the deadliness of truth (*UDH* 9). Here, though, he suggests that "the after-effect of knowledge is determined by a man's temperament," and that it is perfectly possible to imagine a life based on knowledge that is "much simpler and emotionally cleaner than our present life is." Despite having distanced himself from Schopenhauer throughout the chapter, it is at this point that we begin to hear echoes of something like Schopenhauer's contemplative ideal, especially in the beautiful concluding passage where Nietzsche elaborates on the moderate life of the free-spirited knower:

> Though the old motives of violent desire produced by inherited habit would still possess their strength, they would gradually grow weaker under the influence of purifying knowledge. In the end, one would live among men and with oneself as in *nature*, without praising, blaming, contending, gazing contentedly, as though at a spectacle, upon many things for which one formerly felt only fear. (*HH* 34)[28]

From a Moral to a Knowing Mankind

The chapter on "First and Last Things" is followed by a chapter devoted to "The History of the Moral Sensations." In this chapter, we encounter what is in many ways the most novel aspect of Nietzsche's diagnosis of the problem of culture in *Human, All too Human*, and certainly the one that had the greatest implications for his future philosophy. For it is in this chapter that

Nietzsche, for the first time, identifies morality as one of the chief culprits in the barbarization of modern culture. Before we can begin to make sense of this, I need to say something about the two thinkers who form the crucial background out of which Nietzsche's reflections on morality develop.

The first is, once again, Schopenhauer. In the chapter on morality, Nietzsche continues the polemic against his great teacher that he began in the first chapter on metaphysics. For Schopenhauer, the criterion of moral worth in actions consists in the absence of self-interest or egoism, and the only motive that fulfills this criterion is pity or compassion (*Mitleid*), which he defines as "the immediate *participation*, independent of all ulterior considerations, primarily in the *suffering* of another, and thus in the prevention or elimination of it."[29] It is precisely this identification of morality with nonegoistic action and motivation, and especially with the motive of compassion, that Nietzsche rejects in the chapter on morality in *Human, All too Human*. Needless to say, he also rejects Schopenhauer's metaphysical argument that compassion allows the individual to overcome the *principium individuationis* and grasp the unity of the will in itself lying behind phenomena.[30] Finally, he rejects Schopenhauer's attempt to salvage some notion of freedom of the will in his Kantian doctrine of the intelligible character, which holds that freedom applies not to what we do (*operari*) but only to what we are (*esse*).[31]

The second thinker to whom Nietzsche's psychological-historical approach to morality in *Human, All too Human* is much more positively indebted is Paul Rée.[32] Rée completed his *Origin of the Moral Sensations*—which Nietzsche's chapter title obviously echoes—in the fall of 1876 while staying in Sorrento with Nietzsche, and Nietzsche acknowledges his influence on *Human, All too Human* in several aphorisms (*HH* 36–37, 133). In *The Origin of the Moral Sensations*, Rée accepts Schopenhauer's identification of morality with nonegoistic action and motivation, but unlike Schopenhauer, he provides a purely naturalistic explanation of morality thus understood. He defends this naturalistic approach in a passage quoted approvingly by Nietzsche (*HH* 37): "[T]oday, since Lamarck and Darwin have written, moral phenomena can be traced back to natural causes just as much as physical phenomena: moral man stands no closer to the intelligible world than physical man."[33] The crux of his Darwinian, naturalistic account is that, originally, nonegoistic actions were praised because of their utility to the community, while selfish or egoistic actions were condemned for their harmfulness. But eventually, as a result of repetition, habituation, and social reinforcement, this utilitarian origin was forgotten, and the goodness of nonegoistic actions was taken to be a quality inherent in the acts themselves. On this fundamental misinterpretation modern morality rests, though recognizing it, Rée believes, has only theoretical, not practical, implications.[34]

How much Nietzsche's argument in the chapter on morality in *Human, All too Human* owes to Rée is complicated—far more complicated than Nietzsche's later denials that Rée had any influence on him at this time (see *GM* Preface 4; *EH* 3, on *HH* 6). Nevertheless, while Nietzsche certainly agrees with much in Rée's naturalistic account of morality, his ultimate purpose in *Human, All too Human* remains quite different and, needless to say, far more radical.[35] He is not merely interested in the theoretical point that what we now take to be moral action performed for its own sake was originally valued for its contribution to social utility. Such a theoretical point does not call into question the value of morality understood in terms of altruism or nonegoistic action; it merely provides an alternative, utilitarian explanation of its origin. Nietzsche's investigation of morality in *Human, All too Human*, on the other hand, is very much concerned with questioning the value of morality understood in terms of nonegoistic action. For him, the whole distinction between egoism and nonegoism, selfishness and self-lessness, that belongs to morality not only represents a misinterpretation of human motivation; it also constitutes one of the leading factors in the corruption of modern culture.[36]

We must be careful here not to assimilate Nietzsche's critique of morality in *Human, All too Human* too closely to his later critique in the *Genealogy of Morals*, as Nietzsche himself seems to do when he retrospectively comments that what was at stake in *Human, All too Human* "was the *value* of morality," especially "the value of the 'unegoistic,' the instincts of pity, self-abnegation, self-sacrifice, which Schopenhauer had gilded, deified, and projected into a beyond for so long that at last they became for him 'value in itself'" (*GM* Preface 5). While Nietzsche certainly has some critical things to say about pity in *Human, All too Human*, the main thrust of his argument focuses on the way in which morality has been responsible for "blackening" the world, which then gives rise to the intoxicating and narcotizing remedies provided by religion and sometimes art. We "require a *history* of the ethical and religious sensations," he writes, in order "to become clear in our minds as to the origin of that calamitous weightiness we have for so long accorded" things (*WS* 16). The critique of morality thus leads back to the problem of culture.

Connected with its artificial "blackening" of the world, morality has also been chiefly responsible for the oppositional thinking that Nietzsche seeks to overcome in *Human, All too Human*. The fundamental opposition in morality is, of course, between good and evil, and he tries to show in a variety of ways that this opposition is ultimately a false one, that "between good and evil actions there is no difference in kind, but at most one of degree" (*HH* 107). The particular form of this opposition that he focuses on is that between egoistic and nonegoistic actions. As we have seen, this opposition forms the basis of Schopenhauer's moral philosophy as well as Rée's investigations into the origin of the moral sensations. Nietzsche, however, regards it as an utterly false distinction. All our actions have an egoistic basis; there is no such thing as a nonegoistic action: "No man has ever done anything that was done wholly for others and with no personal motivation whatever" (*HH* 133). The self-sacrifice of a woman for her lover, a mother for her child, or a soldier for his country, for example, has nothing unegoistic about it. Rather, in each of these cases the individual divides him- or herself in two and sacrifices one part to another, one desire or inclination to another (*HH* 57). Nietzsche sums up his entire point of view in a little aphorism entitled "Luke 18:14 Improved": "He that humbleth himself wants to be exalted" (*HH* 87).[37]

Nietzsche is particularly suspicious of the nonegoistic sentiment par excellence, pity, which Schopenhauer had made the basis of morality. Pity, he argues, does not have the pleasure of the pitied as its objective but the pleasure of the one who pities. The latter experiences pleasure both in the emotion of pity itself (as in tragedy) and in the feeling of superiority or power over another (*HH* 103). The motives of the one who is pitied are not innocent either. Lacking the power to effect anything else, the unfortunate individual moans, complains, and parades his misfortune in order to hurt those around him and show that he retains at least *that* power: "The thirst for pity is thus a thirst for self-enjoyment, and that at the expense of one's fellow men; it displays man in the whole ruthlessness of his own dear self" (*HH* 50). Nietzsche's unflattering portrait of pity does not lead him to disparage all sympathetic feeling among human beings, but he admires "sharing joy" (*Mitfreude*) more than "sharing suffering" (*Mitleid*), though not because the former is less egoistic than the latter (*HH* 49 and 499; also *HH* 321 and *AOM* 62).[38]

Nietzsche's analysis of pity is notable not only because it unmasks the egoism that underlies this sentiment but because it highlights the prominent role of the desire for power among our egoistic drives. Long before he had formulated the doctrine of the will to power, Nietzsche shows himself to be acutely aware of the manifold ways in which the desire for power motivates human behavior. Not only in pity but in many other actions, we experience pleasure in venting "our power on others" and producing "in ourselves the pleasurable feeling of ascendancy" (*HH* 103). At one point, Nietzsche even identifies pleasure with the "feeling of one's own power" and states that "the struggle for pleasure" thus understood "is the struggle for life" (*HH* 104). Interestingly, as Walter Kaufmann has pointed out, Nietzsche generally associates the lust for power in *Human, All too Human* with behavior he dislikes; "the will to power is essentially an urge of the impotent."[39] This is particularly the case in his discussion of the Christian ascetic, whose tyranny over himself exhibits the most extreme lust for power (*HH* 136–44).

Nietzsche's view in *Human, All too Human* that all action is motivated by egoism or self-interest—a view that goes by the name of psychological ego-ism—seems to link him closely to the French moralist La Rochefoucauld.[40] But while Nietzsche certainly evinces admiration for La Rochefoucauld, citing him approvingly in several aphorisms (see *HH* 35–36, 50, 133), his reasons for exposing the egoistic basis of human action differ sharply from La Rochefoucauld's. The latter thinker was primarily concerned to bring out the hypocrisy of human beings and the discrepancy between their pretence to virtue and the real thing. Far from repudiating Christianity, La Roche-foucauld in many ways ratcheted up its already strenuous demands and un-compromising idealism. Nietzsche has a very different purpose in bringing out the egoism behind our putatively nonegoistic actions. He does not mean to discredit those actions—of the self-sacrificing lover, mother, or soldier, for example—by comparing them to some nonegoistic ideal. Quite the op-posite: he wants to explode the whole notion of the nonegoistic so that it can no longer serve as a basis for self-condemnation and self-contempt. Looking back from a later vantage point, Nietzsche captures this original purpose of his psychological egoism: "The Christian gloominess in La Rochefoucauld which extracted egoism from everything and thought he had thereby *re-duced* the values of things and of virtues! To counter that, I at first sought to prove that there could not be anything other than egoism" (*WP* 362).[41]

In an aphorism from *The Wanderer and His Shadow*, Nietzsche makes clear how his critical analysis of morality differs from the sort of cynical de-bunking of virtue for which La Rochefoucauld was famous. Unlike moralists of the latter sort, Nietzsche does not seek to deny "the grandiose, mighty, self-sacrificing disposition such as is evidenced by Plutarch's heroes, or the pure, enlightened, heat-conducting state of souls of truly good men and women"; rather, he merely seeks to explain such dispositions, revealing the complex motives and "delicate conceptual illusions" woven into them. Nietz-sche is emphatic that his analysis of morality is not to be confused with the analyses of those valet-psychologists "who have no belief at all in these dispositions and states of soul and suppose that greatness and purity are only an outward show concealing behind them a paltriness similar to their own" (*WS* 20).[42]

One of the chief strategies Nietzsche uses to break down the false opposition between egoistic and nonegoistic actions is to return to primitive morality and show that it was based on utility and reciprocal exchange. This strategy is first deployed in an aphorism devoted to the "twofold prehistory of good and evil," which complicates the story Rée had told about how the concept of good originally referred to actions that promoted a single, unitary communal interest. As he later does in *Beyond Good and Evil* and *The Genealogy of Morals*, Nietzsche here argues that good and evil originally designated very different things, depending on whether one belonged to the ruling, powerful caste or the subjected, powerless caste. For the former, good referred to those who were capable of requital, either in the form of gratitude or revenge, and bad (*Schlecht*) referred to those who were too powerless to requite. For the latter, on the other hand, "every other man" is perceived as threatening, dangerous, and therefore evil (*Böse*). Clearly, no community could arise or persist on the basis of the latter disposition, and therefore Nietzsche concludes—in contrast to his analyses in *Beyond Good and Evil* and *Genealogy of Morals*—that "our present morality has grown up in the soil of the *ruling* tribes and castes" (*HH* 45).

Nietzsche elaborates on this idea of requital as the original basis of social morality in his reflections on the origin of justice. Alluding to the Melian Dialogue of Thucydides, he asserts that "justice (fairness) originates between parties of approximately *equal power*" and that equal exchange is its fundamental characteristic. Justice is not something independent of self-interest, but, rather, it is based entirely on "enlightened self-preservation" and egoism. Gradually, though, through habit, education, and emulation, this utilitarian origin of justice has been forgotten and just action has come to be associated with what is nonegoistic. This, of course, is an error—justice is ultimately grounded in egoism and utility—but it is an error upon which the high value accorded justice and the respect it commands depends: "How little moral would the world appear without forgetfulness! A poet could say that God has placed forgetfulness as a doorkeeper on the threshold of the temple of human dignity" (*HH* 92).

Nietzsche's emphasis on the role of forgetting here (see also *WS* 40 on "The Significance of Forgetting for Moral Sensation") is highly reminiscent of Rée, but his account of the origin of justice is quite different. For Rée, the origin of justice lies in the retrospective misinterpretation of the original aim of punishment, which was deterrence. Legal punishment is always a deterrent for future actions rather than a retribution for past ones; and the rightness of punishment does not rest on the feeling of retributive justice but on considerations of social utility. Rée puts his instrumentalist view in the most uncompromising terms: "[J]ust as we lock up or kill vicious dogs, although they do not deserve punishment, so too we will condemn, lock up, and sometimes kill individuals who are harmful to others (thieves, murderers) even though they do not deserve punishment."[43] Nietzsche does not dismiss justice quite so easily. He concedes to Rée that the purpose of punishment is deterrence and that "the utility of mankind" requires the continuance of such punishment. Nevertheless, he denies that such deterrent punishment accords with justice understood as reciprocity or "giving to each what is his own" (HH 105). Justice is an independent consideration and not merely a misinterpretation. And it is on account of our sense of justice, according to Nietzsche, that we are offended more by an execution than a murder; we recoil from "the insight that here a human being is being used as a means of deterring others" (HH 70).

We have seen how Nietzsche's inquiry into the origin of the moral sensations differs from Rée's in a variety of ways. But perhaps the sharpest difference emerges in Nietzsche's discussion of the role of custom (Sitte) in primitive morality. He addresses this theme, which is much more fully developed in Daybreak, in only a handful of aphorisms. His principal point is that good originally referred to what was in accordance with custom and evil to what was not in accordance with it. Contrary to Rée's contention, good and evil had nothing to do with the distinction between egoistic and nonegoistic actions. What more than anything else was necessary for the preservation of the community was adherence to custom or tradition, no matter how irrational (HH 96). Nietzsche here seems to echo Bagehot, who also emphasized the "cake of custom" in primitive society as a means of binding wayward human beings together.[44] In contrast to Rée's idealized portrait of the rational utility of primitive morality, Nietzsche stresses how customary morality originally sacrificed the individual to the community (AOM 89) and stifled the fledgling impulses of science (AOM 90).

In addition to rejecting Rée's rationalization of the origin—at one point he comments that "in the beginning was nonsense" (AOM 22), a sentiment to which Rée took particular exception[45]—Nietzsche also holds out the possibility of moral progress. Here again there are echoes of Bagehot, who envisaged the thick "cake of custom" giving way to a more individualistic "age of discussion."[46] Nietzsche, too, speaks of the "stages of morality." In the first, corresponding to customary morality, the "most dreadful means of inspiring fear have to be pressed into service" for the sake of "preserving the community and warding off its destruction." This is followed by a morality whose commands come from the mouth of God (as in Mosaic law) and, after that, a morality based on the concept of unconditional duty (as in Kant). Further stages include "a morality of *inclination,* of *taste,* finally that of *insight*—which is above and beyond all illusionary motive forces of morality but has a clear realization of why mankind could possess no other" (*WS* 44).

In another evolutionary scenario, Nietzsche speaks of the "three phases of morality hitherto," in which the preference for the common utility over that of the individual is gradually internalized. This corresponds to the morality of nonegoistic action and motivation valorized by Schopenhauer and Rée. But Nietzsche looks forward to an even higher stage of morality, "the morality of the mature individual," in which "it is realized more and more that it is in precisely the most *personal* possible considerations that the degree of utility is at its greatest also for the generality. . . . To make of oneself a complete *person,* and in all that one does to have in view the *highest good* of this person—that gets us further than those pity-filled agitations and actions for the sake of others" (*HH* 94–95).[47] It is not just value of the nonegoistic that Nietzsche calls into question here but the whole static model of moral development that is found in Rée and even Darwin himself. In the end, Nietzsche's "naturalism" incorporates a much more profound sense of historicity than the naturalism of these other writers.

Having shown that the origins of moral goodness and justice lie in considerations of utility, power, and self-preservation, Nietzsche goes on to draw the further conclusion that, insofar as "evil" actions share the same prudential motivation, they do not deserve to be simply condemned: "All 'evil' acts are motivated by the drive to preservation or, more exactly, by the individual's intention of procuring pleasure and avoiding displeasure; so motivated, however, they are not evil" (*HH* 99). The "innocent element" in "evil" or "wicked" actions consists in the fact that they, too, are always carried out for the purpose of self-defense or self-preservation; they are never motiveless or carried out simply for the sake of doing harm. It is true that sometimes we commit such actions for the sake of producing in ourselves "the pleasurable feeling of ascendancy," or the pleasurable "feeling of our own power," but Nietzsche contends that this feeling is essentially connected with self-preservation and also characterizes (as we have already seen) "nonegoistic" sentiments such as pity. Thus, he concludes, "Socrates and Plato are right: whatever man does he always does the good, that is to say: that which seems to him good (useful) according to the relative degree of his intellect, the measure of his rationality" (*HH* 102–4).

The reference to intellect and rationality in the previous quotation is not insignificant, and I will have more to say about it in a moment. But first we need to attend to the sweeping conclusion Nietzsche draws from the fore-going reflections on the egoistic basis of all our actions: namely, that "no one is accountable for his deeds, no one for his nature; to judge is the same thing as to be unjust." Here Nietzsche agrees with Rée's denial of the freedom of the will,[48] not to mention Spinoza's,[49] and goes one step beyond Schopen-hauer, who held that while the actions of men are determined by necessity their natures are not. This last vestige of the "fable of intelligible freedom" and human accountability that Schopenhauer inherited from Kant is firmly rejected by Nietzsche: no one can be held accountable for his nature "insofar as it is altogether a necessary consequence and assembled from the elements of things past and present" (HH 39; see also AOM 33). Human beings are composites of passions and desires that have been inherited from the past and modified in the present. There is no way to get beyond these desires and passions, no way to escape into a realm of transcendental freedom or non-egoistic action. As we have already seen, "it is the individual's sole desire for self-enjoyment (together with the fear of losing it) which gratifies itself in every instance, let a man act as he can, that is to say as he must: whether his deeds be those of vanity, revenge, pleasure, utility, malice, cunning, or those of sacrifice, sympathy, knowledge" (HH 107).

As sweeping as his denial of free will is here, it is not clear from every-thing else that Nietzsche says that he means to proclaim a rigid determinism or a resigned fatalism. Interestingly, the relationship between free will and fate had been the subject of two of Nietzsche's earliest essays, "Fate and History" and "Freedom of Will and Fate," both written in 1862, and both showing the heavy influence of Emerson, especially his essay "Fate." Like Emerson, Nietzsche emphasizes the manifold ways in which human be-ings are subject to fate, but he also maintains that this subjection in no way eliminates human freedom. If fate were the only principle governing our actions, he writes, "man would be the plaything of dark, effective forces," a mere "automaton."[50] Emerson, too, defends human freedom in the face of an all-pervasive fate: "Fate has its lord; limitation its limits . . . If Fate follows and limits power, power attends and antagonizes Fate. . . . Man is not order of nature, sack and sack, belly and members, link in a chain, but a stupen-dous antagonism." And he goes on to argue that "if Fate is so prevailing, man also is part of it, and can confront fate with fate."[51]

Years later, Nietzsche employs this very Emersonian argument in an aphorism from The Wanderer and His Shadow entitled "Turkish Fatalism." Turkish fatalism, which counsels resignation to a fate one cannot control, rests on the belief that fate is something separate from human beings, standing over against them. But this is an error, according to Nietzsche: "In reality every man is himself a piece of fate; when he thinks to resist fate in the way suggested, it is precisely fate that is here fulfilling itself; the struggle is imaginary, but so is the proposed resignation to fate; all these imagining are enclosed within fate" (*WS* 61). Nothing follows practically from Nietzsche's denial of free will, at least as far as opposing or acquiescing to fate is concerned. The belief in fate, which is grounded in science, can be met with either "cowardice, resignation, or frankness and magnanimity," but the belief itself does not dictate any of these responses; "out of this [belief] anything and everything can grow" (*AOM* 363). This point will be relevant when we come to consider the seemingly fatalistic doctrine of the eternal recurrence.

Further complicating the question of Nietzsche's determinism is the fact that, while he denies the freedom of the will, he does not subscribe to Schopenhauer's doctrine of the unalterable character, which holds that an individual's "conduct is fixed and settled even at his birth and remains essentially the same to the very end."[52] He agrees with Schopenhauer that an individual's conduct may not change much over the course of his brief lifetime, but this suggests nothing more than that the motives operating on his conduct "are unable to scratch deeply enough to erase the imprinted script of many millennia." But what if we imagine an individual living eighty thousand years? Then we would see that his character is "totally alterable" (*HH* 41). In other words, while human beings may not be alterable at the individual level, they certainly are at the historical level.

Among the factors that can influence or alter an individual's character, Nietzsche includes circumstances, experiences, and even opinions. "Alter," however, is not quite the right word for what he has in mind. It is not that circumstances, experiences, and opinions actually change who we are; rather, they bring out or illuminate aspects of our character of which we have hitherto been unaware. Thus Nietzsche comments that we "do not know whether or not we have a serpent's tooth until someone has set his heel on us" (*AOM* 36). In the same way, a book can sometimes bring out the "hidden sickness of [our] heart and [make] it visible." He summarizes his general point in this way: "Altered opinions do not alter a man's character (or do so very little); but they do illuminate individual aspects of the constellation of his personality which with a different constellation of opinions had hitherto remained dark and unrecognizable" (*AOM* 58). One might object that Nietzsche here merely substitutes a kind of social determinism for the characterological determinism espoused by Schopenhauer, but this overlooks the degree to which we can control our circumstances, experiences, and opinions, a point Nietzsche will emphatically underline in *Daybreak*.

The charge that Nietzsche is a simple or rigid determinist becomes even harder to draw when we consider the role that he accords to thought or intelligent judgment in our actions. In the passage invoking Socrates and Plato above, for example, he claims that, though our actions are thoroughly determined by what appears good or useful to us, what we deem good or useful is based on the "relative degree of our intellect" and "the measure of our rationality." He elaborates on this point in another aphorism: "Degrees of intelligent judgment decide whither each person will let his desire draw him; every society, every individual always has present an order of rank of things considered good, according to which he determines his own actions and judges those of others" (*HH* 107). It is at this point that Nietzsche recurs to his evolutionary perspective, arguing that the "accepted order of rank of desirable things" is based on a "low, higher, or highest egoism" and that those who are deemed "immoral" are merely "not yet sufficiently sensible of the higher, more refined motives which a new culture has introduced" (*HH* 42). On this view, cruel men and criminals are to be regarded as "retarded," as survivals from earlier cultures that have been left behind: "They show us what we all *were*, and fill us with horror: but they themselves are as little accountable for it as a piece of granite is for being granite" (*HH* 43).[53]

Nietzsche acknowledges that his doctrine of the complete unaccountability and innocence of human beings constitutes the biggest blow to human vanity (*AOM* 50) and "is the bitterest draught the man of knowledge has to swallow" (*HH* 107). Nevertheless, he concludes the chapter on "The History of the Moral Sensations," as he did the chapter on "First and Last Things," by holding out the possibility of a more positive outcome in the transition from a "moral to a knowing mankind." Once again, he emphasizes in Spinozistic fashion[54] the moderation that results from the knowledge of the innocence and unaccountability of human beings, a moderation that is much needed in an age that is "visibly becoming more and more ignited" (*HH* 38):

> Even if the inherited habit of erroneous evaluation, loving, hating, does continue to rule in us, under the influence of increasing knowledge it will grow weaker: a new habit, that of comprehending, not-loving, not-hating, surveying is gradually implanting itself in us on the same soil and will in thousands of years' time perhaps be strong enough to bestow on mankind the power of bringing forth the wise, innocent (conscious of innocence) man as regularly

as it now brings forth—*not his antithesis but necessary preliminary*—the unwise, unjust, guilt-conscious man. (*HH* 107; see also *HH* 56)

Nietzsche's praise of moderation in *Human, All too Human* and the middle works in general is striking, especially given his reputation for passionate excess. Some commentators even see it as anomalous with respect to Nietzsche's other, and especially later, works.[55] There are certainly places where Nietzsche goes very far in his denial of the passions; for example, in a draft preface to *Human, All too Human*, he speaks of the soul of the free spirit as being "without envy and almost desireless [*bedürfnislos*]" (*KSA* 8:25 [2]). But in other places, especially *The Wanderer and His Shadow*, he is careful to distinguish moderation from extirpation of the passions. In one aphorism, for example, he points out that overcoming the passions must be viewed only as a means and not as the goal. It prepares the soil for good works, but if it is taken as the goal of our activity, "all kinds of weeds and devilish nonsense will quickly spring up in the rich soil now unoccupied" (*WS* 53). In the same way, he finds the Christian attempt to kill sensuality self-defeating, for it continues to "live on in an uncanny vampire form and torment [the individual] in repulsive disguises" (*WS* 83). Moderation does not so much involve denying the passions as depriving them of their "terrible character" so that they do not become "devastating torrents." The task is not to eliminate the passions (*Leidenschaften*) but to transform them into joys (*Freudenschaften*) (*WS* 37). In passages such as these, Nietzsche's praise of moderation in the middle period is not altogether discordant with his later outlook as expressed in a note from 1887: "*In Summa: domination* of the passions, *not* their weakening or extirpation!" (*WP* 933; see also 384).

The Artificiality of Religion

The third chapter of *Human, All too Human*, "The Religious Life," forms a bridge between the preceding chapter on morality and the ensuing chapters on art and culture. Religion is connected to morality in Nietzsche's scheme because it heightens the savage passions spawned by the moral interpretation of the world. The "blackening" of the world that results from the false opposition of "good" and "evil" in morality is both intensified by religion and then "lightened" or "cured" by it. This is especially the case with Christianity, which Nietzsche here, for the first time in his published writings, identifies as a major factor in the barbarization of modern culture. It is in its "lightening" or "curative" guise that religion is linked with art. In the notes that he began to write under the title "The Plowshare" after his crisis at the Bayreuth Festival, Nietzsche refers to religion and art as "narcotics" (*Betäubungen*) that "belong to a lower stage of medicine" (*KSA* 8:18 [33]). And he begins his chapter on religion in exactly the same way, complaining that art and religion attack an ill, not by removing its causes, but merely by providing a "momentary amelioration and narcotization (*Narkotisierung*)" (*HH* 108).

Before following up on this insight, Nietzsche leaves the reader in no doubt that he no longer subscribes to the understanding of religion as expressing the truth of things in allegorical form found in Schopenhauer's chapter "On Man's Need for Metaphysics." He concedes that in many ways this romantic understanding of religion was a necessary corrective to the Enlightenment's inadequate appreciation of the significance of religion (see *HH* 26). But romantic thinkers ultimately went too far in their reaction against the Enlightenment. The significance of religion "was appreciated much too highly, inasmuch as the religions were treated with love, almost amorously indeed, and were adjudged to possess a profound, indeed the profoundest possible understanding of the world." Once again, Nietzsche rejects the whole unhistorical notion of "the metaphysical need." And he claims that, had Schopenhauer been born later, he would have been forced to agree that "*a religion has never yet, either directly or indirectly, either as dogma or as parable, contained a truth*. For every religion was born out of fear and need, it has crept into existence along paths of aberrations of reason" (*HH* 110).

Nietzsche elaborates on the last point about the irrationality of primitive religion in the very next aphorism, entitled "The Origin of the Religious Cult." His reflections on primitive religion in this lengthy aphorism show the influence of English anthropological thinkers like Tylor, Bagehot, and Lubbock—indeed, he refers to Lubbock by name—and they go all the way back to the lectures he first gave in the Winter Semester of 1875–76 on "The Worship Service of the Greeks."[56] His overall point is that, far from expressing some sort of symbolic intuition or allegorical truth, the religious practices of primitive societies grew out of a deeply irrational and erroneous understanding of the world. What makes primitive societies and their religious life so difficult for us to understand, according to Nietzsche, is that they lacked any notion of natural law or natural causality. Instead, nature was thought to be governed by irrational forces and magical influences. Whereas modern people believe human beings to be changeable and nature uniform, primitive people believed the opposite: "man is the *rule*, nature is irregularity." The whole of primitive religion was devoted to somehow bringing this irregular, capricious, and also more powerful nature under control, whether through prayers, offerings, worship, treaties, magic, or sorcery. The whole meaning of the primitive religious cult was "to determine and constrain nature for the benefit of mankind" by impressing on it "a regularity and rule of law which it did not at first possess" (*HH* 111). Out of this irrational soil grew the so-called metaphysical need.

At the end of the aphorism on the origin of the religious cult, Nietzsche mentions that, in addition to the ideas of sorcery and magic, ancient religion also rested on "other and nobler ideas" which did not presuppose such inequality between gods and human beings. This was especially the case with Greek religion, where the Olympian gods were certainly nobler and mightier than human beings, but they were not understood to belong to a different species (*HH* 111). Christianity changed all this. In contrast to ennobling and idealizing tendencies of Greek religion, it "crushed and shattered man completely and buried him as though in mud: into a feeling of total depravity it then suddenly shone a beam of divine mercy, so that, surprised and stupefied by this act of grace, man gave vent to a cry of rapture and believed he bore all heaven within him" (*HH* 114). Here we see the dialectical and deceptive relationship between "blackening" and "lightening" alluded to above. Nietzsche goes on to illustrate it through a psychological analysis of the Christian idea of redemption and the Christian ideal of the saint.

The Christian need for redemption arises from a misinterpretation of morality. Human beings either commit or discover tendencies in themselves to commit actions that stand low in "the customary order of rank of actions." This would ordinarily result in no more than a moderate self-dissatisfaction if human beings compared themselves to other fallible and egoistic human beings, but instead they compare themselves with a "being which alone is capable of those actions called unegoistic," namely, God; and it is only because they look into this "brilliant mirror" that their own natures come to appear "so dismal, so uncommonly distorted." Self-contempt is the result of this false comparison with a fictitious God characterized by an impossible unegoism. Fortunately, such self-contempt does not afflict human beings at every moment of their lives, but when it ebbs from time to time, the event seems so incredible, miraculous, and undeserved that human beings erroneously attribute it to divine grace. It is on this double misinterpretation that the Christian need for redemption is built, and Nietzsche optimistically predicts that psychological insight into it will lead to a gradual loss of Christian belief (*HH* 132–35).

The phenomenon of the Christian ascetic and saint exhibits the same double movement of "blackening" and "lightening," making sick and "curing." At the bottom of this phenomenon, Nietzsche argues, is a "lust for power" that the individual seeks to gratify by tyrannizing over parts of his own nature. Oppressed by spiritual boredom and enervation of the will, the Christian ascetic found new excitement in life by transforming himself into a battlefield and waging continual war on himself. Such a war required a perpetual enemy, however, and the Christian ascetic proved particularly adept at finding or creating this enemy, "casting suspicion on everything human" and seeing everything that belongs to human nature as evil or sinful. To this end, the moral demands of Christianity were exaggerated "so that a man *could* not live up to them; the intention [was] not that he should *become* more moral, but that he should feel *as sinful as possible.*" It was this sinfulness that afforded the Christian saint the opportunity to practice a savage self-cruelty that produced a heightened feeling of power and a "rare kind of voluptuousness" in himself and a terrified awe and belief in the miraculous in others (*HH* 136–43).

In *The Wanderer and His Shadow*, Nietzsche states that "it was Christianity which first painted the Devil on the world's wall." And even though we no longer believe in the cure that Christianity offered, "*belief in the sickness* which it taught and propagated continues to exist" (*WS* 78). Nietzsche undoubtedly has Schopenhauer in mind here. Schopenhauer accepted Christianity's pessimistic interpretation of the world, while dispensing with its dogmatic foundations. In this way, he took as an eternal fact of human nature what was actually a historical product of contingent needs and erroneous interpretations. This latter intellectual tendency, Nietzsche claims, is particularly characteristic of "those half-beings, the poetizing philosophers and the philosophizing artists" (*HH* 110). Having disposed of the former, chief among whom is Schopenhauer, in the first three chapters of *Human, All too Human*, he now turns his attention to the "philosophizing artists," a class that includes the other great influence on his early philosophy, Richard Wagner.

Overcoming Romantic Art

With the fourth chapter of *Human, All too Human*, entitled "From the Souls of Artists and Writers," we finally arrive at the issue that, along with the problem of culture in general, originally motivated Nietzsche's inquiry in the book. As we have seen, *Human, All too Human* was born from the rejection of romantic, Wagnerian art, a rejection symbolized by Nietzsche's sudden flight from the first Bayreuth Festival in 1876. It was his break with Wagner that constituted the crisis to which Nietzsche, at the end of his sane life, said the book was a monument. Nietzsche does not mention Wagner by name in the 1878 publication of *Human, All too Human*—he actually deleted explicit references to both Wagner and Schopenhauer after his publisher rejected the idea of publishing the book under a pseudonym[57]—but that Wagner is his principal target, especially in the chapter on art, is unmistakable. Wagner himself fully recognized this when Nietzsche sent him a copy of the book in May 1878. In a condescending letter to Nietzsche's close friend Franz Overbeck, he wrote, "I have done [Nietzsche] the kindness . . . of *not* reading his book, and my greatest wish and hope is that one day he will thank me for this."[58] By the time he wrote *Assorted Opinions and Maxims*, Nietzsche was referring to Wagner explicitly in the section devoted to art (see *AOM* 134, 171).

The first aphorism of "From the Souls of Artists and Writers" recalls the beginning of *Human, All too Human*, where Nietzsche tells us that metaphysical philosophy refuses to see our highest values—truth, beauty, morality—as products of becoming, attributing to them instead "a miraculous source in the very kernel and being of the 'thing in itself'" (*HH* 1). In the same way, the artist promotes the illusion that the work of art is not something that *becomes* but that it springs "into being with miraculous suddenness," the product of divine inspiration. In keeping with the historical approach of the entire book, which detects behind the appearance of the miraculous and the divine a human, all too human origin, Nietzsche states that the "science of art" must counter the illusion of the miraculous origin of the work of art and "display the bad habits and false conclusions of the intellect by virtue of which it allows the artist to ensnare it" (*HH* 145).

This illusion of the miraculous origin of the work of art is nowhere more evident than in the romantic cult of genius. Nietzsche devotes several aphorisms to debunking this idea, arguing that great art has far more to do with hard work than with sudden inspiration. The imagination of artists is productive of a wide assortment of things, good, bad, and mediocre. What distinguishes the great artist is his "power of judgment," which allows him to sift the gold from the dross, the fresh formulation from the cliché: "All great artists have been great workers, inexhaustible not only in invention but also in rejecting, sifting, transforming, ordering" (*HH* 155). Nietzsche sounds like he is describing his almost exact contemporary, Henry James (born in 1843), when he lays out his simple recipe for becoming a good novelist:

> One has only to make a hundred or so sketches for novels, none longer than two pages but of such distinctness that every word in them is necessary; one should write down anecdotes each day until one has learned how to give them the most pregnant and effective form; one should be tireless in collecting

and describing human types and characters. . . . One should continue in this
many-sided exercise some ten years: what is then created in the workshop,
however, will be fit to go out into the world. (*HH* 163)

The cult of genius, with its belief in miraculous origins and divine inspiration, is only one of the illusions that artists partake in. According to Nietzsche, artists are also generally characterized by a rather attenuated sense of
truth or intellectual probity. They "do not wish to be deprived of the glittering, profound interpretations of life" because these interpretations make
their art more "efficacious" (*HH* 146). For this reason, artists have always
been "the glorifiers of the religious and philosophical errors of mankind"
(*HH* 220). Even as the sea of religious faith recedes in the nineteenth century as a result of the growth of science, art "takes over a host of moods
and feelings engendered by religion" and thereby "grows more profound
and soulful, so that it is now capable of communicating exultation and
enthusiasm as it formerly could not" (*HH* 150). This is what happens in
Beethoven's Ninth Symphony (*HH* 153) and, though Nietzsche does not
say so explicitly, in Wagnerian opera.[59] The Enlightenment has not completely succeeded in eradicating religious feelings or the metaphysical need:
"[T]he feelings expelled from the sphere of religion by the Enlightenment
throw themselves into art" (*HH* 150).

It is because artists glorify and perpetuate the old metaphysical and religious errors of mankind that Nietzsche says they do not "stand in the
foremost ranks of the Enlightenment and the progressive *masculinization* of
man." He frequently compares them to children who not only remain attached to "the games of childhood" but also constitute a retrogression to the
mythological and unscientific outlook of earlier times. This childlike condition they then seek to extend to the rest of mankind (*HH* 147, 159). Art no
longer belongs among the progressive forces in history, and for this reason
Nietzsche argues that it must be superseded by science as the fundamental
activity of human beings. Long gone is the sentiment expressed in *The Birth
of Tragedy* that "art represents the highest task and truly metaphysical activity of this life" (*BT* Preface). Instead, in a manner reminiscent of Hegel,
Nietzsche now reflects on the "end of art."[60] The great works of art of the
past—Dante's *Divine Comedy*, Raphael's paintings, the Gothic cathedrals—
all rested on religious and metaphysical presuppositions. Not without a
certain nostalgia, Nietzsche believes he can see the end of this religiously
and metaphysically charged art on the horizon: "A moving tale will one day
be told how there once existed such an art, such an artist's faith" (*HH* 220;
see also 218).

Ever the dialectical thinker, though, Nietzsche does not merely dismiss art but shows how, even if superseded, it will still play a crucial role in our scientific and enlightened future. We owe a debt of gratitude to art because "it has taught us for thousands of years to look upon life in any of its forms with interest and pleasure, and to educate our sensibilities so we at last cry: 'life, however it may be, is good.' This teaching . . . reemerges as an almighty requirement of knowledge. . . . The scientific man is the further evolution of the artistic" (*HH* 222). We are reminded here of what Nietzsche said early on in *Human, All too Human* about the need to take "a retrograde step" after we have recognized the erroneousness of our metaphysical conceptions; otherwise "we will deprive [ourselves] of the best mankind has produced" (*HH* 20). In the same way, he remarks at the end of the chapter on art that, though the "artist will soon be regarded as a glorious relic," we must nevertheless honor him because the "best in us has perhaps been inherited from the sensibilities of earlier ages to which we hardly have any access by direct paths; the sun has already set, but the sky of our life still glows with its light, even though we no longer see it" (*HH* 223).

Most of the aphorisms in the original, 1878 *Human, All too Human* deal with art in general and not with specific historical styles or aesthetic attitudes. But in a lengthy aphorism entitled "The Revolution in Poetry," Nietzsche broaches the latter theme, contrasting the "stern constraint" of the French dramatists of the seventeenth and early eighteenth centuries with the unfettered freedom, formlessness, and naturalism of modern, romantic art. (The praise of the French at the expense the Germans throughout this aphorism is clearly meant as a provocation to the French-hating Wagner.) Whereas the former took their inspiration from the Greeks, the latter models itself on the "great barbarian Shakespeare," whose promiscuous mixing of styles and forms reflects the restlessness of the modern spirit, "its hatred for bounds and moderation." Nietzsche concedes that the latter, unfettered poetry enables us to enjoy the "primitive, wild-blooming, strangely beautiful and gigantically irregular," but it ultimately leads to the corruption of public taste and the valuing of "artistic power for its own sake" (*HH* 221).

The discussion of classic versus romantic art introduced in this aphorism from the original *Human, All too Human* is much more fully developed in the sequels to the book. There Nietzsche consistently contrasts the simplicity, discipline, restraint, moderation, and economy of expression that he associates preeminently with Greek art with the florid, emotionally excessive, unmeasured, and novelty-obsessed character of modern art. Against the "rage for originality" that animates the latter, he holds up the "noble poverty" and "dancing in chains" that distinguish the former (see *AOM* 112–13,

116–18, 162; *WS* 122, 127, 136, 140). Nor is this opposition between classic and romantic art merely an aesthetic matter; it also has profound implications for morality. Nietzsche agrees with Plato about the potentially
harmful effects of certain types of art (*HH* 212). In particular, he worries
about the raptures, convulsions, and indulgence of passions promoted by
modern romantic art. Whereas the ancient Greeks "were tamers of the will,
transformers of animals, creators of men, and in general sculptors and re-
modelers of life," today's great artists "are mostly unchainers of the will"
whose souls resemble "cave[s] of desires, overgrown with flowers, thistles,
and poisonous weeds" (*AOM* 172).

The attack on Wagner that is implicit in these aphorisms becomes explicit
in several places. In an aphorism entitled "How Modern Music is Supposed
to Make the Soul Move," for example, Nietzsche analyzes Wagnerian music
in terms of the classic/romantic dichotomy sketched above. He contends
that, whereas earlier music, with its regular rhythm and "orderly measure,"
constrained the soul to dance, Wagnerian music, with its celebrated "endless
melody" and avoidance of "all mathematical symmetry of tempo," makes
the soul feel as though it is swimming or floating. The danger posed by such
watery music is that it may ultimately deprive the soul of the listener of all
sense of "limit and proportion" (*AOM* 134).

Even here, though, Nietzsche's analysis is not without dialectical com-
plication. He recognizes that at a certain point the delight in order and
mathematical symmetry can become cloying, and then there arises "the
even subtler feeling that enjoyment might also lie in breaking through the
orderly and the symmetrical; when, for example, it seems enticing to seek
the rational in the apparently irrational" (*AOM* 119). In the history of Greek
rhetoric, he points out, the "ever increasing care expended on obedience to
all the ancient rules and self-limitations" finally led to a "painful tension"
and the feeling that "the bow *has* to break." At this point, "the baroque style
of Asia," with its manifold and "marvelous means of expression," became "a
necessity and almost an act of *charity*" (*AOM* 131). It seems that romantic,
Wagnerian art has its uses for the free spirit. Though Nietzsche condemns
modern artists for being "unchainers of the will," he adds, significantly,
that they are "for that reason under certain circumstances liberators of life"
(*AOM* 172). It is in this connection that he praises Laurence Sterne, the
master of ambiguity, irony, and the "endless melody," the enemy of "discipline, compactness, simplicity, [and] restraint," as the most free-spirited of
authors (*AOM* 113).

Despite this dialectical nuance, Nietzsche's final verdict on Wagnerian
music is that it is ultimately reactionary. In its nationalism, attraction to

myth, and "Christian-medieval thirst for ecstatic sensuality and asceticism," the spirit of Wagner's music "wages the *ultimate* war of reaction against the spirit of the Enlightenment" (*AOM* 171). In one place, Nietzsche points to the "religious origin of modern music" and its opposition to the secular and scientific spirit of the Renaissance and Enlightenment (*HH* 219, 237); and in another, he suggests that the "grand tragic-dramatic mode of [modern] musical execution acquires its character through imitating the demeanor of the *great sinner* as Christianity imagines and desires him to be" (*WS* 156). Lest the reader fail to grasp that it is Wagnerian music of which he speaks, Nietzsche follows the latter aphorism with one praising the music of Felix Mendelssohn, the Jewish composer for whom Wagner conceived an almost pathological hatred. In contrast to the torment, guilt, and despair of Wagner's music, Mendelssohn's music exudes gratitude; it "is the music of enjoyment of whatever is good and precedented" (*WS* 157).

This last reflection points to one final problem Nietzsche attributes to modern, romantic art: namely, its distorted understanding of the relationship between art and life. Whereas earlier ages sought self-enjoyment and self-glorification in art, ours desires that "it shall scare away [our] discontent, boredom, and uneasy conscience for moments or hours at a time." For the Greeks, "art was an outflowing and overflowing of their own healthiness and well-being . . . self-enjoyment was what led them to art, whereas what leads our contemporaries to it is—self-disgust" (*AOM* 169). Art and artistic taste should grow integrally out of actuality rather than be used as an escape from or compensation for it. Among his contemporaries, Nietzsche prefers even the vulgar but genuine taste for August Kotzebue's sentimental dramas over the high-minded but artificial taste for Goethe and Sophocles (*AOM* 170). (This is another dig at Wagner, who, in extolling the virtues of the nationalistic Burschenschaft movement in Germany, went so far as to defend the murder of Kotzebue in 1819 by the insane student Karl Sand.)[61]

Nietzsche sums up his point about the distorted relationship between art and life in modern culture in an aphorism entitled "Art in the Age of Work." Because we live in an industrious age, we no longer "bestow our best hours and mornings on art" but treat it as a leisure or "recreational activity." In these circumstances, artists are forced to provide "recreation and distraction" to the "tired and weary," using the most powerful stimulants in their pharmacy. In this pharmacy, they have "the mightiest means of excitation capable of terrifying even the half-dead; they have narcotics, intoxicants, convulsives, paroxysms of tears; with these they overpower the tired and weary, arouse them to fatigued overliveliness and make them beside themselves with rapture and terror." Nietzsche does not blame the composers of "opera, tragedy, and music" for the degraded need to which they must minister, but he does look forward to "an age which shall one day bring back true festivals of joy and freedom [and] have no use for *our* art" (*WS* 170).

What sort of art will characterize this post-romantic age of the future? In the original *Human, All too Human* of 1878, as we have seen, Nietzsche speaks of the end or superseding of art, but in the 1879 *Assorted Opinions and Maxims* he evokes a poetry that will serve as a "signpost of the future," blending "knowledge and art into a new unity." Such poetry will be the exact opposite of the intoxicating and overexcited art of romantic music and opera, appearing instead "to be secluded and secured against the fire and breath of the *passions*." This poetry will not dwell on the alienated and unhappy but, rather, "scent out those cases in which, in the *midst* of our modern world and reality and without any artificial withdrawal from or warding off of this world, the great and beautiful soul is still possible." The characters depicted in this poetry will not be marked by Tristan-like longing and despair but by harmoniousness, "strength, goodness, mildness, purity, and an involuntary inborn moderation" (*AOM* 99).[62] As he does throughout his discussion of art, Nietzsche holds out Goethe as the great forerunner of this anti-tragic, counter-romantic poetry of the future, though in another aphorism he also commends the works of Georg Lichtenberg, Gottfried Keller, and Adalbert Stifter (*WS* 109).[63]

The ideal that Nietzsche sketches in this aphorism is the same ideal of a moderate, serene, and harmonious life based on knowledge that was evoked in the concluding aphorism of chapter 1 (from which I quoted above) and that finds expression in the paintings of Poussin and the philosophy of Epicurus (*WS* 295). It is an ideal that is elaborated in the climactic chapter of *Human, All too Human* devoted to the "higher culture" of the future, a culture based not on art, religion, or metaphysics but on scientific knowledge.

Scientific Culture

The full title of the fifth chapter of *Human, All too Human* is "Marks of Higher and Lower Culture," which immediately alerts us to the evolutionary perspective that frames Nietzsche's argument. We have already encountered this perspective early on in the book, where Nietzsche indicates that human history consists in the movement from a lower culture occupied with "spinning out forms and symbols" to a higher culture marked by a "manly," scientific spirit (*HH* 3). There is a tremendously Hegelian dimension to Nietzsche's historical outlook here, as we will see more clearly the further we get into his argument concerning higher culture. Nevertheless, he is careful to avoid any metaphysical assumptions about the providential character of historical progress. The notion that human history is the self-revelation of an "evolving god," as opposed to a "blind mechanism, a senseless, purposeless confused play of forces," is a thoroughly metaphysical and erroneous idea. On the other hand, given the senseless and purposeless nature of the historical process, Nietzsche sympathetically understands the comfort this idea of an evolving god provides and even urges that we not get annoyed by it. Such an idea at least springs from a serious attempt to come to terms with history, whereas Schopenhauer's mocking of it springs from an ahistorical denial of "the fact of evolution" (*HH* 238).[64]

Another myth about historical progress that Nietzsche immediately dispels is that it necessarily results in advances in all departments of human activity. "It is folly," he writes, "to believe that a new higher stage of mankind will unite in itself all the excellences of earlier stages and be obliged, for example, to include the highest phase of art" (*HH* 239). This, of course, reiterates what he has already said about the "end of art" in scientific culture. Now he predicts that the forces that "condition the production of art"—for example, "delight in lying, in the vague, in the symbolic, in intoxication, in ecstasy"—"could simply die out." And the same goes for religion: "we cannot expect to see the astonishing effects of the religious feeling . . . there will never again be a life and culture bounded by a religiously determined horizon" (*HH* 234).

As Nietzsche develops his argument, however, it appears that these earlier stages of human development are not simply lost but somehow preserved as they are being superseded—or *aufgehoben*, to use the Hegelian term that seems so apposite here. "It is a sign of superior culture," he writes, "to consciously retain certain phases of development which lesser men live through almost without thinking" (*HH* 274). This is the great gift of the modern "historical sense," which is enhanced when individuals recapitulate the earlier stages of cultural development in their own lives. Do not be ashamed, Nietzsche counsels, for having given oneself wholly to art or religion at some point in one's life, for it is through such experiences that one gains a more profound understanding of the "paths taken by earlier mankind" (*HH* 292). The typical course of cultural development begins with religion and passes through metaphysical philosophy and art before arriving at the scientific outlook of higher culture. Nietzsche comments that this course of development "nowadays usually takes place within a man's first thirty years. It is the recapitulation of a curriculum at which mankind has been laboring for perhaps thirty thousand years" (*HH* 272).

Of all the reversals in *Human, All too Human*, perhaps none is so striking as its exaltation of the modern historical sense, the feature of modern cultural life that Nietzsche had so brilliantly criticized in "The Uses and Disadvantages of History for Life." In one of the most Hegelian statements of the book, he writes that "the striving for knowledge of the entire historical past, which ever more mightily distinguishes the modern age from all others," may someday allow us to arrive at "cosmic self-consciousness" (*AOM* 185). This sentiment is echoed in another aphorism, where he argues that self-knowledge ultimately "requires history" or "universal knowledge with respect to all that is past" (*AOM* 223). From these statements it is clear that the knowledge that distinguishes higher or scientific culture is historical knowledge. There is "no honey sweeter" than this sort of knowledge, Nietzsche comments, which reaches its apex in old age and "that gentle sunshine of a constant spiritual joyousness" (*HH* 292).

The perfect historical consciousness that Nietzsche describes as the goal of higher culture is obviously a contemplative ideal, and this provokes his lament that the modern age does not sufficiently value the *vita contemplativa*. "Time for thinking and quietness in thinking are lacking" in the modern world, which is increasingly characterized by the agitation and restlessness epitomized by America. From this "lack of repose," Nietzsche insists, "our civilization is turning into a new barbarism," and therefore "one of the most necessary corrections to the character" of modern humanity is the "strengthening of the contemplative element in it."[65] Even scholars have not escaped the busyness of modern life, feeling ashamed of *otium* or leisure and conducting their investigations with "antlike industry." In this regard, they differ fundamentally from the free spirit, who alone is capable of genuine reflection on knowledge and whose "higher task" therefore is to command "from a lonely position the whole militia of scientific and learned men and [show] them the paths to and goals of culture" (*HH* 282–85).

How one can acquire the leisure necessary for contemplation in our modern, restless, and industrial circumstances is a difficulty that Nietzsche does not omit to consider. On the one hand, he comments dismissively that, "as at all times, so now too, men are divided into the slaves and the free; for he who does not have two-thirds of his day to himself is a slave, let him be what he may otherwise: statesman, businessman, official, scholar" (*HH* 283). On the other, he suggests a more realistic scenario by which the free spirit, without completely opting out of modern economic conditions, can somehow preserve his freedom and leisure within them. "The liberal minded men who live for the sake of knowledge alone," he writes, will not be ambitious in a worldly way but content themselves with minor positions and small incomes that merely allow them to get by. Such men will certainly know "weekdays of unfreedom, of dependence, [and] servitude," but they must also have their "Sunday of freedom" to make it all worthwhile. In this way, each lives a life of "refined heroism which disdains to offer itself to the veneration of the masses . . . and tends to go silently through the world and out of the world" (*HH* 291).

Though historical knowledge appears very much as an end in itself in Nietzsche's conception of higher, scientific culture, it also promises important practical benefits. Nietzsche claims that our age may be considered fortunate in two respects. "With respect to the *past* we have enjoyment of all the cultures there have ever been and of their productions." But on a more practical note, "with respect to the *future* there opens out before us, for the first time in history, the tremendous far-flung prospect of human-ecumenical goals embracing the entire inhabited earth" (*AOM* 179). This is the fundamental practical task that confronts humanity after the death of God, a task that requires (as we have already seen) an "altogether unprece-dented *knowledge of the preconditions of culture*" (*HH* 25).

In the chapter on higher culture in *Human, All too Human*, Nietzsche devotes a number of aphorisms precisely to this practical problem of the "preconditions of culture." In one, entitled the "Bell-Founding of Culture," he compares the construction of culture to the fashioning of a bell. The cas-ing of the bell consists of "coarser commoner stuff" such as untruth and vio-lence, and the question arises: "Has the time now come to remove it? Has what was molten become solid, have the good and advantageous drives, the habits of the nobler disposition grown so secure and general that there is no longer any need to lean on metaphysics and the errors of the religions?" Nietzsche does not answer this question; indeed, in the aphorisms that fol-low he reiterates his dialectical stance that untruth and violence, the errors of metaphysics, religion, and art, cannot simply be cast off in scientific cul-ture. Of one thing, though, he is sure: "There is no longer a god to aid us in answering this question: our own insight must here decide. Man himself has to take in hand the rule of man over the earth, it is his 'omniscience' that has to watch over the destiny of culture with a sharp eye" (*HH* 245).[66]

That we cannot completely dispense with error and illusion Nietzsche makes clear in an aphorism on the "double-brain" required by higher cul-ture. Because it is the *quest* for knowledge that makes science pleasurable, not the possession of it, science will provide us with less and less pleasure the more it accumulates its solid and disillusioning truths. For this reason, Nietzsche suggests that "a higher culture must give to man a double-brain, as it were two brain-ventricles, one for the perceptions of science, the other for those of non-science." In the latter lies the "power-source," and in the former the "regulator." In his new version of the Apollonian–Dionysian dialectic, Nietzsche claims that the brain "must be heated with illusions, one-sidenesses, [and] passions," and then the "perilous consequences of overheating must be obviated with the aid of the knowledge furnished by science." Only in this way can interest and pleasure in scientific truth be preserved so that humanity does not relapse into its earlier delight in error, illusion, and fantasy (*HH* 251). How, exactly, Nietzsche envisions these two brains as coexisting alongside one another, whether in a single individual or in society as a whole, is not made clear in this aphorism, pointing to a persistent problem about the role of error and illusion in scientific culture that runs throughout *Human, All too Human* (see also *HH* 16, 20, 29–34) and in many ways through *Daybreak* and *The Gay Science* as well.

Of one thing he is certain, however: freedom from the errors of morality, religion, and metaphysics is only for the few—at least for the foreseeable future. Nietzsche once again shows that he is not an uncritical disciple of the Enlightenment and its faith in the universal dissemination of knowledge. Chains consisting of the "heavy and pregnant errors" of morality, religion, and metaphysics have been laid on human beings for a very long time, and it is these chains that have succeeded in lifting human beings above the animals. We now stand at a critical juncture in history when these chains can begin to be removed, but Nietzsche insists that we must "proceed with the greatest caution. Only the *ennobled man may be given freedom of spirit*; to him alone does alleviation of life [*Erleichterung des Lebens*] draw near and salve his wounds; only he may say that he lives for the sake of *joy* and for the sake of no further goal; in any other mouth his motto would be perilous." He suggests that there may come a time in the future when all human beings can share in this freedom of spirit, but for now these glad tidings—unlike those announced long ago to the shepherds in the fields around Bethlehem—can only be incorporated without danger by the very few (*WS* 350).

At one point, Nietzsche comments that "interest in education will become genuinely intense only from the moment when belief in God and his loving care is abandoned" (*HH* 242). Therefore, it is not surprising that many of his reflections on the "preconditions of culture" revolve around the cultivation and education of the human type that embodies the ideal of the scientific quest for knowledge, namely, the free spirit. What makes the production of this human type particularly tricky is that, in comparison with the fettered spirit, who never questions tradition and is actuated by a few uncomplicated motives, the free spirit is relatively weak, especially when it comes to action; "he is aware of too many motives and points of view and therefore possesses an uncertain and unpracticed hand" (*HH* 230). In an interesting rejoinder to the Darwinian notion of the struggle for existence, though, Nietzsche claims that it is the weaker natures who bring about human progress and evolution, whereas the stronger natures merely preserve the species (*HH* 224).[67] So the task that confronts the educator of the free spirit is how to make the latter strong enough so that he does not "ineffectually perish" and fail to fulfill his evolutionary mission; the task is to make the free spirit into an *esprit fort* (*HH* 230).

The problem of producing a free spirit with the energy, strength, and endurance to oppose tradition is the same as the problem of producing genius in general (*HH* 231–32). As he does throughout his writings, Nietzsche emphasizes the all-important role of adversity, suffering, cruelty, and evil. These are the things that will spur the creativity of the free spirit and toughen him up for his deviant task. In educating the free spirit, therefore, the educator ought to emulate the harshness of nature: "He who became aware of how genius is produced, and desired to proceed in the manner in which nature usually does in this matter, would have to be exactly as evil and ruthless as nature is" (*HH* 233). History teaches us that the "frightful energies—those which are called evil—are the cyclopean architects and road-makers of humanity" (*HH* 246). It is for this reason that Nietzsche is opposed to the socialist attempt to create an ideal state and "a comfortable life for as many as possible." Such a goal, if accomplished, "would destroy the soil out of which great intellect and the powerful individual in general grows: by which I mean great energy. If this state is achieved, mankind would have become too feeble to still be able to produce the genius" (*HH* 235). The specter of the "last man" looms on the horizon.

For all his talk about the production of genius in the form of the free spirit, though, in *Human, All too Human* Nietzsche ends up being quite critical of the romantic cult of genius. This constitutes another of the book's reversals of his earlier position on the problem of culture, and it certainly reflects his growing disillusionment with the overweening genius of Wagner. There is a tendency among men, he writes, to "overvalue everything big and conspicuous," and this leads them to throw all of their force into a single domain and make of themselves "*one* monstrous organ," even though they would be much happier if they developed all of their powers equally (*HH* 260).[68] We must be careful to guard against the veneration of the genius whose power derives precisely from such hypertrophic development of a single power, for "the system of all that which humanity has need of for its continued existence is so comprehensive, and lays claim to so many and such varying forces, that humanity as a whole would have to pay dearly for any *one-sided* preference . . . to which these individuals would entice it."

Therefore, Nietzsche recommends that "next to the cult of genius and his force there must always be placed, as its complement and palliative, the cult of culture," which understands that the harmonious development of humanity requires a multiplicity of conditions and is "as much the work of ants and cyclops as of genius" (*AOM* 186).

Culture and Politics

The four chapters following the climactic one on culture cover a variety of topics, from vanity, love, and friendship to women and the family. Only one of these chapters, however, "A Glance at the State," directly bears on the theme of culture we have been following throughout our analysis. In this chapter, Nietzsche views modern politics largely through the lens of culture. Like his youthful hero, Friedrich Hölderlin, and his friend and colleague at Basel, Jacob Burckhardt, he worries about the excessive growth of the state and the possibility of its overwhelming the realm of culture.[69] For this reason he speaks out vociferously against "great politics." Some commentators have seen this antipolitical strain in the middle period as anomalous with respect to Nietzsche's advocacy of "great politics" in his later works,[70] but a quick glance at *Twilight of the Idols* shows remarkable continuity in Nietzsche's views on culture and politics. There he writes that "culture and the state . . . are antagonists. . . . All great ages of culture are ages of political decline: what is great culturally has always been unpolitical, even *antipolitical*. . . . [W]hat matters most . . . is always culture" (*TI* Germans 4). Given such statements, it is not surprising that in the last year of his sane life Nietzsche refers to himself as the "last *antipolitical* German" (*EH* 1.3).[71]

This is not to say that Nietzsche ignores the important auxiliary role the state can play with respect to culture. As we saw above, he rejects the Darwinian notion that the struggle for existence is the motor of human evolution, arguing instead that weaker natures are primarily responsible for progress, whereas stronger natures merely preserve the species. Nevertheless, preservation is an important value, and the state plays a crucial role in promoting it, serving as stabilizing force within which weaker, degenerate natures can bring about cultural progress. Quoting Machiavelli, Nietzsche writes that "'the great goal of statecraft should be *duration*.' . . . Only when there is a securely founded and guaranteed long duration is a steady evolution and ennobling inoculation possible" (*HH* 224).

Perhaps the most interesting aspect of Nietzsche's discussion of politics in *Human, All too Human* and its sequels is his treatment of democracy. Again, some commentators have seen this discussion as anomalous with respect to the "aristocratic radicalism" of Nietzsche's later works,[72] but this does not quite capture the nuance of his analysis. It is true that he does not simply reject democracy in *Human, All too Human*. Like Tocqueville, he regards the "democratization of Europe [as] irresistible" (*WS* 275). And he even concedes that such democratization is a legitimate demand on the part of the many: "[I]f the purpose of all politics really is to make life endurable for as many as possible, then these as-many-as-possible are entitled to determine what they understand by an endurable life." Nevertheless, he insists that the narrow-mindedness that belongs to democratic politics must not be allowed to infect all spheres of activity, especially of higher activity; it must not "go so far as to demand that *everything* should become politics in [the democratic] sense, that *everyone* should work according to such a standard." The few must be allowed to "refrain from politics" and assume an "ironic posture" with respect to the "happiness of the many" (*HH* 438; see also 450).

No matter how much Nietzsche concedes to the unavoidability of democracy in the modern world, he still divides humanity into the many and the few. This is made explicit in the aphorism following the one from which I just quoted. There he states: "A higher culture can come into existence only where there are two different castes in society: that of the workers and that of the idle, of those capable of true leisure" (*HH* 439; see also 462). The former are no different from slaves, according to Nietzsche's earlier definition: "he who does not have two-thirds of his day to himself is a slave" (*HH* 283; see also 457). But the idle do not merely enjoy life at the expense of the workers. Indeed, they suffer more than the latter; their "enjoyment of existence is less, [their] task heavier" (*HH* 439; cf. *BGE* 269).

Nietzsche's most favorable assessment of the cultural effects of democracy appears in an aphorism from *The Wanderer and His Shadow* entitled "The Age of Cyclopean Building," but even here the subordinate or auxiliary role of democracy is never lost sight of. Nietzsche suggests that the democratization of Europe may serve as a secure and durable foundation for the cyclopean building of culture in the future. It is the ultimate "prophylactic measure" that makes it "henceforth impossible for the fruitful fields of culture to be destroyed overnight by wild and senseless torrents." In a manner not altogether different from his later political outlook (see *BGE* 242), Nietzsche here conceives of democracy solely as a means and not as an end; it merely provides the protective walls and trellises required by the "supreme artist of horticulture" to carry out his more spiritual task. Such is not the understanding, however, of the present-day advocates of democracy, who "loudly decree that the wall and the trellis *are* the end and final goal" and do not yet see "the gardener or fruit-trees *for whose sake* the trellis exists" (WS 275).

A somewhat less optimistic assessment of the effects of democracy on the state appears in the lengthy and highly nuanced aphorism devoted to "Religion and Government." Here Nietzsche argues that democracy undermines the complementary relationship between religion and the state that exists under an aristocratic, tutelary government. In the latter, the governing classes, while not necessarily believers themselves, cultivate religion among the masses because it promotes a "calm, patient, trusting disposition." Such an instrumental (not to say hypocritical) use of religion, however, presupposes a gulf between governors and governed, a gulf that disappears with democracy, where "the attitude towards religion adopted by the government can only be the same as that adopted towards it by the people; every dissemination of enlightenment must find its echo in their representatives, and an employment and exploitation of the religious drives and consolations for political ends will no longer be so easy."[73] As a result, the state gradually loses its sacred aura, and the individual's relationship to it becomes grounded in utilitarian self-interest. Everyone devotes himself to his momentary, private interest, and (as Tocqueville predicted) no one engages in "undertakings that require quiet tending for decades or centuries if their fruits are to mature." Democracy thus leads to the "decay of the state." Interestingly, though, Nietzsche suggests that "prudence and self-interest" may be able to stave off this inevitable decay for a while, and so he puts his trust in them rather than in the "destructive experiments of the precipitate and overzealous" (HH 272).[74]

This last line points to another feature of Nietzsche's analysis of politics in *Human, All too Human*: its anti-utopian and anti-revolutionary animus. He derides those "political and social fantasists who with fiery eloquence invite a revolutionary overturning of all social orders in the belief that the proudest temple of humanity will then at once rise up as though of its own accord." These fantasies can all be traced back to Rousseau, who believed in the natural goodness of human beings and blamed society for their corruption. History shows, however, that revolutions do not restore a pristine human nature but unleash the "most savage energies." For this reason, Nietzsche prefers "Voltaire's moderate nature, inclined as it was to ordering, purifying, and reconstructing," to the revolutionary optimism of Rousseau, which "has for a long time banished *the spirit of the Enlightenment and of progressive evolution*" (HH 463).[75] Unfortunately, the Enlightenment itself became fanatical when it was yoked to the Rousseau-inspired French Revolution, and therefore anyone who wishes to carry the work of the Enlightenment forward in the future must first extract the violent spirit of the Revolution from it (*WS* 221).[76]

The two revolutionary political movements that Nietzsche focuses his criticisms on are socialism and nationalism, with people in the former seeking to "work as little as possible with their hands . . . [and in] the latter as little as possible with their heads" (*HH* 480). Socialism, he claims, is distinguished by its desire for an excess of state power and an almost complete absence of individual freedom. With considerable political astuteness, he writes: "Socialism is the fanciful younger brother of the almost expired despotism whose heir it wants to be; its endeavors are thus in the profoundest sense reactionary. For it desires an abundance of state power such as only despotism ever had." Unlike democracy, which provides a durable foundation that allows the weaker but culturally richer individual to thrive, socialism seeks to annihilate the individual, "who appears to it like an unauthorized luxury of nature destined to be improved into a useful *organ of the community.*" Only through its negative example can socialism contribute anything to the higher culture of the future. It "can serve to teach, in a truly brutal and impressive fashion, what danger there lies in all accumulations of state power, and to that extent to implant mistrust of the state itself" (*HH* 473).

Nietzsche is no less critical of nationalism. Indeed, it is in *Human, All too Human* that he first espouses the "good Europeanism" that will become a prominent feature of his mature political outlook. Developments in communication and trade are eroding the barriers between nations, and it is only an "artificial nationalism" that seeks to reverse this inevitable trend. Therefore, "one should not be afraid to proclaim oneself simply a *good European* and actively to work for the amalgamation of nations." Nietzsche is particularly concerned about the hatred of the Jews that is being whipped up by nationalists, and he presciently warns that the "literary indecency of leading the Jews to the sacrificial slaughter as scapegoats for every possible public or private misfortune" is rapidly gaining ground. He himself nourishes a dangerous stereotype by referring to the repulsive "stock-exchange Jew," but he goes on to pay moving homage to the Jews as a people who have "had the most grief-laden history of any people and whom we have to thank for the noblest human being (Christ), the purest sage (Spinoza), the mightiest book, and the most efficacious moral code in the world" (*HH* 475).

Related to his discussion of nationalism, Nietzsche takes an ambivalent stance on war, arguing on the one hand that it is indispensable for revitalizing a feeble and over-cultivated European humanity (*HH* 477), and on the other advocating disarmament as the "means to *real* peace" (*WS* 284). In the concluding aphorism of the chapter on the state, however, he comes down decisively against the prosecution of costly wars in the pursuit of "great politics." The identification of great politics here with nationalism and war—i.e., with Bismarckian politics—clearly differentiates it from the sort of philosophical legislation Nietzsche has in mind when he uses this phrase in his later works. His opposition to great politics in *Human, All too Human* is once again driven by his preoccupation with culture. The problem with great politics is that it sacrifices the talent and energy previously dedicated to culture on the "'altar of the fatherland or of the national thirst for honor." The pursuit of great politics—and with it great wars—comes at tremendous spiritual and cultural cost: "[T]he political emergence of a people almost necessarily draws after it spiritual impoverishment," sacrificing the "more spiritual plants and growths" to the "coarse and gaudy flower of the nation" (*HH* 481).

Having concluded my analysis of *Human, All too Human*, let me highlight one more time the thread that runs through it. I have argued that Nietzsche's reflections on culture constitute the climax of his argument in the book and the axis around which all his other reflections—on metaphysics, morality, religion, and art—revolve. In *Human, All too Human*, he rejects the romantic notion of culture to which he had earlier subscribed and which he chiefly identified with Wagner: the notion that art represents the highest cultural activity, taking over from religion the function of grounding, unifying, and inspiring a people. Instead, he defends a view of culture in which knowing—especially historical knowing—constitutes the supreme human activity. The free-spirited knower replaces the artist-priest as the bearer of higher culture.

We have seen that, in order to sustain this notion of a culture based on knowledge, Nietzsche critiques the moral and metaphysical presuppositions of the older, romantic conception of culture. He begins by exposing the religious foundations of the romantic conception of art. Like religion, romantic art depicts the world in dramatic shades of light and dark, offering redemption from the world of suffering in the form of aesthetic rapture and exaltation. But this world of dramatic lights and shadows rests on an erroneous interpretation of existence. It is only by artificially blackening existence that religion, and later art, can then rapturously redeem it. This misinterpretation of the world does not, of course, originate with religion and romantic art but derives even more fundamentally from the oppositional thinking that belongs to morality and metaphysics. Morality, especially Christian morality, introduces into the world the erroneous distinction between egoistic and nonegoistic, good and evil, actions. And the belief in opposite values in general—for example, between truth and falsity, being and becoming, the divine and the human, all too human—belongs to the metaphysical way of thinking that stretches from primitive humanity all the way to Schopenhauer.

Nietzsche's reflections on the problem of modern culture thus lead him to ever more fundamental reflections on metaphysics, morality, and religion. These latter considerations assume an increasingly central position in his writings after *Human, All too Human*, beginning with *Daybreak*, while the theme of culture seems to recede. Nevertheless, it does not disappear; it remains an animating theme in the second and third works of the free-spirit trilogy, though much less explicitly than in *Human, All too Human*. What does change in these works, however, is that the problem of modern culture comes to be less and less defined by Nietzsche's formative struggle against romanticism. It is this struggle that accounts for some of the peculiar features of *Human, All too Human*—its hostility to violent passion and its unDionysian emphasis on repose, moderation, and contemplation—and ultimately gives the work its transitional character. As Nietzsche moves farther away from Wagner and Bayreuth, the target of his cultural criticism subtly shifts. We begin to see this shift in *Daybreak*.

TWO

Daybreak and the Campaign
against Morality

Nietzsche completed *The Wanderer and His Shadow* in September 1879, and it was published in December of that year. By this time, having resigned his professorial chair at the University of Basel, he had begun the itinerant existence that was to characterize his life for the next decade. In February 1880, he traveled to Venice with his friend Heinrich Köselitz (aka Peter Gast), and there he began to compile notes for a new book, provisionally titled *L'Ombra di Venezia* (*KSA* 9:3). In July, he left for Marienbad, where he stayed until the end of August. After a trip to Naumberg to visit his mother, Nietzsche finally arrived in Genoa toward the beginning of November. There he completed his new book, now titled *The Plowshare: Thoughts on the Prejudices of Morality*, in January 1881 (*KSA* 9:9).

A word about this title. It will be remembered that the notes Nietzsche began to write after his flight from Bayreuth in 1876 were given the title "The Plowshare" (*Die Pflugschar*). This title was accompanied by a quote from a medieval German poem, *Der Meier Helmbrecht*: "If you would follow me, farm with the plow. Then many will benefit from you, certainly the poor man and the rich man will benefit from you, the wolf and the eagle and indeed all creatures will benefit from you" (*KSA* 8:18 [1]). Later in the same notebook, Nietzsche underlined the theme of universal benefaction in this quote by stating that his book will improve both the good man and the evil man, the humble and the mighty (*KSA* 8:18 [62]). This theme continues to resonate in *Daybreak*, where Nietzsche paraphrases the plowshare quote in an aphorism that argues against the vengeful punishment of criminals and in favor of treating them as mental patients in need of relief and healing. Instead of punishing judges, we need physicians who will act as plowshares for the benefit of all (*D* 202; see also 146).

In the event, Nietzsche did not end up calling the book *The Plowshare*. When Köselitz returned a fair copy of the manuscript, he included a verse from the Rig Veda: "There are so many dawns [*Morgenröten*] that have not yet broken." Nietzsche liked the quote and decided not only to use it as an epigraph but to call the book *A Daybreak* (*Eine Morgenröte*), later just *Daybreak* (*SB* 6:61, 73, 83). He found this title to be a little more upbeat than the previous one and thought it would nicely counterbalance the otherwise depressing contents of the book: "If one didn't come to the book with a bit of hope for the morning," he wrote to Köselitz in February 1881, "then it would be too gloomy!" (*SB* 6:63). Interestingly, Nietzsche would later characterize *Daybreak* as a "Yes-saying book" (*EH* 3.D.1 and *GS*).

In a letter to his publisher, Ernst Schmeitzner, from February 1881, Nietzsche also calls the book "a decisive step" (*SB* 6:66), and in a letter to his sister a few months later, "a decisive book" (*SB* 6:84). This raises the complicated question of how *Daybreak* stands with respect to *Human, All too Human*. To begin with the obvious, the analysis of morality to which one chapter of *Human, All too Human* (and a section in each of the supplements) was dedicated has now grown to take up the bulk of *Daybreak*. While he was writing the latter book, Nietzsche wrote to Köselitz: "[M]eanwhile I go on digging zealously in my moral mine, and sometimes seem to myself wholly subterranean" (*SB* 6:28). This image of the "subterranean man" reappears later in the 1886 Preface to *Daybreak* (*D* Preface 1). In *Ecce Homo*, Nietzsche states that with *Daybreak* "my campaign against morality began" (*EH* 3.D.1). Clearly, the critique of morality is far more central to *Daybreak*—the subtitle of which is *Thoughts on the Prejudices of Morality*—than to *Human, All too Human*. But this does not mean that the culture theme that pervaded *Human, All too Human* completely disappears. Indeed, we will see that culture still looms quite large in books 3 and 5 of *Daybreak*.

Of course, the more important question is whether, apart from becoming more central, Nietzsche's analysis of morality in *Daybreak* actually changes from that of *Human, All too Human*. Maudemarie Clark and Brian Leiter maintain that there is a radical shift in Nietzsche's thinking about morality from *Human, All too Human* to *Daybreak*. In the former work, they claim, Nietzsche is completely in the grips of the doctrine of psychological egoism. Like La Rochefoucauld, he is primarily concerned to bring out the egoistic motivation behind our actions and thereby expose the hypocrisy behind our appeals to nonegoistic motivation, but he never questions the value of nonegoistic motivation itself. In this respect, Nietzsche still remains under the spell of Schopenhauer in *Human, All too Human*: "[I]t appears that Nietzsche rejects Schopenhauer's view that unegoistic actions exist, but completely agrees with him about their higher value." It is only in *Day-break* that Nietzsche repudiates his earlier psychological egoism and begins "to raise his characteristic questions about the value of the unegoistic and, ultimately, morality." For this reason, *Daybreak* must be seen as "the real beginning of Nietzsche's own path on the topic of morality."[1]

We have already seen that the understanding of *Human, All too Human* upon which Clark and Leiter draw this contrast with *Daybreak* is erroneous. In that work, Nietzsche is not engaged in a La Rochefoucauldian exposure of the discrepancy between our basely egoistic behavior and the nonegoistic ideals to which we appeal and still presume to be valuable. Nevertheless, there are important, if somewhat subtler, differences between these two works, many of which I hope to bring out over the course of this chapter. One of the most crucial of these has to do with Nietzsche's deepening skepticism about the utilitarian interpretation of the origins and development of morality found in Darwinian writers like Rée. We have seen that as late as *The Wanderer and His Shadow* Nietzsche is still invoking Rée's understanding of morality as having a utilitarian origin that gradually comes to be forgotten as the result of habituation (see *WS* 40). But we have also seen that he sometimes diverges from this utilitarian understanding of morality, especially in his remarks on the irrationality of primitive or customary morality. It is significant that Nietzsche's excavation of customary morality is much more fully developed in *Daybreak*, with the concomitant consequence that his emphasis falls increasingly on the erroneousness and irrationality of morality. Throughout the book, he denies that utility has anything to do with origins: "When one has demonstrated that a thing is of the highest utility, one has thereby taken not one step towards explaining its origin" (*D* 37).

Nietzsche does not engage Rée directly in *Daybreak*, though his disenchantment with the latter's analysis of morality is evident in a note from the fall of 1880: "Not the forgotten motive and the habituation to certain movements is the essential thing, as I previously assumed; rather, the purposeless drives of pleasure and displeasure" (*KSA* 9:6 [366]). But there is another Darwinian thinker with whom he was much occupied during this period: Herbert Spencer. Shortly after finishing *The Wanderer and His Shadow*, Nietzsche wrote to Schmeitzner, requesting that he publish a translation of Spencer's 1879 *Data of Ethics* (*SB* 5:466; also 474). He eventually procured a German translation of the book, but having left it at his mother's house in Naumberg, he sent several urgent letters from Venice asking her to send it to him (*SB* 6:13, 15, 16, 18). Nietzsche's notebooks from 1880 are full of negative references to Spencer. He has two fundamental problems with the latter's evolutionary ethics. First, he rejects Spencer's optimistic belief that morality consists in the ever-more efficient and expedient adjustment of actions to ends, his claim that our "moral intuitions are the results of the accumulated experiences of utility" (see *KSA* 9:6 [456]).[2] For Nietzsche, Spencer (like Rée) unhistorically "confuses the system of morals 'as it should be enacted' with the origin of morals" (*KSA* 9:1 [106]). Second, he rejects Spencer's belief that human evolution consists in the progress from egoism to altruism, or to the ideal point where the two merge into one another. For Nietzsche, such an evolution represents the weakening of humanity, the reduction of humanity to "soft pulp, smooth sand." In opposition to it, he advocates "evolution toward the individual" (*KSA* 9:6 [163]).[3]

It is this critical attitude toward the morality of pity and social adaptation exemplified by Spencer that constitutes the genuinely new element in *Daybreak*. In *Human, All too Human*, Nietzsche questioned the existence of nonegoistic motivation and action but he did really not question the *value* of such motivation and action. His concern there was with the oppositional thinking of morality that leads to the blackening of existence and calls forth the radical cures of religion and romantic art. In *Daybreak*, he begins to move away from his earlier preoccupation with romanticism—though he by no means abandons it—and he evinces an increasing concern with the "cult of philanthropy" that seeks to eliminate all danger and suffering from life and threatens to abolish the individual and transform humanity into sand, "small, soft, round, unending sand" (*D* 132, 174). It is here that Nietzsche's later critique of herd morality and the last man definitively begins to emerge, and it is in this respect that *Daybreak* can be said to mark the inauguration of Nietzsche's "campaign against morality."

In addition to jettisoning the elements of Rée's Darwinian utilitarianism that can still be found in *Human, All too Human*, Nietzsche also provides a far more complex picture of the self in *Daybreak* with which to criticize the notion of nonegoistic or altruistic action. Instead of pointing out the egoistic basis of all human action, as he did in the earlier work, he now questions the very notion of a unified ego. What we refer to as the "self" or "ego" turns out to be in actuality a complex mechanism of drives and desires whose ultimate law we cannot know. From this new theory of the self as a multiplicity Nietzsche draws the practical implication that the unity of the self must be artistically made, not found. Though there are glimmers of this notion of the aesthetic self in *Human, All too Human*, it is only in *Daybreak* that Nietzsche fully develops it.

There is one final difference between *Daybreak* and *Human, All too Human* that deserves preliminary notice. It concerns Nietzsche's conception of the very activity that defines his ideal of the free spirit, namely, the quest for knowledge. Whereas in *Human, All too Human* Nietzsche emphasized the role of knowledge in calming or moderating the passions, in *Daybreak* he speaks of the quest for knowledge as itself a passion. Marco Brusotti has argued that this new emphasis on the "passion for knowledge" (*Leidenschaft der Erkenntnis*) in *Daybreak* constitutes a radical break with the ideal of moderation and repose of soul found in *Human, All too Human*.[4] While this may exaggerate the difference between the two works somewhat—as we will see, the free spirit in *Daybreak* continues to be marked by a certain coldness, detachment, moderation, and mildness—it nevertheless points to an important change in Nietzsche's outlook. And like the change in his critique of morality, this one too reflects a shift in Nietzsche's critical attention away from the overpassionateness of romanticism to the blandness and lack of individuality and heroism that belong to utilitarianism.

All of this needs to be further explored and established in this chapter. As far as the organization of the chapter is concerned, I have for the most part followed Nietzsche's lead. In each section, I take up a different book of the five that make up *Daybreak*. Unlike the chapters of *Human, All too Human*, the books of *Daybreak* do not have titles, and it is not always clear how the aphorisms within each book relate to one another. Nevertheless, I do not agree with Arthur Danto's claim that "the 'thoughts' of one book seldom relate more closely to the other thoughts in it than they do to those in the other books."[5] In each of the books of *Daybreak*, Nietzsche focuses on a certain set of themes that are related to one another, albeit in a complex and prismatic way. It is the task of the interpreter to bring out the unity underlying each of these books and, of course, the book as a whole.

The Irrational Origins of Morality

The very first aphorism of *Daybreak*, which points out the "origin in unreason" of all the things we regard as rational, signals Nietzsche's sharper emphasis on the irrationality of origins and his clear rejection of Rée's attribution of utilitarian rationality to the origin of morality. For Nietzsche, the rationality that belongs to things is supplied after the fact, thus concealing the irrationality of the origin, and this is what the good historian needs to expose (*D* 1). Formerly, philosophers believed that they would discover in the origin of things "something of incalculable significance for later action and judgment." But this is no longer the case for the scientific knower. The closer we get to the origin, the more meaningless and nonsensical it appears (*D* 44). Clearly, Nietzsche has absorbed the lesson of Darwin. "Formerly," he writes, "one sought the feeling of the grandeur of man by pointing to his divine *origin*: this has now become a forbidden way, for at its portal stands the ape, together with other gruesome beasts, grinning knowingly as if to say: no further in this direction!" (*D* 49). No matter how exalted a thing has become, if we trace it back far enough, we always arrive at the *pudenda origo* (*D* 42).

Book 1 of *Daybreak* is largely concerned to bring out the shameful origins of morality and Christianity. Before Nietzsche undertakes his specific investigations of these origins, however, he discloses the overall philosophy of history that governs his analysis, much as he did at the beginning of *Human, All too Human*. In an aphorism entitled "Everything Has its Day," he asserts that just as human beings once believed that everything in nature had a sex, so they have "ascribed to all that exists a connection with morality and laid an *ethical significance* on the world's back." He predicts that this latter view will one day "have as much value, and no more, as the belief in the masculinity or femininity of the sun has today" (*D* 3). There is not much of an argument here; all the work in the aphorism is being done by the analogy of morality to primitive beliefs that have given way to more enlightened views. What the aphorism does bring out, however, is the intellectualism of Nietzsche's approach to morality in *Daybreak*, an intellectualism that also characterized his approach in *Human, All too Human*. The fundamental problem with morality is that it rests on intellectual errors. As Nietzsche puts it later on in the book: "I deny morality as I deny alchemy" (*D* 103).[6]

Nietzsche goes on to elaborate on his philosophy of history, and once again we are reminded of *Human, All too Human* and its view of history as consisting in the progress from a "lower culture" based on spectacular errors to a "higher culture" marked by a manly, scientific spirit that values "little unpretentious truths" (*HH* 3). "We must again rid the world of much *false* grandeur," he writes, because it offends our sense of intellectual justice. Much of this false grandeur—in Christianity, Schopenhauerian pessimism, and Wagnerian tragedy, for example—comes from imagining the world to be more disharmonious than it really is (*D* 4). Science is crucial to evacuating the world of false grandeur. In contrast to the "art of the conjuror," which charms us by seeing "a very simple causality where in truth a very complicated causality is at work," science shows us that even the "'simplest' things are *very complicated*" (*D* 6). Science also reduces "the *extent of space* between the highest happiness and the deepest unhappiness [that] has been produced only with the aid of imaginary things" (*D* 7).

In *Human, All too Human*, Nietzsche predicted that a kind of equanimity and moderation would replace the violent highs and lows that had been produced by the errors of morality and metaphysics. In *Daybreak*, he again does not see desolation as the only possible result of the disenchantment of the world by science. He speculates that were Raphael, the great transfiguring artist of Christianity, living today, he would no longer see the world as divided between "those who suffer helplessly, those who dream confusedly, [and] those who are entranced by things supernatural"; rather, "he would behold a new transfiguration" (*D* 8).

From these more general considerations about origins and the nature of historical progress, Nietzsche moves in the ninth aphorism to a more specific analysis of the morality of custom. This analysis, along with that of Christianity, takes up the rest of book 1. As I have already pointed out, the depth of Nietzsche's analysis of primitive morality in *Daybreak* is one of the things that distinguishes it from *Human, All too Human*. It also suggests an important difference between the general perspectives of the two works. In *Daybreak*, we find a much stronger emphasis on the irrational origins of morality in primitive society, and this only serves to further distance Nietzsche's general account of morality from the rationalist-utilitarian accounts of his friend Rée and other writers in the Darwinian tradition. Of course, one might raise questions about the historical veracity of Nietzsche's speculations about primitive morality, but it is important to recognize that he is not merely making it all up but drawing heavily on the most advanced anthropological knowledge of his day, found in writers like Bagehot, Lubbock, and Tylor.[7] Whatever their ultimate scientific validity, these anthropological speculations spring from an authentic historical impulse to understand primitive beliefs and practices in all their otherness instead of anachronistically assimilating them to the familiar contours of utilitarian rationality.

It is precisely the radical difference between current beliefs and those of primitive humanity that Nietzsche emphasizes in the lengthy opening aphorism devoted to the "Concept of the Morality of Custom" (*Begriff der Sittlichkeit der Sitte*). Because we moderns are used to thinking of morality in terms of individual utility—in this respect, following in the footsteps of Socrates—we find it extraordinarily difficult to comprehend primitive morality, the chief proposition of which was: "[M]orality is nothing other (therefore *no more!*) than obedience to customs, of whatever kind they may be; customs, however, are the *traditional* way of behaving and evaluating." Nietzsche places the greatest emphasis in his account of customary morality on its anti-individualistic character. The demands that customary morality imposes on individuals are made, "*not* on account of the useful consequences [they] may have for the individual, but so that the hegemony of custom, tradition, shall be made evident in despite of private desires and advantages: the individual is to sacrifice himself." The community enforces these demands strictly because, as Nietzsche (following Bagehot) points out, punishment for breaches of custom is understood to fall not merely on the individual but on the community as a whole (D 9).[8]

Nietzsche concludes the ninth aphorism by saying that "under the dominion of the morality of custom, originality of every kind has acquired a bad conscience" (D 9). As a result, anyone who wished to break "the yoke of custom" (Bagehot's phrase) and introduce a new idea into the rigid framework of society had to assume the guise of a madman. Madness made it appear that the individual did not speak merely for himself but as the voice of the divinity. Here Nietzsche draws on Lubbock to buttress his claim that madness alone aroused the dread and reverence necessary to allow new ideas to get a hearing in primitive societies. He refers to the Indian medicine-man, the angekok of Greenland, and the Brazilian pajee—all examples taken from Lubbock—to illustrate his point about the role of madness in the innovation of customary morality (D 14).[9]

Nietzsche devotes many aphorisms in book 1 to bringing out the irrationality and arbitrariness of primitive customs, thus countering the rationalistic assumption found in Rée and Spencer that these customs somehow accord with utility. In the first place, customary morality rests on a complete distortion of the relationship of cause and effect. Chance events are misinterpreted as punishments for breaches of custom or offenses against demonic powers. There is no interest in investigating the real, natural causes of phenomena; rather, everything is attributed to supernatural causes. As a result, "one spoils one's sense for reality and one's pleasure in it, and in the end accords reality a value only *insofar as it is capable of being a symbol*" (D 33; also 10–13). The unscientific character of customary morality can be clearly discerned in what it considers as "proof" of its prescriptions. Nietzsche once again draws on Lubbock to show how in rude ages "very little was required for a thing to be regarded as *demonstrated*." Take the prescription, "you shall not throw an animal bone into the fire or give it to dogs," for "if you do so you will have no luck in hunting." But, Nietzsche claims, "one almost always has in some sense 'no luck in hunting.'" The "proof" of the prescription turns out to be unfalsifiable (D 24).[10]

But though the utility of particular customs or moral prescriptions proves to be quite small when considered by themselves, Nietzsche still seems to concede that these customs and prescriptions do ultimately serve some useful purpose. Considering a species of customs whose sole purpose appears to be custom itself—his examples come from the Kamshadales of eastern

Russia[11]—Nietzsche argues that these seemingly arbitrary customs serve to remind individuals "of the constant proximity of custom, the perpetual compulsion to practice customs." Without such compulsion, primitive society would fall apart. The "first proposition of civilization" is that "any custom is better than no custom" (*D* 16). Here Nietzsche echoes Bagehot argument that what primitive communities needed more than anything else in order to survive was "a comprehensive rule binding men together. . . . What this rule is does not matter so much. A good rule is better than a bad one, but any rule is better than none."[12]

Apart from rigid obedience, Nietzsche highlights one other aspect of the morality of custom in book 1 of *Daybreak*, an aspect that distinguishes his account from all other Darwinian accounts and that has tremendous implications for his later philosophy. In an aphorism entitled "The Morality of Voluntary Suffering," he asks: "Of all pleasures, which is the greatest for men of that little imperiled community which is in a constant state of war and where the sternest morality prevails?" The answer comes back: "the pleasure of *cruelty*." In language that anticipates the later *Genealogy of Morals*, he writes that "cruelty is one of the oldest festive joys of mankind." Living in fear and feeling powerless in the face of enemies and the elements, primitive man enjoys "the highest gratification of the feeling of power" in the exercise of cruelty (*D* 18; see also *GM* 2.6).

This is the first time the feeling of power (*Machtgefühl* or *Gefühl der Macht*) is mentioned in *Daybreak*. In *Human, All too Human*, we saw the desire for power play an important role in Nietzsche's explanation of human conduct, especially in his analysis of the Christian ascetic. In *Daybreak*, it plays an even greater role. We see this concept suddenly come to the fore in Nietzsche's notes from the summer of 1880.[13] There, as in *Human, All too Human*, he often sees the desire for power arising out of the feeling of impotence (*KSA* 9:4 [177, 202]).

So what is the connection between the delight in cruelty and the morality of voluntary suffering? Nietzsche argues that primitive humanity inferred from its own delight in cruelty that the gods too must enjoy the spectacle of suffering. It was just such a spectacle that humans offered to the gods when they engaged in self-torture. Virtue thus came to be associated with voluntary suffering. Indeed, anyone who sought to stir up "the inert but fertile mud of their customs" (a phrase recalling Bagehot's "cake of custom") needed to exhibit not only madness but also voluntary self-torture in order to inspire belief and counteract the bad conscience that always accompanied innovation. Nor does this voluntary suffering and self-torture belong simply to the primitive past. Nietzsche points out here, as he does later in

Beyond Good and Evil and the *Genealogy of Morals,* that "every step in the field of free thought . . . has always had to be fought for with spiritual and bodily tortures. . . . Nothing has been bought more dearly than that little bit of human reason and feeling of freedom that now constitutes our pride" (*D* 18; see also *BGE* 229–30; *GM* 2.3, 6).

Human beings' delight in cruelty exhibits itself not only in voluntary suffering but also in the striving for distinction that belongs to virtue. What we really seek when we strive to be virtuous, according to Nietzsche, is "to make the sight of us *painful* to another and to awaken in him the feeling of envy and of his own impotence and degradation." Behind humility lies the desire to torture, and behind the chastity of the nun lies "joy in revenge" and the feeling of superiority over other women (*D* 30; see also 275). In general, "the striving for distinction is the striving for domination over the next man." The history of culture in many ways constitutes a long ladder of different methods of satisfying this drive to domination, and at the top of the ladder "stands the *ascetic* or martyr." Recalling his analysis of the ascetic saint in *Human, All too Human,* Nietzsche here maintains that the ascetic derives the "liveliest feeling of power" from the sight of his own self-torment. Never before has there been such "voluptuousness of power" (*D* 113).

Nietzsche brings out the dialectical relationship between the feeling of impotence and the desire for the feeling of power by considering primitive beliefs in animism. Once again, he relies on Lubbock and to some extent Tylor for his anthropological data.[14] Because primitive human beings believed that physical things in the world were animated by spirits that were not automatically compliant to human purposes, the feeling of impotence was much more prevalent than it otherwise would have been. This was the source of many of the superstitious practices by which primitive human beings sought to compel, constrain, flatter, or bribe these spirits so that they would not thwart their purposes. Through this useless activity, fearful and impotent human beings regained a certain sense of control and power. Nietzsche concludes grandly that over the course of time the means for producing the feeling of power evolved in subtlety; indeed, "the means discovered for creating this feeling almost constitute the history of culture" (*D* 23).

Prominent among the means devised by culture to produce the feeling of power is religious and artistic intoxication. Nietzsche devotes several aphorisms to this theme, and these aphorisms serve as a bridge to his discussion of Christianity in the second half of book 1. By means of religious and artistic intoxication, human beings experience a momentary feeling of exaltation and power. Unfortunately, after the ecstasy has passed, one returns to ordinary life more dissatisfied with oneself and the world (*D* 50). This is the seedbed of the world-weariness that pervades pessimistic philosophies like Schopenhauer's. "It has been the means of comfort," Nietzsche comments, "that have bestowed on life that fundamental character of suffering it is now believed to possess." The temporary relief provided by religious and artistic intoxication has "often had to be paid for with a general and profound worsening of the complaint." The supposed cure ends up intensifying the sickness (*D* 52). For this reason, Nietzsche takes it as his fundamental task to "calm the imagination of the invalid" (*D* 54).

These reflections on religious and artistic intoxication are reminiscent of Nietzsche's critique of romanticism in *Human, All too Human*, as is the aphorism immediately preceding the series devoted to Christianity entitled "The Apostate of the Free Spirit." Nietzsche does not mention the name of this apostate, but it is clear that he is talking about the composer of *Parsifal*. He begins by saying that the simple faith of pious people does not arouse his disgust; indeed, he respects and takes pleasure in it. "But whence comes that sudden deep repugnance without apparent cause which we feel for him who once *had* all freedom of spirit and in the end *became* 'a believer'? . . . Would we not turn our back even upon the person we most revered if he became suspicious to us in this respect?" At this point, the aphorism turns intensely personal, as Nietzsche questions why he feels so strongly about this betrayal of spiritual freedom. Is it that he feels unsure of himself, that he worries about changing his opinion in the future out of weakness? He rejects these doubts and explains his strong reaction to the "tremendous *dishonesty*" of the apostate as similar to that of a physician when he encounters someone with a repulsive disease: "physical disgust at something fungous, softened, bloated, suppurating, momentarily overpowers reason and the will to help" (*D* 56). This is perhaps Nietzsche's most graphic description of his revulsion at Wagner's sudden collapse before the Christian cross.

The analysis of Christianity that follows this aphorism picks up on the theme of intoxication and the feeling of power that accompanies it. In contrast to the "sages of antiquity," who taught self-control and "advised men against the affects," Christianity encourages the most extreme indulgence of the affects. It "condemns rationality in general and challenges the affects to reveal themselves in their extremest grandeur and strength" (*D* 58). As part of its condemnation of reason, Christianity demands that belief come about miraculously: "What is wanted are blindness and intoxication and an eternal song over the waves in which reason has drowned" (*D* 89). All of this emotional indulgence is tied to producing the feeling of power. In this regard, Nietzsche indicates that there are two different "recipes" for producing the feeling of power: the first, which he associates with Brahminism, is to exercise control over oneself; the second, which he associates with Christianity, involves intoxication and is designed for those incapable of self-control (D 65).

Nietzsche brings together the various elements of his critique of Christianity in a lengthy psychological analysis of "the first Christian," St. Paul, whom he also refers to as the "Jewish Pascal." Paul's story revolves around the difficulties of fulfilling the Jewish law, a law that took "the fantasy of moral sublimity" further than any previous moral code. At first, Paul exercised his "extravagant lust for power" by persecuting those who transgressed against the law. But soon he realized that "he himself—fiery, sensual, melancholy, malevolent in hatred as he was—*could* not fulfill the law," that, indeed, the law was unfulfillable. At that point, he turned against the law and sought to destroy it. Jesus provided him with the crucial insight on the road to Damascus: "Sick with the most tormented pride, at a stroke [Paul] feels himself recovered, the moral despair is as if blown away, destroyed— that is to say, *fulfilled*, there on the Cross." This is the great liberating and intoxicating insight. Unable to fulfill the law, he now destroys it and enjoys the most extraordinary feeling of power. Here "the intoxication of Paul is at its height, and likewise the importunity of his soul—with the idea of becoming one with Christ all shame, all subordination, all bounds are taken from it, and the intractable lust for power reveals itself as an anticipatory reveling in *divine* glories" (D 68).

Once again, we are reminded of the pattern of blackening and lightening found in Nietzsche's discussion of Christianity in *Human, All too Human*. This pattern is especially prominent in Nietzsche's analysis of the Christian emphasis on the miraculous in the sphere of morality. Like its Hebrew predecessor, the New Testament set up a "canon of *impossible virtue*." The whole point of this canon was to make individuals "*despair* of virtue, and in the end *throw themselves on the bosom* of the merciful." Only by making the individual feel as sinful as possible could Christianity "bring about that ecstatic moment when he experiences the 'breakthrough of grace' and the moral miracle." Only after first blackening the world could Christianity then shine its bright redemptive light (D 87; cf. HH 132–35).

Many of the aphorisms in book 1 of *Daybreak* are devoted to bringing out the various ways in which Christianity blackens the world: by condemning the passions as evil; by diabolizing Eros, which paradoxically makes it more interesting; by transforming the earth into a torture chamber and "vale of misery"; and so forth (*D* 76, 77). The supreme genius in this blackening enterprise turns out to be Pascal, who is mentioned in these aphorisms more often than any other figure (see *D* 63, 64, 68, 79, 86, 91). Nietzsche's depiction of Christianity is not, however, monochromatically negative. In one aphorism, he characterizes the "highest Catholic priesthood" as comprising "the most refined figures in human society that have ever yet existed," the most beautiful examples of the interpenetration of the body by the spirit (*D* 60). And generalizing from this single instance of historical justice, he claims that if one is to fairly judge the evaluations of the past, "one has voluntarily to *live through* them once again" and engage in "rigorous comparison" (*D* 61).

Nietzsche concludes book 1 by pointing to the demise of belief in Christianity and God. As far as Christianity is concerned, it has been adapted to bourgeois secularity and turned into a "gentle moralism" that prizes "benevolence and decency of disposition" above all—a far cry from Pascal's tortured suicide of reason. Nietzsche calls this the "*euthanasia* of Christianity" (*D* 92). As for God, he argues that the historical disclosure of how belief in God has arisen and "acquired weight and importance" constitutes the "definitive refutation" of this belief (*D* 95). He said something similar in *Human, All too Human*—"with the insight into the origination [of the belief in God] that belief falls away" (*HH* 133)—and this comes dangerously close to what is referred to as the "genetic fallacy," the fallacy of confusing the origin of a belief with its validity. Nietzsche is much more careful in his later writings to avoid this fallacy.[15] In *The Gay Science*, for example, he states that "even if a morality has grown out of an error, the realization of this fact would not so much as touch on the problem of its value" (*GS* 345). And in a note from 1885–86, he says much the same thing but adds significantly: "[T]he insight into some *pudenda origo* certainly brings with it *a feeling* of a diminution in value of the thing that originated thus and prepares the way to a critical mood and attitude toward it" (*WP* 254). Nietzsche's inquiries into the origins of morality and Christianity in book 1 of *Daybreak* are best seen as propaedeutics in this way rather than as definitive refutations.

Deconstructing the Ego

Book 2 of *Daybreak* is in many ways a breakthrough book. As in *Human, All too Human*, Nietzsche is here concerned to expose the errors involved in altruism and freedom of the will. But instead of relying on the conventional doctrine of psychological egoism and pointing out the egoistic basis of all human action, he questions the very notion of the ego. In *The Wanderer and*

His Shadow, Nietzsche famously states that "every word is a prejudice" (*WS* 55), and of no word is this more true than that of "ego." For what this word designates as a simple unity turns out to be in actuality a complex mechanism of drives and desires whose ultimate law we cannot really know. There is a hint of this new outlook on the ego in *Human, All too Human*, when Nietzsche speaks of the human being as a *dividuum* as opposed to an *individuum* (*HH* 57). But it is only in book 2 of *Daybreak* that he develops this insight fully, thereby deepening his moral psychology and giving birth to his distinctive understanding of the fathomless self.[16]

Before undertaking his deconstruction of the ego, Nietzsche begins book 2 with some general reflections on morality. Once again, he emphasizes the fundamental point that morality hitherto has rested on errors (*D* 100, 102), and this leads him to make an important statement about the nature of his critique of morality. There are two different ways of denying morality, he claims. The first denies "that the moral motives which men *claim* have inspired their actions really have done so." This is the way of La Rochefoucauld, and it is primarily concerned to expose the hypocrisy of those reputed to be virtuous.[17] The second way, which Nietzsche identifies as his own, denies "that moral judgments are based on truths": "I deny morality as I deny alchemy." It is not that our judgments about what is right or wrong, good or evil, do not often serve as motives for our actions; it is merely that these judgments do not correspond to anything real or true. Though some commentators have seen this as an important step in the development of Nietzsche's critique of morality, it is important to note that his denial of morality here does not rise to the radical level of his later immoralism.[18] Indeed, he makes it clear that the point of this denial is not to license all sorts of actions that have hitherto been designated as immoral; rather, his point is to get us to think differently about the basis upon which we make the distinction between moral and immoral actions. Thus he writes: "It goes without saying that I do not deny—unless I am a fool—that many actions called immoral ought to be avoided and resisted, or that many called moral ought to be done and encouraged—but I think the one should be encouraged and the other avoided *for other reasons than hitherto*" (*D* 103).

What sorts of errors in our moral judgments and evaluations does Nietzsche have in mind? He provides a clue in the aphorisms immediately following the one above, which call into question the benefit of morality for either the individual or humanity in general. With respect to the individual, he argues that most people adopt the evaluations that they acquire in childhood and that do not necessarily coincide with their individual needs or desires (D 104). In this regard, most people are not truly egoistic at all: they "do nothing for their own ego" but, rather, act on behalf of "the phantom of their ego which has formed itself in the heads of those around them." As a result, "they all of them dwell in a fog of impersonal, semi-personal opinions, and arbitrary, as it were poetical evaluations" that have nothing to do with their real interests (D 105). It is interesting to note the change of tack from *Human, All too Human* here. Instead of pointing to the egoistic basis of our putatively nonegoistic actions, Nietzsche shows that our putatively egoistic actions are not egoistic at all.[19] The question of the *value* of these actions for the individual suddenly moves to the fore.

A similar question arises with respect to the connection postulated between morality and the welfare of mankind. Many writers on ethics—and Nietzsche seems to have Spencer especially in mind—define the goal of morality as the "preservation and advancement of mankind." But Nietzsche regards this as an empty formula. "Preservation *of what?*" he asks; and "Advancement *to what?*" How we answer these questions makes all the difference. Do we seek the longest possible existence for human beings or the "greatest possible deanimalization"? Do we seek the highest happiness that an individual can attain or the greatest amount of happiness for all (D 106)? In the absence of a universally recognized goal for mankind, it is irrational to impose the same moral demands on everyone. Nevertheless, Nietzsche does allow that it is perfectly permissible to "*recommend* a goal to mankind," which, if found appealing, could then lead mankind to impose a moral law on itself (D 108).

With these general considerations about morality out of the way, Nietzsche turns his attention to the deconstruction of the self or ego that constitutes the most innovative aspect of his analysis in book 2. He introduces this theme with a discussion of self-mastery and the various methods by which the vehemence of a drive can be combated. These methods include avoiding opportunities for gratification of the drive, imposing strict regularity on its satisfaction, inducing satiety and disgust with the drive, associating it with a painful idea, directing one's energy to the satisfaction of another drive, and finally weakening and depressing one's entire system. All of this is compatible with the traditional picture of self-mastery. But where Nietzsche diverges from this picture is in his denial that the very desire to combat a drive lies within our power or emanates from some unified self or reason: "What is clearly the case is that in this entire procedure our intellect is only the blind instrument of *another drive* which is a *rival* of the drive whose vehemence is tormenting us." It is not a matter of reason supervening on passion but of one drive complaining about another. The self does not conflict with the drives but is merely the site where the drives themselves conflict (*D* 109).

Suddenly the prospect opens up that we neither control what we are doing nor even know exactly what we are doing. Nietzsche develops this humbling insight in an aphorism entitled "The Unknown World of the 'Subject.'" The most difficult thing for human beings to understand and accept has been their unavoidable ignorance of themselves. Ever since primeval times, human beings have suffered from the delusion that they know "quite precisely in every case *how human action is brought about.*" Even the great doubters Socrates and Plato showed themselves to be "innocently credulous" in this regard by subscribing to "that most fateful of prejudices, that profoundest of errors, that 'right knowledge *must be followed* by right action.'"[20] Nietzsche denies that this is ever the case. All our actions remain "essentially unknown" to us, and therefore the gulf between knowledge and action can never be bridged (*D* 116). Whenever we act, we often consider the consequences of various courses of action and choose the one that seems most advantageous. But Nietzsche denies that this motive or reason is what really determines our action. There is a whole host of motives of which we remain unconscious that exert an enormous influence on what we do. They, too, probably struggle with one another—as in the case of self-mastery above—but the struggle remains largely invisible to us (*D* 129).

Part of the unconscious process that Nietzsche uncovers in book 2 has to do with the "nutriment" of the drives that make up our being. He conjectures that every one of our experiences serves as potential prey or nourishment for one or the other of our drives—which one is largely a matter of chance—with the result that some drives starve and others are overfed: "Every moment of our lives sees some of the polyp-arms of our being grow and others of them wither," depending on the nutriment that the moment does or does not provide. To avoid starvation, our drives sometimes avail themselves of "dream food," which is able "to *compensate* to some extent for the chance absence of 'nourishment' during the day." By engaging in "*very free*, very arbitrary interpretations" of the nervous stimuli we feel while asleep, our drives gratify themselves in a way that they were not able to do during waking life. But Nietzsche does not want to draw a sharp distinction between waking and dreaming. Indeed, he claims that "our moral judgments and evaluations too are only images and fantasies based on a physiological process unknown to us" and "all our so-called consciousness is a more or less fantastic commentary on an unknown, perhaps unknowable, but felt text" (*D* 119).[21]

Nietzsche's portrayal of human action as determined, not by reason, intellect, or reflective consciousness, but by unconscious drives and struggles between drives clearly undermines any sort of notion of freedom of the will. In the past, he writes, human beings have posited "the existence of two realms, the realm of *purposes* and *will* and the realm of *chance*." The Greeks referred to the latter realm, which constantly thwarts human purposes, as Moira. Even more unbelievably, Christianity reinterpreted the realm of chance in terms of the inscrutable purposes of a loving God. For Nietzsche, though, there are not two realms but only one, that of chance and necessity. In this realm, "all is not purpose that is called purpose, even less is all will that is called will!" What we call purpose and will are merely shallow interpretations of a complicated process that goes on beneath the level of consciousness. In those cases where our actions seem to follow from our will or purposes, it is merely chance playing its game with us: "Those iron hands of necessity which shake the dice-box of chance play their game for an infinite length of time: so that there *have* to be throws which resemble purposiveness and rationality of every degree. *Perhaps* our acts of will and our purposes are nothing but just such throws" (D 130).[22]

In book 2 of *Daybreak*, Nietzsche arrives at the same conclusion about the innocence and unaccountability of human actions that he arrived at in *Human, All too Human*. But whereas in the latter work he denied freedom of the will on the basis of the unavoidably egoistic character of human action, in *Daybreak* he does so on the basis of our ultimate ignorance of ourselves and of the deepest wellsprings of our actions. In the same way, he denies the possibility of altruism, not on the basis that all our actions are egoistic, but on the basis that the complicated mechanism of our drives makes the distinction between egoistic and altruistic actions nonsensical. There is no single, unified ego that can either assert or deny itself; there are only a multiplicity of drives that seek satisfaction in ways of which we have only the vaguest notion.

Nietzsche's most direct assault on altruism comes in the sustained discussion of pity in the aphorisms immediately following the one devoted to will and purposes (D 131–47). These aphorisms raise the question not merely of the possibility of pity but—and again, this is the new element in *Daybreak*—of its value. Nietzsche begins by pointing out that the ancients had no use for the morality of pity. To think of and live for others was regarded as a sign that one was too boring or ugly to be thought of oneself (D 131). One might think that the reversal of this ancient disdain for pity appeared with Christianity, but Nietzsche argues that the valorization of pity was more of an aftereffect of Christianity and no part of its original intention. Christianity was originally quite egoistic, with its intense preoc-cupation with personal salvation. As this aspect of Christianity weakened, however, the subsidiary belief in love of one's neighbor came to the fore; so much so that in the nineteenth century, in thinkers like Comte, Mill, and Schopenhauer, all that remains of Christianity is the "cult of philanthropy" or the religion of pity. The most current version of the morality of pity, ac-cording to Nietzsche, can be found in Spencer's view that "society is on the way to *adapting* the individual to general requirements, and that the *happi-ness and at the same time the sacrifice of the individual* lies in feeling himself to be a useful member and instrument of the whole." This view is the immedi-ate precursor to the complete "abolition of the *individual*" (D 132).[23]

Nietzsche goes on from here to investigate the deeper, often uncon-scious, motives that lie behind pity or compassion. As he did in *Human, All too Human,* he traces these motives back to some sort of egoism or self-interest: when we act compassionately, we are rarely thinking of the other person and very much thinking of ourselves. But his analysis of this egoism or self-interest is much subtler in *Daybreak,* in keeping with his more com-plicated understanding of the self, and it is not nearly as censorious. There are many reasons why we are affected when an accident befalls someone else: the accident makes us aware of our own impotence; it suggests that we too might be in danger or vulnerable in some way; we would look bad if we didn't help; and so forth. It is our own suffering that we seek to relieve through acts of compassion. And sometimes it is our own pleasure that we seek to enhance: the pleasure that comes from feeling how fortunate we are in contrast to the victim; from praise and recognition; from displaying one's competence; from discharging one's indignation at injustice; and so forth. In short, Nietzsche concludes, we never act compassionately from a single motive alone. And with respect to the many subtle things that constitute "pity," he writes: "[H]ow coarsely does language assault with its one word so polyphonous a being" (D 133; see also 145).

This is about as neutral as Nietzsche's analysis of pity gets. In other apho-risms, his emphasis falls again on the harmfulness of this emotion. In the first place, pity adds our own suffering to the suffering that already exists and thereby "*increases* the amount of suffering in the world." The person who attempts to cultivate this passion and increase his sensitivity to all the misery in the world will "inevitably grow sick and melancholic" and thereby incapacitate himself to serve as a physician to mankind (D 134). Finally, by making ourselves gloomy in this way, we become a burden to others and render ourselves incapable of aid and comfort. We would have a much more positive impact on our fellow human beings if we closed our ears to their lamentation instead of serving as an echo of it (*D* 144).

The greatest danger posed by the growth of pity, however, remains the one already alluded to in connection with Spencer: the general weakening and potential destruction of the individual. Behind the call for ever greater sympathy for others Nietzsche senses a timidity that seeks to remove "*all the dangers* which life once held." Above all, this timidity wants "security," which leads Nietzsche to ask: "Are we not, with this tremendous objective of obliterating all the sharp edges of life, well on the way to turning mankind into *sand*? Sand! Small, soft, round, unending sand!" Wouldn't we end up benefiting others more if, instead of anxiously awaiting their cries of distress, we created something out of ourselves that others could "behold with pleasure: a beautiful, restful, self-enclosed garden perhaps, with high walls against storms and the dust of the roadway but also a hospitable gate" (*D* 174)?

Nietzsche's attack on pity thus appears to be motivated by enlightened benevolence. He develops this benevolent aspect of his critique of pity by asking whether it is "truly moral" to act only with a view to the most immediate consequences of our actions on others. Wouldn't a higher morality than this "narrow and petit bourgeois one" consist in pursuing "more distant goals *even at the cost of the suffering of others*"? Nietzsche mentions the pursuit of knowledge as one of these heroic goals that certainly brings doubt and grief to others as well as to oneself. But if we are willing to sacrifice ourselves for such a goal, why not our neighbor as well? Isn't this in keeping with the golden rule too? Such sacrifice is needed "because a new plowshare is needed to break up the ground and make it fruitful for all." Here Nietzsche alludes to the original title of the book. Through such sacrifice on the part of our neighbor and ourselves, he adds, we "strengthen and raise higher the general feeling of human *power*, even though we ourselves might not attain to more" (*D* 146).

In the concluding aphorism of book 2, Nietzsche returns to his main point: namely, that the definition of moral actions in terms of nonegoism or altruism and freedom of the will rests on a set of intellectual errors; there are no such actions. So what becomes of "moral actions" once one has freed oneself from the errors involved in altruism and freedom of the will? Nietzsche admits that, because these actions were accorded a higher value by virtue of being differentiated from egoistic and unfree actions, realigning them with the latter will inevitably lead to a reduction in their value, not because there is anything wrong with egoistic or unfree actions, but only because of the disappointment caused by previous errors. On the positive side, though, he claims that "we shall restore to men their goodwill towards the actions decried as egoistic and restore to these actions their *value—we shall deprive them of their bad conscience*" (D 148).

Here, for the first time, we get a distinct glimpse of the project that will move more and more to the center of Nietzsche's mature thought and that he will refer to under the rubric of "revaluation." In *Ecce Homo*, Nietzsche suggests that the new morning alluded to in the epigraph of *Daybreak* consisted in "a *revaluation of all values*, in a liberation from all moral values, in saying Yes to and having confidence in all that has hitherto been forbidden, despised, and damned. This Yes-saying book pours out its light, its love, its tenderness upon ever so many wicked things" (EH 3.D.1). This no doubt exaggerates the extent of Nietzsche's revaluation of values in *Daybreak*. Though he seeks to restore our good conscience toward egoistic actions, he stops short of praising forbidden, wicked, or evil ones. Indeed, as we saw in the important aphorism on the two different ways of denying morality, he characterizes his revaluative project in rather modest terms. He does not deny that many actions called immoral ought to be avoided and many actions called moral ought to be encouraged. His main point is that "the one should be encouraged and the other avoided *for other reasons than hitherto*" (D 103). We do not yet have the full thrust of Nietzsche's immoralism.[24] For that we have to wait for *The Gay Science*.

At the end of the aphorism on the two different ways of denying morality, Nietzsche adds an observation that is absolutely crucial for understanding how he sees the relationship between his philosophical critique of morality and the practical reform of morality, between theory and practice: "We have to *learn to think differently*—in order at last, perhaps very late on, to attain even more: *to feel differently*" (D 103). Changing the way we feel is of fundamental importance for Nietzsche because our feelings, especially our moral feelings, exert the most powerful influence on the way we act. Children acquire these feelings by imitating the adults around them. At some point they feel the imperative to justify or provide a rational account of their moral feelings, but Nietzsche is clear that feelings come first and moral justification comes later (D 34). The powerful role of feelings is demonstrated by the fact that, long after we have ceased to believe in a particular teaching or doctrine, we continue to adhere to it in action: "our feelings make us do it" (D 99).[25]

Despite the importance of moral feelings in motivating action, Nietzsche still maintains that they are "nothing final or original; behind feelings stand judgments and evaluations." For this reason, he finds the advice to trust one's feelings the ultimate evasion of responsibility; it amounts to giving "more obedience to one's grandfather and grandmother and their grand-parents than to the gods which are in *us*: our reason and experience" (*D* 35; see also 104). This is where Nietzsche's philosophical project of revaluation comes in. By changing our judgments and evaluation of things, especially of our drives, we can affect the way we feel about them, reduce the guilt or bad conscience that attaches to them, and thus increase human happiness, well-being, and power. By learning to think differently, we can hope someday to feel differently—and to feel better. For by depriving our egoistic actions of their bad conscience, we will "remove from the entire aspect of action and life its *evil appearance*. This is a very significant result! When man no longer regards himself as evil he ceases to be so" (*D* 148; see also 76).

Before leaving this topic, it is perhaps worth distinguishing Nietzsche's complex view on theory and practice from the intellectualism he associates with philosophers like Socrates and Plato. These latter thinkers, he believes, overestimated the role of knowledge in action and underestimated the role of feeling. In a passage I have already quoted, he claims that Socrates and Plato were "innocently credulous in regard to that most fateful of prejudices, that profoundest of errors, that 'right knowledge *must be followed* by right ac-tion'" (*D* 116). And he argues against their intellectualism that the "most confident knowledge or faith cannot provide the strength or ability needed for a deed, it cannot replace the employment of that subtle, many-faceted mechanism which must first be set in motion if anything at all of an idea is to translate itself into action" (*D* 22). This is where Nietzsche's view on theory and practice differs subtly but importantly from that of Socrates and Plato. He does not deny that knowledge—for example, the exposure of the intellectual errors involved in altruism and free will—plays a crucial role in action, but this knowledge is ultimately directed, not to providing rational purposes or goals, but to changing our value-feelings, which ultimately play a more efficacious role in the "subtle, many faceted mechanism" referred to above.[26]

The Aesthetic Self

I want to skip over book 3 of *Daybreak* for the time being and go directly to book 4 because it is in this book that Nietzsche draws out the practical implications of the theory of the self that he elaborated in book 2. The psy-chological observations found in book 4 largely revolve around the theme of self-presentation, self-management, and self-fashioning. In this connec-tion, Nietzsche begins to deploy the metaphors of art and gardening that become prominent in his theory of the self from this point on in his writings. Though there are glimmers of this notion of the aesthetic self in *Human, All too Human* (see, e.g., *HH* 279), it is only in *Daybreak* that Nietzsche fully develops it. The reason for this is that the notion of the aesthetic self depends crucially on the understanding of the self as a multiplicity that also emerges in *Daybreak*. As Alexander Nehamas points out, by conceiving of the subject as a multiplicity, Nietzsche makes the "unity of the self . . . not something given but something achieved, not a beginning but a goal."[27] A passage from Nietzsche's notebooks nicely captures this point about the self as something artistically made, not found: "It is mythology to believe that we will find our authentic selves. . . . Rather, making ourselves, shaping a form out of all the elements—that is the task! Always that of a sculptor, a productive man!" (*KSA* 9:7 [213]).[28]

The first aphorism of book 4 summarizes concisely the nerve of the argument in the first three books concerning the false concepts of free will, responsibility, and punishment: "'And in *summa*: what is it you really want changed?'—We want to cease making causes into sinners and consequences into executioners" (*D* 208). Here Nietzsche essentially repeats what he has said a few aphorisms prior to this one when attacking "our detestable criminal codes": "Let us do away with the concept *sin*—and let us quickly send after it the concept *punishment*" (*D* 202). The erroneous interpretation of cause and effect in terms of sin and punishment has "robbed of its innocence the whole purely chance character of events" and led to the unnecessary darkening of human existence. It is as though, Nietzsche comments, "the education of the human race had hitherto been directed by the fantasies of jailers and hangmen" (*D* 13). In order to reeducate the human race, we need to eliminate the concepts of sin and punishment and grasp through knowledge the thoroughgoing innocence of existence.

But don't we need something more to guide us? At the very least, don't we need something to organize and integrate the bundle of drives and desires that make up the self and over which we seem to have so little control according to the argument of book 2? It is to this question that Nietzsche addresses himself in book 4, and he does so initially by invoking the analogy of art mentioned above. In an aphorism entitled "To Deploy One's Weaknesses Like an Artist," he argues that, while we all unavoidably have certain weaknesses, we also have "sufficient artistic power" to arrange these weaknesses in such a way as to create a desire for our virtues. How, if at all, this "artistic power" differs from the free will Nietzsche has already denied is a question that will occupy us in a moment. Here he indicates that it is a power that great composers like Beethoven, Mozart, and Wagner have possessed in abundance. All intersperse their music with passages of dry recitative, cloying sweetness, or restless dissonance that produce in us "a ravenous hunger for their virtues and a ten times more sensitive palate for every drop of musical spirit, musical beauty, musical goodness" (*D* 218; see also 344 on Homer).

Nietzsche uses the analogy of music at several points in book 4, and interestingly not always favorably. In an aphorism entitled "Hint for Moralists," for example, he reproduces his critique of romantic, Wagnerian music with a view to bringing out the comparable sorcery that belongs to morality (hence the title). "Our composers," he writes, "have made a great discovery: *interesting ugliness* too is possible in their art!" These composers deploy ugliness in much the same way that they were said to deploy their weaknesses in the previously discussed aphorism: to set off their virtues or musical beauties. But here Nietzsche's tone is disapproving. In a manner reminiscent of his analysis of the dialectical relationship between blackening and lightening in *Human, All too Human*, he claims that composers have made the corrupting discovery that against a "dark-colored background . . . a ray of beautiful music, however paltry, acquires the luster of gold and emerald. . . . Composers have discovered contrast: only now are the most powerful effects possible—and *cheap*" (*D* 239; see also 561).[29] In the field of morality, Christianity exploited contrast in a similar way: it is only by creating profound feelings of guilt and despair that "the gloomy propylaea of Christian salvation can open up" (*D* 321).

In a couple of places, Nietzsche distinguishes between innocent music and guilty music. Guilty music is, like the Wagnerian music described above, concerned primarily with producing cheap effects; it is demagogic. Innocent music, on the other hand, is music that "thinks wholly and solely of itself . . . and has forgotten the world in contemplation of itself—the self-resounding of the profoundest solitude, which speaks to itself of itself and no longer knows that outside there are hearers and listeners and effects and failures" (*D* 255; see also 223; cf. RWB 8). The significance of this distinction is that it reminds us of the nuances of Nietzsche's conception of art and, by implication, of the nuances of his aesthetic conception of the self. It is not enough to simply point out that he analogizes the integrated or unified self to a work of art, for works of art can themselves be good or bad, innocent or guilty, authentic or demagogic. Within the aesthetic, there is a hierarchy of value; sheer aesthetic unity or coherence is not sufficient.

Interestingly, examples of the inauthentic aesthetic self outnumber those of the authentic aesthetic self in book 4. Nietzsche describes the artistic composition of the vain self in this way: "We are like shop windows in which we are continually arranging, concealing, or illuminating the supposed qualities others ascribe to us—in order to deceive *ourselves*" (D 385). Many aphorisms describe how the lack or deficiency of certain qualities leads people to compensate by affecting precisely those qualities. "It is where our deficiencies lie," Nietzsche remarks, "that we indulge our enthusiasm. The command 'love your enemies!' had to be invented by the Jews, the best haters there have ever been" (D 377). Similarly, the most embittered and mistrustful human beings find happiness in the unconditional trust that belongs to love (D 216); the timid dress themselves up in the accouterments of authority (D 220); phlegmatic natures are often prone to fanaticism (D 222); those who are tenderhearted seek to conceal their softness by appearing harsh and severe (D 233); the strong strive after charm and the weak after coldness (D 238); the power-hungry want to feel overcome and sink into powerlessness (D 271); and practical men propound idealistic theories, while contemplative natures take pride in being ruthlessly realistic (D 328). Nietzsche's favorite example of this sort of compensatory behavior remains, of course, the ascetic saint, who exterminates his sensual drives precisely because he is consumed by lust (D 294, 331, 377).

We know from both *Human, All too Human* and book 1 of *Daybreak* that Nietzsche associates the ascetic saint with the craving for the feeling of power, so it comes as no surprise that a number of aphorisms in book 4 also deal with this craving. He writes: "Not necessity, not desire—no, the love of power is the demon of men" (D 262). And, as he does in so many other places, he sees people trying to satisfy this craving for the feeling of power through enthusiastic devotion to a cause, fanatical acts of self-sacrifice, and the intoxications of romantic art (D 215, 298). To those who seek to cure the afflictions of their souls by these extreme remedies, Nietzsche offers some homely advice: instead of resorting to intoxication, try something more modest: a "change of diet and hard physical labor" (D 269); or even better, "plenty of sleep" (D 376).[30]

As in the rest of *Daybreak*, most of Nietzsche's references to the feeling of power in book 4 are negative. But in one aphorism he makes an important distinction that seems to open the way to a more positive assessment of this feeling. Whereas the person "who wants to acquire the feeling of power resorts to any means and disdains nothing that will nourish it," the person who already has it becomes "very fastidious and noble in his tastes" and "finds few things to satisfy him" (D 348). To put it in the terms of Nietzsche's later philosophy: there is a crucial difference between the will to power of the weak and the will to power of the strong. In another aphorism, he holds up the example of Napoleon as someone in whom the lust for the feeling of power has achieved complete dominance and attained a high degree of subtlety. Insofar as he indulged this drive in everything he did—for example, when he revenged himself on his poor speaking ability by speaking even worse than he could—"Napoleon belongs to the mankind of antiquity," which was marked by "the simple construction and the inventive elaboration and variation of a single motif" (*D* 245).[31]

Let us return now to Nietzsche's conception of the aesthetic self, in particular to the favorable interpretation he gives to it in his gardening metaphors. He invokes this metaphor once in book 4, but his most developed elaboration of it appears in book 5. Because it raises a number of important issues, I quote the aphorism in full:

> *What we are at liberty to do.*—One can dispose of one's drives like a gardener and, though few know it, cultivate the shoots of anger, pity, curiosity, vanity as productively and profitably as a beautiful fruit tree on a trellis; one can do it with the good or bad taste of a gardener and, as it were, in the French or English or Dutch or Chinese fashion; one can also let nature rule and only attend to a little embellishment and tidying-up here and there; one can, finally, without paying any attention to them at all, let the plants grow up and fight their fight out among themselves—indeed, one can take delight in such a wilderness, and desire precisely this delight, though it gives one some trouble, too. All this we are at liberty to do: but how many know we are at liberty to do it? Do the majority not *believe in themselves* as in complete *fully developed facts*? Have the great philosophers not put their seal on this prejudice with the doctrine of the unchangeability of character? (*D* 560)

One is immediately struck by the voluntarism of this aphorism and how it jars with the denials of free will that we have seen Nietzsche repeatedly make so far. By appealing to the liberty to dispose of one's drives like a gardener—or to the power to deploy one's weaknesses like an artist (*D* 218)— does he merely smuggle something like free will in through the back door?[32] We observed in *Human, All too Human* that Nietzsche's denial of free will is not as global or deterministic as it sometimes seems. And toward the end of the previous section, we noted that he insists that the way that we think about things and evaluate them can have a profound effect on our actions. This does not mean, however, that there isn't an awful lot about ourselves that is given or natural or even undeniable. That is the point of the gardening and artistic metaphors. They put the emphasis, not on denying or exterminating our drives or other natural aspects of ourselves, but on working with and arranging what is given. There is no question here of something above the drives—reason, spirit, or the like—combating or suppressing them, a position we have already seen Nietzsche reject (see *D* 109). Rather, our liberty extends only to arranging, cultivating, nourishing, and composing what is already there. This creative activity is powerfully circumscribed by the natural facts that make up our being, but we are still far from being "fully developed facts" prior to this activity.

Toward the end of the quoted aphorism, Nietzsche distinguishes his position on our liberty to shape ourselves from Schopenhauer's doctrine of the unalterable empirical character. Brian Leiter, who emphasizes the deterministic aspects of Nietzsche's moral psychology, argues that his position is not as different from Schopenhauer's fatalistic doctrine as this passage suggests, especially when one takes into account that Schopenhauer acknowledges an "acquired character" in addition to our unalterable empirical character. This acquired character consists of "the most complete knowledge of our individuality" and "puts us in a position to carry out, deliberately and methodically, the unalterable role of our own person."[33] But Schopenhauer's notion of the acquired character is ultimately quite different from Nietzsche's conception of the aesthetic or horticultural self. The notion of the acquired character still assumes that deep down or latent within us there is an essential self of which we can gain knowledge in order to deliberately realize it. Nietzsche's conception of the aesthetic self, on the other hand, involves no such belief in a stable, antecedently given essential self; rather, it maintains that the self is a multiplicity of drives that do not form a predetermined order but can be shaped, arranged, composed, and harmonized in a variety of ways on the basis of our opinions and circumstances.

With respect to our circumstances, too, Nietzsche believes we have far more control than we often suppose. He insists that we should not live in an environment that makes us grow dissatisfied with ourselves, for then we will not achieve the best of which we are capable: "But who gives thought to such things, to possessing a *choice* in such things! One speaks of one's 'destiny,' and spreads one's broad back, and sighs: 'what an unhappy Atlas I am!'" (*D* 364). The particular danger of living in such a self-dissatisfaction-making environment is that it also makes one vengeful. Thus, Nietzsche warns that clever women who have been "confined to a petty, dull environment" eventually end up revenging themselves "on everything that has escaped from their dog-kennel" (*D* 227). We can also become victims of the self-dissatisfied individuals around us, whose vengefulness fills the air with "arrows of malice, so that the sun and sky of life are darkened by them—not only their sky but ours too." In this case, Nietzsche advises that we change *our* environment and seek out solitude (*D* 323). Circumstances can even magnify or diminish our power, he claims: "One should regard oneself as a variable quantity whose capacity for achievement can under favorable circumstances perhaps equal the highest ever known." He concludes that "one should thus reflect on one's circumstances and spare no effort in observing them" (*D* 326). It is to just such reflection and observation that I would like to turn next in connection with Nietzsche's discussion of culture in *Daybreak*.

The Problem of Modern Culture (Again)

Although the theme of culture is more subordinate in *Daybreak* than it was in *Human, All too Human*, it still figures prominently in book 3 and, as we shall see in the next section, to some extent in book 5. In book 3, Nietzsche takes up a wide variety of topics, including the nature of commercial culture, the differences between German culture and Greek (and French) culture, the relationship between culture and politics, art, education, and aristocracy, but it is the culture theme that loosely holds them together. Framing the whole discussion is the contrast between romanticism, with its glorification of the past, the unmeasured, and raw emotion, and the Enlightenment, which Nietzsche associates with skepticism, moderation, and reason. As he did in *Human, All too Human*, Nietzsche continues in *Daybreak* to bear the banner of the latter cultural movement: "This Enlightenment we must now carry further forward" (*D* 197).

Book 3 begins, however, on a much less grandiose note. In an aphorism entitled "The Need for Little Deviant Acts," Nietzsche criticizes free spirits and nonbelievers for deferring to customs they no longer believe in simply because they don't want to offend those around them or be accused of being pedantic. The atheist who gets married in a church or lets his child be baptized, the opponent of nationalism who serves in the army—such seemingly unimportant acts of acquiescence to societal conventions actually end up lending crucial support to these irrational conventions and perpetuating them. For this reason, Nietzsche insists that it is not enough merely to entertain deviant opinions; one must express those opinions outwardly in "little deviant acts" (*D* 149). This may seem a small point, but in many ways it articulates one of the cardinal tenets of Nietzsche's earliest thinking about culture: namely, that a genuine culture is marked by the unity of inner and outer, content and form. No matter how profound we may be in our inner subjectivity, this counts for nothing unless we can endow that subjectivity with an outer form and embody it in visible acts (UDH 4).

The next couple of aphorisms in book 3 deal with marriage and the way in which, especially in the modern world, it has been handed over to chance and the capriciousness of romantic love (*D* 150–51). Nietzsche comments that this "makes a grand rational progress of mankind impossible." (I will pass over his sexist comments about little women plucking to pieces the achieved humanity of their husbands.) Here, again, the connection to the culture theme may seem oblique. The family, of course, plays a crucial role in cultural transmission, and in these aphorisms Nietzsche lays a great deal of emphasis on the harmful effects of irrational marriages on children. But beyond this, his discussion of marriage serves as a metaphor for the kind of self-conscious control of culture that he thinks is necessary in the wake of God's death. It is interesting that he begins one of the aphorisms by stating, "If I were a god, and a benevolent god, the *marriages* of mankind would make me more impatient than anything else." The point is that, once belief in God has disappeared, we must become our own benevolent gods and take responsibility for all the things that we have hitherto left to chance (cf. *HH* 25, 242). Among other things, this means that we must "take marriage enormously more seriously" than we have in the past.

From these preliminary considerations, Nietzsche moves to the main features of his critique of modern culture. He begins with the familiar point that modern culture is fundamentally defined by its desire for security and the removal of all danger from life. The result of this quest for security, as we have already seen, is that humanity is gradually transformed into sand: "small, soft, round, unending sand!" (*D* 174). Nietzsche imagines an "old-style fighting man" who despises civilization precisely because it removes all risks and makes "the good things of life—honors, plunder, beautiful women—accessible to cowards" (*D* 153). And he contrasts our situation in this regard with the way of life of the Greeks, for whom "perils and upheavals were always present." But this does not mean that danger and heroism will necessarily disappear from modern life. Nietzsche holds out the possibility that they may someday be transferred to the quest for knowledge, which, paradoxically, the Greeks saw as a refuge from the perilousness of life (*D* 154). We will explore this possibility further in the next section.

Connected with the modern preoccupation with security is the general softening of human beings and the indulgence of all sorts of emotions that call for tears, especially pity. Here Nietzsche begins to touch more closely on the problem of romanticism in modern culture. And once again, he uses the Greeks as a foil, contrasting their emotional restraint and moderation with the indulgence of the emotions—the "cult of natural sounds," as he calls it—found in modern culture. In this regard, he cites Plato's critical attitude toward tragedy and tragic emotion; but he also indicates that for the

Greeks of an earlier generation, whose disposition was fundamentally hard and warlike, tragedy provided a needed release. Needless to say, this is no longer the case for the soft, easily moved, and excessively emotional souls of the modern age. For such souls, tragedy and music can only worsen the malady, though Nietzsche also envisages a coming age of danger in which music can again perform the salutary role that tragedy once played for the Greeks in the age of Aeschylus (*D* 157, 172).

From the romantic cult of feeling, Nietzsche moves on to consider romantic art, leveling many of the same criticisms that we saw him make in *Human, All too Human*. Like all artists, modern artists reflect the world around them and therefore they "depict beauty as bloated, gigantic and nervous." Again, this contrasts with the Greeks, who, "under the spell of their morality of moderation, saw and depicted beauty as the Apollo Belvedere" (*D* 161).[34] Similarly, modern architecture is characterized by massiveness, while Greek architecture builds on a smaller, but by no means less effective, scale. Finally, Greek art reflects the simplicity of the Greek soul, while modern art, especially romantic music, reflects the labyrinthine character of ours (*D* 169). Modern, romantic art has a peculiar relationship to its audience, providing "greedy, insatiable, undisciplined, disgusted, harassed men of the present day" with an escape from the misery and dissoluteness of their lives. Against this psychiatric function of modern art Nietzsche offers the example of Corneille, whose art is continuous with the noble lives of his audience and therefore can exercise an improving effect on them as opposed to providing sheer escape, intoxication, or narcosis (*D* 191; cf. *AOM* 169).

One of the fruits of romanticism was a deeper appreciation of and empathy for the past, which blossomed into the modern historical sense. Here Nietzsche seems to retreat from his positive assessment of this recent development in *Human, All too Human* and return to the more critical attitude of "The Uses and Disadvantages of History for Life." He says at one point that "the danger that lies in the study of history as soon as it gets the upper hand of an entire age" is that "too much energy is thrown away on all possible resurrections of the dead. Perhaps the whole movement of romanticism can best be understood from this point of view" (*D* 159). The modern historical sense allows modern individuals to digest too many things, and this results in the inner chaos and lack of wholeness that Nietzsche detailed so brilliantly in his earlier essay on history (*D* 171). And as he did in that essay, he here lambastes modern classical education for offering food to those who do not hunger for it and for treating the ancients as mere objects of detached knowledge instead of as models to emulate (*D* 195).

Of all the national cultures of Europe, Germany's has been the one that has been most deeply influenced by romanticism, according to Nietzsche. In an aphorism entitled "German Hostility to Enlightenment," he spells out how in the first half of the nineteenth century the romantic impulse seeped into almost every department of German intellectual life. In philosophy, for example, the Germans "retreated to the first and oldest stage of speculation" (D 197). Of no philosophy was this more true than of the "silver-glistering idealism" of Schiller, Humboldt, Schelling, Hegel, and Schleiermacher, which displayed a "heartfelt repugnance for 'cold' or 'dry' reality" and "for every kind of philosophical temperance and skepticism" (D 190). German historians likewise exhibited the romantic spirit by attempting to revive the "older, primitive sensibilities" of Christianity, the medieval world, and so forth. And German natural scientists fought against the mechanistic universe of Newton and sought to infuse nature once again with an "ethical and symbolical significance." In general, "the cult of feeling was erected in place of the cult of reason," and knowledge was denied to make room for faith. At the end of the aphorism on the German rebellion against the Enlightenment, however, Nietzsche adds an extra twist to his argument. Though originally serving a reactionary purpose, "the study of history, understanding of origins and evolutions, [and] empathy for the past" that animated German romanticism now provide intellectual support for "*that very Enlightenment* against which they were conjured up" and which "we must now carry further forward" (D 197; cf. HH 26).

Connected to their romanticism, in Nietzsche's mind, is the Germans' attraction to all things unconditional: in particular, unconditional homage and unconditional obedience (D 167, 207). Such unconditional feelings fly in the face of the skepticism, moderation, and graduated judgment that he associates with the Enlightenment. As he puts it in one place: "[R]omantic prostration before 'genius' and the 'hero' . . . is contrary to the spirit of the Enlightenment" (D 298). If the Germans are to transform themselves from being "a nation of credulous emulation and blind and bitter animosity" to one "of conditional consent and benevolent opposition," Nietzsche believes they should take to heart the maxim of the great French republican Carnot: "What matters is not persons but things" (D 167).

Nietzsche often uses the French as a foil to highlight the deficiencies of German culture. One of the things he admires most about the French is the way they harmonize their inner spirit and their outer form. This is the theme of one of the stranger aphorisms of book 3, in which Nietzsche praises the French as the most Christian nation on earth. What impresses him about the Christianity of the French is the way "the most difficult Christian ideals have there been transformed into men and not remained merely ideas, beginnings, falterings." As examples of this perfectly embodied Christianity, he mentions Pascal, Fénelon, Madame Guyon, de Rancé (the founder of the Trappist monasteries), and the Huguenots. Such unity of inner and outer, content and form, spirit and body, among the French stands in stark contrast to the Germans. Whereas a great Frenchman "always preserves his surface, a natural skin to cover his content and depths," a great German keeps his depths "enclosed in an intricate capsule, in the same way an elixir seeks to protect itself against the light and against frivolous hands by the hardness and strangeness of its casing." Lest the reader be confused about his intention in this aphorism, Nietzsche adds that the unity of outer surface and inner depth that marks French Christianity can also be found in unchristian French free-spiritedness (*D* 192; see also 60).

Most of the reflections I have discussed so far revolve around the romantic elements in modern culture. But Nietzsche also considers the commercial and industrial aspects of modern life in book 3. Of course, these two dimensions of modern culture are not as unrelated as they may seem, as we saw in *Human, All too Human*. Romantic art is designed precisely to provide stimulants and distraction to the weary and harassed in the age of work (*WS* 170). In *Daybreak*, Nietzsche decries the way in which the young are "worn out daily" in the modern work-economy and thereby prevented from developing into full or mature human beings (*D* 178). Behind the modern glorification of work he sees a "fear of everything individual": "[H]ard industriousness . . . keeps everyone in bounds and can mightily hinder the development of reason, covetousness, desire for independence" (*D* 173). Indeed, he considers the whole idea of commercial culture to be antiindividualistic insofar as it demands that the individual appraise everything "*according to the needs of the consumer*, not according to his own needs" (*D* 175). His revulsion at the features of modern economic life to which we have all become accustomed erupts into violent complaint when he exclaims that it is "disgusting" that one is forced "to be part of a system in which one must either be a wheel and nothing else, or get run over by the other wheels"; a system in which one becomes a useful commodity, a "common piece of nature's pottery" (*D* 166).

Nietzsche's antipathy to modern economic life represents nothing new in his outlook; it goes back to his earliest writings. And the same is true of his condemnation of modern politics. He pities the ambitious young men who are consumed with politics in the belief that they somehow belong to the "chariot of history." He pities them because such political activity deprives these young men of "all genuine productivity" and insures that "the profound speechlessness of pregnancy never comes to them" (*D* 177). The most gifted spirits in society ought not to waste their time and energy on political and economic affairs but, rather, leave these to "lesser heads." The goals of politics and economics, which are directed to "universal security," are mediocre goals and should not "be pursued by the highest instruments . . . which ought to be *saved up* for the highest and rarest objectives" (*D* 179). In all of these reflections on politics, Nietzsche remains very much the antipolitical German.

One of the most ominous features he discerns in modern politics is the way it is used to gratify the craving for the feeling of power, especially among the masses. The masses are actuated more by the desire for intoxication than by the desire for bread: "[I]ntoxication means more to them than nourishment—that is the bait they will always take!" The masses take this bait from the "man of the people," who holds out to them "the prospect of conquests and grandeur." Peace and plenty pale in comparison to the "mad-making power" of these other aims (*D* 188). It would be hard to confuse Nietzsche with the Nazis in this aphorism; or in the one that follows, on "great politics" (*Grosse Politik*), of which he takes—as in *Human, All too Human*—a rather dim view. Great politics is grounded in the "need for the feeling of power," again especially on the part of the masses, who from time to time are "*ready* to stake their life, their goods, their conscience, their virtue so as to acquire that higher enjoyment and as a victorious, capriciously tyrannical nation to rule over other nations." The "prudently calculating prince" can exploit this lust for power on the part of the masses by mouthing "the pathetic language of virtue" and giving them a good conscience in their conquest of other nations. Nietzsche mordantly comments: "Strange madness of moral judgments!" (*D* 189).

Though Nietzsche has little good to say about politics in the conventional sense as it relates to the activities of the modern state, he does display an intense interest in politics in a broader sense as it relates to social classes. The little platoons (as Burke referred to them) that comprise society embody concrete ways of life, with habits, traditions, and modes of transmission that make them far more important as bearers of culture than the abstract state.[35] Nietzsche devotes several aphorisms toward the end of book 3 to these little platoons, beginning with aristocracy.

In the first of the aphorisms dedicated to this social class—"We are Nobler"—he takes the somewhat unexpected position that the contemporary aristocracies of Europe, which are "still chivalrous and feudal in nature," surpass the aristocracy of the ancient Greeks in nobility. Citing the shamelessness of characters like Odysseus and Themistocles, he claims that the

Greeks were far less inclined to risk their lives for the sake of honor and far more concerned with mere fame and the feeling of power than the European descendents of the age of chivalry. Here again, the desire for the feeling of power has a negative connotation for Nietzsche and is associated with ignobility. Motivated by this desire, the Greek aristocrat was willing to do almost anything—lie, murder, betray his friends, sell his city—in order to achieve power over his peers. For such a man justice was "extraordinarily difficult," indeed, "nearly incredible," and the happiest life was understood to be the life of the tyrant. Such is not the case for the contemporary European aristocrat, an observation from which Nietzsche once again draws an antipolitical implication: "[P]eople whose lust for power no longer rages as blindly as that of those noble Greeks also no longer require the idolization of the concept of the state with which that lust was formerly kept in check" (*D* 199).

But Nietzsche is less interested in defending the current aristocracy than in painting a picture of a future aristocracy based on the quest for knowledge: "[T]hanks to the work of our free spirits, it is now no longer reprehensible for those born and raised in the aristocracy to enter the orders of knowledge and there to obtain more intellectual ordinations, learn higher knightly duties, than any heretofore." Again, he draws an antipolitical implication: for such an aristocracy of knowledge "it will be *indecent* to engage in politics." But perhaps even more interesting is the very different implication he draws concerning the value of power, in many ways corresponding to the distinction he made in book 4 between the person who wants to acquire the feeling of power and the person who already has it. In the erect posture of the aristocrat and his calm demeanor in difficult situations, "the consciousness of power is constantly playing its charming game in [his] limbs." Here there is an "actual feeling of superiority," which will reveal itself in a sublimated form in the new aristocracy of knowledge of the future (*D* 201).

One of the groups that Nietzsche believes will play an important role in this new aristocracy is the Jews. In a remarkable aphorism entitled "Of the People of Israel"—which Leo Strauss called the "most profound and most radical statement on assimilation I have ever read"[36]—he argues that the Jews "have gone through an eighteen-century schooling" that has conferred on them extraordinary psychological and spiritual resources. As a result of this discipline, they "are going to ally themselves with the best aristocracy of Europe" and attain a nobility of spiritual and bodily demeanor that will make those they dominate unashamed to have them as masters. In the end, the "abundance of passions, virtues, decisions, renunciations, struggles, [and] victories of every kind" that constitutes Jewish history will issue in "great men and great works" (D 205). This aphorism, which contains perhaps the most positive assessment of the Jews in Nietzsche's entire oeuvre,[37] is remarkable in the context of the increasing anti-Semitism of late nineteenth-century Germany, a prejudice Nietzsche knew firsthand from his acquaintance with Wagner, his publisher Schmeitzner, and his sister's future husband, the rabid anti-Semite Bernhard Förster.

In the very next aphorism, Nietzsche turns his attention to the opposite end of the social spectrum and takes up the plight of the working class. Though his analysis is not notable for its political-economic acuity, it does reveal a concern for the working class that is not often evident in his other writings. To the "factory slaves" who are "used, and *used up*, as part of a machine and as it were a stopgap to fill a hole in human invention," he addresses the question: "[W]here is your inner value if you no longer know what it is to breathe free?" He does not think the "flutings of the Socialist pied-pipers" will be of much help to the worker in this situation, being designed primarily to "enflame wild hopes" rather than offer genuine relief. A much more effective solution would be for European workers to emigrate to other countries and become their own masters, in this way protesting "against the machine, against capital, and against the choice now threatening them of being *compelled* to become either the slave of the state or the slave of a party of disruption" (D 206).

Nietzsche shows a similar solicitude toward the last and lowest class of human beings that he considers in book 3: the class of criminals. As in *Human, All too Human* and its sequels, his discussion of criminals here reflects his general thesis about the total unaccountability of human beings for their actions.[38] Therefore, he advocates that we treat the criminal, not as an evildoer whose guilt cries out for punishment, but as "a mental patient" in need of "the prudence and goodwill of a physician." We should do everything we can to cure the patient, whether it be by giving him a change of air, company, or occupation, or by extinguishing, transforming, or sublimating his criminal drives: "[O]ne should neglect nothing in the effort to restore to the criminal his courage and freedom of heart; one should wipe pangs of conscience from his soul as a matter of cleanliness." Above all, we need to get rid of the spirit of revenge that currently presides in "our detestable criminal codes" and replace it with the "science and art of healing." For all of his fulminations against pity, Nietzsche shows a humanitarianism here—and, indeed, in all of his discussions of criminal punishment—that complicates the conventional picture of his philosophy as devoid of compassion. This humanitarianism is evident in the conclusion of the aphorism, where he invokes the image of the plowshare that served as the original title for *Day-*

break and at the same time quotes the dictum of universal beneficence from *Der Meier Helmbrecht*: "[I]f thou wouldst cultivate the land, cultivate it with the plow: then the bird and the wolf who follow behind the plow shall rejoice in thee—*all creatures shall rejoice in thee*" (*D* 203; see also 236).

The Passion for Knowledge

In book 3, Nietzsche alludes to the role that knowledge and science will play in culture, notably in his discussion of the aristocracy of the future, but he does not elaborate on this aspect of his cultural teaching which had occupied such a central place in *Human, All too Human*. He makes good this defect, however, in book 5, which is concerned throughout with the quest for knowledge and the life of the free-spirited knower. It is here that Nietzsche enunciates the idea of knowledge as a passion that I mentioned at the outset of this chapter. This idea is something we did not see in *Human, All too Human*, which generally emphasized the role of knowledge in calming or moderating the vehemence of the passions. While references to this moderating effect of knowledge are still present in *Daybreak*, it is the new emphasis on knowledge as a passion that catches our attention. One can see this new emphasis emerging quite distinctly in Nietzsche's notes from the end of 1880, where he speaks repeatedly of the "passion for knowledge" (*Leidenschaft der Erkenntnis*), the heroism of science, dying for knowledge, and the "tragedy of knowledge" (*KSA* 9:7 [19, 20, 139, 159, 165, 171, 197, 302, 304]).[39] There is nothing utilitarian or bourgeois about the quest for knowledge for Nietzsche, and this gives his appropriation of the Enlightenment its peculiar, one might say romantic, quality. He celebrates an Enlightenment that has been deepened by the experience of *Tristan and Isolde*.

Nietzsche introduces the theme of the passion for knowledge in an aphorism entitled "The New Passion." Acknowledging that the ignorant barbarians of previous ages were happier than we are, he asks why the idea of reverting to such barbarism fills us with revulsion: "The reason is that our *drive to knowledge* has become too strong for us to be able to want happiness without knowledge, or the happiness of a strong, firmly rooted delusion." We delight in the restlessness and dissatisfaction of the quest for knowledge in the same way that the lover delights in his unrequited love. It is precisely because we seek knowledge in spite of the suffering it brings that makes it a passion. Nietzsche suggests that perhaps "mankind will even perish of this passion for knowledge," asking with Tristan-like significance, "Are love and death not brothers?" He has not abandoned his earlier position that the truth may be deadly, but he now views that possibility in a different light—as a temptation to passion and an opportunity for heroism. And in any case, what is the alternative? Nietzsche lays out the choice confronting humanity in terms that anticipate Zarathustra's alternative of the last man versus the superman: "[I]f mankind does not perish of a *passion* it will perish of a *weakness*: which do you prefer? This is the main question. Do we desire for mankind an end in fire and light or one in sand?" (*D* 429).

The idea of passion is connected with the idea of self-sacrifice, and both ideas are connected in Nietzsche's mind with the notion of tragedy. As far back as the essay on "Richard Wagner in Bayreuth," he argued that the "individual must be consecrated to something higher than himself—that is the meaning of tragedy"; and the only hope and guarantee "for the future of humanity . . . consists in its *retention of the sense for the tragic*" (RWB 4). In an aphorism entitled "A Tragic Ending for Knowledge," he now finds such a goal to which humanity can sacrifice itself in knowledge: the "knowledge of truth" remains "as the one tremendous goal commensurate with such a sacrifice, because for this goal no sacrifice is too great" (*D* 45). The idea of self-sacrifice also figures in what Nietzsche refers to as the "magnanimity of the thinker": "[T]he fairest virtue of the great thinker is the magnanimity with which, as a man of knowledge, he intrepidly . . . offers himself and his life as a sacrifice" (*D* 459). And tragic self-sacrifice for the sake of knowledge is also at the heart of the fable Nietzsche tells of the "Don Juan of knowledge," a figure who "has the spirit and appetite for and enjoyment of the chase and intrigues of knowledge . . . until at last there remains to him nothing of knowledge to hunt down except the absolutely *detrimental*" (*D* 327).

Nietzsche finds countless ways to evoke the heroism of the quest for knowledge—he is in many ways the great poet of this quest. It is not surprising, therefore, that one of the most important virtues he associates with the quest for knowledge is courage. Courage, of course, does not exist in the absence of danger, and therefore Nietzsche insists that he "wants no knowledge anymore without danger" (*KSA* 9:7 [165]). What may we hope for from the courage that does not shrink from the dangers of knowing? "Perhaps there will come a time when this courage in thinking will have grown so great that, as the supreme form of arrogance, it will feel itself *above* man and things—when the sage will, as the most courageous man, also be the man who sees himself and existence farthest beneath him?" (*D* 551). The other virtue that Nietzsche considers to be vital for the quest for knowledge—he calls it the "youngest virtue"—is "honesty" (*Redlichkeit*) (*D* 456).[40] Though implicit in *Human, All too Human*, the emphasis on this quintessential virtue of the free spirit in his later works dates from *Daybreak*.[41]

Insofar as the quest for knowledge is arduous and full of danger, the free spirit needs from time to time to rest and recuperate. Life itself can offer a momentary respite from the rigors of this quest, which prompts Nietzsche to observe that, whereas the Greeks sought refuge from the perils of everyday life in knowledge and reflection, we "have transferred this perilousness into knowledge and reflection" and recover from it with life (*D* 154, 572). Art, too, can play this recuperative role, but only if one does not seek from it artificial stimulation to compensate for a boring life, as romanticism would have it, but precisely the opposite: "For that element into which one formerly wanted to drive for a few moments through the gateway of art is the element in which one now continually dwells." To throw aside for a while the tense excitement of thinking and "dream oneself a child, beggar, and fool—can from now on occasionally give us pleasure" (*D* 531). Finally, in a remark that recalls the image of the "double-brain" in *Human, All too Human* (*HH* 251), Nietzsche points out that we cannot always dwell in the realm of truth if the latter is to retain its power: we must "*find relief* from [truth] from time to time in untruth—otherwise it will become boring, powerless, and tasteless to us" (*D* 507).

Nietzsche's views on the relationship between knowledge and art in book 5 are actually more complicated than the remark quoted in the previous paragraph suggests. For he sees art as providing not only a respite from the rigors of knowing but also an image of the happiness involved in knowing. Defining beauty in art as "*the imitation of happiness,*"[42] he argues that the realism of contemporary art suggests that "*our* happiness lies in realism, in possessing the sharpest possible senses and in the faithful interpretation of reality." In this way, our artists can be seen as "glorifiers of the 'delights' of science" (*D* 432; see also 244). Nietzsche uses his favorite analogy of landscape architecture to explain this new appeal of the real. In the same way that wild, romantic gardens once displaced the stylized nature of rococo gardens, so we now find the "mightiest beauty in precisely the 'wild, ugly' sides of science, just as once it was only from the time of Rousseau that one discovered a sense for the beauty of high mountains and desert" (*D* 427). The *vita contemplativa* does not involve ascetic renunciation (*D* 440). In the quest for knowledge we find both beauty and supreme happiness (*D* 550).

So far we have concerned ourselves with the value—especially the cultural value—that Nietzsche ascribes to the quest for knowledge in book 5, but we have not said much about his understanding of the nature of knowledge and its relation to reality. Nietzsche himself does not say a great deal here about this fundamental topic, which he explored much more fully in the first chapter of *Human, All too Human*, but what he does say hews fairly closely to what he argued in the earlier work. In the very first aphorism of book 5, "In the Great Silence," he gives us a haunting prose-poem that evokes the "tremendous muteness" of the sea, which causes him "to hate speech, to hate even thinking; for do I not hear behind every word the laughter of error, of imagination, of the spirit of delusion?" (*D* 423). Once again, we seem to be back to Nietzsche's "error theory" of knowledge, in which everything we think or say about the world somehow falsifies it. Nietzsche sums up this metaphysical position concisely in another aphorism: "Why does man not see things? He is himself standing in the way: he conceals things" (*D* 438).

Such a metaphysical view would seem to lead to a radical skepticism about knowledge and ill comport with the celebration of the quest for knowledge that runs through book 5. In a dialogue between A and B, however, Nietzsche makes clear that he does not accept that the unknowability of the thing in itself necessarily leads to skeptical consequences. The case for skepticism is put by A: "Learn to know! Yes! But always as a man! . . . Never to be able to see into things out of any other eyes but *these*? . . . What will mankind have come to know at the end of all their knowledge?—their organs! And that perhaps means: the impossibility of knowledge!" B comes back with Nietzsche's nonskeptical response: "This is a serious attack—*reason* is attacking you! But tomorrow you will be again in the midst of knowledge and therewith also in the midst of unreason, which is to say *delight* in the human. Let us go down to the sea!" (*D* 483). Yes, he seems to be conceding, we cannot see things out of any eyes but these—"we behold all things through the human head" (*HH* 9), as he put it in *Human, All too Human*—but this does not preclude the possibility of knowledge. We cannot know the thing in itself, but this still leaves the human world, a rich compound of reason and unreason, as an object of ever-increasing knowledge.

The aphorism that best captures Nietzsche's complex position on the nature of knowledge is the one entitled "Colorblindness of Thinkers." The Greeks, he argues, saw the world in a very different way from the way we do because they lacked the ability to discern green and blue and substituted brown and yellow instead. This gave their world a much more human coloration, since "blue and green dehumanize nature more than anything else does." This is what made the Greeks such great anthropomorphizers. Nietzsche goes on to claim that this is a metaphor for a more general supposition: "Every thinker paints his world in fewer colors than *are actually there*, and is blind to certain individual colors." This is not necessarily a deficiency, since it "introduces harmonies of colors *into the things themselves,* and these harmonies possess great charm and can constitute an enrichment of nature." Gradually, however, more colors are introduced and harmonized, and "even today many an individual works himself out of a partial colorblindness into a richer seeing and distinguishing" (*D* 426). Nietzsche denies that we can ever completely overcome our colorblindness. Nevertheless, he implies that it is possible to move beyond the anthropomorphic simplifications of reality found in earlier humanity and to incorporate more of what is actually there into a "richer seeing and distinguishing."

As beguiling as this aphorism is, it is not without its difficulties. With his metaphor of colorblindness we once again encounter Nietzsche's paradoxical "error theory" of knowledge. In our knowing activity, he suggests, we somehow falsify the world out there; we paint the world "in fewer colors than *are actually there*." But what exactly is the character of this world out there? And how do know enough about it to be able to claim that our concepts falsify it? Nietzsche does not help his cause by equating this world with "things themselves," especially since we have already seen him reject the notion of a metaphysical world in itself as nonsensical. A more promising way of thinking about this world is suggested in a note from roughly the time of *Daybreak*: "Man does not ultimately discover the world, but rather his taste-organs and feelers" (*KSA* 9:10 [83]). It is this world that is disclosed by our "taste-organs and feelers" that we simplify, falsify, and make sense of with our concepts; and it is this world that we can gradually incorporate more of in order to develop a "richer seeing and distinguishing." In a much later note, Nietzsche corroborates something like this understanding of the world that simultaneously serves as the material of our knowledge and is also inevitably falsified by it. He writes that the antithesis to the phenomenal world shaped by our logical concepts "is not 'the true world,' but the formless unformulable world of the chaos of sensations—*another kind* of phenomenal world, a kind 'unknowable' for us" (*WP* 569).[43]

In addition to the nature of knowledge, Nietzsche also takes up in book 5 the question of how the free spirit goes about acquiring knowledge. Here the key aphorism is the one that begins: "There are no scientific methods which alone lead to knowledge! We have to tackle things experimentally, now angry with them and now kind, and be successively just, passionate, and cold with them" (*D* 432). This is one of the first places that Nietzsche clearly articulates the crucial role played by the affects in enabling knowledge, anticipating the famous passage on perspectivism in *The Genealogy of Morals*: "There is *only* a perspective seeing, *only* a perspective 'knowing'; and the *more* affects we allow to speak about one thing . . . the more complete will our 'concept' of this thing, our 'objectivity,' be. But to eliminate the will altogether, to suspend each and every affect, supposing we were capable of this—what would that mean but to *castrate* the intellect?" (*GM* 3.12).[44] In this passage and the earlier one from *Daybreak*, Nietzsche unambiguously rejects the purely spectatorial theory of knowledge that belongs to Schopenhauer, who frequently refers to the "pure, will-less subject of knowledge." Knowledge is acquired not by suspending the will or suppressing the affects but by using them in a controlled way—in the passage from the *Genealogy*, Nietzsche speaks of the ability *to control* one's Pro and Con"—in order to disclose various aspects of the world. This controlled deployment of the affects to disclose various aspects of the world is to be sharply distinguished from the emotivism that makes passion or conviction the criterion of truth, as Nietzsche makes clear in another aphorism from book 5 entitled "Do not Make Passion an Argument for Truth" (*D* 543). This latter view constitutes not merely a modification of the concept of "objectivity" but a total denial of it.

In addition to the affects, Nietzsche explores a number of other conditions of knowledge in book 5, chief amongst which is solitude. Other people constitute a threat to our fine objectivity. "How can one see this rejoicing crowd," he asks, "without feeling with them and being moved to tears?" We have to flee such experiences, "if we are not to lose our *reason*" (*D* 448). We especially need to flee those whom we love because for their sake we become "inveterate transgressors against truth" (*D* 479). It is only when we are alone, Nietzsche insists, that we see things in a "fairer and clearer light" (*D* 485). The more solitary we become, the more our sympathy "for *all* that is human"—and not merely for what immediately surrounds us—grows (*D* 441). Then our glance becomes colder, and we regard our fellow human beings with a certain detachment, as if "gazing out of the windows of [a] castle" (*D* 471).

It is not only detachment from others that Nietzsche regards as crucial for knowledge but also a certain detachment from oneself as well. He ascribes the genius of Plato, Spinoza, and Goethe, for example, to the fact that, in them, "the spirit seems to be only *loosely attached* to the character and temperament, as a winged being who can easily detach itself from these and then raise itself high above them." In this respect, they differ fundamentally from Schopenhauer, who "could *never get free* of [his] temperament" (*D* 497). The "purifying eye" that Nietzsche ascribes to Plato, Spinoza, and Goethe here has nothing to do with absence of passion; in another aphorism, he praises these very same thinkers, again over and against Schopenhauer, because their thoughts "constitute a passionate history of the soul" (*D* 481). Rather, their purity consists in the detached stance they are capable of taking with respect to their passions and even more specifically in their ability not to get stuck in a single passion. This enables them to experience much and hence to know much.

Nietzsche pushes the idea of detachment farthest—and almost to the point of returning to Schopenhauer's contemplative ideal of "pure, will-less knowing"—in an aphorism called "The Third Eye." Here he suggests that, instead of going to the theater, we should look for tragedy and comedy in the actual world around us. He concedes that "it is not altogether easy . . . to remain a mere spectator in these cases—but learn it! And then, in almost every situation you find hard and painful you will have a little portal to joy and a refuge even when your own passions assail you" (*D* 509). What differentiates Nietzsche's position in this aphorism from Schopenhauer's is that he is not advocating escape from the passions into contemplation as a general principle but only as a temporary measure to avoid being overwhelmed by them. Such prudent management of the passions is necessary if we are going to be able to employ them for the sake of knowledge. We come back to the general point that knowledge does not involve eliminating the affects or passions—that would be to castrate the intellect—but it does require that one be able control the affects or passions so that one can deploy them in a productive way.

Though he rejects Schopenhauer's notion of pure, will-less knowing, Nietzsche clearly defends the life of knowledge, science, and in that sense contemplation in book 5. Contemplation here does not mean passive reception but active, passionate experimentation; nevertheless, it is understood to be different from and superior to the life of action. It is marked by a self-sufficiency that contrasts with the lust for the feeling of power that drives so much of the *vita activa*. (It is noteworthy that the notion of the feeling of power, which looms so large in the first four books of *Daybreak*, is virtually absent in the fifth.)[45] The life of action, on the other hand, involves "flight from oneself," according to Nietzsche, in this instance agreeing with Pascal (*D* 549). It requires the suspension of all doubt and skepticism so that one can come to a decision quickly and not be caught hesitating or vacillating. But knowledge thrives on doubt and skepticism. Nietzsche captures the essential difference between the *vita activa* and the *vita contemplativa* in a brief aphorism: "If you want to act you have to close the door on doubt—said a man of action.—And aren't you afraid of thus being *deceived?*—replied a man of contemplation" (*D* 519).

As he did in *Human, All too Human*, Nietzsche sees the greatest threats to the *vita contemplativa* coming from the need to arrive at a definitive answer or to achieve absolute certainty.[46] In the past, the belief in an immortal soul made this need especially urgent. One's salvation "depended on knowledge acquired during a brief lifetime, men had to *come to a decision* overnight—'knowledge' possessed a frightful importance." Now that belief in an immortal soul has receded, mankind "no longer needs to rush precipitately forward or gulp down ideas only half-tasted." There is now time, plenty of time, "for error, for experimentation, for accepting provisionally." The way stands open for "tasks of a vastness that would to earlier ages have seemed madness and a trifling with Heaven and Hell" (*D* 501). Nor is it only the belief in immortality that has thus hindered the progress of science, according to Nietzsche; human mortality has had a similarly arresting effect. Again, human beings have wanted to encompass the whole of knowledge within a single lifespan. As a result, the "small single questions and experiments were counted contemptible: one wanted the shortest route." The individual thinker wanted to "solve everything at a stroke" and unriddle the secrets of the universe. It is this "tyrannical" impulse that must be resisted by thinkers in the future, over whose doors, therefore, Nietzsche would put the motto "What do I matter!" (*D* 547; see also 270, 494).

Nietzsche's most sustained discussion of the threats to the contemplative life of the thinker and knower comes in an aphorism entitled "The Philosopher and Age." It is one of the longest aphorisms in the whole of *Daybreak*, and it details the various ways in which weariness, not wisdom, informs the judgments of the aged thinker. As in the aphorisms previously considered, it is impatience and anxiety in the face of expiring time that leads the aged philosopher to abandon the path of rigorous thought and seek more immediate and practical satisfactions: "[N]ow, like one who can afford to lose no more time, he reaches for coarser and broader means of satisfaction, that is to say for the satisfactions of active, dominant, violent, conquering natures: from now on he wants to found, not structures of thought, but institutions which will bear his name." No longer capable of enduring the "dreadful isolation in which every spirit lives who flies on out ahead," the aged philosopher becomes an apostle of community and even invents a religion to support such community. Finally, having come to the end of his own thought, he seeks to make himself the end of all thought, the last thinker beyond whom no one in the future may go. At this point, Nietzsche comments, the end is near: "Whenever a great thinker wants to make of himself a binding institution for future mankind, one may be certain that he is past the peak of his powers and is very weary, very close to the setting of his sun" (*D* 542).

In the very last aphorism of the book, "We Aeronauts of the Spirit!," Nietzsche returns to this image of the aged thinker coming to a halt in his quest for knowledge, as a bird comes to a halt in the open sea, finding a mast or bit of rock to perch on: "All our great teachers and predecessors have at last come to a stop and it is not with the noblest or most graceful of gestures that weariness comes to a stop." But this is no reason to infer that humanity can fly no farther. Nietzsche affirms that "*other birds will fly farther*," and buoyed by this faith he wonders whether it is "our fate to be wrecked against infinity? Or, my brothers. Or?—" (*D* 575). In *Ecce Homo*, having characterized *Daybreak* as a "Yes-saying book," he boasts that "it is the only book that closes with an 'Or?'" (*EH* 3.D.1).

This would be the logical place to conclude my analysis of *Daybreak*, but I would like to consider one final aphorism that complicates my interpretation of the theory/practice, contemplation/action relationship in the book and also raises a question about the practical or legislative role of philosophy that will confront us again in *The Gay Science* and increasingly preoccupy Nietzsche in his works thereafter. The aphorism is simply entitled "The Practical," and it argues that it is "we thinkers who first have to determine the *palatableness* of things and, if necessary, decree it. Practical people in the end take it from us, their dependence on us is inconceivably great . . . however much they may love to ignore us impractical people" (*D* 505). The distinction between the contemplative life of the thinker and the more superficial life of the practical man of action is maintained in this aphorism, but the new twist is that the former is seen as ultimately having a more profound practical impact on the world than the latter. Contemplation is the ultimate form of *praxis*, or, as Nietzsche puts it later in *Zarathustra*: "[T]he greatest events . . . are not our loudest but our stillest hours. Not around the inventors of new noise, but around the inventors of new values does the world revolve" (*Z* 2.18).

Between the aphorism on "The Practical" in *Daybreak* and this passage from *Zarathustra* lies, of course, *The Gay Science*. To what extent this work develops the theme of the practical or legislative role of philosophy and intimates the figure of the "superman" or "new philosopher" beyond that of free-spirited knower are questions that must occupy us next.

THREE

The *Gay Science* and the Incorporation of Knowledge

After making the final corrections to the proofs of *Daybreak*, Nietzsche traveled to Switzerland at the end of June 1881. He originally intended to spend the summer in St. Moritz, but he ended up staying in the nearby village of Sils-Maria. It was there, at the beginning of August, that the idea of the eternal recurrence came to him. His notebooks record this momentous discovery of "the eternal return of the same" (*die ewige Wiederkunft des Gleichen*) with the words: "Beginning of August 1881 in Sils-Maria, 6,000 feet above the sea, and much higher above all human things!" (*KSA* 9:11 [141]).[1] On 14 August 1881, he wrote excitedly to his friend and scribe, Köselitz, about his discovery: "On my horizon, thoughts have arisen such as I have never seen before—I will not speak of them, but will keep my unshakable peace. I really shall have to live a few more years! . . . [I am] filled with a glimpse of things which put me in advance of all other men" (*SB* 6:112). One year later, in the penultimate aphorism of the original edition of *The Gay Science*, Nietzsche presented the idea of the eternal recurrence to the public for the first time (*GS* 341).

In the same notebook entry in which he recorded his discovery of the eternal recurrence, Nietzsche introduced another idea that was to play a crucial role in the argument of *The Gay Science*: the idea of "incorporation" (*Einverleibung*). The entry presents an outline of a projected work that culminates in the doctrine of the eternal recurrence. The stages leading up to this doctrine are listed as follows:

The incorporation of fundamental errors.
The incorporation of passions.
The incorporation of knowledge and of renunciatory knowledge. (Passion for knowledge)

The innocent man. The individual as experiment. The alleviation of life [*Er-leichterung des Lebens*], humbling [*Erniedrigung*], weakening [*Abschwächung*]—transition.

The new *heavy weight* [*Schwergewicht*]: *the eternal return of the same*. Infinite importance of our knowing, erring, habits, ways of living for all that is to come. What shall we do with the *rest* of our lives—we who have spent the majority of our lives in the most profound ignorance? We shall *teach the doctrine*—it is the most powerful means of *incorporating* it into ourselves. Our kind of blessedness, as teachers of the greatest doctrine. (*KSA* 9:11 [141])

The word "incorporation" can mean quite literally to take into the body, ingestion, digestion. Here it refers to the process by which something becomes useful or serviceable for life and ultimately contributes to the preservation or enhancement of life. As we shall see, it is the issue of the "incorporation of knowledge" mentioned in the third item that is at the heart of the argument of *The Gay Science*. Hitherto humanity has incorporated only its errors. The question now is "how far *knowledge* and *truth* can be **incorporated**" (*KSA* 9:11 [141]). In one of the most important aphorisms of *The Gay Science*, Nietzsche will repeat this question, calling it "the ultimate question about the conditions of life" (*GS* 110; see also 11).[2]

One of the most intriguing features of the notebook entry from August 1881 is the distinction it draws between the third and fourth stages of incorporation. The third stage is identified with the "passion for knowledge." This, of course, was one of the key notions that Nietzsche introduced in *Daybreak*. What, we want to know, is added to it in the transition to the fourth stage of the "innocent man," the "individual as experiment," and "the alleviation of life"?[3] Nietzsche actually provides an explanation of this fourth stage in the rest of the note. Referring to it under the rubric of the "philosophy of indifference [*Gleichgültigkeit*],"[4] he claims that this stage is marked by a detached attitude that looks on the errors that have exerted such a powerful influence on human beings in the past as a "game," something to be "aesthetically enjoyed"; "we adopt a child's attitude towards what used to constitute the *seriousness of existence*." The emphasis here on indifference, playfulness, and aesthetic detachment contrasts with the "renunciatory" character of knowledge that Nietzsche associates with the third stage of incorporation. It also contrasts with the self-sacrificing and even tragic character attributed to the passion for knowledge in *Daybreak* (*D* 45, 429). Is this the "gay" (*fröhliche*) element that distinguishes the free spirit's quest for knowledge in *The Gay Science*?

Nietzsche goes on to explain that the fourth stage is also characterized by a much greater appreciation of the role of error in life and especially in the life of the knower. The highly suggestive passage must be quoted at length:

> The seriousness of our striving, though, is to understand everything as becoming, to deny ourselves as individuals, to look into the world through as *many* eyes as possible, to *live in* drives and activities so as to create eyes for ourselves, *temporarily* abandoning ourselves to life **so as** to rest our eye on it temporarily afterwards: to *maintain* the drives as the foundation of all knowing, but to know at what point they become the enemies of knowing: in sum to *wait and see* how far knowledge and truth can be *incorporated*—and to what extent a transformation of man occurs when he finally lives only *to know*.—This is the consequence of the passion for knowledge: there is *no way of ensuring its existence* except by preserving as well the sources and powers of knowledge, the errors and passions; from the *conflict* between them it draws its sustaining strength. (*KSA* 9:9 [141])

Among the many noteworthy aspects of this passage is the unmistakable anticipation of Nietzsche's later doctrine of perspectivism, which holds that increasing our knowledge involves allowing "*more* affects" to speak about a thing and using "*more* eyes, different eyes" to observe it (*GM* 3.12; see also *D* 432).

I will have occasion to return to this passage—and, indeed, several other notes from this remarkable 1881 notebook—in the course of my analysis of *The Gay Science*. Before getting to that analysis, however, it is important to understand something of the genesis of this book, which Nietzsche continued to work on during the months following his vision of the eternal recurrence in Sils-Maria. Interestingly, up until the end of January 1882, he conceived of the book as a "continuation of *Daybreak* (books 6–10)" (*SB* 6:150; also 156, 163). On 25 January 1882, for example, he wrote to Köselitz that he had

> finished a couple of days ago Books VI, VII, and VIII of *Daybreak*, and with that my work for this time is done. Books 9 and 10 I will reserve for next winter—I am not ripe enough for the fundamental thoughts that I want to depict in these concluding books. Among those thoughts is one that in fact needs a "thousand years" in order to become something. Where do I get the courage to express it! (*SB* 6:159)

The fundamental thought requiring "a thousand years" to develop is obviously the thought of the eternal recurrence.

In the event, Nietzsche did not have to wait until the following winter to finish his book. In a letter to Köselitz written less than two weeks after the one above, he refers his friend to "the 9th book of *Daybreak*" to correct a misimpression the latter had gotten from reading one of the earlier aphorisms (*SB* 6:167). After this letter of 5 February, it is a little unclear what gets written over the next couple of months. During this time, Rée visited Nietzsche in Genoa, the two of them traveled to Monte Carlo together, Nietzsche then traveled alone to Messina, where he wrote his *Idylls*, and finally, at the end of April, he arrived in Rome for his momentous first meeting with Lou Salomé. By the beginning of May, however, he is writing to his publisher, Schmeitzner, that he will have a new manuscript for him by the fall, the title of which is "*Die fröhliche Wissenschaft*" (*SB* 6:191). This letter suggests that two important changes have occurred in Nietzsche's conception of his book since late January: first, he no longer envisages a fifth book for his "continuation" of *Daybreak*; and second, he no longer conceives of the book as a whole as a mere "continuation" of *Daybreak*.

These changes are clearly bound up with the section of the book Nietzsche was working on between February and April 1882, the one originally conceived of as the ninth book of *Daybreak* but which ultimately became the fourth book of *The Gay Science*. Nietzsche gave this book the title "Sanctus Januarius" in honor of the martyred saint whose congealed blood, preserved in a church in Naples, periodically becomes liquefied. The title also celebrates the mild and cloudless January—"the most beautiful of my life" (*SB* 6:161)—that Nietzsche had spent in Genoa writing *The Gay Science*. In letters to friends such as Burckhardt, Köselitz, Rée, and Gersdorff, Nietzsche repeatedly highlights the importance and deeply personal nature of book 4 of *The Gay Science* (*SB* 6:235, 238, 247, and 248). To Rée, for example, he writes that *The Gay Science* is "the most personal of all my books" and instructs him to "read Sanctus Januarius once through in this connection. There is gathered my private morality, as the sum of my conditions for existence" (*SB* 6:247). The most revealing comment about book 4 appears in a letter to Overbeck: "If you have read the 'Sanctus Januarius' you will have remarked that I have crossed a tropic. Everything that lies before me is new, and it will not be long before I catch sight also of the *terrifying* face of my more distant life task" (*SB* 6:255).

What tropic had Nietzsche crossed? Only a complete analysis of book 4 and, indeed, of the whole of *The Gay Science*, will give us a definitive answer to this question, but provisionally we may state that Nietzsche had arrived at the limits of the free-spirit ideal and begun to glimpse another, higher ideal on the horizon. This is strongly suggested in some of the letters he wrote while making the final corrections to the manuscript of *The Gay Science* over the summer of 1882. In many of these letters, he conveys an acute sense that an important chapter in his philosophical career is coming to an end. On 27 and 28 June, for example, he writes to Lou Salomé: "With [*The Gay Science*] that series of writings that began with *Human, All too Human* comes to a conclusion: in all of them taken together, 'a new image and ideal of the free spirit' has been erected. That this is not the 'free man in fact' you will have long guessed" (*SB* 6:213). Apart from the final sentence, this is virtually the same statement Nietzsche put on the back of the original edition of *The Gay Science*. Similar attempts to "place" his free-spirit writings appear in other letters as well. Again writing to Lou, Nietzsche reports that he has "just finished the very last part of the manuscript [of *The Gay Science*] and therewith the work of six years (1876–82), my entire *Freigeisterei*. O what years! What tortures of every kind, what solitudes and weariness with life" (*SB* 6:217). And to Malwida von Meysenbug he writes that *The Gay Science* "forms the conclusion of that chain of thoughts [*Gedanken-Kette*] that I began to put together in Sorrento. . . . My life now belongs to a higher goal and I do nothing that is not of benefit to it" (*SB* 6:223).

Perhaps the most intriguing remark in these letters from the summer of 1882 is the one where Nietzsche suggests that Lou will have long guessed that the free spirit is not the "free man in fact." Wherein does the lack of freedom of the free spirit consist? In a note written in the winter of 1882–83, Nietzsche already intimates the answer to this question, an answer that he will amplify in his later writings, most notably in the famous aphorism entitled "How We, Too, Are Still Pious" from the fifth book of *The Gay Science*: the free spirit is still in the grips of morality or the ascetic ideal; "The *Freigeisterei* itself was moral activity: 1) as honesty; 2) as bravery; 3) as justice; 4) as love" (*KSA* 10:6 [1]). In a series of notes written shortly after finishing the final revisions to *The Gay Science*, he also indicates that it is precisely this moral activity of the free spirit that ultimately leads to the overcoming of morality. "Why do I love the *Freigeisterei*?" he asks in one of these notes. "As the last consequence of morality. To be just toward everything" leads morality to the insight that "enables it to preserve its opposite" (*KSA* 10:1 [42]). The unconditional honesty and justice of the free spirit "arrives at the insight that life is essentially unjust" (*KSA* 10:1 [28]). "Morality dies at the hands of morality" (*KSA* 10 1 [76]).[5]

All of this underlines the point that, shortly after writing *The Gay Science*, and even while making the final corrections to the book, Nietzsche no longer regarded the free spirit as his highest ideal or the quest for knowledge as his ultimate goal. He makes this point very strongly—perhaps too strongly—in a letter to Lou Salomé from November 1882: "Spirit [*Geist*]? What is spirit to me? What is knowledge to me? I value nothing but impulses . . . Look through this phase in which I have lived for several years—look beyond it! Do not deceive yourself about me—surely you do not think that the 'free spirit' is my ideal! I am . . ." (*SB* 6:282).

A tropic had indeed been crossed, and the fourth book of *The Gay Science*, which begins with the resolution to *amor fati* and concludes with the announcement of the eternal recurrence and the introduction of *Zarathustra*, marks the critical moment of this crossing. But the fourth book cannot simply be detached from the three preceding ones. The discussion of the death of God in book 3, for example, is clearly relevant to the teaching of book 4, and books 1 and 2 were written after Nietzsche had his vision of the eternal recurrence in August 1881. Also, Nietzsche made revisions to the first three books after he had finished the fourth in order to bring them into conformity with the latter.[6] So it is not merely book 4 that forms the shadow-line between Nietzsche's free-spirit writings and his later philosophy but *The Gay Science* as a whole. This is what makes the book so interesting and important. As Jorg Salaquarda has put it: "*The Gay Science* was for Nietzsche the conclusion of the preceding project of the 'Freigeisterei' and the prelude to the new project [of *Zarathustra*]. . . . From this in-between position results the uniqueness and significance of the writing."[7] By studying *The Gay Science*, we may hope to deepen our understanding not only of the break that occurs between these two phases of Nietzsche's philosophical development but also of the considerations that led him from one phase to the other and thereby of the profound continuities between them.

As in previous chapters, I organize my analysis here in accordance with Nietzsche's division of the original edition of *The Gay Science* into four books—I will postpone my analysis of the fifth book, added in 1887, until the next chapter—taking up a different book in each of the sections that follow. The rationale for this procedure is even greater with respect to *The Gay Science* than it was for *Daybreak* because *The Gay Science* has a more coherent organization both within each of its constituent books and across them than does *Daybreak*.[8] Nietzsche indicates his aspiration to greater artistic and philosophical unity in *The Gay Science* in a letter to Rée from August 1881. He tells his friend that he hopes in his new work to place his "poor piecemeal philosophy" in a larger context that reveals the "golden chain" that binds it together (*SB* 6:124). His hopes were certainly fulfilled, for *The Gay Science* represents not only a crucial bridge in Nietzsche's philosophical development but a profoundly imagined artistic and philosophical whole.

The Most Amazing Economy

As in *Daybreak*, the individual chapters or books that comprise the original edition of *The Gay Science* (with the exception of book 4, "Sanctus Januarius") are not titled. This, of course, increases the difficulty of knowing what Nietzsche thought the unifying theme of each book to be. Fortunately, in a note from the spring of 1882, he gives a chapter outline of *The Gay Science* that corresponds fairly closely to the contents of the final, published version. In addition to "Sanctus Januarius," the outline includes a chapter "On Artists and Women" (corresponding to book 2), a chapter containing "Thoughts of a Godless Man" (corresponding to book 3), and a collection of epigrams entitled "Joke, Cunning, and Revenge" (corresponding to the Prelude in German Rhymes). By process of elimination, the chapter listed in the note as "From the 'Moral Diary'" would seem to be Nietzsche's descriptor for book 1 of *The Gay Science* (*KSA* 9:19 [12]). As one casts a glance over the aphorisms contained in book 1, it does indeed seem that most of them are concerned with morality in one way or another, especially in relation to the question of what preserves and advances the species.

This is certainly the case in the magnificent opening aphorism entitled "The Teachers of the Purpose of Existence." In this aphorism, Nietzsche returns to his long-running dispute with Darwinian thinkers like Rée and especially Spencer, who hold that our "judgments of 'good' and 'evil' sum up experiences of 'expedient' and 'inexpedient.'" According to these thinkers, what is called good supposedly preserves the species, while what is called bad supposedly harms it. Nietzsche regards this Darwinian-utilitarian view, however, as utterly myopic; it fails to grasp that "in any large-scale accounting" what is called evil has played an absolutely crucial role in the preservation of the species: "Hatred, the mischievous delight in the misfortunes of others, the lust to rob and dominate, and whatever else is called evil belongs to the most amazing economy of the preservation of the species" (*GS* 1, 4).[9] In his notebooks, he criticizes Spencer specifically for failing to appreciate the important role of the evil instincts in the grand economy of the preservation of the species: "These glorifiers of selection on the basis of expediency (like Spencer) believe that they know what the most favorable conditions for development are! and do not count evil among them!" (*KSA* 9:11 [43]; see also 11[73]).

Here, for the first time in his middle works, Nietzsche explicitly affirms the value of instincts and actions that have hitherto been considered evil, and in doing so he enunciates the immoralism that will characterize his moral outlook for the rest of his philosophical career. Hints of this immoralism were certainly present in *Daybreak*, especially in Nietzsche's critical remarks about the "cult of philanthropy," Spencerian adaptation and altruism, and the moral objective of removing all the dangers from life (see *D* 132, 174). But nowhere in that work did he actually come out and praise evil. Indeed, he even insisted that, in criticizing morality, he did not mean to deny that "many actions called immoral ought to be avoided and resisted, or that many called moral ought to be done and encouraged"; he merely wanted to show that the former ought to be avoided and the latter encouraged "*for other reasons than hitherto*" (*D* 103). The critique of morality in *The Gay Science* goes considerably beyond this reinterpretive task.

Let us return to the first aphorism. After pointing out the crucial role of evil in the grand economy of the preservation of the species, Nietzsche quickly discloses the dwarfing effect such a large-scale perspective has on our conceptions of individual worth, meaning, and purpose. Not only are we incapable as individuals of completely grasping what, in the grand scheme of things, actually preserves or harms the species; we may not even be able any longer to do anything that harms the species or fails to preserve it: "Pursue your best or your worst desires, and above all perish! In both cases you are probably still in some way a promoter or benefactor of humanity and entitled to your eulogists" (*GS* 1). It becomes a little clearer why, in the note from August 1881 quoted above, Nietzsche associates this stage of knowledge with "humbling" (*KSA* 9:11 [141]). From the cosmic perspective of the grand economy of the preservation of the species, the individual looks very small indeed; and everything that the individual has hitherto taken seriously appears comical.[10] The only conceivable response to this grim insight into our situation is laughter—and a rather inhuman laughter at that. It is here that Nietzsche provides the first important gloss on his notion of "gay science":

> To laugh at oneself as one would have to laugh in order to laugh *out of the whole truth*—to do that even the best so far lacked sufficient sense for truth, and the most gifted had too little genius for that. Even laughter may yet have a future. I mean, when the proposition "the species is everything, one is always none" has become part of humanity, and this ultimate liberation and irresponsibility has become accessible to all at all times. Perhaps laughter will then have formed an alliance with wisdom, perhaps only "gay science" will then be left. (*GS* 1)

But Nietzsche adds a dialectical twist to this most dialectical of aphorisms. He indicates that humanity has not yet achieved the "gay" perspective just described. The "comedy of existence has not yet 'become conscious' of it-self . . . we still live in the age of tragedy, the age of moralities and religions," which is also the age of "heroes." The dialectical point is that these "tra-gedians," these "teachers of the purpose of existence," also "promote the interests of the species" in their own way by *"promoting the faith in life."* No matter how false and antinatural these ethical teachings are, they still make life more *interesting* and heroic for human beings. They have also created in human beings "the need for the ever new appearance of such teachers and teachings of a 'purpose.' Gradually, man has become a fantastic animal that has to fulfill one more condition of existence than any other animal: man *has to* believe, to know, from time to time *why* he exists" (*GS* 1).

What follows practically from this dialectic of comedy and tragedy, gay science and morality, that Nietzsche has laid out in this aphorism? Clearly, we cannot do without either side of the dialectical opposition. On the one hand, laughter is necessary to correct for the antinaturalness of ethical sys-tems; on the other, human beings need teachings of ethical purpose to give their lives meaning and gravity. Thus, the "most cautious friend of man" will remind the skeptical free spirit that "'not only laughter and gay wis-dom but the tragic, too, with all its sublime unreason, belongs among the means and necessities of the preservation of the species.' Consequently—." It is with the sentences following this "consequently" that Nietzsche raises the dialectical irony of the aphorism to its highest pitch: "Consequently. Consequently. O, do you understand me my brothers? Do you understand this new law of ebb and flood? There is a time for us, too!" (*GS* 1). But who is Nietzsche identifying himself with here, the free-spirited gay scientists or the tragedians? Certainly the former; but given that the final aphorism of *The Gay Science* is entitled "*Incipit Trageodia*" and that the penultimate apho-rism announces the idea of the eternal recurrence, which is designed to give human existence a new, albeit very different, gravity, it would seem that he also identifies with the latter as well.

The dialectical ebb and flood described in the first aphorism is a defining feature of book 1 as a whole. In the second aphorism, for example, which contains Nietzsche's beautiful and oft-cited celebration of the "intellectual conscience," it is his inability to believe that the great majority of people lack this quality that is the subject of the reflection. Nietzsche finds it in-comprehensible—and contemptible—that some people can "stand in the midst of this *rerum concordia discors* and of this whole marvelous uncertainty and rich ambiguity of existence *without questioning*, without trembling with the craving and rapture of such questioning." But he also recognizes that to expect everyone to share in this passion for knowledge and "desire for certainty" is unjust. It is, he says, "my type of injustice," and in saying so acknowledges a higher dialectical justice (*GS* 2).

Nietzsche continues this reflection on the relationship between the exception and the majority in the next aphorism, entitled "Noble and Common." The common person is defined by a heightened sense of self-interest and expediency: "What distinguishes the common type is that it never loses a sense of its advantage, and that this thought of purpose and advantage is even stronger than the strongest instincts." It is precisely this utilitarian sense of expediency that makes the common type suspicious and ultimately scornful of all noble, magnanimous feelings. The noble individual, by contrast, does not act according to utilitarian calculation, he succumbs to his instincts, and in this regard he is "more *unreasonable*" than the common person. Such unreason is the essence of passion for Nietzsche, including the "passion for knowledge." Again, though, he draws attention to the fact that noble or exceptional human beings often fail to appreciate that their passion is singular, idiosyncratic, and not shared by the masses. Because "such exceptional people do not see themselves as the exception," they are unable to "understand the common type and arrive at a fair evaluation of the rule. . . . This is the eternal injustice of those who are noble" (*GS* 3).

The contrast (and eternal misunderstanding) between noble and common, exception and rule, individual and herd runs throughout book 1 of *The Gay Science*. This contrast is paralleled by others, including passion versus utility or expediency, change versus order or stability, new versus old, and evil versus good. The former member of each of these antitheses has played a vital role in preserving and especially advancing the species, according to Nietzsche. Once again, he flashes his newfound immoralism: "The strongest and most evil spirits have so far done the most to advance humanity: again and again they relumed the passions that were going to sleep . . . and they reawakened again and again the sense of comparison, of contradiction, of the pleasure in what is new, daring, untried" (*GS* 4). The "evil" inclinations that lead exceptional human beings to contradict prevailing opinion, mistrust accepted beliefs, and think in uncustomary ways have been especially important for the advance of knowledge and science (see *GS* 25, 33, 35).

All of this, of course, is at odds with stable, ordered society. Nietzsche claims that "all ordered society puts the passions to sleep" (*GS* 4). Therefore, it is necessary that societies from time to time undergo "corruption." With corruption comes the luxuriant growth of superstition, which Nietzsche regards as much more conducive to experiment and knowledge than orthodox religion. He calls superstition "second order free spirit" and argues that, with its "delight in individuality," it is "actually a symptom of *enlightenment*." In a corrupt society, the passions that were formerly spent in war now find subtler and more multifarious expression in private life, and as a result "the flame of knowledge flares up into the sky." Furthermore, the decay of morals in a corrupt society leads to the emergence of tyrants, "the precocious harbingers of *individuality*," under whose protection the individual ripens and culture attains "its highest and most fruitful stage" (GS 23).

Nietzsche provides a variation on this argument in the aphorism immediately following the one on corruption. Here he contrasts what he calls the "weak and quasi-feminine type of the dissatisfied," who "has a sensitivity for making life more beautiful and profound," with the "strong or masculine type," who "has a sensitivity for making life better and safer." It is the former, feminine, dissatisfied type that has been most responsible for the "celebrated European capacity for change" which has made its culture so dynamic. Nietzsche worries, however, that the "socialists and state idolaters" of his day may end up bringing about Chinese stagnation in Europe "with their measures for making life better and safer." Therefore, he expresses gratitude for the "sicklier, tenderer, more feminine dissatisfaction and romanticism" of European culture insofar as it will serve as a bulwark against this spiritless fate (GS 24; cf. HH 224).

But Nietzsche does not forget the other side of the dialectical opposition that frames the argument of book 1. In yet another aphorism on the noble versus the common human being, he highlights once again the injustice of the former's judgments concerning the latter. The "passion that attacks those who are noble is peculiar, and they fail to realize this. It involves the use of a rare and singular standard and almost a madness." This standard has been crucial for all higher aspiration in human history, but it has also "involved an unfair judgment concerning everything usual, near, and indispensable—in short, that which most preserves the species and was the *rule* among men hitherto." Therefore, Nietzsche suggests that, instead of slandering the rule in favor of the exceptions, the "ultimate noblemindedness" might consist in becoming "the advocate of the rule" (GS 55).

He elaborates on this argument in an aphorism in book 2 entitled "The Greatest Danger." Discipline of mind and uniformity of thinking among the majority of human beings has been absolutely crucial to the preservation of humanity; and "the eruption of madness—which means the eruption of arbitrariness in feeling, seeing, and hearing, the enjoyment of the mind's lack of discipline, the joy in human unreason"—has posed the greatest danger. Society requires agreement about many things in order to survive; it requires "the universal binding force of a faith." But it is precisely this faith

that "the most select spirits bristle at . . . the explorers of *truth* above all."
This is merely to repeat what Nietzsche has already said about the role of
"evil" spirits in breaking down the boundaries of conventional society and
the constraints of customary opinion. But instead of emphasizing how this
destructive activity advances the species, here he warns about its disruptive
effects on the bonds that hold society together:

> Thus virtuous intellects are needed—oh, let me use the most unambiguous
> word—what is needed is *virtuous stupidity*, solid metronomes for the slow
> spirit, to make sure that the faithful of the great shared faith stay together
> and continue their dance. It is a first-rate need that commands and demands
> this. *We others are the exception and the danger*—and we need eternally to be
> defended.—Well, there actually are things to be said in favor of the exception,
> *provided that it never wants to become the rule.* (GS 76)

Nietzsche's contention that the exception or free spirit should never
want to become the rule is nothing new in his writings from the middle
period. As far back as *Human, All too Human* and its sequels, he insisted that
freedom of spirit—that is, freedom from the errors of religion, morality, and
metaphysics—is only for the very few (WS 350). Such freedom can have a
beneficial effect only if it rests on the secure and durable foundation made
up of the rule (HH 224; WS 275). In *The Gay Science,* this issue of how the
free-spirited quest for knowledge can be reconciled with ordered society is
connected to the larger issue of how knowledge can lose its corrosiveness
and ultimately become a condition of life. This is the issue of "incorporation" to which I alluded at the beginning of the chapter. It is an issue that
pops up in many of the notes from the period leading up to *The Gay Science,* including the important note from August 1881 (KSA 9:11 [141, 162,
164]), and it occupies a central place in the book itself.

Nietzsche introduces the notion of the incorporation of knowledge in
an aphorism devoted to the subject of consciousness. "Consciousness," he
writes, "is the last and latest development of the organic and hence also
what is most unfinished and unstrong." For the most part, it has laid hold of
only what is most superficial—a point Nietzsche illustrates in the aphorisms
leading up to this one by disclosing how much of our interior selves we remain unconscious of (GS 8–10)—and as result, it has given rise to "countless errors," "misjudgments," and "fantasies." Indeed, humanity would long
ago have perished of these errors of consciousness, if it had not been for the
conserving role of the instincts. Fortunately, the belief that consciousness
constitutes the essence of human beings, something that they possess as

an original birthright, has prevented them from exerting themselves to acquire it. But now, it appears, consciousness is finally beginning to be something other than error; it has begun to lay hold of genuine knowledge, and this suggests a new task to Nietzsche: "To this day the task of *incorporating* knowledge and making it instinctive is only beginning to dawn on the human eye and is not yet clearly discernible; it is a task that is seen only by those who have comprehended that so far we have incorporated our errors and that all our consciousness relates to errors" (GS 11).

This passage does not go very far in explaining what exactly Nietzsche means by the "incorporation of knowledge" or "making it instinctive." In order to gain greater clarity, we need to jump momentarily to book 3 and the important aphorism on the "Origin of Knowledge." As he did in the aphorism on consciousness, Nietzsche here argues that "over immense periods of time the intellect produced nothing but errors." Some of these errors—for example, that there are enduring things, equal things, substances, that the will is free, and so forth—proved to be useful and were thereby "incorporated." It was only very late, Nietzsche tells us, that these errors were "denied and doubted" and that "truth emerged—as the weakest form of knowledge." He helpfully explains that "the *strength* of knowledge does not depend on its degree of truth but on its age, on the degree to which it has been incorporated, on its character as a condition of life. Where life and knowledge seemed at odds there was never any real fight, but denial and doubt were simply considered madness" (GS 110).

So how did true knowledge eventually acquire strength and become incorporated? Nietzsche provides two scenarios: first, where two contradictory sentences were compatible with the life-preserving errors, it was possible to debate about their relative utility for life; and second, where propositions were neither useful nor harmful to life, it was possible to consider them in an intellectually playful fashion. The crucial step in the process of incorporation came, however, when the affects and drives, especially the "lust for power" (*Machtgelüst*), got involved in the debate over these propositions: "Not only utility and delight but every kind of impulse took sides in this fight about 'truths.' The intellectual fight became an occupation, an attraction, a profession, a duty, something dignified—and eventually knowledge and the striving for the true found their place as a need among other needs." Having become a piece of life and been incorporated to a certain degree, true knowledge is now able to come into conflict with the "basic primeval errors" that have hitherto supported life in a way that it never could before. Nietzsche describes this fundamental conflict as it takes place in the person of the thinker in the following way:

A thinker is now that being in whom the impulse for truth and those life-preserving errors clash for their first fight, after the impulse for truth has proved to be also a life-preserving power. Compared to the significance of this fight, everything else is a matter of indifference: the ultimate question about the conditions of life has been posed here, and we confront the first attempt to answer this question by experiment. To what extent can truth endure incorporation? That is the question; that is the experiment. (GS 110)

I will come back to this question of the degree to which truth can endure incorporation in a moment. First, though, let us consolidate what we have learned about the notion of the incorporation of knowledge from the aphorisms just discussed. The key to this notion seems to be cathexis, the harnessing of knowledge to the affects, drives, and impulses of human beings.[11] This is what Nietzsche means when he identifies the task of incorporating knowledge with "making it instinctive." It is also what lies behind his repeated characterization of knowledge, beginning with *Daybreak*, as a passion. In the note from August 1881 in which he first introduced the idea of the incorporation of knowledge, Nietzsche explicitly linked it with the passion for knowledge (*KSA* 9:11 [141]). Not coincidentally, in the aphorism "On the Aim of Science" that immediately follows the one in which we first encounter the idea of the incorporation of knowledge in *The Gay Science*, Nietzsche emphasizes the relationship between science and pleasure (and displeasure). Up till now, science has mainly been "known for its power of depriving man of his joys and making him colder, more like a statue, more stoic. But it might yet be found to be the *great dispenser of pain*" and, at the same time, to possess "the immense capacity for making new galaxies of joy flare up" (GS 12).

We may now return to the "ultimate question" as to the degree to which truth can endure incorporation. Nietzsche addresses this question in a number of notes from the late summer and fall of 1881, and he consistently points out that there are limits to the amount of truth that can be incorporated; some degree of error is unavoidable and ineradicable in all knowing. "In order for there to be some degree of consciousness in the world," he writes in one note, "an unreal world of errors must arise" in opposition to the world of "absolute flux." The "ultimate truth of the flux of things cannot withstand incorporation, our organs (for life) are arranged for error." Thus arises in the thinker the struggle alluded to above between his drive for knowledge and the life-preserving errors upon which his activity rests: "Life is the condition of knowing. Error is the condition of life. . . . We must love and cultivate error as the womb of knowing." In this note,

Nietzsche invokes the dialectical ebb and flood that frames the entire argument of book 1 of *The Gay Science*: "So we discover here a night and day as living-conditions for us. Wanting-knowledge and wanting-error are the ebb and flood. If one rules absolutely, man perishes" (*KSA* 9:11 [162]; see also 11 [141, 156, 325]).

This note anticipates the point Nietzsche later makes in the opening aphorism of the section on the free spirit in *Beyond Good and Evil* about knowledge resting on the "solid, granite foundation of ignorance" (*BGE* 24).[12] Interestingly, an early draft of this aphorism appears in the notes from the fall of 1881. Nietzsche writes there: "In what strange simplification of things and men do we live! How we have made everything easy and convenient and given our senses a passport for superficial observation, our thinking for the maddest, most courageous leaps and mistaken conclusions!" (*KSA* 9:15 [1]). As he later does in the aphorism from *Beyond Good and Evil*, Nietzsche here insists that scientific knowledge is not the opposite of error but its refinement: man "gives birth to an abundance of errors and limited views" and "science only leads this monstrous process further" (*KSA* 9:15 [7]). Already Nietzsche's perspectival conception of knowledge is on the horizon: "Our knowledge is no knowledge in itself . . . it is the magnificent result, developing over thousands of years, of necessary optical error—necessary because we generally want to live—errors because all laws must be perspectives, errors in themselves" (*KSA* 9:11 [9]). And as I observed earlier, from this perspectival conception of knowledge Nietzsche draws the same inference about the task of science that he will later draw in *The Genealogy of Morals* (*GM* 3.12): our task is "to look into the world through as *many* eyes as possible, to *live* in drives and activities so as to create eyes for ourselves, *temporarily* abandoning ourselves to life so as to rest our eye on it temporarily afterwards" (*KSA* 9:11 [141]; see also 11 [65]).

These notes from the late summer and fall of 1881 about the limits of our ability to incorporate truth and about the unavoidability of error and perspective are extremely helpful as we approach one of the most important aphorisms of book 1 of *The Gay Science*, "The Consciousness of Appearance." Nietzsche comments that he finds his position with respect to existence wonderful, gruesome, and ironic in the light of his insight that "the human and animal past, indeed the whole primal age and past of all sentient being continues in me to invent, to love, to hate, and to infer."[13] But the persistence of the basic primeval errors in our thinking and knowing does not invalidate that thinking or knowing or relegate it to the realm of "appearance" in contradistinction to an error- or perspective-free "essence." As he did in *Human, All too Human*, Nietzsche here denies that this distinction between appearance and essence or thing in itself is meaningful; there is no point in trying to think of what the world would look like once one's head has been cut off (see *HH* 9, 16). "What is appearance for me now?" he asks. "Certainly not the opposite of some essence: what could I say about any essence except to name the attributes of its appearance! Certainly not a dead mask that one could place on an unknown *x* or remove from it! Appearance is for me that which lives and is effective." Once again, scientific knowledge is not the opposite of life-preserving error but, rather, builds upon it, extends it, refines it. Nor does scientific knowledge seek to wake us permanently from the dream that began with the childhood of the race (or, even earlier, with the first stirrings of organic life). Nietzsche concludes, beautifully, that knowledge is not opposed to life:

> that among all these dreamers, I, too, who "know," am dancing my dance; that the knower is a means for prolonging the earthly dance and thus belongs to the masters of the ceremony of existence; and that the sublime consistency and interrelatedness of all knowledge perhaps is and will be the highest means to *preserve* the universality of dreaming and the mutual comprehension of all dreamers and thus also *the continuation of the dream*. (*GS* 54)

How exactly can science contribute to the prolongation of the "earthly dance" and the "continuation of the dream" referred to in this passage? As he did in *Human, All too Human*, Nietzsche argues that once the path leading from the apparent world back to some metaphysical "true" world has been blocked off, a door opens up to unprecedented empirical research of the "marvelously variegated world" of which we have been the colorists (see *HH* 16, 23). "So far," he writes, "all that has given color to existence still lacks a history." Therefore, anyone who is interested in making a study of moral matters must engage in a comprehensive historical investigation of the various passions, evaluations, and perspectives that have animated individuals and peoples in the past. Nietzsche lays out an impressive array of topics for such investigation: the history of love, avarice, envy, conscience, pious respect for tradition, and cruelty; the comparative history of law, punishments, ways of dividing up the day, and diet; the study of the manners of scholars, businessmen, and artists; and so forth (*GS* 7).

Nor is it only historical study that is required for this immense empirical project; we also need to engage in active experimentation. This represents a departure from the more contemplative ideal of *Human, All too Human*, in which Nietzsche claims that the labors of science will culminate in a complete "history of the genesis of thought" (*HH* 16). Here he argues that, after science has completed its historical investigations, the "most insidious question of all" emerges as to whether it "can furnish goals of action after it has proved that it can take such goals away and annihilate them." In order to answer this question, "experimentation [*Experimentiren*] would be in order that would allow every kind of heroism to find satisfaction—centuries of experimentation that might eclipse all the great projects and sacrifices of history to date" (*GS* 7; see also 51). Nietzsche mentions the need for experimentation at several points in his notebooks, and interestingly he invokes the authority of Darwin. Darwin can be used not only to justify the status quo, as in Rée and Spencer, but also to justify the use of experiments to determine what conditions actually do promote the enhancement of the species: "The age of experiments [*Experimente*]! The assertions of Darwin need to be proved—through experiments [*Versuche*]. Likewise the origin of the highest and lowest organisms. Experiments [*Versuche*] for thousands of years must be conducted. To educate the ape to man!" (*KSA* 9:11 [177]; see also 10[42]).[14]

In connection with his empirical or scientific approach to morality, Nietzsche devotes a number of aphorisms in book 1 to breaking down the false opposition between good and evil, egoistic and nonegoistic action, that has dominated moral thinking up till now. This is familiar territory in the middle works, and Nietzsche's treatment of it here does not differ substantially from his discussions in *Human, All too Human* and *Daybreak*. Using a variety of examples, he shows that actions that are categorized as good or evil actually spring from a common source, namely, the egoistic desire for power. Benefiting and hurting others, for example, are simply different "ways of exercising one's power upon others." Benefiting others is generally more pleasant than hurting them because the latter is often "a sign that we are still lacking power." But *whom* one benefits varies depending on whether one is strong or weak. The strong disdain easy prey and therefore confer benefits only on equals, while the weak seek out the poor and the suffering and achieve a feeling of power through pity (*GS* 13). It is worth noting that, though the aphorism in which these observations appear is entitled "On the Doctrine of the Feeling of Power," there are far fewer references to the "feeling of power" in *The Gay Science* than we found in *Daybreak*.

Nietzsche makes a similar argument about the egoistic basis of putatively nonegoistic feelings in an aphorism entitled "The Things People Call Love." Avarice and love are merely two different names for the same desire to possess. The former is used by those who already possess something and fear to lose it, the latter by those who feel a lack and "lust for new possessions." Though we tend to idealize love, Nietzsche insists that it is nothing more than the lust for possession. This is especially true of sexual love, which seeks "unconditional and sole possession" of the beloved. He finds it ironic that the "wild avarice and injustice of sexual love has been glorified and deified so much in all ages—indeed, that this love has furnished the concept of love as the opposite of egoism while it actually may be the most ingenuous expression of egoism" (GS 14).

In yet another aphorism, Nietzsche unmasks the selfishness that lies behind society's praise of selflessness. By praising virtues such as industriousness or obedience, society has its own advantage in mind, not that of the individual. While these virtues may benefit society, they harm the individual by transforming him into a "mere function of the whole" and depriving him of "his noblest selfishness and the strength for the highest care of the self." Of no virtue is this more true than industriousness, the most exalted virtue in this "most industrious of all ages." Nietzsche sounds an almost Marxian note when he argues that, while "blindly raging industriousness" certainly creates wealth and honors for the individual, it also deprives his "organs of their subtlety, which alone would make possible the enjoyment of wealth and honors." Society's praise of such a virtue is "far from selfless" insofar as it involves the stunting and mutilation of the individual for society's benefit (GS 21).

As in his previous writings from the middle period, Nietzsche denies that there is any such thing as a selfless or nonegoistic action. Even the so-called man of renunciation makes sacrifices only because "he strives for a higher world, he wants to fly further and higher than all men of affirmation." In this respect, he is no less a "man of affirmation" than anyone else is (GS 27). Magnanimity, too, is not at all selfless. When the magnanimous man forgoes revenge and forgives his enemy, it is not out of some sort of nonegoistic motive. Rather, Nietzsche imagines the magnanimous man as a particularly vengeful person who merely drains the cup of his revenge so quickly in his imagination that the resulting satiety produces the opposite feeling in him: "Magnanimity contains the same degree of egoism as does revenge, but egoism of a different sort" (GS 49).

And what of the selflessness of pity? At several points in book 1, Nietzsche highlights the desire for power and possession that lies behind pity, echoing his earlier analyses of this sentiment in *Human, All too Human* and *Daybreak*. In the final aphorism of book 1, he returns to this subject and suggests that the craving to help the poor and the suffering that spurs "millions of young Europeans" springs largely from boredom and their inability "to create for themselves, internally, their own very authentic distress." They

want unhappiness to approach them *"from the outside* and become visible";
they want to turn the distress of others "into a monster so that they can fight
a monster." Here again it is not selflessness that motivates but the selfish
need for neediness (*GS* 56).

The Good Will to Appearance

The second book of *The Gay Science* is devoted to art and the individuals
Nietzsche regards as being supremely artistic, namely, women (see *GS* 361).
The book constitutes Nietzsche's most sustained discussion of art since the
chapter on the "Souls of Artists and Writers" in *Human, All too Human;*
it also marks a major reversal of the attitude toward art expressed in that
earlier chapter.[15] In *Human, All too Human,* and very much in reaction to
his earlier attachment to Wagner, Nietzsche criticized artists for glorifying
and perpetuating the old metaphysical and religious errors of mankind. He
claimed they did not "stand in the foremost ranks of the Enlightenment"
and would someday be regarded as "glorious relics" (*HH* 147, 220, 223).
Nietzsche did not stick with this purely reactive position very long. In the
1879 supplement to *Human, All too Human, Assorted Opinions and Maxims,*
he evoked a non-romantic art that would serve as a "signpost of the future"
and blend "knowledge and art into a new unity" (*AOM* 99). This attempt
to reconcile art with science can also be found in *Daybreak,* where Nietzsche
defends realism in contemporary art as an expression of the happiness
found in "knowledge of reality"; realist artists, as opposed to romantic ones,
are "glorifiers of the 'delights of science'" (*D* 433).

In *Daybreak,* reflection on art takes a back seat to the critical investigation
of morality. This is emphatically not the case in *The Gay Science,* in which
art is of central importance—a fact reflected in the title of the book, with
its reference to *la gaya scienza* of the troubadours, as well as in the Prelude
in Rhymes.[16] The salience of art in *The Gay Science* has much to do with the
Nietzsche's increased emphasis, evident in book 1, on the role of error in
knowledge and the inescapability of appearance. Art is the "good will to appearance" (*GS* 107). In the same note in which he insists that we "must love
and cultivate error as the womb of knowing," Nietzsche also asserts: "Art as
the cultivation of illusion—our cult" (*KSA* 9:11 [162]). The centrality of art
to *The Gay Science* is above all made clear in the 1887 Preface to the book,
where Nietzsche claims that we "no longer believe that truth remains truth
when the veils are withdrawn" and praises the Greeks for stopping "courageously at the surface, the fold, the skin, to adore appearance, to believe in

forms, tones, words, in the whole Olympus of appearance. . . . Are we not, precisely in this respect, Greeks? Adorers of forms, of tones, of words? And therefore—*artists*?" (*GS* Preface 4).

The discussion of art in book 2 of *The Gay Science* takes place on several different levels. In the broadest context, art refers to the whole constructed, apparent, and even erroneous character of the world that concerns us and of which we can have knowledge. This is the meaning of art that is invoked in the passage from the Preface above. Nietzsche also invokes art in relation to the construction, fashioning, and aesthetic shaping of the self. We saw this notion of the aesthetic self emerge definitively in *Daybreak*, and it continues to play a prominent role in *The Gay Science*. Finally, Nietzsche discusses art in the narrower, more conventional context of aesthetic activities such as poetry and music. Here, as in the previous middle works, he rejects the romantic notion of art as intoxication, but he abandons his earlier attempt to blend "knowledge and art in a higher unity" and instead emphasizes their productive tension.

The first three aphorisms of book 2 take up art in its broadest, metaphysical meaning as constitutive of reality. To the realists who believe that reality stands unveiled before them—as in the Preface, he alludes to Schiller's poem "The Veiled Image of Sais"—by virtue of their sobriety, objectivity, and insulation from passions and fantasies, Nietzsche addresses the question: even "in your unveiled state are not even you still very passionate and dark creatures compared to fish, and still far too similar to an artist in love? And what is reality to an artist in love?" He refers again to the fundamental insight disclosed in the aphorism on "The Consciousness of Appearance" in book 1: "You are still burdened with those estimates of things that have their origin in the passions and loves of former centuries." Every perception of reality that we have is shot through with primeval error, prejudice, and perspective. There is no reality for us that is devoid of "human contribution," that is not the product of "your descent, your past, your training—all of your humanity and animality." Despite the element of error in all knowing and of drunkenness in all sobriety, Nietzsche does not mean to proclaim a radical subjectivism that renders knowledge or science meaningless. At the end of the opening aphorism of book 2, he tells the naïve realists that "perhaps our good will to transcend intoxication is as respectable as your faith that you are altogether incapable of intoxication" (*GS* 57).

In the next couple of aphorisms, Nietzsche continues to develop his radically idealistic conception of reality that denies us access to anything beyond the world of appearance. He claims that "what things *are called* is incomparably more important than what they are." This name or evaluation of a thing, which originally is "almost always wrong and arbitrary, thrown over things like a dress and altogether foreign to their nature and even to their skin," is passed down through the generations and "gradually grows to be part of the thing and turns into its very body. What at first was appearance becomes in the end, almost invariably, the essence and is effective as such." To become aware of the constructed character of our reality does not in any way destroy it: "We can destroy only as creators," that is, only by creating "new names and estimations for things" (GS 58). As in the earlier aphorism on "The Consciousness of Appearance," Nietzsche claims here that the awareness that we are dreaming brings with it the imperative that we continue to dream lest we perish. As loving, desiring, and feeling beings, we are "somnambulists of the day" and above all artists (GS 59).

From these reflections on art in relation to reality, Nietzsche goes on to devote a number of aphorisms to the nature of women (GS 60–75). The reason he does so, as the aphorisms themselves make abundantly clear, is that he identifies women with art, appearance, idealization, and beauty. As he puts it later in the fifth book of *The Gay Science*: "Woman is so artistic" (GS 361). And though he admits that "one cannot be too kind about women" (GS 71), he also suggests that their preoccupation with appearance and illusion is not altogether misplaced; for what lies underneath—"reality"—is ugly, a pudendum. Women understand the need for veils (GS 64; see also Preface 4). The reverse side of this identification of women with art and appearance is that they are not suited for knowledge or science (see GS 293). Nietzsche draws this implication in a note from the fall of 1881—and later in *Beyond Good and Evil*[17]—where he confesses that the idea of the world as a "continuously growing phantom of the human brain, on which we all in complete blindness work, write, love, and create," offends his "manly instinct"; whereas it is something with which "women and artists, in conformity with their instincts and affinity for all that is fantastical, like to amuse themselves" (KSA 9:15 [2]).

Immediately following his reflections on women, Nietzsche devotes one final aphorism to art in the broad, metaphorical sense. I have already discussed this aphorism, entitled "The Greatest Danger," in connection with Nietzsche's understanding of the relationship between the exception and the rule. But the aphorism also needs to be grasped in the context of his reflections on art. Once again, the greatest danger is the "eruption of madness—which means the eruption of arbitrariness in feeling, seeing, and hearing, the enjoyment of the mind's lack of discipline, the joy in human unreason." To guard against this danger, human beings need universal agreement on certain things, "regardless of whether these things are true or false." Such universal agreement is the product of art, not reason. And though exceptional seekers after truth may bristle at it, the universal binding force of this agreement is absolutely necessary so that "the faithful of the great shared faith stay together and continue their dance" (GS 76). Thus, not only the rule, but art in the broadest sense of binding fiction is necessary for the preservation of society.

The remaining aphorisms in book 2 deal with art proper: music, drama, poetry, and so forth. The first of these, "The Animal with a Good Conscience," is noteworthy because it introduces a new aspect to Nietzsche's philosophy of art: namely, the celebration of illusion, the cult of the false. In *Daybreak*, it will be remembered, he celebrated realism in contemporary art as a reflection of our newfound delight in science (D 433). The aphorism in *The Gay Science* begins with an appreciation of the vulgar element in the art of Southern Europe, which Nietzsche identifies above all with the "delight in masks and the good conscience in using any kind of mask." This vulgar delight in masks corresponds to a great need in human beings, the need for a "universal language" of which Nietzsche spoke in the previous aphorism. It also relates to the animal side of man, which Nietzsche associates with the tendency to simplify or falsify things and make erroneous inferences. As we have seen in other aphorisms, he insists that this simplifying, error-producing tendency from our animal past continues to operate in us today. Here he makes the same point: "And you, my dear fellow man, are still an animal in spite of everything." The vulgar art of Southern Europe—and of antiquity—lets this animal tendency run free; it is not ashamed of it; it gives it a good conscience (GS 78).

Nietzsche continues to celebrate the simplifying and transfiguring function of art in the next aphorism, applying it to the fashioning of the self. "Only artists, and especially those of the theater," he writes, "have given men eyes and ears to hear with some pleasure what each man *is* himself . . . only they have taught us the art of viewing ourselves as heroes—from a distance and, as it were, simplified and transfigured—the art of staging and watching ourselves" (GS 78). Here Nietzsche picks up the theme of the aesthetic self introduced in *Daybreak*. It is a theme that he will develop later on in *The Gay Science* in one of the most famous aphorisms of the book: the one in which he describes the "great and rare art" of giving style to one's character (GS 290).

What is novel in Nietzsche's discussion of art in book 2 is the emphasis he places on the illusory, unrealistic, unnatural character of art. This emphasis was evident in his celebration of the mask in vulgar art. And it appears again in his discussion of the unnaturalness of Greek drama. In

Greek drama, we find no naturalistic "stammering and screaming"; rather, passion is forced to "speak well," and everything is transmuted into "reason and words." With its narrow stage, its use of masks, and its stylized gestures, Greek drama went very far, "alarmingly far," in this antinaturalistic direction. But Nietzsche sees the same tendency in modern, non-Wagnerian opera, only here the unnaturalness consists in the complete substitution of music for words: "With just a little more impertinence, Rossini would have had everybody sing nothing but la-la-la-la—and that would have made good, rational sense. . . . [T]hat is the beautiful *unnaturalness* for whose sake one goes to the opera" (GS 80; see also 81). Nietzsche finds the same lack of concern for what is real or true reflected in the Roman approach to translation, which was concerned primarily to assimilate everything to "the Roman present" and remained unacquainted with "the delights of the historical sense" (GS 83).

There is one other aphorism that belongs to this effort to establish the unnatural, unrealistic, and irrational character of art, the aphorism devoted to "The Origin of Poetry." This is an incredibly complicated aphorism, and one which in many ways epitomizes Nietzsche's ability to pack a multitude of meanings and suggestive trains of thought in a brief essay. In addition to being about poetry, the aphorism serves as an occasion for Nietzsche to revisit his running dispute with the utilitarian outlook that accounts for the origin of human practices in terms rational utility. He begins by apparently siding with the utilitarians—"after all, they are so rarely right that it is really pitiful"—against those defenders of instinctive morality who see the "wild and beautiful irrationality of poetry" as a refutation of utilitarianism. But he quickly subverts this apparent agreement with utilitarianism by arguing that the utility that originally belonged to poetry was not rational but "superstitious." It was believed that putting one's petitions in the form of rhythmic speech would make them more appealing to the gods, also more compelling, and even allow them to be heard over longer distances. Even more strangely, rhythmic speech was credited with the power of discharging the vengeful emotions of the gods so that they would then leave human beings in peace. Finally, rhythmic speech or poetry was assumed to have a magical power, the ability to summon or gain the assistance of spirits or deities. Nietzsche adds one more ironic twist to his argument. He claims that the superstitious belief in the magical power of poetry persists to this day, as can be seen when serious philosophers appeal to poets "to lend their ideas force and credibility." He adds, "And yet it is more dangerous for a truth when a poet agrees with it than when he contradicts it," and caps his point by quoting a poet: "For as Homer says: 'Many lies tell the poets'" (GS 84).

The final sentences of this amazingly polysemous aphorism open up a new, more critical line of thought in Nietzsche's reflections on art, suggesting the inferiority of the artist to the thinker, the philosopher, the truly independent spirit. In the very next aphorism, he announces that "artists continually *glorify*—they do nothing else—all those states and things that are reputed to give man the opportunity to feel good for once, or great, or intoxicated, or cheerful, or well, or wise." Artists are not, as Shelley suggested, "the unacknowledged legislators of the world"; they merely echo and amplify the appraisals of happiness made by the true legislators. They are "always among the first to glorify the *new* good" enunciated by the moral and religious teachers, but they themselves do not lay down any new tables of good (*GS* 85). As Nietzsche puts it early on in *The Gay Science*: the poets have always been the "valets of some morality" (*GS* 1).

In the next couple of aphorisms, Nietzsche intensifies his questioning of art, returning to some of his earliest criticisms of the intoxicating, narcotizing art that he associates with Wagner. In an aphorism on the theater, he states that, after a day of "strong and elevated feelings," he knows "what sort of music and art I do *not* want—namely, the kind that tries to intoxicate the audience and to force it to the height of a moment of strong and elevated feelings." Evoking the disgust expressed in "Richard Wagner in Bayreuth" and the *Human, All too Human* series about the distorted relationship between art and life in the modern world,[18] he claims that the intoxicating art of the present day is "designed for those everyday souls who in the evening are not like victors on their triumphal chariots but rather like tired mules who have been whipped too much by life." Art here serves to exalt the weary and distract the bored. It "gives the mole wings and proud conceits—before it is time to go to sleep, before he crawls back in his hole." It enacts passions before an audience that has never felt them before. Nietzsche concludes: "Theater and music as the hashish-smoking and betel-chewing of the European! Who will ever relate the whole history of narcotica?—It is almost the history of 'culture,' of our so-called higher culture" (*GS* 86).

He continues this critique of romantic, intoxicating—Wagnerian[19]—art in the ensuing aphorism on "The Vanity of Artists." Actually, the critique is surrounded by a moving homage to Wagner, who is said to be "a master at discovering the tones out of the realm of suffering, depressed, tormented souls and at giving speech even to dumb animals. Nobody equals him in the colors of late fall, the indescribably moving happiness of the last, the very last, very briefest enjoyment." The problem with Wagner is that his vanity wants him to be more than this. He is the "master of the very small," but he wants to be a painter of "audacious frescoes." Nietzsche captures both the greatness and the self-delusion of Wagner in one of the most beautiful passages that has ever been written about an artist:

> He fails to see that his spirit has a different taste and urge and likes best of all to sit quietly in the nooks of houses that have collapsed; there, concealed, concealed from himself, he paints his real masterpieces, all of which are very short, often only a single measure in length; there he becomes wholly good, great, and perfect—perhaps only there.—But he does not know it. He is too vain to know it. (GS 87)

Perhaps the most scathing criticism Nietzsche levels at artists appears in the aphorism entitled "In Praise of Shakespeare." Here again he uses irony and paradox to maximum effect, praising Shakespeare for criticizing himself in *Julius Caesar*. The greatness of Shakespeare is nowhere more clearly evidenced than in his belief in Brutus and his supreme virtue, "independence of soul." This is the quintessential virtue of the free spirit for Nietzsche (see *BGE* 29, 41), and as he speaks of it here in connection with Brutus's relationship to Caesar there is more than an echo of his own relationship to Wagner. For such independence of soul, he writes, "no sacrifice can be too great. . . . [O]ne must be capable of sacrificing one's dearest friend for it, even if he should also be the most glorious human being, an ornament of the world, a genius without peer—if one loves freedom as the freedom of great souls and he threatens this kind of freedom." It is precisely this independence of soul that the poet lacks, a fact that Shakespeare himself self-critically acknowledges when he brings a poet onstage twice in *Julius Caesar* only to have scorn heaped upon him (GS 98).

Independence of soul is the quintessential virtue of the free spirit and the philosopher, but by criticizing artists for lacking it Nietzsche does not mean to imply that they should be more like free spirits and philosophers. Indeed, he suggests that when artists try to become more philosophical in order to prove that they are serious about truth, they end up appropriating only what is most superficial in a philosopher and merely "playing with knowledge" (GS 88). He makes this point emphatically in a lengthy aphorism entitled "Schopenhauer's Followers," in which he once again engages with Wagner. What, he asks, have Schopenhauer's German followers taken from the master? Not "his sense for hard facts" or his "clarity and reason." Not his "intellectual conscience" or "his cleanliness in questions about the church and the Christian God." No, what has enchanted Schopenhauer's followers in Germany are his "mystical embarrassments and subterfuges," his "unprovable doctrine of the *One Will*," his *"denial of the individual,"* his "ecstatic reveries about *genius*," and his "nonsense about *pity*." On no one has this baleful influence of Schopenhauer been greater than on Wagner, who in making his art "a companion piece and supplement to Schopenhauer's philosophy" has renounced the "loftier ambition of [its] becoming a companion piece and supplement to human knowledge and science." Nietzsche prefers the pre-Schopenhauerian Wagner who celebrated the innocent, amoral passion of Siegfried—he quotes a famous passage from his early essay "Richard Wagner in Bayreuth"—to the Wagner who has absorbed Schopenhauer's Christian-Buddhistic resignationism and set it to music in *Parsifal* (GS 99).[20]

Having disclosed his deepest reservations about the intellectual laxity, obsequiousness, and vanity of artists, Nietzsche comes back in the final aphorism of book 2 to express his "ultimate gratitude to art." This aphorism, which he seems to have been revising up until the last minute before publication,[21] contains his most considered statement on the relationship between science and art and, by implication, on the meaning of "gay science." Without art and the "cult of the untrue," he writes, "the realization of general untruth and mendaciousness that now comes to us through science—the realization that delusion and error are conditions of human knowledge and sensation—would be utterly unbearable. *Honesty* would lead to nausea and suicide" (GS 107). This is in many ways the same point that Nietzsche later makes in his oft-quoted remark that "we have art lest we perish of the truth" (WP 822), but it makes explicit just what the deadly truth consists in from which art must save us: namely, "the realization that delusion and error are conditions of human knowledge and sensation." This was the general point Nietzsche made in the very first aphorism of book 2: the most fundamental truth we possess is that we can never possess a truth outside of appearances. To put it even more paradoxically: the truth that art makes bearable for us is the realization that reality is thoroughly artistic. Art, therefore, is the "good will to appearance" (GS 107), to the unavoidably apparent character of the world.

Nietzsche goes on to specify just how art renders existence "*bearable* for us"—and by "us" he clearly means we free spirits, we men of knowledge. He focuses on the distancing, simplifying, and transfiguring function of art that was highlighted earlier in the first aphorism in which he first expressed his gratitude toward art (GS 78): "[A]rt furnishes us with eyes and hands and above all the good conscience" to transform ourselves into an aesthetic phenomenon. "At times we need a rest from ourselves by looking upon, by looking *down* upon, ourselves and, from an artistic distance laughing *over* ourselves or weeping *over* ourselves. We must discover the *hero* no less than the *fool* in our passion for knowledge." In *Daybreak*, Nietzsche emphasized the heroic aspect of the quest for knowledge (see *D* 45, 327, 459, 551). Here, in keeping with the theme of "gay science," he places the greatest emphasis on the fool. Recalling the first aphorism of the book on the gravity of the teachers of the purpose of existence, he claims that "precisely because we are at bottom grave and serious human beings—really more weights than human beings—nothing does us so much good as a *fool's cap*: we need it in relation to ourselves—we need all exuberant, floating, dancing mocking, childish, and blissful art lest we lose the *freedom above things* that our ideal demands of us" (*GS* 107; cf. *D* 531).

Mention of "our ideal" leads us to ask whether anything new has been introduced into Nietzsche's ideal of the free spirit here. I think there has, and it comes out in the lines immediately following the ones just quoted: "It would mean a *relapse* for us, with our irritable honesty, to get involved entirely in morality and, for the sake of the over-severe demands that we make on ourselves in these matters, to become virtuous monsters and scarecrows. We should also be *able* to stand *above* morality . . . to *float* above it and *play*" (*GS* 107). What receives articulation here for the first time—or almost the first time (see *D* 510)—is Nietzsche's recognition that the scientific quest for knowledge is itself implicated in morality, that it is the last expression of the faith in morality, of the ascetic ideal, of religious piety. This is a theme he develops much more fully later on (see, e.g., *GS* 344), and it suggests a significant modification of the ideal of the free spirit that has hitherto informed the middle works. It suggests a standpoint beyond the quest for knowledge insofar as this quest remains mired in morality and asceticism. Art is indispensable to achieving this standpoint, which, insofar as it floats above morality, can be understood as the quintessence of gay science.

The Death of God

In the dialectical ebb and flood that defines the structure of *The Gay Science*, book 3 represents a return from art and gaiety to science and tragedy. In this book, Nietzsche draws the ultimate and fateful consequence of his scientific skepticism, namely, the death of God. He announces the death of God in the first aphorism of the book, and he goes on to develop the meaning of this momentous event in the central and very famous aphorism on "The Madman." Of course, this is not first time in his writings that Nietzsche has acknowledged the death of God. In many ways, the death of God, the loss of religion and myth, and the secularization of the modern age were always at the heart his reflections on culture, from *The Birth of Tragedy* on (see, e.g.,

BT 10, 18, 23; SE 4). In *Human, All too Human*, for example, the loss of belief
in God and his providential oversight suggested that humanity now had to
take responsibility for itself and set "goals embracing the whole earth" (*HH*
25). Nevertheless, these earlier reflections on the death of God—which are
also fairly commonplace in the context of *fin de siècle* Europe—don't quite
capture all that Nietzsche has in mind when he takes up the theme in *The
Gay Science*, as will become clear when we analyze the peculiar story he tells
in "The Madman."

The death of God is, of course, one of the ideas that plays an absolutely
critical role in Nietzsche's mature philosophy. Another such idea, the eternal recurrence, is announced for the first time at the end of book 4. That
these two ideas are profoundly related to one another is indicated not only
by their appearing together in *The Gay Science* but also by their almost si-
multaneous emergence in Nietzsche's notebooks from the late summer and
fall of 1881, where they grow out of theoretical reflections on the necessary,
mechanistic, purposeless, and inhuman character of the world of becoming.[22] In the analysis of books 3 and 4 that follows, I begin to suggest how
the ideas of the death of God and the eternal recurrence are related to one
another. But because Nietzsche announces the eternal recurrence only at the
end of book 4, deferring its full development until *Zarathustra*, I focus for
most part on the death of God and its implications for the free spirit.

As I have mentioned, Nietzsche announces that "God is dead" in the
first aphorism of book 3. He does so, however, almost as a side note to the
main point that, even after his demise, the shadows of God may continue
to haunt human beings for thousands of years to come. Therefore, "we still
have to vanquish his shadow" (GS 108). This leads directly into the very important aphorism entitled "Let Us Beware," which details the various ways
in which the shadows of God may continue to inform our conceptions of
nature and the universe. These shadows consist chiefly in our habit of an-
thropomorphizing the universe by conceiving of it either as a living organism, or as a machine designed for a specific purpose, or as a law-governed
entity. Against these "aesthetic anthropomorphisms," Nietzsche asserts that
the "total character of the world . . . is in all eternity chaos—in the sense not
of a lack of necessity but of lack of order, arrangement, form, beauty, wisdom."[23] And he hints at the connection between this idea of chaos and the
idea of eternal recurrence by claiming that the "whole musical box repeats
eternally its tune which may never be called a melody."[24] He concludes the
aphorism by holding out the prospect of the naturalization of humanity
through the dehumanization of nature: only after we have completed the

"de-deification of nature" can we "begin to '*naturalize*' humanity in terms of a pure, newly discovered, newly redeemed nature" (*GS* 109).

The dehumanization and de-deification of nature that Nietzsche calls for in this aphorism receives considerable attention in the notes surrounding his first reflections on the eternal recurrence. In several of these notes, he repeats the phrase "let us beware" in connection with the tendency to anthropomorphize nature, and he regards such anthropomorphization as evidence that we continue to worship the shadows of God: "The modern-scientific counterpart to the belief in God is the belief in the universe as an organism: this nauseates me" (*KSA* 9:11 [201]; see also 11 [157, 205]). Our task, therefore, is to dehumanize nature and thereby naturalize humanity (*KSA* 9:11 [211]; see also 11 [197, 238, 293]). Related to the notes on the dehumanization of nature are several others that enigmatically refer to the "dead world" and "dead nature" in opposition to the erroneousness of the "sentient world": "The 'dead' world! Always in motion and without error, power versus power! And in the sentient world everything false, vainglorious! It is a feast to pass from this world into the 'dead world'" (*KSA* 9:11 [70]; see also 11 [7, 21, 125]). From these notes on the dead, dehumanized, purposeless, and eternally chaotic world it is but a small step to Nietzsche's initial attempts to scientifically prove the eternal recurrence of things based on the limited quantity of force in the universe and the infinity of time (*KSA* 9:11 [148, 202]). The idea of the "circular course of things," he remarks in one note, does not stand in contradiction to the purposeless and chaotic necessity of the universe but follows logically from it (*KSA* 9:11 [225]).[25]

Before moving on, there is one other note from this group that we need to consider. Dated 26 August 1881, the note sketches the four parts or books of a projected work devoted to a "new way of living." The theme of the first book is "*Chaos sive natura: 'of the dehumanization of nature'*" (*KSA* 9:11 [197]).[26] The allusion here is obviously to the *Deus sive Natura* of Spinoza, a philosopher with whom Nietzsche was much occupied while writing *The Gay Science*. In a letter to Overbeck of 30 July 1881, he excitedly announced that "I have a *precursor*, and what a precursor!"—namely, Spinoza: "Not only is his overall tendency like mine—making knowledge the *most powerful* affect—but in five main points of his doctrine I recognize myself . . . : he denies the freedom of the will, teleology, the moral world order, the unegoistic, and evil" (*SB* 6:111).[27] As this comment suggests, what Nietzsche found so congenial in Spinoza was the latter's denial of anything beyond or outside of nature and his conception of nature as a nonanthropomorphic and nonmoral system of necessity. Unlike Nietzsche, however, Spinoza conceived of necessity in terms of rational intelligibility and thereby did not escape the shadow of God. Nietzsche's substitution of "chaos" for "Deus" is meant to rectify this weakness in Spinoza's naturalism. We will return to this relationship between Nietzsche and Spinoza when we analyze the important aphorism on *amor fati* in book 4.[28]

Following the aphorism in which he cautions us against the anthropomorphization of nature, Nietzsche devotes several others to considering the relationship between human knowledge and the dehumanized, de-deified world just disclosed. The first of these, on the "Origin of Knowledge," I considered above in connection with the issue of incorporation. As we saw there, Nietzsche argues that for most of human history the only knowledge that has been incorporated has been based on errors such as the belief in enduring things, equal things, substances, and so forth. Only recently has truth emerged as a life-preserving power, and with this development the ultimate question has been posed as to how far truth can endure incorporation (GS 110). It turns out that there is a limit to how much truth human beings can incorporate. As Nietzsche puts it in one note: "In order for there to be some degree of consciousness in the world, an unreal world of errors must arise" in opposition to the world of "absolute flux"; the "ultimate truth of the flux of things cannot withstand incorporation, our organs (for life) are arranged for error" (KSA 9:11 [162]).

He elaborates on the unavoidability of error and falsification in the ensuing aphorisms on the "Origin of the Logical" and "Cause and Effect." With respect to logic, though the categories of equality and substance involved a tremendous simplification and falsification of reality, the animals that possessed them had an advantage in the struggle for existence over those animals who "saw everything 'in flux'" (GS 111). Likewise, cause and effect represent artificial disruptions and dismemberments of a process that is in fact a "continuum" and a "flux." We certainly have gotten better at describing this process, discerning a complex manifold where primitive human beings "saw only two separate things." But still such description nowhere amounts to a full explanation. "[H]ow could we possibly explain anything?" Nietzsche asks. "We operate only with things that do not exist: lines, planes, bodies, atoms, divisible time spans, divisible spaces. How should explanations be at all possible when we first turn everything into an *image*, our image! It will do to consider science as an attempt to humanize things as faithfully as possible" (GS 112; see also 246).[29]

The final sentence in the passage just quoted suggests that Nietzsche does not mean to dispense with all distinctions between true and false or better and worse descriptions. Though all knowing involves some simplification, selection, and falsification of reality, there are epistemically meaningful differences in the way we go about constructing knowledge and the honesty we bring to bear on it. Thus, Nietzsche writes: "As soon as we see a new image, we immediately construct it with the aid of all our previous experiences, *depending on the degree* of our honesty and justice. All experiences are moral experiences, even in the realm of sense perception" (GS 114). Though scientific thinking never completely escapes the humanized world, it does struggle against the grosser simplifications and falsifications that human beings have perpetrated on reality to make it more bearable and manageable. For this reason, the impulses to doubt, negate, wait, and patiently collect that belong to science operated for the longest time as poisons on human beings. Still, Nietzsche holds out the possibility—returning to the question of how far truth can endure incorporation—that there will be a time in the future "when artistic energies and the practical wisdom of life will join with scientific thinking to form a higher organic system in relation to which scholars, physicians, artists, and legislators—as we know them at present—would have to look like paltry relics of ancient times" (GS 113).

From these epistemological considerations Nietzsche shifts abruptly to moral ones, but the underlying point remains the same: simplification, falsification, and error have been an inextricable part of our experience of the world. In the case of morality, such simplification and falsification take the form of herd judgment in contradistinction to what is ineffably individual. This is the first time Nietzsche refers to "herd" morality in his published writings, though his point largely echoes his analysis of the morality of custom in *Daybreak*.[30] Morality, he writes, "trains the individual to be a function of the herd and to ascribe value to himself only as a function. . . . Morality is herd instinct in the individual" (GS 116). This subordination of the individual to the herd was, of course, greatest during the "longest and most remote periods of the human past," when "nothing was more terrible than to feel that one stood by oneself," when individuality, freedom of thought, and egoism were considered painful, and the desire to live "according to one's own weight and measure" was considered "madness." In the modern world, human beings have learned to think and feel differently about themselves, so much so that it is difficult for them to grasp the crudity of primitive morality: "Today one feels responsible only for one's will and actions, and one finds pride in oneself. All our teachers of law start from this sense of self and pleasure in the individual as if this had always been the fount of law" (GS 117; cf. D 9).

Analogous to his belief in the possibility of greater faithfulness and honesty in science, Nietzsche certainly believes that we can go further in the direction of individual responsibility and self-cultivation. Thus, he argues that the ancient medical-moral formulation that "virtue is the health of the soul" needs to be changed to "*your* virtue is the health of *your* soul. For there is no health as such." We must allow the "unique and incomparable to raise its head once again" and attempt to find the peculiar virtue and the peculiar health that belong to each individual. Indeed, even health may too narrowly define our ultimate objective, given that the quest for knowledge may require a certain amount of illness. From this enlarged perspective, the "will to health alone" may in fact be a "prejudice, cowardice, and perhaps a bit of very subtle barbarism and backwardness" (GS 120).

Nietzsche's reflections on both knowledge and morality in book 3 grow out of his earlier glimpse into the dehumanized, de-deified world whose character is "in all eternity chaos—in the sense not of a lack of necessity but of a lack of order, arrangement, form, beauty, wisdom, and whatever other names there are for our aesthetic anthropomorphisms" (GS 109). It is not possible for humans to live in accordance with this world, and so we have "arranged a world in which we can live—by positing bodies, lines, planes, causes and effects," and so forth. But Nietzsche once again reminds us that the fact that these simplifications and falsifications of reality are necessary or useful for life does not make them true: "Life is no argument. The conditions of life might include error" (GS 121). Intellectual probity has led us to dehumanize and de-deify the world; it has led us not only to the conclusion that God is dead but to the resolution to vanquish his shadows. Nietzsche addresses the implications of this tremendous event of the death of God in the climactic aphorism of book 3 on "The Madman." But before doing so, he says a few things about the sources of the skeptical, scientific impulse that has brought this event to pass.

In the first place, he points out that Christianity has played an important role in the development of scientific skepticism and the modern intellectual conscience: "Christianity, too, has made a great contribution to the Enlightenment, and taught moral skepticism very trenchantly and effectively, accusing and embittering men, yet with untiring patience and subtlety." It was this moral skepticism of Christianity that exposed the vanity and self-deception that lay behind the pagan virtue in which the ancients took such naïve pride. Having been trained in the Christian school of skepticism, we modern scientific investigators now read the treatises of moralists like Seneca and Epictetus with a certain sense of embarrassment "as if a child were talking before an old man, or an over-enthusiastic beauty before La Rochefoucauld." Nietzsche goes on to say that "we have applied this same skepticism also to all *religious* states and processes" and now feel the same sense of "subtle superiority" with respect to Christian books (*GS* 122). That Christianity was the source of the scientific skepticism that eventually destroyed it is a notion that appears in several places in Nietzsche's later works (see, e.g., *GS* 357). The other point Nietzsche makes about the scientific outlook that discloses the de-deified world of eternal chaos is familiar to us from the opening aphorisms of *The Gay Science* as well as from *Daybreak*: namely, that this outlook is not a mere means to something else—honor, virtue, technological power, or amusement—but has itself become a passion (*GS* 123). This is a new development in human history, and it renders us incapable of abjuring science even when it leads to the loss of the comforting beliefs that have hitherto made us happy. As Nietzsche put it in *Daybreak*: the passion for knowledge "has become too strong for us to be able to want happiness without knowledge or the happiness of a strong, firmly rooted delusion" (*D* 429).

We are now ready to approach the climactic aphorism of book 3, "The Madman," in which Nietzsche announces the death of God—or more precisely, the death of the Christian God, belief in whom has become unbelievable (*GS* 343)—and graphically draws out the nihilistic implications of this historic event. This, of course, is one of the most famous and frequently commented upon passages in the whole of Nietzsche's oeuvre. It is also one of the strangest, with its story about a madman who carries a lantern into the marketplace in the bright morning hours and shouts to a crowd of uncomprehending atheists that God is dead. Why does Nietzsche put this world-shattering pronouncement in the mouth of a madman? And why does he adopt such an apocalyptic tone and employ such extreme language and imagery? These are questions that any analysis of this disturbing aphorism must address. I will address them in the course of analyzing the three aspects of the death of God that Nietzsche emphasizes most in the aphorism: (1) the sheer cataclysmic horror of the event; (2) the failure of the multitude to appreciate its significance; and (3) the fact that *we* are responsible for it.

Let us begin with the first aspect, since it focuses on what is commonly seen as the most fundamental consequence of the death of the Christian God, namely, nihilism. The madman speaks of the entire horizon being wiped away, the absence of any sense of up or down or backward or forward, the "straying as through an infinite nothing," and again the "breath of empty space." The reason the madman needs a lantern in the morning is that night is "continually closing in around us" (*GS* 125). All of this dramatic imagery points toward a total loss of meaning and orientation in the world, a total loss of "gravity" (*Schwergewicht*). As Nietzsche explains in a note from 1885, as a result of the death of the Christian God, "it will seem for a long time as if all gravity has departed from things" (*KSA* 11:34 [5]). In an even later note, he writes that this event will lead to the loss of the "center of gravity by which we have lived" for two thousand years (*KSA* 12:11 [148]).

Above all, the death of the Christian God spells the end of Christian morality. As we have already seen in *The Gay Science*—not to mention the other middle works—the same scientific mentality that has led to the de-deification of nature has also led to the complete undermining of Christian morality, with its false opposition of good and evil and its erroneous notions of selflessness, sin, free will, and responsibility. Only a couple of aphorisms prior to the one on the madman, for example, Nietzsche argues that the moral skepticism that Christianity applied to pagan morality has now been applied to "all *religious* states and processes, such as sin, repentance, grace, [and] sanctification" (*GS* 122). And in his later gloss on the death of God in the fifth book of *The Gay Science*, he claims that few people realize "how much must collapse now that this faith [in the Christian god] has been undermined because it was built upon this faith, propped up by it, grown into it; for example the whole of our European morality" (*GS* 343; see also *TI* Expeditions 5).

Connected to this last point is the second aspect of the death of God that Nietzsche emphasizes in his aphorism on the madman: namely, that the vast majority of human beings do not grasp the significance of this momentous event. This is dramatically evoked when the easygoing atheists make fun of the madman's anxious cries that he seeks God. They show no understanding of the gravity of their situation in the wake of God's death, which provokes the madman to exclaim, "I have come too early; my time is not yet. This tremendous event is still on its way, still wandering; it has not reached the ears of men" (*GS* 125). Indeed, it is partly the incomprehension of the multitude that makes the madman seem mad—although we will soon see that there are ways in which the madman really is mad. Again, Nietzsche's later gloss on the death of God captures this same point. Even though the "greatest recent event that 'God is dead,' that the belief in the Christian god has become unbelievable—is already beginning to cast its first shadows over Europe," only a few exceptional individuals are able to discern them. "The event itself is far too great, too distant, too remote from the multitude's capacity for comprehension even for the tidings of it to be thought of as having *arrived* as yet" (*GS* 343).

We are now ready to tackle third and in many ways strangest aspect of the aphorism on the madman: the emphasis on *our* responsibility for the death of God. The madman repeatedly insists that it is *we* who have killed God, that *we* are the "murderers of all murderers" (*GS* 125). This point is also prominent in Nietzsche's early drafts of the aphorism (*KSA* 9:12 [77] and 14 [26]), though he sometimes adds the twist that God merely used us to kill himself—we were "only his hands" (*KSA* 9:12 [157]). One of the things Nietzsche highlights with this violent imagery is the way in which *our* scientific skepticism has brought about the death of God and the de-deification of the universe. This to some extent is what we have learned in the aphorisms leading up to the one on "The Madman"; and the Copernican overtones of the madman's references to the earth being unchained from its sun and the breath of infinite empty spaces only serve to confirm it. Again in a later note, Nietzsche evokes the nihilistic consequences of modern natural science: "[E]ver since Copernicus, man rolls from the center into an x" (*KSA* 12:2 [127]). It is under the knives wielded by science that the "holiest and mightiest" of our beliefs have bled to death.

But this only takes us so far in understanding the bizarre imagery of the madman's speech. For this imagery not only highlights our responsibility for God's death but even more emphatically our guilt: "'How shall we comfort ourselves, the murderers of all murderers?'" the madman cries out in anguish. "'What was holiest and mightiest of all that the world has yet owned has bled to death under our knives: who will wipe this blood off us? What water is there for us to clean ourselves? What festivals of atonement, what sacred games shall we invent? Is not the greatness of this deed too great for us?'" (*GS* 125). It is his morbid obsession with guilt that alerts us to the fact that the madman does not necessarily speak for Nietzsche here; that, indeed, he is a character Nietzsche is using to bring out not only the fateful consequences of the death of God but also the limitations of certain kind of response to this event.[31] Far from being liberated by the death of God, the madman remains imprisoned in the guilt and self-contempt that are part and parcel of religion. In this respect, he resembles the "ascetic of the spirit" in *Zarathustra*, whose self-contempt and nausea betray that he has not fully incorporated his "ugly truths," that he has not yet "learned laughter or beauty." In what seems to be a reference to the death of God, Nietzsche comments that the deed of the ascetic of the spirit "still lies on him as a shadow: the hand still darkens the doer. As yet he has not overcome his deed" (*Z* 2.13). Nietzsche points to the same inability to overcome his deed, when discussing the "ugliest man," the "murderer of God," in part 4 of *Zarathustra* (*Z* 4.7).

All of this suggests that the madman has not vanquished the shadow of God referred to in the first aphorism of book 3—a point reinforced by the

fact that he runs into the marketplace crying, "I seek God! I seek God!" Even
he seems to realize his inadequacy to the world-shattering message that he
bears when he asks: "Is not the greatness of this deed too great for us?" The
madman is no terminus but must be superseded by a higher humanity that
has liberated itself from the ascetic self-cruelty that brought about God's
death. Again he asks: "Must we ourselves not become gods simply to be
worthy of [this deed]? There has never been a greater deed; and whoever is
born after us—for the sake of this deed he will belong to a higher history
than all history hitherto" (GS 125).[32]

That the madman does not simply speak for Nietzsche but remains
mired in the ascetic presuppositions of religion is confirmed when we look
at the very different, much more cheerful response to the death of God
that Nietzsche evokes in book 5 of *The Gay Science*. He does not, of course,
ignore the terrifying aspect of the death of God in this later aphorism. He
refers to the "long plenitude and sequence of breakdown, destruction, ruin,
cataclysm that is now impending," and to the "monstrous logic of terror"
that portends an "eclipse of the sun whose like has probably never yet occurred on earth." But he also indicates that we free spirits "look forward to
the approaching gloom without any real sense of involvement and above
all without any worry and fear for *ourselves*." Thinking only of the consequences for *himself*, the free spirit experiences the death of God as a kind
of "dawn" (*Morgenröte*): "At long last the horizon appears free to us again,
even if it should not be bright . . . all the daring of the lover of knowledge is
permitted again; the sea, *our* sea, lies open again; perhaps there has never yet
been such an 'open sea'" (GS 343). Nor is it only in the later book 5 that we
find this less morbid, more cheerful response to the death of God; in many
ways, it is implicit in book 4.

Before we can begin to explore this claim, we need to complete our analysis of the argument of book 3. Not surprisingly, many of the aphorisms
in the rest of the book (GS 128–52) are concerned with religion and specifically Christianity. This might seems superfluous in the light of the madman's pronouncement that God is dead, but Nietzsche is aware that, while
intellectual probity and scientific skepticism have removed a central pillar
in the belief in the Christian God and thereby rendered that belief more
unbelievable, there are other, more practical reasons why one might continue to believe. One might value Christianity for its utility, its "cash value"
(in William James's wonderfully American phrase). Indeed, Nietzsche acknowledges this pragmatic justification of religion in general in a very funny
aphorism on "The Value of Prayer," where he suggests that prayer has been

invented to keep the masses occupied so that they don't disturb the few individuals who do experience genuine elevations of the soul (GS 128).[33] The scientific de-deification of the world alone is not sufficient to undermine Christianity. Therefore, the post-madman aphorisms in book 3 are concerned to show that Christianity is unappealing on a practical level. As Nietzsche succinctly summarizes this aspect of his argument: "What is now decisive against Christianity is our taste, no longer our reasons" (GS 132).

Prominent in his aesthetic arguments against Christianity is the claim, familiar to us from as far back as *Human, All too Human*, that Christianity artificially blackens the world: "The Christian resolve to find the world ugly and bad has made the world ugly and bad" (GS 130; see also 138). St. Paul, of course, played a crucial role in this Jewish-Christian uglification of the world, having "an evil eye for the passions," which made them seem "dirty, disfiguring, and heartbreaking" and led to the impossible quest to annihilate them. By contrast, the Greeks "loved, elevated, gilded, and deified" the passions (GS 139). The other side of Nietzsche's argument about Christianity's artificial blackening of the world is that it made the redemptive light of Christianity seem all the more miraculous. It was only against the gloomy, Jewish landscape in which Jesus lived that the "rare and sudden piercing of the gruesome and perpetual general day-night by a single ray of sun [was] experienced as if it were a miracle of 'love' and the ray of unmerited 'grace'" (GS 137; cf. *HH* 132–35).

As can be seen from these aphorisms, Nietzsche emphasizes the Jewish roots of Christianity and contrasts them with the more affirmative outlook of the Greeks. He claims, for example, that Christianity inherited its notion of sin from the Jews. This notion rests on the belief in a "powerful, overpowering being" who regards every violation of his commands as a slight to his honor. It is not the actual harm resulting from an action that makes it sinful but, rather, the fact that it is an offense against God, whom Nietzsche refers to as an "honor-craving Oriental":[34] "[E]very deed is to be considered *solely with respect to its supernatural consequences*, without regard for its natural consequences; that is what Jewish feeling demands, for whatever is natural is considered ignoble." Again, this contrasts with the Greeks, who had no notion of sin and believed that sacrileges of the sort committed by Prometheus and Ajax possessed a certain nobility (GS 135).

Nietzsche develops his aesthetic critique of Christianity (and Judaism) by celebrating the advantages of polytheism over monotheism. Against monotheism, which holds that there is "one normal type and ideal" for all human beings, polytheism allows the individual "to posit his own ideal and to derive from it his own law, joys, and rights." It is only with polytheism that the "luxury of individuals was first permitted" and the "rights of individuals" first honored. And it is only with polytheism that the ability to view the world through a multiplicity of perspectives, an ability that distinguishes human beings from other animals, first develops: "In polytheism the free-spiriting and many-spiriting of man attained its first preliminary form—the strength to create for ourselves our own new eyes—and ever again new eyes that are even more our own: hence man alone among all the animals has no eternal horizons and perspectives" (GS 143). This same appreciation for diversity and individuality informs Nietzsche's positive evaluation of religious wars (GS 144) and the failure of general reformations of religion among the Greeks (GS 149).

Nietzsche's critique of Christianity in book 3 concludes with another familiar point about the "brutality" of Christian virtue, that it was designed to make the saint feel superior by engendering self-contempt in others (GS 150; cf. D 30). This aphorism is followed by three others that in many ways bring the central argument in book 3 about the de-deification of the world to a conclusion. The first criticizes Schopenhauer's notion of the so-called metaphysical need, arguing that it corresponds to nothing permanent in human beings but, rather, grows out of the "uncomfortable emptiness" that follows upon the destruction of religious ideas. These religious ideas themselves do not grow out of any sort of permanent need but out of a primitive "*error* in the interpretation of certain natural events, a failure of the intellect" (GS 151). This denial of the metaphysical need goes back to Nietzsche's earliest critique of religion in *Human, All too Human,* and it also serves to highlight how little his de-deification of the world in *The Gay Science* rests on the historical arguments about the origin of religion that he previously regarded as the "definitive refutation" of belief in God (D 95; see also HH 133).

The next aphorism is entitled "The Greatest Change," and it details how ancient humanity experienced the world in a superstitious way that we moderns can no longer completely understand. His examples of ancient superstition seem to include certain Christian beliefs—"What was joy in ages when one believed in devils and tempters? What was passion when one saw demons lying in wait nearby? What was philosophy when doubt was experienced as . . . sacrilege against eternal love?"—and what is perhaps surprising is that he seems to regard this superstitious view of the world as in many ways richer than our own: "We have given things a new color; we go on painting them continually. But what do all our efforts to date avail when we hold them against the colored splendor of that old master—

ancient humanity?" (GS 152) A note of regret about the de-deification of the world seems to creep into Nietzsche's voice at this point. At the very least, he acknowledges that it results in a less colorful world.

The third of these aphorisms marks not only the conclusion of the central argument of book 3 but also in many ways the transition to book 4. Entitled "Homo Poeta," it describes the whole process by which humanity—speaking here in the first person singular—originally created morality and religion and has now recently destroyed them: "I myself, having made this tragedy of tragedies all by myself . . . I, having first tied the knot of morality into existence . . . I myself have now slain all gods in the fourth act, for the sake of morality."[35] Book 3, of course, corresponds to the fourth act in which the Christian God has died at the hands of Christian skepticism and honesty. "Now what is to become of the fifth act? From where am I to take the tragic solution?—Should I begin to think about a comic solution?"(GS 153). Here it becomes ambiguous whether it is humanity that is still speaking or Nietzsche himself. He invokes the dialectic of tragedy and comedy that frames the argument of *The Gay Science*, from the first aphorism to the last. If book 4 is taken to be the fifth act, is Nietzsche suggesting that it represents a comic solution to the slaying of the gods in the fourth act? This is a question we will take up in the next section.

The rest of book 3 consists of 122 short aphorisms on a wide variety of topics. Though it is difficult to discern a single theme that unifies them all, there does seem to be a thread that links the final eight aphorisms (GS 268–75). As with the concluding aphorism of book 2, Nietzsche seems to have been revising these final aphorisms of book 3 until the last minute before publication.[36] In each he asks a single question, and the answers he gives point to major themes that he will develop in book 4 as well as in his later works. Perhaps the most important of these answers is the one he gives to the question "In What Do You Believe?": "In this, that the weights of all things must be determined anew" (GS 269). This is followed by an aphorism in which he states for the first time, "You shall become the person you are" (GS 270; see also 335). And the final three aphorisms all have to do with the importance of "no longer feeling ashamed in front of oneself" (GS 273–75; see also 107). The affirmative note that will dominate book 4 is here already struck at the end of book 3. That Nietzsche considered these final aphorisms to be of the utmost importance he makes clear retrospectively in *Ecce Homo*, where he writes: "[A]t the end of the third book [of *The Gay Science*] one reads the granite words in which a destiny finds for the first time a formula for itself, for all time" (EH 3.GS).

The Ethics of a Free Spirit

Book 4 of *The Gay Science* is titled "Sanctus Januarius," in honor of the martyred saint whose congealed blood, preserved in a church in Naples, periodically becomes liquefied. This title and the poem that accompanies it suggest a great thawing of the spirit, a rebirth after a long, cold winter. And there can be little doubt that Nietzsche associates this winter with the death of God announced in book 3, or, perhaps more precisely, with the renunciatory, comfort-denying skepticism that killed him. In his 1886 Preface to *The Gay Science*, he speaks of winter and thawing ice in connection with the book as whole, but his remarks seem to be especially pertinent to book 4: "It seems to be written in the language of the wind that thaws ice and snow . . . and one is instantly reminded no less of the proximity of winter than of the triumph over the winter that is coming, must come, and perhaps already has come." He adds that the book exudes gratitude, "the gratitude of a convalescent" who has endured "exhaustion, disbelief, icing up in the midst of youth" and who now experiences "the rejoicing of strength that is returning, of a reawakened faith in a tomorrow and the day after tomorrow, of a sudden sense and anticipation of a future, of impending adventures, of seas that are open again, of goals that are permitted again, believed again" (GS Preface 1).

These retrospective remarks provide a clue to understanding the relationship between book 4 and the death of God announced in book 3, between the cheerfulness of the former and the terrifying character of the latter. As we saw in the previous section, Nietzsche believes that two different responses to the death of God are possible: there is the terrified, guilt-obsessed response of the madman, who focuses on the nihilistic consequences of the death of God; and there is the cheerful response of the free-spirited seeker after knowledge, for whom the death of God signifies a new dawn and a completely open sea. For the most part, book 4 seems to embody the second, more cheerful response. This is Nietzsche's own response, as his frequent references to the deeply personal character of the book in letters to friends such as Burckhardt, Köselitz, Rée, and Gersdorff confirm (*SB* 6:235, 238, 247, and 248).

But how does the idea of the eternal recurrence introduced at the end of book 4 fit into this scheme? It does not seem to be a particularly cheerful idea, as the title alone of the aphorism in which it is introduced—"The Heaviest Weight"—suggests. And yet the eternal recurrence seems to be the grand idea toward which the rest of book 4 is building. Or is it? Here I think some caution is needed before making the idea of the eternal recurrence too central to the overall interpretation of book 4—or, indeed, of *The Gay Science* as a whole.[37] Though the ideas of the death of God, the de-deification of nature, the reign of chance, necessity, purposelessness, and chaos that run through *The Gay Science* are certainly connected to the eternal recurrence, the latter idea ultimately goes beyond the horizon of the free spirit and the quest for knowledge that remain the focus of *The Gay Science*. It is for good reason that Nietzsche waits until the penultimate aphorism of book 4 to announce the idea of the eternal recurrence and then follows it with the introduction to *Zarathustra*. This announcement marks the beginning of the latter work, not the culmination of *The Gay Science*.[38]

This general reading of the argument of book 4 needs, of course, to be demonstrated through a detailed analysis of the aphorisms that comprise it. It receives at least partial confirmation from Nietzsche's September 1882 letter to Overbeck from which I have already quoted. There he writes: "If you have read the 'Sanctus Januarius' you will have remarked that I have crossed a tropic. Everything that lies before me is new, and it will not be long before I catch sight also of the *terrifying* face of my more distant life task. . . . This whole interim state between what was and what will be, I call 'in media vita'" (*SB* 6:255). The last phrase alludes to the title of an important aphorism (*GS* 324) that I will analyze below. In general, the letter suggests that book 4 intimates but does not yet belong to Nietzsche's "more distant life task," which undoubtedly revolves around the teaching of the terrifying idea of the eternal recurrence.

As we turn to the first aphorism of book 4, however, we seem to encounter a potential difficulty with my reading. In this aphorism, Nietzsche makes *amor fati*, love of fate, his motto and resolves to be "only a Yes-sayer." It would be hard to deny the connection here to the idea of the eternal recurrence, which represents the supreme formula of Yes-saying affirmation. But it is also important to note that Nietzsche speaks of *amor fati* in connection with the free spirit's quest for knowledge, and he does so in the most personal terms: "I still live, I still think: I still have to live, for I still have to think. *Sum, ergo cogito: cogito, ergo sum*" (*GS* 276). The emphasis here is on thinking or knowing, to which life seems to be a means rather than an end.

Perhaps the most intriguing sentence in this famous aphorism is the one in which Nietzsche declares that he wants "to learn more and more to see as beautiful what is necessary in things; then I shall be one of those who make things beautiful" (*GS* 276). Here again we seem to encounter the recurring theme of the incorporation of knowledge—by making it beautiful and desirable—but Nietzsche adds a few interesting twists. First, there is the idea of necessity, which recalls the aphorism on the de-deification of nature in book 3. There Nietzsche claims that the world is characterized throughout by necessity or chaos, the latter idea signifying not "lack of necessity" but a "lack of order, arrangement, form, beauty, wisdom, and whatever other names there are for aesthetic anthropomorphisms" (GS 109). The necessity that characterizes the world is not in and of itself beautiful (see also GS 299), therefore Nietzsche wants to *learn* to see it as beautiful. As he puts it later in book 4, seeing something as beautiful and loving it does not happen naturally; it, too, "has to be learned" (GS 334). But why learn to see as beautiful what is necessary in things? Nietzsche answers, so that he can become "one of those who make things beautiful." It is only by accepting and affirming the necessity of things, which is to say their ultimate purposelessness, that we can begin to make them beautiful through our own creative activity. The link between necessity (or chaos) and creativity that is introduced in this aphorism will run through book 4.[39]

Before following the theme of the free-spirited quest for knowledge in the rest of book 4, let me pause to note the echoes of some of Nietzsche's philosophical heroes in this aphorism. The first is Spinoza, whom we have already considered in relation to Nietzsche's understanding of the universe in terms of immanent necessity. As we saw there, though, Nietzsche's understanding of immanent necessity in terms of chaos differs radically from Spinoza's understanding of it in terms of rational intelligibility. The same difference undergirds their respective notions of *amor fati* and *amor intellectualis Dei*. For Spinoza, the latter is a love of the order that inheres in nature insofar as it is governed by universal and rational laws. For Nietzsche, on the other hand, *amor fati* is a love of that necessity that is indistinguishable from chaos and that serves as the presupposition for radical creativity. Not fatalistic contemplation of order but aggressive creation of order lies at the bottom of Nietzsche's notion of *amor fati*.

The other echo that sounds in this aphorism on *amor fati* is that of Emerson. Emerson, of course, wrote an essay entitled "Fate," and Nietzsche was very familiar with it.[40] Interestingly, Emerson refers to "beautiful necessity" in that essay. This theme is echoed in the quote from Emerson's essay on "History" that Nietzsche chose for the epigraph to the original edition of *The Gay Science*: "To the poet and sage, all things are friendly and hallowed, all experiences profitable, all days holy, all men divine."[41] Nietzsche jotted down a more faithful rendering of this quote in his notes from February and March 1882 (*KSA* 9:18 [5])—at the very time he was writing book 4—and in general, his notes from this period show a deep engagement with Emerson. A notebook from the beginning of 1882, for example, contains many excerpts from Emerson's *Essays* (*KSA* 9:17). And a note from the fall of 1881 reads: "Emerson: Never have I felt so much at home in a book, and in my own home—I am not permitted to praise it because it stands so close to me" (*KSA* 9:12 [68]).[42]

To return to the ideal of the free-spirited quest for knowledge, nowhere is this ideal evoked more emphatically than in the aphorism entitled "In Media Vita" (the Latin phrase used in the letter to Overbeck referred to above). The aphorism begins with another personal affirmation of life—the life of the knower—in the spirit of *amor fati*: "No, life has not disappointed me. On the contrary, I find it truer, more desirable and mysterious every year— ever since the day the great liberator came to me: the idea that life could be an experiment [*Experiment*] for the seeker for knowledge." As he has elsewhere in *The Gay Science*, Nietzsche points to the experimental character of the free spirit's knowledge (see *GS* 7, 110; also 319). Relatedly, he celebrates the quest for knowledge, not because it is *sine ira et studio*, but because it is a "world of dangers and victories in which heroic feelings, too, find a place to dance and play." And he connects this heroic dimension of the quest for knowledge with the overarching theme of "gay science": "'*Life as a means to knowledge*'—with this principle in one's heart one can live not only boldly but even gaily [*fröhlich*] and laugh gaily, too" (*GS* 324).

Nietzsche develops this idea of the heroic quest for knowledge in one of the most famous aphorisms of book 4, "Preparatory Human Beings," in which he declares that he welcomes "all signs that a more virile, warlike age is about to begin," an "age that will carry heroism into the search for knowledge and that will *wage wars* for the sake of ideas and their consequences." This aphorism contains the oft-quoted passage in which Nietzsche exhorts his fellow seekers after knowledge to "*live dangerously*! Build your cities on the slopes of Vesuvius! Send your ships into uncharted seas!" What is perhaps most interesting about this aphorism is that Nietzsche envisages the present age in which the free spirit lives at war with his contemporaries, isolated, alienated, and alone, as preparatory to a future age in which "the search for knowledge will reach out for its due; it will want to *rule* and *possess*, and you with it!" (*GS* 283). It is not entirely clear what he has in mind here, but the suggestion seems to be that the free spirit is preparatory to some higher type of human being who will not merely wage war against the age but rule over it. It is a suggestion that points toward Nietzsche's later reflections on the *Übermensch* and the new philosophers.

Nietzsche brings out the role of heroic feelings in the quest for knowledge in a variety of ways in book 4. For example, he argues that science would never have developed as it did if magicians, alchemists, astrologers, and witches had not first created "a thirst, a hunger, a taste for *hidden* and *forbidden* powers" (*GS* 300).[43] He even suggests that there is a lesson for preachers of morals in this. Instead of appealing to the masses by speaking of the advantages to be derived from morality, these preachers should try denying morals and thereby "withdraw the mob's easy acclaim from them as well as their easy currency." They should make morals "once again concealed secrets of solitary souls; say *that morality is something forbidden. That way* [they] might win over for these things the kind of people who alone matter: I mean those who are *heroic*" (*GS* 292). Science is only for the few who can endure the virility of its air and the "severity of its service" (*GS* 293). And yet, for all its severity, scientific thinking is not ponderously serious but involves laughter and gaiety (*GS* 327).

All of these aphorisms underline the point that Nietzsche first made in *Daybreak* (see *D* 432) that knowledge is not a matter of dispassionate or disinterested inquiry but, rather, is intimately bound up with desire and all the other affects that motivate human behavior. His notes from the period of *The Gay Science* are full of observations on this point. In one, he writes: "To seek 'truth for its own sake'—superficial. We want not to be deceived, it insults our pride" (*KSA* 9:11 [66]). In another, he states that science does not involve the silencing of the will: "In truth all our drives are active" (*KSA* 9:11 [119]). In book 4, he makes this point by taking issue with Spinoza's claim that knowing is independent of the affects—independent of laughing, lamenting, and detesting.[44] In fact, knowing involves all three of these instincts, each struggling with the others to impose its one-sided interpretation of a thing or event. This struggle goes on for the most part beneath the level of consciousness. It is only the final reconciliation between the warring instincts that rises to consciousness, and this is what gives us the misimpression that knowledge is something calm, impersonal, and essentially opposed to the instincts (*GS* 333; see also 307).

Nietzsche further undermines the identification of knowing with calm, rest, and tranquility when he evokes the restless striving that belongs to it. In one aphorism he has the familiar figure of the free-spirited "wanderer" complain: "This penchant and passion for what is true, real, non-apparent, certain—how it aggravates me! Why does this gloomy and restless fellow keep following and driving *me*? I want to rest, but he will not allow it" (*GS* 309). The same restlessness and endless striving is evoked in the aphorism following this one, "Will and Wave," albeit with a more joyful, less exasperated, affect. Here Nietzsche compares willing to the activity of ever-questing, never-disappointed waves crashing upon the beach (*GS* 310). Though he speaks of willing instead of knowing, the context in which this aphorism appears, as well as the way in which willing is described in it, makes it difficult to imagine that he does not also have the activity of knowing in mind. Indeed, like many of the other aphorisms in book 4, this one seems to suggest the identity of willing and knowing.

In addition to restlessness, these aphorisms also highlight the pathos of knowledge, the fact that the passion for knowledge drives us rather than the other way around. This is especially clear in the aphorism about the exasperated wanderer. But pathos runs through book 4. Nietzsche speaks of it explicitly in a beautiful aphorism called "Looking Back," in which he observes that the "true pathos of every period of our life rarely becomes clear to us as long as we live in this period" (GS 317). Pathos is also present in his discussion of "brief habits," which he considers to be "inestimable means for getting to know *many* things and states." In every brief habit there is the faith in eternity that belongs to all passion, but "one day its time is up; the good thing parts from me, not as something that has come to nauseate me but peacefully and sated with me as I am with it" (GS 295). Pathos is even evident in the aphorism entitled "Star Friendship," which is generally taken to be a commentary on Nietzsche's friendship with Wagner. He speaks of breaking off with his friend when the "almighty force of our tasks drove us apart again into different seas and sunny zones. . . . That we have to become estranged is the law *above* us" (GS 279).

Though the passion and pathos of knowledge is characterized by a certain restlessness and striving, this is to be sharply distinguished from the frenetic busyness that Nietzsche associates primarily with Americans, whose "breathless haste" with respect to work "is already beginning to infect old Europe with its ferocity and spreading spiritlessness like a blanket. Even now one is ashamed of resting, and prolonged reflection almost gives people a bad conscience" (GS 329; see also 6). As in his other writings from the middle period, Nietzsche remains here an implacable foe of the "age of work" (WS 170) and a defender of the contemplative ideal. In an aphorism entitled "Architecture for the Search for Knowledge," he complains that what "is lacking in our big cities" are "quiet and wide, expansive places for reflection." Churches can no longer fulfill this function for the *vita contemplativa* of the free spirit; the language they speak is "far too rhetorical and unfree": "[W]e who are godless could not think *our thoughts* in such surroundings. We wish to see *ourselves* translated into stones and plants, we want to take walks in *ourselves* when we stroll around these buildings and gardens" (GS 280).

As this quote makes clear, the object of contemplation for Nietzsche is humanity, not God. But the other wrinkle he goes on to add to his contemplative ideal is that this object is not merely passively received by the contemplative thinker but actively created by him. "What distinguishes the higher human beings from the lower," he writes, echoing a similar comment he made on the order of rank in the aphorism on the intellectual conscience (GS 2), "is that the former see and hear immeasurably more, and see and hear more thoughtfully. . . . For anyone who grows up into the heights of humanity the world becomes ever fuller; ever more fishhooks are cast in his direction to capture his interest." The contemplative human being, however, fails to appreciate the creative aspect of his activity: "[H]e fancies he is a *spectator* and *listener* who has been placed before the great visual and acoustic spectacle that is life," when in fact he is "the poet who keeps creating this life." It is the contemplative thinker who continually fashions "something that had not been there before: the whole eternally growing world of valuations, colors, accents, perspectives, scales, affirmations, and negations." These values do not inhere in nature, for "nature is always valueless. . . . Only we have created the world *that concerns man*" (GS 301).

This is perhaps Nietzsche's clearest rejection of the spectator-view of contemplation that he originally found in Schopenhauer's philosophy and continued to pay homage to in *Human, All too Human*. In *Daybreak*, he began to emancipate himself from this spectator-view, especially in the aphorism on the "Colorblindness of Thinkers," where he claims that "every thinker paints his world in fewer colors than *are actually there*" and in doing so introduces harmonies into things themselves that "can constitute an enrichment of nature" (D 426). But it is here, in *The Gay Science*, that he elicits the creative aspect of contemplation most clearly. Gone is any reference to "things themselves" which our concepts falsify; and the emphasis now falls not on painting the chaotic and valueless world of sensations in "fewer colors than *are actually there*" but on continually fashioning out of it "something that had not been there before."

Nietzsche draws an interesting implication from this understanding of the creativity that lies behind contemplation: namely, that contemplative life has a certain primacy over practical life; that the latter is merely derivative of the truly creative activity of the former. It will be remembered that he drew a similar conclusion in *Daybreak*, arguing that thinkers "determine the *palatableness* of things," which practical people then adopt and act upon (D 505). In *The Gay Science*, he expresses it this way: the poem that is invented by contemplative human beings "is continually studied by the so-called practical human beings (our actors) who learn their roles and translate everything into flesh and actuality" (*GS* 301). Here the knowing activity of the free spirit merges quietly with the creative and legislative activity that Nietzsche will later ascribe to the "new philosopher."[45] In *The Gay Science*, the distinction between these two figures is not yet clearly drawn.

In his discussion of the creative character of contemplation, Nietzsche also points out that the contemplative human being "always becomes at the same time happier and unhappier" (*GS* 301). He made this point earlier with respect to science (*GS* 12), and he now goes on to elaborate on it in several aphorisms that deal with the risks and dangers that accompany the highest happiness. In one, he evokes the happiness of one who has "refined senses" for the "most exquisite things of the spirit" and who is "impelled by the longing for undiscovered worlds and seas, people and gods." But the flip side of this highest, "Homeric happiness" is that one also becomes "more capable of suffering than any creature under the sun" and "ever more refined in pain" (*GS* 302). One way to avoid such suffering is the way of the Stoic, who "trains himself to swallow stones and worms, slivers of glass and scorpions without nausea." But in doing so, he becomes indifferent to the most refined and spiritual pleasures as well. For this reason, Nietzsche opts for the "irritable, intellectual constitution" of the Epicurean over the "hard hedgehog skin" of the Stoic (*GS* 306; see also 326).

Linked to these reflections on happiness are others that question the value of moralities that preach self-denial and self-control. Like Stoicism, these moralities assume a defensive posture in the face of the accidents of nature. They condemn all instincts and inclinations as evil, and as a result the individual experiences a "constant irritability in the face of all natural stirrings and inclinations" and becomes incapable of entrusting himself to "any instinct or free wingbeat." In this way, the individual becomes "cut off from the most beautiful fortuities of his soul" and, most importantly, deprives himself of the opportunity of learning anything new; for "one must be able to lose oneself occasionally if one wants to learn something from things different from oneself" (*GS* 305; see also 294, 303). For all of these reasons, Nietzsche insists that he does not like "negative virtues" (304).

But he does not preach a mere "letting go" with respect to one's natural instincts and inclinations either. Instead, he argues that he we should arrange them as artists do the elements of a landscape or gardeners their plants and flowers. Here he returns to the theme of the aesthetic self that he began to explore in *Daybreak* (see *D* 218, 560). Indeed, here he gives this theme its most famous expression in the aphorism that begins, "To 'give style' to one's character—a great and rare art!" It is not a matter of denying our instincts or inclinations but of fitting them into an "artistic plan"—adding

emphasis here, obscuring in shadow there, moving one thing into the foreground while viewing another from a distance. Strong characters find delight in a highly stylized nature, while weaker ones prefer a freer, wilder,
more disorderly nature, but the key is that they all give pleasure to themselves. "For one thing is needful," Nietzsche asserts: "that a human being
should *attain* satisfaction with himself, whether it be by means of this or
that poetry or art" (*GS* 290; see also 78, 299).

It is in the context of the aesthetic management of the self that several
of the aphorisms devoted to pain and suffering should be viewed. Pain
serves as a helpful signal of how strong or weak we are. We are not always
strong, and when we are not, we should take in our sails in the same way
the sailor does when a storm approaches. In what may seem like unchar-
acteristic modesty and prudence, Nietzsche comments that we "must learn
to live with diminished energies, too." But he does not sound this prudent
note for long. He points out that there are other sorts of people—the heroic types—"who hear precisely the opposite command when great pain
approaches." For them such pain serves as a tonic, not as a signal to lower
the sails. These are the "great *pain bringers* of humanity," and they too "contribute immensely to the preservation and enhancement of the species" (*GS*
318; see also 312, 314, 325).

Nietzsche endorses both the prudent submission to pain and the heroic
embracing of it, but he condemns the manipulative exaggeration of pain by
preachers of morals. These latter "try to con men into believing that they
are in a very bad way and need some ultimate, hard, radical cure." Such
cures include Schopenhauer's denial of the will to live and, once again,
Stoic "petrification." Nietzsche insists, however, that we need not resort to
such radical measures. There exist "innumerable palliatives against pain"
that fall far short of self-annihilation: "We know quite well how to drip
sweetnesses upon our bitternesses, especially the bitternesses of the soul . . .
a loss is a loss for barely one hour" (*GS* 326). In this connection, we should
recall Nietzsche's prescription against ennui and melancholy in *Daybreak*:
"plenty of sleep" (*D* 376). It is in reaction to the manipulative exaggeration of pain and suffering by Schopenhauer and other preachers of morals
that Nietzsche declares, in his meditation on the oblivious chatter of "life-
thirsty people" prior to the departure of an emigrants' ship, that it makes
him "happy that men do not want at all to think the thought of death!"
(*GS* 278) and that, like Raphael, he never wants to "paint another image of
torture" (*GS* 313).

The reflections on happiness and aesthetic self-fashioning that we have
been following grew out of Nietzsche's original concern with the happiness

of the contemplative life of the free-spirited knower. They constitute what Nietzsche referred to as his "private morality, as the sum of my conditions for existence, which only prescribe an ought in the event I *want* myself" (*SB* 6:247), and what I have referred to as the "ethics of a free spirit." In many ways, this aspect of Nietzsche's argument reaches its dramatic climax in the aphorism "Long Live Physics!" In this critical aphorism, the link between knowledge of necessity and self-creation that was hinted at in the first aphorism of book 4 is fully explained. "Physics" here, of course, does not refer to knowledge of the mechanics of the physical universe but to knowledge of the complex mechanism of the self.[46] This knowledge, self-knowledge, is the most elusive of all: "Each is farthest from himself," Nietzsche comments, using a phrase that he will repeat again in the Preface to the *Genealogy of Morals* (*GM* Preface 1). And yet it is precisely on the subject of self-knowledge that everyone considers himself to be most expert (*GS* 335).

The object of Nietzsche's attack in "Long Live Physics!" is the unquestioning faith people have in the truth of their moral judgments about what is right and wrong. The denial of precisely this faith—the demonstration that our moral judgments are based on errors—was always the central thrust of Nietzsche's critique of morality in the middle period, as the crucial aphorism on "two kinds of deniers of morality" in *Daybreak* made clear (*D* 103). In "Long Live Physics!" he excoriates those who appeal to their conscience as an infallible basis for their moral judgments. This moral conscience itself needs to made a matter of conscience, of "intellectual conscience." It is not some God-given voice of nature but has a "pre-history in your instincts, likes, dislikes, experiences, and lack of experiences. '*How* did it originate there?' you must ask, and then also: 'What is it that impels me to listen to it?'" Nietzsche goes on to list a variety of weaknesses and stupidities that might impel one to listen to one's conscience. And he shows how the firmness of one's moral judgment may have less to do with moral strength than with personal abjectness, stubbornness, and lack of imagination. The same goes for Kant's categorical imperative, which rests on selfishness insofar as it makes one's personal judgment a universal law, and on timidity insofar as it "betrays that you have not yet discovered for yourself nor created for yourself an ideal of your own, your very own" (*GS* 335; see also 5, 319).

The greatest defect of the Kantian categorical imperative—and of any morality that is based on universal laws—is that it fails to recognize that "there neither are nor can be actions that are the same; that every action that has ever been done was done in an altogether unique and irretrievable way." Nietzsche's claim here to some extent rests on his earlier analysis of how judgments of sameness and equality rest on simplifications and

falsifications of the seamless flux of reality and on crude comparisons between what is unique and incomparable (see *GS* 110–17, 120). Echoing
a point he made in *Daybreak* (*D* 116), he insists that all of our actions are
essentially unknowable and that all moral regulations about them "relate
only to their coarse exterior." He does grant that "our opinions, valuations,
and tables of what is good certainly belong among the most powerful levers
in the involved mechanism of our actions," echoing another point from
Daybreak (*D* 35, 148), but he still maintains that "in any particular case the
law of their mechanism is indemonstrable" (*GS* 335).

So what, practically, follows from this knowledge of our unavoidable
ignorance about the complex mechanism of our actions? Having acknowledged the important role of our opinions and valuations, it is not surprising that he recommends that we "*limit* ourselves to the purification of our
opinions and valuations and to the *creation of our own new tables of what is
good*." What exactly does this mean? In *Daybreak*, the purification of our
opinions and valuations consisted mainly in the exposure of the intellectual
error involved in altruism, thus depriving egoistic actions of their bad conscience (see *D* 148). In "Long Live Physics," insight into the unknowability
and uniqueness of actions leads to the overturning of the identification of
moral value with universality. As Nietzsche points out: "Sitting in moral
judgment should offend our taste" (*GS* 335). This evacuation of moral judgment opens the door to the task of creating "our own new tables of what is
good." Nietzsche gives us some idea of what this sort of creation involves
when he calls on "new philosophers" to provide every individual with an
"overall philosophical justification of his way of living and thinking" that
serves as "a sun that shines especially for him and bestows warmth, bless-
ing, and fertility on him" (*GS* 289; see also 120).

The conclusion to "Long Live Physics" contains a powerful statement of
the importance of knowledge to the project of self-creation:

> We . . . *want to become those we are*—human beings who are new, unique,
> incomparable, who give themselves laws, who create themselves. To that end
> we must become the best learners and discoverers of everything that is lawful
> and necessary in the world: we must become *physicists* in order to become *cre-
> ators* in this sense—while hitherto all valuations and ideals have been based
> on *ignorance* of physics or were constructed so as to *contradict* it. (*GS* 335)

Peter Berkowitz quotes this passage in support of his claim that Nietzsche
holds that "right making is based on right knowing,"[47] but we must be careful to distinguish in exactly what way this is so. Knowledge alone cannot

provide goals for action—Nietzsche's notes make this clear. "Can science provide goals?" he asks in one, and he answers "No": "our drives form according to our ideal and with the help of science," but it is "as artists" that we "create our ideal" (*KSA* 9:8 [2]). In another note, he writes: "Science has many uses . . . [but] it cannot be entrusted to know the way; rather, only if one knows whither? can it be of use" (*KSA* 9:8 [98]). Scientific knowledge can, however, be enormously helpful in uncovering the errors upon which our valuations and ideals have hitherto been based—the errors of altruism, free will, and universality—and thereby clear the way for us to create our own ideals and become the people we are. Most important of all, though, the de-deified necessity disclosed by "physics" makes clear that knowledge alone will never be enough to enable us to become those we are; we must creatively fashion something out of this formless chaos. The self we become is ultimately made not found. To bring it back to the aphorism on *amor fati* with which we began this section, necessity serves here not as model for imitation but as the ground for radical self-creation.

The Heaviest Weight

The aphorism following "Long Live Physics!" is entitled "Nature's Stinginess." It is a short aphorism and does not seem to have much to do with the aphorisms that precede it. Echoing Aristotle's complaint that nature fails to neatly distinguish masters from slaves by giving them different body types,[48] Nietzsche asks why "nature has been so stingy with human beings that it did not allow them to shine—one more, one less, each according to the plenitude of his own light." Such a visible distinction between higher and lower human beings would make life on earth infinitely less ambiguous (*GS* 336). The very strangeness of this aphorism, at least with respect to what has gone before, alerts us that something new is about to enter the picture. Nietzsche complains about the lack of a principle in nature that would unambiguously establish an order of rank among human beings. The idea of the eternal recurrence, introduced five aphorisms later, provides just such a principle.

In the next aphorism, "The 'Humanness' of the Future," Nietzsche takes up the "historical sense," which he calls present-day humanity's "distinctive virtue and disease." Like the previous one, it is not immediately clear why this aphorism is placed here or what it has to do with the lead-up to the eternal recurrence. If we look back at the note in which Nietzsche records his discovery of the eternal recurrence, however, we seem to get a clue. There he writes: "The new *heavy weight: the eternal return of the same.* Infinite importance of our knowing, erring, our habits, ways of living for all that is to come" (*KSA* 9:11 [141]). Our historic knowing, errors, habits, and perspectives are not simply to be sloughed off; they constitute our "accumulated treasure," as Nietzsche put it as far back as *Human, All too Human*, and it is on this accumulated treasure that the "value of our humanity depends" (*HH* 16). He makes a similar point in *Zarathustra*—significantly, in the chapter "On Old and New Tablets" that immediately precedes Zarathustra's acceptance of the eternal recurrence. There Zarathustra laments how the past is reduced by the rabble to the immediate needs and pleasure of the present. To counteract this shallow presentism of the rabble, Zarathustra calls for a "new nobility" to preserve the past (*Z* 3.12:11).

With these hints as to its relevance to the eternal recurrence, let us return to Nietzsche's discussion of the historical sense in *The Gay Science*. The disease of historical consciousness he of course brilliantly anatomized in "The Uses and Disadvantages of History for Life," and here he repeats that this sense can be a sign of "stealthily approaching old age," full of grief and melancholy and nostalgia for one's lost youth. But he also holds out the possibility—seemingly informed by his rereading of Emerson[49]—that the historical sense can provide us with a tremendous sense of continuity with the past that inspires both gratitude and a sense of obligation: here the individual becomes "a person whose horizon encompasses thousands of years past and future, being the heir of all the nobility of all past spirit—an heir with a sense of obligation, the most aristocratic of old nobles and at the same time the first of a new nobility—the like of which no age has yet seen or dreamed of." The reference to a "new nobility" here not only anticipates *Zarathustra* but is echoed in Nietzsche's notebooks, where he speaks of the historical sense as providing us with our "noble family tree, our heraldry" (*KSA* 9:12 [76]; see also 15 [70]). In the conclusion of the aphorism, Nietzsche speaks of a happiness resulting from the historical sense that is both godlike and radically humanistic, using another image that will reappear in "On Old and New Tablets": "the happiness of a god full of power and love, full of tears and laughter, a happiness that, like the sun in the evening, continually bestows its inexhaustible riches, pouring them into the sea, feeling richest, as the sun does, only when even the poorest fisherman is still rowing with golden oars! This godlike feeling would then be called—humanness [*Menschlichkeit*]" (*GS* 337; cf. *Z* 3.12:3).[50]

The aphorism following the one on the historical sense is devoted to pity, and it, too, does not initially seem to have much to do with the idea of the eternal recurrence whose announcement is imminent. Once again, though, the critical note from August 1881 provides a clue. After stating that the past *"will* and must repeat itself eternally,"* Nietzsche writes there: "If we are not to be overwhelmed by [this idea], our pity must not be great. Indifference needs to have worked away deep inside us, and enjoyment in contemplation, too. Even the misery of future humanity must *not* concern us" (*KSA* 9:11 [141]). Pity is incompatible with the idea of the eternal recurrence because it increases the amount of suffering in the world (see *D* 134) and thereby makes the idea even more unbearable than it would otherwise be. And why the remark about the misery of future humanity? Though Nietzsche does not really explain, the suggestion seems to be that, because the idea of the eternal recurrence itself will inevitably increase the misery of a substantial portion of humanity in the future, the call upon our pity, and therefore also the danger posed by it, will also increase.

Turning back now to the aphorism on pity in *The Gay Science*, we find Nietzsche raising two questions about it: Is it good for the one who pities? And is it good for the one who is pitied? With respect to the second question, he points out that pity "strips away from the suffering of others whatever is distinctively personal"; it devalues the struggles, risks, and distress that make any individual's life meaningful. It is the first question, though, that seems to interest him most and partially accounts for the strategic placement of this aphorism at the end of book 4. It is as if, before leaving the subject of the free spirit, he needs to consider for one last time the distinctive danger of this figure, the danger that threatens to divert him from his distinctive task. "How is it at all possible to keep to one's own way?" Nietzsche asks, and he goes on to argue that pity provides the great excuse in our age to lose one's way and dodge one's goal. Interestingly, he says war does the same, offering individuals a "detour to suicide . . . with a good conscience." He concludes the aphorism with another statement of his personal morality, the ethics of a free spirit: "Live in seclusion so that you *can* live for yourself. Live in *ignorance* about what seems most important to your age. Between yourself and today lay the skin of at least three centuries." And with respect to your true friends, *"share not suffering but joy* [*Mitfreude*]" (*GS* 338; see also 56).[51]

While the preceding three aphorisms take up considerations that in one way or another bear on the idea of the eternal recurrence, it is only with the one called "Vita Femina" that we unmistakably enter the shrouded precincts of this idea. Nietzsche seems to be casting a glance back at the whole of *The Gay Science* as he writes: "For seeing the ultimate beauties of a work, no knowledge or good will is sufficient; this requires the rarest of luckiest accidents." Not only that, but the unveiling of these beauties "must have been accomplished by our own soul because it needed some external expression and parable"; and "what does unveil itself for us, *unveils itself for us once only"* (*GS* 339). Is Nietzsche talking about the course of the argument of *The Gay Science* so far? Or is he about to unveil something new and important? Without discounting the former alternative, we certainly know the latter to be true. In the letter to Overbeck from which I have quoted already, Nietzsche intimated that he had crossed a tropic in book 4 (*SB* 6:255). If it were possible to locate the exact point of crossing, this would be it.

Nietzsche prefaces his announcement of the eternal recurrence with an aphorism devoted to "The Dying Socrates." This is a theme that he had treated in his very first book, *The Birth of Tragedy* (*BT* 13, 15). But whereas in that first book the dying Socrates epitomized the theoretical optimism that killed Greek tragedy, here it epitomizes the theoretical pessimism against which Nietzsche's entire philosophy, and especially the idea of the eternal recurrence, is directed. Socrates last words about sacrificing a rooster to Asclepius suggest that he regarded life as a disease from which we needed to be cured. Was Socrates a pessimist? Did he suffer life? Did he ultimately seek revenge on life? These are the questions that Socrates enigmatic last words evoke in Nietzsche. By highlighting Socrates in this strategically important aphorism, Nietzsche makes clear that the pessimistic outlook against which he is reacting goes back even further than Christianity—Christianity is merely "Platonism for 'the people'" (*BGE* Preface).[52] Ever since *The Birth of Tragedy*, Nietzsche regarded Socrates as the "one turning point and vortex of so-called world history" (*BT* 15), the single most important influence on the Western philosophical tradition. Insofar as Nietzsche hopes to overturn that tradition and the pessimistic outlook on life that is inherent in it, he must overcome Socrates: "Alas, my friends, we must overcome even the Greeks!" (*GS* 340).

The stage is now set for the climactic aphorism that introduces the idea of the eternal recurrence. One of the most interesting and oft-commented upon features of this aphorism is that it presents the idea of the eternal recurrence as a hypothetical:

> What if some day or night a demon were to steal after you into your loneliest loneliness and say to you: "This life as you now live it and have lived it, you will have to live once more and innumerable times more; and there will be nothing new in it, but every pain and every joy and every thought and sigh and everything unutterably small or great in your life will have to return to you, all in the same succession and sequence—even this spider and this moonlight between the trees, and even this moment and I myself. The eternal hourglass of existence is turned upside down again and again, and you with it, speck of dust!" (*GS* 341)

Many interpreters cite this passage as evidence that Nietzsche regarded the eternal recurrence as merely a hypothetical thought experiment, not as a scientific or metaphysical theory about the nature of the universe.[53] But the notes from this period (and not merely from the later *Will to Power*) suggest otherwise. In the note recording his original discovery of the eternal recurrence, for example, he states clearly that "this piece of human history *will* and must repeat itself eternally; we can leave *that* out of account, we have no influence over it" (*KSA* 9:[141]). The only real question is the extent to which we can "incorporate" this deadly truth. And in several other notes—which appear in the context of his reflections on the nonanthropomorphic, nonteleological, necessary, mechanistic, and chaotic character of the universe—he lays out his scientific proof of the eternal recurrence, arguing that the amount of force in the universe is limited, as are the "number of positions, alterations, combinations, and developments of this force," and yet time is infinite; consequently, "all possible developments must already have been" and will recur infinitely in the future (*KSA* 9:11 [202]; see also 11 [148]; cf. *WP* 1066).[54]

Though the preponderance of recent scholarship argues otherwise, it seems hard to deny that Nietzsche originally thought of the eternal recurrence as some sort of propositional truth about the nature of the universe. Nevertheless, this is not what made him so excited on that day in August 1881when he first beheld the idea. Rather, it was the potential practical effects of the idea that fired his imagination. This is clear from the way in which the relevant aphorism in *The Gay Science* develops: "If this thought [of the eternal recurrence] gained possession of you, it would change you as you are or perhaps crush you. The question in each and every thing, 'Do you desire this once more and innumerable times more?' would lie upon your actions as the greatest weight" (*GS* 341). The echo here of the title of the aphorism, "The Greatest Weight" (*Das grösste Schwergewicht*), underlines that the practical, transformational effect of the idea of the eternal recurrence is the crucial point for Nietzsche. Again, the notes offer confirmatory evidence: "If you incorporate the thought of thoughts within yourself, it will change you. The question in everything that you want to do: 'is it the case that I want to do it countless times?' is the *greatest* weight" (*KSA* 9:11 [143]).

The emphasis on heaviness or gravity here is, of course, in sharp contrast to the lightness and gaiety that characterizes the rest of *The Gay Science*. This is one of the reasons for seeing the idea of the eternal recurrence as belonging more to Nietzsche's project in *Zarathustra* than to his *Freigeisterei*. The contrast between the heaviness of the idea of the eternal recurrence and the lightness of the free-spirited quest for knowledge is especially pronounced in Nietzsche's initial note on the former idea. In the outline of the five stages of incorporation there, the stage corresponding to *The Gay Science*—the stage of the "innocent man," the "individual as experiment," and the "philosophy of indifference"—involves the adoption of "a child's attitude towards what used to constitute the seriousness of existence"; here life takes on the aspect of a *"children's game* under the gaze of the wise man." The transition to the stage of the eternal recurrence of the same is sudden and sharp: "But now comes the heaviest (*schwerste*) knowledge, one which prompts the terrible reconsideration of all forms of life" (*KSA* 9:11 [141]). One is reminded of the dialectic of comedy and tragedy in the very first aphorism of *The Gay Science*, and only now can one fully appreciate the exquisite ambiguity of the inference Nietzsche draws from it: "Do you understand this new law of ebb and flood? There is a time for us, too!" (*GS* 1).

But why is heaviness or gravity needed? Why is the lightness of the free spirit not sufficient? The answer lies in the problem of nihilism that Nietzsche dramatically evoked in the aphorism on the madman and the death of God. The problem of nihilism, as we saw there, is the problem of weightlessness.[55] The death of the Christian God leads to the departure of gravity from things (*KSA* 11:34 [5]), the loss of the "center of gravity by which we have lived" for two thousand years (*KSA* 12:11 [148]). In the absence of God and an eternal background, our actions no longer have any weight or significance. Nothing matters except the fleeting happiness of the individual. There is no reason to defer momentary pleasure or make sacrifices for the future. In his notes, Nietzsche refers to this as the problem of "secularization" (*Verweltlichung*), which entails "belief in the *world* and a deliberate ignoring of the 'beyond' and the 'afterworld.' Its goal is the well-being of the **fleeting** individual: which is why its fruit is socialism, i.e. *fleeting* **individuals** want to conquer happiness through socialization—they have no reason to *wait*, as do human beings with eternal souls and eternal becoming and future improvement" (*KSA* 9:11 [163]). This diagnosis of the problem of modern culture goes all the way back to *The Birth of Tragedy*, where Nietzsche maintains that "when a people begins to comprehend itself historically" and becomes "secularized," it is no longer able to find rest from "the burden and greed of the moment. Any people—just as, incidentally, also any individual—is worth only so much as it is able to press upon its experiences the stamp of the eternal; for thus it is, as it were, desecularized" (*BT* 23).[56]

As we saw in our analysis of the aphorism on the madman, the free spirit remains largely immune to the terrifying, nihilistic implications of the death of God; for him this event signifies the cheerful prospect of open seas that invite the daring of the lover of knowledge. For this reason, the free spirit does not really address the problem of nihilism or secularization in a completely satisfying way. Something more is needed, a new gravity, and this is what the doctrine of the eternal recurrence aims to provide. In his note on secularization and the absence of an eternal horizon, Nietzsche continues:

> My doctrine says: the task is to live your life in *such* a way that you have to *want* to live again—you will *in any case*! If striving gives you the highest feeling, then strive; if rest gives you the highest feeling, then rest; if fitting in, following, obedience give you the highest feeling, then obey. Only **make sure** *you become aware of* **what** gives you the highest feeling and then stop at *nothing*! *Eternity* is at stake! (*KSA* 9:11 [163])[57]

The phrase "you will in any case" in this passage once again suggests that Nietzsche regards the eternal recurrence as a descriptive fact about the world. It also raises in a pointed way the issue of fatalism in Nietzsche's doctrine of the eternal recurrence. What difference does the imperative to live your life in certain way make if you will live the very same life "in any case"? Martin Heidegger puts this question in an especially illuminating way: "[I]f everything recurs as it once was, then all thinking and planning become superfluous . . . we must take everything as it comes; and all is indifferent. Instead of providing us with a burden, the thought deprives us of the ballast and the steadying weight of all decision and action. . . . It ends by causing us to founder in sheer inaction—we let it all slide."[58] Heidegger goes on to show that Nietzsche's doctrine of the eternal recurrence does not lead to such indifference and fatalism. We cannot know what once was in a previous cycle; we always experience things as if for the first time. Therefore, that which was and recurs again is paradoxically "whatever will be in the next moment. If you allow your existence to drift in timorousness and ignorance, with all the consequences these things have, they will come again, and they will be that which already was. And if on the contrary you shape something supreme out of the next moment . . . then this moment will come again and will have been what already was."[59] We are reminded of Nietzsche's reflection on "Turkish Fatalism" in *The Wanderer and His Shadow*. Fate is not something separate from our response to it; the choice to resist or resign oneself to it is itself a part of fate (*WS* 61). As Emerson put it in an essay Nietzsche read as a youth: "[I]f Fate is so prevailing, man is also a part of it, and can confront fate with fate."[60]

Of course, the eternal recurrence does not just affect individual actions;

it also favors (or disfavors) certain ways of life and systems of valuation. Nietzsche points out that the eternal recurrence "would be horrible if we still believed in sin. . . . If the thought of the eternal recurrence of all things is not to overpower you, then there must be no guilt." This thought only becomes bearable if we believe in the innocence of becoming and the "play of life" (*KSA* 9:11 [144]). In other words, eternal recurrence demands the revaluation of values that Nietzsche alluded to earlier in *The Gay Science* (*GS* 269; see also *KSA* 9:11 [76]). Nietzsche stresses the connection between recurrence and revaluation in a letter to Overbeck from March 1884: "If [the idea of the eternal recurrence] is *true*, or rather: if it is believed to be true—then *everything* changes and spins around, and *all* previous values are devalued" (*SB* 6:485). He makes the same point in a couple of notes from the same year: "Means of *enduring* [the idea of the eternal recurrence]: the revaluation of all values. No longer joy in certainty but in uncertainty" and "all kinds of experimentalism" (*WP* 1059–60).[61]

The revaluation of values that the idea of the eternal recurrence encourages has in many ways already been sketched in the rest of *The Gay Science*, especially book 4. It includes the reappraisal of "evil" and egoistic actions, the jettisoning of the notions of free will, responsibility, and guilt, and the construction of an aesthetic model of the self, among other things. No longer is Stoic endurance, anxious self-control, or vengeful renunciation enough; rather, we must lead our lives more artistically, more creatively, and with a view to attaining the "highest feeling." The life of the knowing, dancing, laughing free spirit seems to fulfill these requirements, and Nietzsche indicates that it proves to be well suited to enduring the idea of the eternal recurrence. Again: "If we are not to be overwhelmed by [this idea], our pity must not be great. Indifference needs to have worked away deep inside of us, and enjoyment in contemplation, too" (*KSA* 9:11 [141]). Indeed, he hints in his notes that he wanted to elaborate the sort of life that would flourish under the eternal recurrence before presenting the doctrine itself:

> We want to experience a work of art over and over again! We should fashion our life in this way, so that we have the same wish for each of its parts! This is the main idea! Only at the end will the *doctrine* be presented of the repetition of everything that has been, once the tendency has been implanted to *create* something which can *flourish* a hundred times more strongly in the sunshine of this doctrine! (*KSA* 9:11 [165])

In addition to promoting the revaluation of values, the idea of the eternal recurrence also serves as a selecting, sifting principle, elevating the healthy and the strong, eliminating the sickly and the weak. This selecting, "breeding" aspect of the eternal recurrence looms large in Nietzsche later notes, provoking some of his most notorious statements (see *WP* 55, 56, 462, 862, 1053–58); but it is also present in his earliest reflections on the eternal recurrence. Thus he refers to the possibility that the idea of the eternal recurrence might "crush you"; and he complains about "nature's stinginess" in not allowing human beings "to shine—one more, one less, each according to the plenitude of his own light" (*GS* 336). The notes from the period of *The Gay Science* are even more unambiguous. In one, Nietzsche claims that the "weaker, emptier, sicker, and more needy" human beings will "catch the new infection" caused by the doctrine of the eternal recurrence first—and presumably die as a result (*KSA* 9:11 [147]). And in another, he exults that those who are unable to bear the idea of the eternal recurrence "must ultimately *die out* in accordance with their nature," while "only those who consider their existence to be capable of eternal repetition will *remain*" (*KSA* 9:11 [338]).

It is clear that it is the practical and psychological consequences of the doctrine of the eternal recurrence that most intrigue Nietzsche. But these consequences do not follow unless the doctrine is true in some sense. If the eternal recurrence is merely a myth or a fantasy or a heuristic device, it is no longer able to act as the "heaviest weight" on our actions, to motivate us to change our lives or revalue our values, or to weed out the weak. Unfortunately, Nietzsche's attempts to scientifically prove the eternal recurrence as a cosmological theory all seem to fail.[62] It is true he argues that even the *possibility* that the doctrine is true could produce the desired results: "Even if the circle-repetition is only probable or possible, the thought of such a possibility can disturb and transform us. . . . What an effect the possibility of eternal damnation has had!" (*KSA* 9:11 [203]).[63] But this seems a bit of a stretch, especially since the possibility of the eternal recurrence seems far more remote to modern human beings than the possibility of eternal damnation was to earlier humanity. All this is not to deny that the idea of the eternal recurrence can serve as a representation or ideal of an affirmative attitude toward life and *amor fati*,[64] but Nietzsche himself seems to have had much more ambitious plans for this idea when he introduced it at the end of *The Gay Science*.

The concluding aphorism of *The Gay Science* is, of course, the opening section of *Thus Spoke Zarathustra*. This is perhaps the clearest sign that, with the introduction of the idea of the eternal recurrence, we have left the horizon of *The Gay Science* behind and entered a new dimension. This transition is also signaled by the title of the final aphorism—"Incipit Trageodia."

Zarathustra himself seems to be a somewhat different figure from the free spirit. For ten years he has lived in his cave in the mountains, perhaps as a free spirit and a practitioner of gay science, but now he declares that he is sick of his (gay) wisdom, "like a bee that has gathered too much honey; I need hands outstretched to receive it; I want to give away and distribute until the wise among men enjoy their folly once again and the poor their riches" (GS 342). This aspect of benevolence and giving that is so characteristic of Zarathustra contrasts with the somewhat self-occupied quest for knowledge of the free spirit. And as the latter remained aloof from the nihilistic consequences of the death of God, so the former now seeks to address them with his doctrine of the eternal recurrence of the same. What this new project means for our understanding of the place of the free spirit in Nietzsche's philosophy as a whole is a question that we must pursue in the next chapter.

FOUR

The Later Works:
Beyond the Free Spirit

In the summer of 1882, while making the final corrections to *The Gay Science*, Nietzsche indicated in letters to his friends that a crucial period in his philosophical career was coming to an end. To Lou Salomé he wrote at the end of June: "With this book that series of writings that began with *Human, All too Human* comes to a conclusion: in all of them taken together, 'a new image and ideal of the free spirit' has been erected. That this is not the 'free man in fact' you will have long guessed" (*SB* 6:213). In July, he wrote to Malwida von Meysenbug that *The Gay Science* "forms the conclusion of that chain of thoughts that I began to put together in Sorrento. . . . My life now belongs to a higher goal and I do nothing that is not of benefit to it" (*SB* 6:223). Several months later, he repeats to Lou that he no longer regards the free spirit as his ultimate ideal: "Look through this phase in which I have lived for several years—look beyond it! Do not deceive yourself about me—surely you do not think that the 'free spirit' is my ideal!" (*SB* 6:282). And several months after that, having just completed the first part of *Zarathustra*, he writes to Carl von Gersdorff: "I have a long, difficult period of asceticism of the spirit behind me. . . . The past six years have been in *this* respect the years of my greatest self-overcoming. . . . Enough—I have risen also *above* this stage of my life—and what remains . . . must now give complete and full expression to that for which I have endured life at all" (*SB* 6:386).

Nietzsche no doubt simplifies his philosophical development here, ex-aggerating the break between his free-spirit writings and the emerging out-look of his later works. *The Gay Science*, for example, as my analysis in the previous chapter showed, can hardly be said to be animated by an "asceti-cism of the spirit"; the title alone suggests a very different spirit. As we will see in this chapter, Nietzsche offers a more nuanced picture of his free-spirit ideal in several of his later writings, in particular *Beyond Good and Evil*, book

5 of *The Gay Science*, and the 1886 prefaces to his middle works—so much so that it sometimes seems that this ideal blends seamlessly into the higher ideal he refers to above.

Nuances aside, however, Nietzsche's comments to his friends do point to a fundamental shift in his thinking. At the heart of this shift and marking the boundary between the "asceticism of the spirit" of the free-spirit writings and the "higher goal" of the later ones is the idea of the eternal recurrence. This idea came to him, as we know, just as he was beginning to write *The Gay Science*, but he did not use that book to develop it. While he introduces the idea of the eternal recurrence for the first time in the penultimate aphorism of *The Gay Science*, he quickly follows it with a final aphorism that contains the opening of *Zarathustra*, thus indicating that it is to this latter book that the development of the idea will belong. That, indeed, is what *Zarathustra* exists for: "The fundamental conception of this work [is] the idea of the eternal recurrence" (*EH* 3.Z.1).

It is not only the idea of the eternal recurrence, however, that distinguishes *Zarathustra* from Nietzsche's earlier writings. The book also introduces the new ideal of the *Übermensch* and the notion of the will to power. It is true that the latter notion is not altogether new to Nietzsche's outlook; we have seen him talk about power, and especially the feeling of power, throughout the middle works. But it is only in *Zarathustra* that the will to power begins to take on a more systematic philosophical meaning. Eternal recurrence, the *Übermensch*, and the will to power—these are the great, and portentous, themes of Nietzsche's later philosophy, to which he will add the new philosophers, the revaluation of values, and the order of rank in the works following *Zarathustra*. What is the relationship between these great themes of Nietzsche's later philosophy and the ideas that we have been following in the middle works?

A common view of the relationship between Nietzsche's middle and later works is that in the latter he abandons the commitments to scientific objectivity, empirical knowledge, and Enlightenment rationality that are evident in the former and celebrates radical subjectivity and the unfettered exercise of the will to power instead.[1] This is clearly an inadequate view. As I will show in this chapter, Nietzsche does not abandon in his post-*Zarathustra* writings the commitments to intellectual honesty and the free-spirited quest for knowledge that animate his middle works, though he certainly places these commitments in a larger context that deprives them of their ultimacy. What leads him to subordinate his ideal of the free spirit to the *Übermensch* and later the new philosopher is a deeper understanding of what is necessary to address the civilizational crisis of nihilism. Though he dramatically evoked this crisis in his reflections on the death of God in *The Gay Science*, he did not offer a solution to it that went beyond the personal happiness of the free spirit. Something more than the quest for knowledge was needed to bring about the regeneration of modern culture that he had long dreamed of: nothing less than the complete revaluation of the values that have hitherto governed humanity.[2] It is around this grand, and in a peculiar way political, project that the other themes of the late works—eternal recurrence, the *Übermensch*, the new philosophers, and the order of rank—organize themselves.

In this chapter, I will consider this grand project in relation to Nietzsche's middle works, focusing specifically on how it builds upon and ultimately goes beyond the ideal of the free spirit that is found in those works. I begin with *Zarathustra*, in which Nietzsche introduces the new ideal of the *Übermensch* and connects it, albeit enigmatically, to the ideas of the eternal recurrence and the will to power. In the next section, I take up *Beyond Good and Evil*, focusing on the relationship between the free spirit and the new philosopher and on the role of the latter in the project of revaluing values and establishing an order of rank. In the third section, I turn to Nietzsche's *Genealogy of Morals* and consider it in relation to Nietzsche's psychological and historical investigations of morality in his middle works. Finally, in the fourth section I carefully examine the fifth book of *The Gay Science* along with Nietzsche's prefaces to the middle works, both of which were written in 1886. These writings contain Nietzsche's definitive statement of the place of his free-spirit ideal in the context of his mature philosophy as a whole.

This is obviously a significant amount of ground to cover in a single chapter, and it goes without saying that my discussion of Nietzsche's great later works—with the exception of book 5 of *The Gay Science*—will be highly schematic. Nevertheless, such a discussion is important to undertake for two different reasons. First, any analysis of the middle works would be incomplete without considering them in relation to the later, more canonical works. But second, approaching the later works from the vantage point of the middle ones can cast new light on them and help to dissolve the image of the post-*Zarathustra* Nietzsche—the Nietzsche most firmly planted in both the popular and scholarly imaginations—as an essentially irrationalist thinker.[3]

The New Ideal

No book, of course, has done more to reinforce the image of Nietzsche as an antiscientific exponent of irrationality and subjectivity than *Thus Spoke*

Zarathustra. Its exaggerated, rhetorical, and often bombastic style marks a radical departure from the cool, dry skepticism of the middle works. Nietzsche himself was well aware of this, remarking in *Ecce Homo* that if he had published *Zarathustra* under a different name no one would have guessed that "the author of *Human, All too Human* is the visionary of *Zarathustra*" (*EH* 2.4). But the style of *Zarathustra*—which is far more complicated, controlled, and ironic than the popular view of it suggests—should not blind us to the continuities with the middle works and the philosophical issues raised there. As Nietzsche intimated to Köselitz in a letter written shortly after he had completed the first part of the book, with *Zarathustra* "the 'free spirit' is fulfilled" (*SB* 6:353). Of course, he then adds, "Or?" suggesting that it is not *merely* a matter of continuity.

The opening scene of the book, in which Zarathustra tells the sun of his decision to descend from the mountaintop, is already familiar to us from the final aphorism of *The Gay Science*. Zarathustra has grown weary of his (gay) wisdom and, "like a bee that has gathered too much honey," longs for "hands outstretched to received it." He wants to "give away and distribute, until the wise among men find joy once again in their folly, and the poor in their riches" (*Z* Prologue 1). Zarathustra's desire to give to others here contrasts sharply with the birdlike aloofness that we have come to associate with the free spirit. Zarathustra's beneficence is further amplified in the next scene when he tells the saint that he loves man and brings him a gift (*Z* Prologue 2). Once again, we seem to have left the cheerful indifference of the gay scientist far behind. The contrast between the redemptive figure Zarathustra represents and the more aloof figure of the free spirit is captured well in a later passage from *The Genealogy of Morals*: "But some day, in a stronger age than this decaying, self-doubting present, he must yet come to us, the *redeeming* man of great love and contempt, the creative spirit whose compelling strength will not let him rest in any aloofness or any beyond" (*GM* 2.24).

The gift Zarathustra brings to man is his teaching of the *Übermensch*. This teaching is intimately bound up with the fact that God is dead, a fact that is mentioned almost as an aside after Zarathustra's encounter with the saint. In the notebook in which references to the *Übermensch* begin to appear with some frequency, we find the following note: "God is dead: and it is at the time that the *Übermensch* lives" (*KSA* 10:4 [132]; see also *Z* 1.22:3). The world that Zarathustra has come to redeem is one in which all the goals and ideals that have traditionally given life meaning have disappeared. Zarathustra offers humanity a new goal to strive for: the *Übermensch*. In Zarathustra's initial speeches on the *Übermensch*, we do not learn a great deal more than that the *Übermensch* represents a further stage in the evolution from ape through man (*Z* Prologue 3). It is not until we absorb the idea of the eternal recurrence that we can fully grasp what exactly is involved in the ideal of the *Übermensch*: the *Übermensch* is most precisely the being who can live with, incorporate, and ultimately embrace the idea of the eternal recurrence. As Nietzsche put it in a note from 1883: "We created the heaviest thought—now let us create the being who can cope with it" (*KSA* 10:21 [6]).

The people in the marketplace scoff at Zarathustra's teaching of the *Übermensch*, so he decides to speak to them of the other human possibility in the post-death-of-God world: the last man. Though the *Übermensch* represents a genuinely new idea in Nietzsche's philosophy up to this point, the last man is merely a new expression for Nietzsche's long-held anxiety about the fate of modern humanity. This anxiety begins to be seen in *Daybreak* and the notes surrounding it, especially in connection with Spencer's ideal of the reconciliation of egoism and altruism. In *Daybreak*, Nietzsche wonders whether the "tremendous objective" of removing all the dangers of life will someday turn mankind "into *sand*? Sand! Small, soft, round, unending sand!" (*D* 174). And in another aphorism, he seems to anticipate the alternative posed in *Zarathustra* between *Übermensch* and last man: "This is the main question. Do we desire for mankind an end in fire and light or one in the sand?" (*D* 429; see also *KSA* 9:1 [123], 6 [163]). In one place, Nietzsche even speaks of the "enduring man" (*Dauermensch*) that results from Spencerian evolution: "I doubt whether that enduring man, which the expediency of species selection finally produces, stands much higher than the Chinese" (*KSA* 9:11 [44]; see also 11 [43]).

The last man is not hard to understand, but the *Übermensch* is more elusive.[4] Perhaps the best place to start in order to understand this new ideal—and certainly the place most relevant to this study—is with Nietzsche's attempt to differentiate between the *Übermensch* and the free spirit in Zarathustra's first speech "On the Three Metamorphoses." These figures are symbolized by the lion and child respectively, but before the spirit can metamorphose into either of them it must first begin as a camel. The camel represents the strong, reverent spirit who assumes the most difficult duties and heroically seeks out the most arduous tasks.[5] The lion or free spirit in some ways grows out of this heroic will, but instead of loyally sacrificing itself on behalf of traditional values it breaks all fetters and says "No" to all "Thou shalts." Such activity is purely destructive, however, and the crucial limitation of the free spirit is that it is unable to create new values: "To create new values—that even the lion cannot do; but the creation of freedom for oneself for new creation—that is within the power of the lion." The creation of new values belongs to the third metamorphosis of the spirit, the child, who represents the *Übermensch*: "Why must the preying lion still become a child? The child is innocence and forgetting, a new beginning, a game, a self-propelled wheel, a first movement, a sacred 'Yes.' For the game of creation, my brothers, a sacred 'Yes' is needed: the spirit now wills his own will" (Z 1.1).

Though the *Übermensch* is the new ideal articulated in *Zarathustra*, the free spirit continues to play an important role in the book both as a precursor to the *Übermensch* and as a figure that falls short of the highest ideal. The only explicit reference to the free spirit in the first three parts of *Zarathustra* appears in the speech "On the Famous Wise Men." There the severity of the free spirit's will to truth is contrasted with the laxness of the famous wise men, who are more interested in justifying the prejudices of the people than in seeking the truth. Like the lion in the "Three Metamorphoses," the free spirit is the "enemy of fetters" and the destroyer of traditional reverences: "Truthful I call him who goes into godless deserts, having broken his revering heart. . . . Hungry, violent, lonely, godless: thus the lion-will wants itself. . . . It was ever in the desert that the truthful have dwelt, the free spirits, as masters of the desert." It is in this speech that Nietzsche brings out for the first time the cruelty that lies behind the free spirit's quest for knowledge: "Spirit is the life that cuts into life: with its own agony it increases its own knowledge" (Z 2.8).[6]

In addition to the lion, Nietzsche also uses the image of youth to capture the unrest, self-dissatisfaction, and self-torture of the newly liberated free spirit. In a note from the time of the composition of *Zarathustra*, he writes: "One must also overcome the youth in oneself, if one wants to become a child again" (*KSA* 10:5 [1:5]). And in the speech "On the Tree on the Mountainside," he portrays a youth crying out in despair about the self-distrust, loneliness, and self-contempt that the quest for knowledge and freedom has engendered in him. Zarathustra tells the youth that he is "not yet free, you still *search* for freedom. You are worn out from your search and over-awake." In this respect, the immature free spirit remains a prisoner: "And even the liberated spirit [*der Befreite des Geistes*] must still purify himself. Much prison and mustiness still remain in him: his eyes must still become pure" (Z 1.8).

The reference to pure eyes here recalls the hermit's observation in the Prologue that Zarathustra has changed since the hermit last saw him carrying his ashes to the mountain: "His eyes are pure, and around his mouth there hides no disgust. Does he not walk like a dancer? . . . Zarathustra has become a child" (*Z* P 2). The reference to Zarathustra as a dancer suggests that he has moved from renunciatory knowledge to gay science during his ten-year stay in the mountains. At the very least, the imagery of the hermit's remark suggests that at the beginning of his going down Zarathustra, while not yet an *Übermensch*, is at a more mature stage of freedom of spirit than the self-lacerating youth of "On the Tree on the Mountainside." I will have more to say about where exactly Zarathustra fits on the spectrum extending from the free spirit to the *Übermensch* in a moment.

A little later in part 1, Nietzsche highlights the preparatory character of the free spirit in the speech "On War and Warriors," which parallels the aphorism on "Preparatory Human Beings" in *The Gay Science*. The warriors Zarathustra addresses in this speech are warriors of knowledge, whom he exhorts to wage wars "for your thoughts. And if your thought be vanquished, then your honesty [*Redlichkeit*] will find cause for triumph in that." As in the aphorism from *The Gay Science*, Nietzsche emphasizes here that such warriors of knowledge are ultimately suited more for obedience than for command or rule: "Your nobility should be obedience. Your very commanding should be an obeying. To a good warrior 'thou shalt' sounds more agreeable than 'I will.' And everything you like you should first let yourself be commanded to do" (*Z* 1.10; see also *GS* 283). The task of commanding once again belongs to a type higher than the free spirit, namely, the *Übermensch*.

In the speech "On War and Warriors," Zarathustra also refers to the ugliness of the free spirit: "You are ugly? Well then, my brothers, wrap the sublime around you, the cloak of the ugly" (*Z* 1.10). This theme is picked up in the speech "On Those Who Are Sublime," which I alluded to in the previous chapter in connection with the madman and which more than any other speech in the first three parts of *Zarathustra* highlights the limitations of the free spirit. Zarathustra refers to the sublime individual as an "ascetic of the spirit" who is most proud of his "ugly truths, the spoil of his hunting." Such a spirit falls short of the ideal insofar as "he has not learned laughter or beauty. Gloomy this hunter returned from the woods of knowledge." In this respect, the ascetic of the spirit also seems to fall short of the free spirit whose science is gay. Alluding to the death of God accomplished by the free spirit, Zarathustra indicates that the ascetic of the spirit "has not yet overcome his deed"; his "deed itself still lies on him as a shadow; the hand still darkens the doer." In order to become beautiful, the ascetic of the spirit must first "discard his heroic will." But precisely "the *beautiful* is the most difficult thing for the hero. No violent will can attain the beautiful by exertion." The heroic free spirit must ultimately be superseded by the "overhero" (Z 2.13).

For all their ugliness, though, the ascetics of the spirit still seem to stand higher on the scale of human types than the poets, according to Zarathustra. The middle works began with Nietzsche's profound disillusionment with art, specifically romantic, Wagnerian art, and even in *The Gay Science* he criticizes artists for their vanity and tendency to be valets of the dominant morality (see *GS* 1, 85, 87). He repeats many of these criticisms in *Zarathustra* and, as in *The Gay Science* (*GS* 84), accuses the poets of lying too much. Like the famous wise men, the poets are not really interested in truth but "believe in the people and their 'wisdom.'" Zarathustra finds them "shallow" and "superficial," and he believes their poetry to be largely in the service of "lust and boredom." He also claims that they are not "clean enough for me: they all muddy their waters to make them appear deep." Finally, they are vain: "[T]heir spirit is the peacock of peacocks and a sea of vanity! The spirit of the poet craves spectators." For all of these reasons, Zarathustra says he has "grown weary of the poets," and he foresees that they will grow weary of themselves. In the end, they will be superseded by the ascetics of the spirit: "I have already seen the poets changed, with their glances turned back on themselves. I saw ascetics of the spirit approach; they grew out of the poets" (Z 2.17).

In the privately circulated fourth part of *Zarathustra*, which describes Zarathustra's comic experiences with various "higher men" after the main action of the book—the acceptance of the eternal recurrence—has been completed, Nietzsche returns to the theme of the free spirit. In the chapter on the leech, Zarathustra accidently steps on the "conscientious man," whose intellectual conscience in the form of the leech sucks his blood. The conscientious free spirit tells Zarathustra that it was his dictum that "spirit is the life that cuts into life" that seduced him to his doctrine: "And verily, with my own blood I increased my own knowledge" (Z 4.4; see also 4.15). Once again, Nietzsche emphasizes the asceticism and self-cruelty involved in the free-spirited quest for knowledge.

In another chapter, Zarathustra's shadow, who is referred to as a "free spirit and wanderer," complains about the endless quest for knowledge that leaves him emaciated and homeless. With Zarathustra, he has striven "to penetrate everything that is forbidden, worst, remote"; and he has broken "whatever my heart revered; I overthrew all boundary stones and images." All this has left the shadow, however, without anything to love, without a goal, without a home: "'Where is—my home?' I ask and search and have searched for it, but I have not found it. O eternal everywhere, O eternal nowhere, O eternal—in vain!" (Z 4.9; cf. GS 309). Here the quest for knowledge threatens to end in nihilism.

As in the works from the middle period, Nietzsche's treatment of the free spirit in *Zarathustra* is multifaceted, highlighting different aspects depending on the context and purpose. In some places, he emphasizes the truthfulness and courage of the free spirit, as in the speeches on the warriors of knowledge, the famous wise men, and the poets. In other places, he stresses the asceticism, ugliness, and even nihilism of the free spirit, as in the speeches on the ascetics of the spirit, the conscientious man, and the shadow. What is important about all these speeches is that they reveal the continuity between Nietzsche's outlook in *Zarathustra* and his outlook in the middle works; and they also suggest why Nietzsche came to regard the free-spirit ideal as incomplete and the move to the *Übermensch* ideal as necessary. The free spirit is good at stripping away comforting illusions, exploring possibilities, and experimenting with ideas, but in the end it is unable to provide new goals, create new values, or assume the role of commander. For these tasks the *Übermensch* is necessary. This latter figure, so easy to caricature and misunderstand, is not an arbitrary excrescence on Nietzsche's defense of knowledge, skeptical reason, and the Enlightenment in the middle works but a logical outgrowth of it.

And where does Zarathustra himself stand on the spectrum that leads from the free spirit to the *Übermensch*? A great deal of scholarly ink has been spilled over the question of whether Zarathustra is or becomes an *Übermensch*.[7] He begins, of course, as the herald of the *Übermensch*; but when he finally incorporates the idea of the eternal recurrence in the chapter on "The Convalescent," he seems to have become the thing he heralded (Z 3.13). Nevertheless, the fact that Zarathustra is designated as the "*teacher of the eternal recurrence*" in this chapter suggests that he remains primarily the figure who is responsible for ushering in the new order of the *Übermensch* rather than being the consummate product of it.[8] Many of Nietzsche's retrospective comments reinforce this distinction between Zarathustra and the *Übermensch* and point to his affinity with the free spirit. In *The Antichrist*, for example, he calls Zarathustra a "skeptic" (AC 54); and in a late note, he comments that Zarathustra "is, of course, only an old atheist" (KSA 13: 17 [4]; see also Z 3.5). Even more tellingly, in *Ecce Homo* he characterizes Zarathustra's supreme virtue as "truthfulness" and credits him with the accomplishment that constitutes the chief consequence of the free spirit's relentless honesty: the "self-overcoming of morality" (EH 4.3). All of this is not to suggest that Zarathustra is merely a free spirit; I have already indicated that in his redemptive capacity he is something more. Rather, he is, like

Nietzsche himself, a figure poised perfectly between the free spirit and the *Übermensch*, teaching the eternal recurrence and initiating the revaluation of values that will make the latter possible.

We may now turn to the second of the three major concepts around which the argument of *Zarathustra* revolves: the will to power. Unlike the notion of the *Übermensch*, the concept of the will to power is one that we have already encountered, at least in certain forms, in the middle works. In *Human, All too Human* and especially *Daybreak*, Nietzsche traces a good deal of human behavior—from religious asceticism to artistic intoxication—back to the desire for the feeling of power. At one point, he even claims that the "means discovered for creating this feeling almost constitute the history of culture" (*D* 23). And though he generally refers to the "feeling of power" (*Machtgefühl* or *Gefühl der Macht*) in these works, there are several references to the "will to power" (*Wille zur Macht*) in the notebooks from 1880 and 1881 (see, e.g., *KSA* 9:4 [239]; 9 [14]; 11 [346]).

Nietzsche's reflections on the desire for power in his middle works grew out of his effort to overcome the dualism of selfishness and selflessness, egoism and unegoism, that lay at the root of traditional moral psychology. Despite this naturalistic objective, he nevertheless resisted the Darwinian tendency to reduce all human behavior to the desire for self-preservation or the struggle for mere existence. Human motivation was more complicated than that and required a more dynamic principle of explanation. In a note from 1875, for example, while arguing that stability makes us stupid and that weakness and corruption are necessary for progress, he states: "The struggle for existence is not the important principle" (*KSA* 8:12 [22]). In another note, this one from 1876–77, he criticizes Schopenhauer's notion of the "will to life" for being too bourgeois in character: "It is not true that one wants existence at any price" (*KSA* 8:23 [12]). Finally, in a note from 1881, he flatly declares that "there is no self-preservation drive" (*KSA* 9:11 [108]).

It is important to recall these reflections on power from Nietzsche's middle period because they point to the psychological basis of the doctrine of the will to power found in the past-*Zarathustra* writings.[9] Nevertheless, they do not constitute a full-fledged doctrine themselves. This only begins to take place in *Zarathustra*. Though the phrase "will to power" appears in only three places in the book, it does so at three critical junctures in the argument. The sudden salience of the concept of the will to power in *Zarathustra* is ultimately to be explained in terms of its connection to the book's fundamental concern with the revaluation of values. The will to power does not merely describe the basic motive that lies behind our actions; it names the fundamental principle of life. As such, it becomes the basis for evaluating our actions and ultimately our values themselves. Those actions or values that express or promote the will to power are more in accord with life and therefore more valuable than those that do not. This is obviously somewhat simplistic, so we need to look more closely at how Nietzsche develops the concept of the will to power in *Zarathustra*.

The first reference to the will to power in *Zarathustra* appears in the speech "On the Thousand and One Goals." Here we learn that the will to power is intimately connected with "esteeming" (*Schätzen*), valuing, and establishing standards of good and evil. "No people," Zarathustra asserts, "could live without first esteeming," and what a people esteems most is whatever seems difficult to them and makes them "rule and triumph and shine, to the awe and envy of their neighbors." The tablet of good and evil that hangs over every people "is a tablet of their overcomings"; it is the "voice of their will to power." Zarathustra adduces the Greeks, the Persians, the Jews, and the Romans as examples of such value-creation on the part of peoples (Z 1.15). And he sharply distinguishes peoples united in this way by a love and a substantive conception of the good from the modern, neutral state—that "coldest of all cold monsters"—which unites individuals only in terms of their egoistic needs and appetites (Z 1.11).

The second reference to the will to power in *Zarathustra* appears in part 2 of the book, in the speech "On Self-Overcoming." This speech, in which Zarathustra uses the phrase "will to power" no less than seven times, represents the most extended discussion of the concept in the entire book. Zarathustra picks up here where he left off in the speech "On the Thousand and One Goals": with the creation of tablets of good and evil for peoples. He informs those "who are wisest" that what they refer to as the "will to truth" is really a "will to power": "You still want to create the world before which you can kneel: that is your ultimate hope and intoxication." It is from this act of world- and value-creation on the part of the wisest that the unwise people take their particular understanding of good and evil. And what ultimately brings the sway of a particular conception of good and evil to an end is nothing other than a new act of value-creation on the part of the wisest, a new expression of the will to power, which Zarathustra now refers to as "the unexhausted procreative will of life" (Z 2.12).

He goes on to elaborate on this identification of life with the will to power. Everything that lives seeks to overcome that which is weaker. Even those who serve and obey seek to become master over something in themselves that is weaker still. Not life but power is the fundamental will of all that lives. It is for the feeling of power that heroes risk their lives and sacrifice themselves; and it is for this same feeling that the lover of knowledge cruelly deprives himself of comforting illusions in the quest for truth. As he did in earlier writings, Nietzsche here rejects Schopenhauer's notion of the "will to existence": "For, what does not exist cannot will; but what is in existence, how could that still want existence? Only where there is life is there also a will: not a will to life but—thus I teach you—will to power." Once again, Zarathustra points out that this will to power expresses itself most essentially through esteeming and the creation of values. And such creation necessarily involves the annihilation of old values. Therefore, "good and evil that are not transitory, do not exist. Driven on by themselves, they must overcome themselves again and again" (Z 2.12).

The chapter "On Self-Overcoming" comes immediately after the one entitled "The Tomb Song." This latter chapter, along with the chapter "Upon the Blessed Isles," celebrates the creative will that is finally named and defined in "On Self Overcoming." In "Upon the Blessed Isles" Zarathustra calls creation "the great redemption from suffering and life's growing light." He indicates that he himself has passed through a hundred souls in his lifetime, "a hundred cradles and birth pangs," but just this constitutes the happiness of the creative will: "Whatever in me has feeling, suffers and is in prison; but my will always comes to me as my liberator and joy-bringer. Willing liberates" (Z 2.2). This theme is taken up again "The Tomb Song," albeit initially in a melancholy key. Zarathustra laments how all the visions and apparitions of his youth have died. Many of these visions are reminiscent of Nietzsche's own disappointed hopes and shattered ideals. For instance, the "dearest singer" who dashed Zarathustra's hopes for dancing when he "struck up a horrible dismal tune" and "tooted like a gloomy horn" seems to refer to Wagner. And the allusion to *The Gay Science* is unmistakable when Zarathustra grieves: "'All days shall be holy to me'—thus said the wisdom of my youth once; verily, it was the saying of a gay wisdom. But then you, my enemies, stole my nights from me and sold them into sleepless agony; alas, where has this gay wisdom fled now?" Though the pathos is palpable here, Zarathustra concludes the chapter on a triumphant note, once again invoking the liberating power of the creative will: "How did I get over and overcome such wounds? How did my soul rise again out of such tombs? Indeed, in me there is something invulnerable and unburiable, something that explodes rock: that is *my will*. . . . [F]or me, you are still the shatterer of all tombs. Hail to thee, my will! And only where there are tombs are there resurrections" (Z 2.11).

But as the drama of part 2 of *Zarathustra* unfolds, it turns out that the liberation or redemption offered by the will—and the will to power—is not as unproblematic as the chapters on the blessed isles and the isle of tombs suggest. In the crucial chapter "On Redemption," which contains the third and final reference to the will to power in the book, Zarathustra elucidates the difficulty to which the will is unavoidably subject. After referencing his earlier contention that the will is the "name of the liberator and joy-bringer," he adds:

> But now learn this too: the will itself is still a prisoner. Willing liberates; but what is it that puts even the liberator in fetters? 'It was'—that is the name of the will's secret melancholy. Powerless against what has been done, he is an angry spectator of all that is past. The will cannot will backwards; and that he cannot break time and time's covetousness, that is the will's loneliest melancholy. (Z 2.20)

"Time's covetousness" refers to the general problem of change or becoming. This is the fundamental problem of willing: nothing stays, everything passes away.

But this is only the beginning of the will's problems. For, given its self-overcoming nature, the will also tries to liberate itself from its fetters; but it does so foolishly: "Alas, every prisoner becomes a fool; and the imprisoned will redeems itself foolishly." Unable to master the past or prevent the passage of time, the will exercises its will to power negatively by wreaking revenge and hurting: "This, indeed this alone, is what *revenge* is: the will's ill will against time and its 'it was.'" The philosophers have been absolutely critical in this project of revenge. As Zarathustra points out, "*The spirit of revenge*, my friends, has so far been the subject of man's best reflection." Beginning with Plato and running from Christianity through Schopenhauer, philosophers have taken revenge on the will's inability to will backwards by interpreting willing and life itself as a punishment. Finally, madness preaches: "Everything passes away; therefore everything deserves to pass away. And this too is justice, this law of time that it must devour its children." This descent into nihilism culminates in Schopenhauer's denial of the will to live, his demand that "willing should become not willing" (Z 2.20).

Will to power is not only the great liberator and the principle of human creativity; it is also the source of the will's revenge against time and its "it was." The deliverance of humanity from this revenge now becomes Zarathustra's supreme task: "For *that man be delivered from revenge*, that is for me the bridge to the highest hope, and a rainbow after long storms" (Z 2.7). In the final reference to the will to power in the book, Zarathustra states that in order to overcome the spirit of revenge, the "will that is the will to power must will something higher than any reconciliation"; and he goes on to ask, "but how shall this be brought about" (Z 2.20). We know that the eternal recurrence is going to be the solution to this fundamental problem of the will. With the final reference to the will to power, the doctrine of the eternal recurrence appears on the horizon.

The idea of the eternal recurrence is the third major concept presented in *Zarathustra*. Unlike the concepts of the *Übermensch* and the will to power, the idea of the eternal recurrence had already been articulated prior to the writing of *Zarathustra*, in *The Gay Science*. Nevertheless, the presentation of the idea in *Zarathustra* crucially depends on the other two concepts insofar as it serves as their enabling condition. The idea of the eternal recurrence delivers the will to power from the revenge to which it has hitherto been subject, allowing it to express itself in a positive, creative manner instead of denying itself. This deliverance of the will to power from revenge also makes possible the *Übermensch*, a type of humanity free of the bonds that have hitherto fettered creativity and wholly given over to the innocence of becoming. How the idea of the eternal recurrence accomplishes these objectives is what we must investigate next, always keeping in view the question of how this idea—the "fundamental conception" of *Zarathustra*—modifies Nietzsche's outlook in the middle period.

Zarathustra's first presentation of the idea of the eternal recurrence appears toward the beginning of part 3 in the chapter "On the Vision and the Riddle." Zarathustra is climbing a mountain, and on his shoulder sits a dwarf, the spirit of gravity, the vengeful spirit that informs moralities, religions, and pessimistic philosophies and leads humanity to deny the will to power and the reality of becoming. He shows the dwarf a gateway that stands for the present and two paths leading from it, one stretching infinitely into the past, the other stretching infinitely into the future. Given that the path stretching into the past is infinite, that "behind us lies an eternity," Zarathustra argues: "Must not whatever *can* walk have walked on this land before? Must not whatever *can* happen have happened, have been done, have passed by before? And if everything has been there before—what do you think, dwarf, of this moment? Must not this gateway too have been there before?" He concludes with imagery that recalls the initial presentation of the idea of the eternal recurrence in *The Gay Science*: "And this slow spider, which crawls in the moonlight, and this moonlight itself, and I and you in the gateway, whispering together, whispering of eternal things—must not all of us have been there before? And return and walk in the other lane, out there before us, in this long dreadful lane—must we not eternally return?" (Z 3.2).

With respect to the dichotomy between the cosmological and existential interpretations of the eternal recurrence, this presentation of the idea looks more like the former than the latter. No longer is the idea presented as a hypothesis, as it was in *The Gay Science*. And though he does not mention the crucial assumption of finite force here, Nietzsche continues to put tremendous emphasis on the infinite character of time in his demonstration of the eternal recurrence, as he did in his first attempts at a scientific proof of the idea in his notes from 1881 (see *KSA* 9:11 [148, 202]). Similar attempts to scientifically prove the eternal recurrence litter his later notebooks. In a note from 1888, for example, he writes: "If the world may be thought of as a certain definite quantity of force . . . it follows that, in the great dice game of existence, it must pass through a calculable number of combinations. In infinite time, every possible combination would at some time or another be realized; more: it would be realized an infinite number of times" (*WP* 1066; see also 55, 708, 1062–64).

But though he seems to consider the eternal recurrence to be a propositional truth about world, the most important thing for Nietzsche remains our ability to "incorporate" this potentially deadly truth. This problem of "incorporation" had been at the center of the very first note he devoted to the idea of the eternal recurrence (see *KSA* 9:11 [141]), and it now receives graphic representation in Zarathustra's vision of the young shepherd gagging on a black snake that has crawled down his throat. What makes the shepherd gag is the thought that, among all the things that recur, the rabble, the last man, the small man must recur eternally. As Zarathustra explains later: "The great disgust with man—*this* choked me and had crawled into my throat . . . 'Eternally recurs the man of whom you are weary, the small man'—thus yawned my sadness" (*Z* 3.13; see also 2.6). This "blackest" and "heaviest" aspect of the eternal recurrence is what Zarathustra sees the shepherd bite off, after which he is transformed into an *Übermensch*: "No longer shepherd, no longer human—one changed, radiant, *laughing*! Never yet on earth has a human being laughed as he laughed! O my brothers, I heard a laughter that was no longer human" (*Z* 3.2).[10]

The drama of part 3 of *Zarathustra* is the drama by which Zarathustra eventually overcomes his nausea and incorporates the idea of the eternal recurrence. This drama reaches its denouement in the chapter on "The Convalescent," in which Zarathustra recounts how the "monster" of the eternal recurrence "crawled down my throat and suffocated me. But I bit off its head and spewed it out." Throughout this chapter, Nietzsche highlights the horror involved in incorporating the idea of the eternal recurrence by contrasting it with the serene, detached, contemplative attitude of Zarathustra's animals toward the idea. The "hurdy-gurdy song" they make of the eternal recurrence completely drains the idea of its terror: "Everything goes, everything comes back; eternally rolls the wheel of being. Everything dies, everything blossoms again, eternally runs the year of being."[11] In the end, they reveal to Zarathustra his ultimate destiny: "[B]ehold, *you are the teacher of the eternal recurrence*—that is your destiny" (Z 3.13). Once again, we are brought back to Nietzsche's very first note on the eternal recurrence, where he wrote that teaching the doctrine "is the most powerful means of *incorporating* it in ourselves. Our kind of blessedness, as teachers of the greatest doctrine" (KSA 9:11 [141]).

With the announcement that Zarathustra's destiny is to teach the eternal recurrence and "proclaim the *Übermensch*," ushering in "the great noon of earth and man," the drama of *Zarathustra* comes to an end: "Thus *ends* Zarathustra's going down" (Z 3.13). I will come back to the notion of the "great noon" in a moment, but before doing so, I must first clarify how the idea of the eternal recurrence solves the problem of willing that originally motivated it in the chapter "On Redemption."

The crux of the problem, it will be remembered, was the will's inability to will backwards, which leads it to exercise its frustrated will to power by wreaking revenge on itself. The eternal recurrence solves this problem by making the past something that the will can will eternally for the future. A somewhat less formalistic way of grasping Nietzsche's point is by thinking of the problem of willing in terms of the problem of flux or becoming: the problem that the will can never achieve lasting satisfaction because it no sooner fulfills one desire than ten new ones appear; nothings stays, everything is fleeting, which gives rise to the feeling of "in vain." This is the problem with willing that Schopenhauer first identified,[12] and it is the problem that the Schopenhauerian soothsayer encapsulates in his doctrine that "All is empty, all is the same, all was" (Z 2.19).[13] The eternal recurrence solves this problem by conferring eternity on all of our actions; nothing is ever really lost or dead. In several notes, Nietzsche speaks of the eternal recurrence as providing "redemption from flux" (KSA 10:4 [94], 5 [1] 160; see also WP 1065); but such redemption does not come from escaping into a fictional world of being beyond the world of becoming; rather, it comes by finding eternity within becoming. As he puts it in a crucial note: "That *everything recurs* is the closest *approximation of a world of becoming to a world of being*—high point of the meditation" (WP 617).[14]

By overcoming "time's covetousness" in this way, the idea of the eternal recurrence delivers the will to power from revenge and enables it to express itself in a genuinely positive and creative fashion. This marks a fundamental turning point in human history; Zarathustra refers to it as "the great noon when man stands in the middle of his way between beast and *Übermensch*" (*Z* 1.22). There are many references to the "great noon" in *Zarathustra* (see *Z* 3.5, 10, 12 [3, 30]; 4.13, 20), and many more in the notes, usually in conjunction with the idea of the eternal recurrence. Indeed, "Noon and Eternity" is one of the most frequently recurring phrases in the notes.[15] As in *Zarathustra*, the references to "noon" or the "great noon" in the notes generally indicate that the idea of the eternal recurrence represents a decisive turning point in human history, a time of the "*most terrible* clearing up" (*WP* 134), a "period of greatest danger" (*WP* 1057), the "decisive moment" (*KSA* 12:2 [71]).[16]

For Nietzsche, the irruption of the idea of the eternal recurrence into human history brings with it two critical practical—and political—consequences: the revaluation of values and the establishment of an order of rank. With respect to the first, already in *The Gay Science* Nietzsche stated that his fundamental conviction was that "the weights of all things must be determined anew" (*GS* 269). The idea of the eternal recurrence is the instrument—the "hammer," as he often refers to it (*WP* 1054, 1055)—which brings this revaluation about. Without the revaluation of values, the idea of the eternal recurrence would be unendurable. In a world deprived of (or delivered from) purpose and given over wholly to chance (see *Z* 3.4), a world understood as "in all eternity chaos" or dehumanized necessity (*GS* 109), those who value being, permanence, stability, certainty, calm, and rest are doomed to despair. Belief in the eternal recurrence brings about the devaluation of those values, as Nietzsche indicated in his letter to Overbeck from March 1884 (*SB* 6:485). Only those who embrace becoming, change, uncertainty, experimentalism, creativity, and self-overcoming—in a word, will to power—will flourish in the shade of this doctrine. Thus Nietzsche writes in one of his notes: "Means of *enduring* [*the idea of the eternal recurrence*]: the revaluation of all values. No longer joy in certainty but uncertainty; no longer 'cause and effect' but the continually creative; no longer will to preservation but to power" (*WP* 1059). And in another: "To *endure* the idea of recurrence one needs: freedom from morality . . . the enjoyment of all kinds of uncertainty, experimentalism, as a counterweight to this extreme fatalism" (*WP* 1060).

In *Zarathustra*, the three chapters preceding the one in which Zarathustra finally incorporates the idea of the eternal recurrence are devoted to the revaluation of values. In "On the Three Evils," Zarathustra weighs the three worst reputed things—sex, the lust to rule, and selfishness—and finds that they have been misweighed on the scales of traditional morality. He continues this revaluation of values in the chapter "On Old and New Tablets," arguing that the good and the just have always done the least to advance humanity: "For the good are *unable* to create; they are always the beginning of the end: they crucify him who writes new values on new tablets; they sacrifice the future to *themselves*—they crucify all man's future" (*Z* 3.12 [26]). This, of course, picks up the immoralism that Nietzsche had already begun to enunciate in *The Gay Science*. Its placement in the argument of part 3 of *Zarathustra* underlines the crucial connection he sees between the idea of the eternal recurrence and the revaluation of all values.

The second major consequence of the irruption of the idea of the eternal recurrence into human history has to do with the establishment of an order of rank based on strength and weakness. This selective function of the eternal recurrence is not emphasized in *Zarathustra*, but it is prominent in Nietzsche's notes. There he argues that the weak "will experience the belief in the eternal recurrence as a curse." In this way, the idea "brings to light the weaker and less secure among [men] and thus promotes an order of rank" (*WP* 55). It is a "doctrine that sifts men—driving the weak to decisions, and the strong as well" (*WP* 56). It is the "great cultivating idea: the races that cannot bear it stand condemned; those who find it the greatest benefit are chosen to rule" (*WP* 1053; see also 862, 1055, 1056, 1058).

The last-cited note highlights the political dimension of the idea of the eternal recurrence, as does another note, which speaks of the idea's "place in history as a *mid-point*. Period of greatest danger. Foundation of an oligarchy *above* peoples and their interests: education to a universally human politics" (*WP* 1057). Perhaps nothing differentiates Nietzsche's outlook in his post-*Zarathustra* writings from that of his middle works more than this new, albeit highly ambiguous, emphasis on "great politics." In the middle works, the free spirit tended to remain aloof from politics, living a life of "refined heroism" either buried in the midst of society (*HH* 291) or "hidden in forests like [a] shy deer" (*GS* 283). Even Zarathustra, prior to part 3, exhibits a free-spirited reluctance to rule, and he is duly chastised by his "stillest hour": "This is what is unforgiveable in you: you have the power, and you do not want to rule" (*Z* 2.22). All of this changes in part 3, where Zarathustra seeks to establish a "new nobility" and insists that "the best should rule, the best also want to rule" (*Z* 3.12 [21]). In a couple of notes from 1883, Nietzsche makes clear that part 3 of *Zarathustra* was meant to effect this transition from the apolitical free spirit to the responsibility to rule: "Z 3: against the comfortableness of the wise—against the '*fröhliche Wissenschaft*'" (*KSA* 10:15 [17]); and "Z 3: the *transition* from the free spirit and hermit to the having to *rule*" (*KSA* 10:16 [51]). We will see this movement from the free spirit to great politics further developed in *Beyond Good and Evil*.

From the Free Spirit to the New Philosopher

In *Beyond Good and Evil*, Nietzsche articulates the ideas of *Zarathustra* in a less poetic, less prophetic—and yet hardly prosaic—fashion. As he described the book to his revered friend Jacob Burckhardt: "[I]t says the same things as my *Zarathustra*, but differently, very differently" (*SB* 7:254). But from the perspective of the middle works, what is most interesting about *Beyond Good and Evil* is that Nietzsche originally intended the book to be a second edition of *Human, All too Human*, revised so as to bring it into accord with his post-*Zarathustra* outlook. His plan was to buy back the unsold copies of the original edition of *Human, All too Human* in order to make room for a new one, but when his publisher, Schmeitzner, informed him of the large number of copies that remained unsold, he reluctantly had to give up on this plan.[17] His next thought was to make the new book a companion volume to *Daybreak*, but he soon gave up on that idea as well.[18] Finally, at the end of March 1886, he decided the new book needed a title of its own, and in letter to Köselitz on 27 March he referred to *Beyond Good and Evil: Prelude to a Philosophy of the Future* for the first time (*SB* 7:167).[19]

Traces of Nietzsche's original conception of *Beyond Good and Evil* as a new edition of *Human, All too Human* can be seen in the structure and even some of the specific aphorisms of the book. Like *Human, All too Human*, it contains nine chapters; and like that earlier book, it begins with a chapter on the metaphysical and epistemological errors of previous philosophy, "The Prejudices of Philosophers." The second aphorism of the book self-consciously echoes the first aphorism of *Human, All too Human* when it raises the question, "How *could* anything originate out of its opposite? for example, truth out of error? or the will to truth out of the will to deception? or the pure and sunlike gaze of the sage out of lust?" (*BGE* 2). Both aphorisms—indeed, both books—identify *"the faith in opposite values"* as the fundamental faith that has animated the metaphysical philosophy of the past. Additionally, the third chapter of *Beyond Good and Evil*, "The Religious Nature," recalls the third chapter of *Human, All too Human* on "The Religious Life"; and the eighth chapter of the former book, "Peoples and Fatherlands," picks up the political themes of the eighth chapter in the latter, "A Glance at the State." Finally, both books contain important chapters on the "Natural History of Morals" or the "History of the Moral Sensations."

The latter chapter from *Human, All too Human* contains an aphorism on the "Twofold History of Good and Evil" (*HH* 45) that anticipates the famous aphorism in *Beyond Good and Evil* on the two basic types of morality, master and slave (*BGE* 260).

Despite these similarities, *Beyond Good and Evil* departs from *Human, All too Human* in fundamental ways that reflect the impact of *Zarathustra*. First and foremost, *Beyond Good and Evil*, like *Zarathustra*, no longer regards the free spirit as the ultimate ideal or the most complete human being; rather, the free spirit is seen as a precursor to a higher type, the "new philosopher." This latter figure, unlike the free spirit, legislates new values and is charged at this crucial moment in human history with the "revaluation of all values" and the establishment of an "order of rank." Both of these ideas reflect the more political orientation of *Beyond Good and Evil*, as compared with the antipolitical posture of *Human, All too Human*. *Beyond Good and Evil* takes up the task of "great politics" that Nietzsche began to sketch in *Zarathustra*. As Laurence Lampert has insightfully put it, though the book is anti-Platonic in its philosophical commitments, it is "Platonic in the scope and aim of its philosophical politics."[20]

In order to grasp Nietzsche's distinction between the free spirit and the new philosopher in *Beyond Good and Evil*, we must turn first to the chapter on "The Free Spirit." Lampert considers this to be the most important chapter of the book because it seeks to persuade Nietzsche's "indispensable audience" of the reasonableness of the new teaching of *Zarathustra*.[21] From the point of view of the middle works, the chapter is important because it constitutes the most sustained discussion of the free spirit in the later works, with the exception of the fifth book of *The Gay Science*. The chapter cannot, of course, be considered separately from the chapter that precedes it, "On the Prejudices of the Philosophers." The honesty and truthfulness that mark the free spirit are precisely the qualities that have been missing in philosophers hitherto. As Nietzsche puts it in a late note: "I understand by 'freedom of spirit' something quite definite: being a hundred times superior to philosophers and other disciples of 'truth' in severity towards oneself, in cleanliness and courage" (*WP* 465). In a note from the fall of 1883, he draws the distinction in this way: "In place of the philosopher I put the free spirit, who is superior to the scholar, researcher, and critic and continues to live through many ideals: who, without becoming a Jesuit, nevertheless fathoms the unlogical nature of existence" (*KSA* 10:16 [14]).

The reference to Jesuitism in the last note may seem puzzling, but it points to an important theme in *Beyond Good and Evil*. In the Preface to the book, Nietzsche refers to Jesuitism as one of the two great movements in modern European history to "unbend the bow" and relax the "magnificent tension of the spirit"—the other being democracy (*BGE* Preface; see also 206). What exactly he has in mind only becomes clear in the notes leading up to *Beyond Good and Evil*. There he contrasts the Jesuits with Pascal, that "brilliant sign of the terrible tension [of the bow]," who in his *Provincial Letters* attacked the Jesuits for their lax attitude toward truth and honesty as evidenced in their doctrines of mental reservation and probable opinion (*KSA* 11:34 [163]). Jesuitism defends the practice of telling lies—or at least of not telling the whole truth—for the sake of preserving the status quo and not disturbing the happiness of the many (*KSA* 10:7 [203, 238]). Nietzsche's most interesting reference to the Jesuit tendency toward deception and the perpetuation of illusion appears in a critical comment on his earliest works: "Grinning from behind my first period is the face of Jesuitism: I mean the conscious holding on to illusion and the forcible incorporation of that illusion as the basis of culture" (*KSA* 10:16 [23]).[22]

Nietzsche's critical remarks about Jesuitism highlight the rejection of self-conscious illusion and the affirmation of truth-seeking that had been the hallmark of the middle works in contradistinction to the early ones. But the paradoxical result of the free spirit's quest for truth is the discovery of the "unlogical nature of existence." This paradox is at the heart of the theme-laying first aphorism of *Beyond Good and Evil*, where Nietzsche states: "The will to truth which will still tempt us to many a venture, that famous truthfulness of which all the philosophers so far have spoken with respect—what questions has this will to truth not laid before us! What strange, wicked, questionable questions!" Among these wicked, questionable questions, there are two that especially concern Nietzsche in *Beyond Good and Evil*. The first is: "*What* in us really wants 'truth'?" What more fundamental will lies behind the will to truth? The answer to this question turns out to be the will to power. The second, "even more basic question," is: What is the *value* of the will to truth? "Suppose we want truth: *why not rather* untruth? and uncertainty? even ignorance?" (*BGE* 1). This is the fundamental question that will occupy Nietzsche not only in the rest of *Beyond Good and Evil* but also, as we shall see, in the third essay of the *Genealogy of Morals* and the fifth book of *The Gay Science*. And while the question does not necessarily deny the importance of the free spirit's quest for truth—again, Nietzsche does not intend to relapse into Jesuitism—it certainly points beyond it.[23]

Nietzsche begins his inquiry into the value of truth by first pointing out the lack of truthfulness among philosophers hitherto. He remarks that the latter are simply "not honest enough in their work, even though they all make a lot of virtuous noise when the problem of truth is touched even remotely." These philosophers act as if they had arrived at their opinions "through the self-development of a cold, pure, divinely unconcerned dialectic," when in fact their opinions are the product of very personal passions, drives, affects, interests, and perspectives (*BGE* 5; see also 6). In addition to this dishonesty and self-deception, philosophers ever since Plato have fallen prey to the "dogmatist's error" that denies the perspectival character of all knowledge (*BGE* Preface). There is no such thing as pure truth unalloyed with error, partiality, or perspective. Without the simplification or falsification of reality, there would be no life. But such falseness, Nietzsche claims, "is for us not necessarily an objection to a judgment; in this respect our new language may sound strangest. The question is to what extent it is life-promoting, life-preserving, species-preserving, perhaps even species-cultivating." Arguing that "without accepting the fictions of logic, without measuring reality against the purely invented world of the unconditional and self-identical, without a constant falsification of the world by means of numbers, man could not live," he concludes with the famous pronouncement that "untruth [is] a condition of life" (*BGE* 4; see also 3, 11).

Again, it is important to underline that Nietzsche is not here celebrating untruth or endorsing the kind of Jesuitical holding on to illusion that we saw him criticize above. His claim that "untruth [is] a condition of life" does not represent a brand new insight in his philosophy but goes back to his reflections on the incorporation of truth in *The Gay Science* (*GS* 110–13). There he argued that there is a limit to how much truth human beings can incorporate. Because the absolute flux of things cannot ultimately be incorporated by human beings, they end up simplifying and falsifying reality with numbers, lines, planes, atoms, causes, and effects. But this does not mean that science cannot overcome the grosser simplifications and falsifications of reality and develop a richer, more complex understanding of it. Science may not be able to escape the humanized world completely, but it can "attempt to humanize things as faithfully as possible." So, while untruth may be a condition of life, Nietzsche's ultimate aspiration is to determine the extent to which truth can also be made a condition of life and thereby endure incorporation.

These considerations lead directly to the first aphorism of the chapter devoted to "The Free Spirit," a draft of which appears in a notebook from the fall of 1881 when Nietzsche was writing *The Gay Science* (*KSA* 9: 15 [1]). The aphorism opens with Nietzsche once again pointing to the "strange simplification and falsification" in which human beings live. Because there would be no life without such simplification and falsification, the knowledge sought by the free spirit cannot altogether escape it: "[O]nly on this now solid, granite foundation of ignorance could knowledge rise so far—the will to knowledge on the foundation of a far more powerful will: the will to ignorance, to the uncertain, to the untrue! Not as its opposite, but—as its refinement!" (*BGE* 24). This is no doubt paradoxical, but it is the very paradox that runs through many of Nietzsche's reflections on scientific knowledge in the middle period, especially in *The Gay Science* (see especially *GS* 54). In scientific knowledge we do not have access to a "true" world that is opposed to the apparent world formed by our optical errors and perspective estimates. Nevertheless, science constitutes a "refinement" of our will to ignorance insofar as it enables us to look at that apparent world through many different eyes, rendering our knowledge of it richer, more complex, and variegated. Yes, "science at its best seeks most to keep us in this *simplified*, thoroughly artificial, suitably constructed and suitably falsified world," but it does so by extending the dimensions of that world, making it more subtly colorful and interestingly audible than it ordinarily appears to a cruder seeing and hearing (*BGE* 24; cf. *D* 426 and *GS* 301).[24]

That his perspectivism does not undermine the possibility of genuine knowledge or the meaningfulness of the free spirit's quest for it Nietzsche makes clear several aphorisms later. Once again he refers to the "*erroneousness* of the world in which we think and live," and he repeats that "there would be no life at all if not on the basis of perspective estimates and appearances." Nevertheless, our knowledge of the unavoidably apparent world can be greater or lesser, richer or more impoverished. In order to maintain the distinction between scientific knowledge and useful fiction, it is not necessary "to suppose that there is an essential opposition of 'true' and 'false.'" Rather, it is "sufficient to assume degrees of apparentness and, as it were, lighter and darker shades of appearance—different 'values,' to use the language of painters" (*BGE* 34; again cf. *D* 426).

The good will toward appearance announced in the opening aphorism of the chapter on the free spirit suggests that Nietzsche's discussion will emphasize the "gay" aspects of the quest for knowledge rather than the ascetic aspects stressed in *Zarathustra*. It comes as no surprise, therefore, that after this "gay" (*fröhliche*) beginning Nietzsche goes on to warn: "Take care, philosophers and friends of knowledge, and beware of martyrdom! Of suffering 'for truth's sake'!" Such moral posturing destroys the "innocence and fine neutrality" of the free spirit's intellectual conscience, as does "moral indignation" (*BGE* 25). In contrast to *Zarathustra*'s image of the free spirit as a hungry and violent lion who tears to pieces the child in him and finally ends up eating himself (*Z* 2.8; *KSA* 10:4 [218]), Nietzsche here counsels the lover of knowledge to avoid the morally indignant individual and "whoever perpetually tears and lacerates himself with his own teeth" (*BGE* 26). He also cautions the free spirit against the "wrathful and reverent attitudes characteristic of youth" in a way that recalls the speech "On the Tree on the Mountainside" in *Zarathustra*. In its quest for an unconditional Yes and No, "the young soul, tortured by all kinds of disappointments, finally turns suspiciously against itself, still hot and wild, even in its suspicion and pangs of conscience—how angry it is with itself! how it tears itself to pieces, impatiently!" (*BGE* 31; see *Z* 1.8).

Nietzsche canvasses a number of qualities that belong to the knowledge-seeking free spirit in the chapter devoted to this figure: curiosity about the average human being (*BGE* 26); a *presto* tempo in thinking and writing (*BGE* 27–28); independence (*BGE* 29, 41); esotericism and a love of masks (*BGE* 30, 40); suspicion (*BGE* 33–34); and hardness and lack of illusions (*BGE* 39). But as was the case throughout the middle works, the quality or virtue that most defines the free spirit is honesty (*Redlichkeit*) (*BGE* 227). In his notebooks, Nietzsche refers to it as the "ultimate virtue, *our* virtue" (*KSA* 12:1 [145]). And he claims that, insofar as it is a virtue that *we* free spirits cannot get out of, "we immoralists" are "men of duty" too (*BGE* 226).

Nietzsche's discussion of honesty in *Beyond Good and Evil* appears in the chapter entitled "Our Virtues." There he explains that this quintessential virtue of the free spirit is based, like everything else in higher culture, on the "spiritualization of *cruelty*." By refusing to rest satisfied with the conventional understanding of things, the seeker after knowledge goes against the basic inclination of the human spirit, which seeks to simplify what is manifold in experience and assimilate everything new to what is old and familiar. The free-spirited knower delights in hurting this basic inclination to mere appearance and simplification, insisting instead "on profundity, multiplicity, and thoroughness, with a *will* that is a kind of cruelty of the intellectual conscience and taste." Why? This is the question Nietzsche asks at the end of the two aphorisms devoted to the cruelty involved in the free spirit's quest for knowledge. What is it that motivates the "strange and insane task" of deconstructing the "many vain and overly enthusiastic interpretations and connotations that have so far been scrawled on the eternal basic text of *homo natura*"? (*BGE* 229–30). Though he does not answer this question explicitly, the implication seems to be that it is the will to power that lies behind the self-cruelty of the free spirit—and an ascetic will to power at that.

The most consequential example of the free spirit's ascetic self-cruelty is his skeptical undermining of belief of God—to use the madman's more graphic language, the free spirit's murder of God. In the chapter devoted to religion in *Beyond Good and Evil*, Nietzsche describes three fundamental stages on the "great ladder of religious cruelty." In the first, one sacrificed human beings to one's god; in the second, one sacrificed one's strongest instincts; and in the third, corresponding to the scientific outlook of the free spirit, one sacrificed all that was "comforting, holy, healing," including God himself. Nietzsche comments that this final cruelty, the nihilistic sacrifice of God for the nothing, has been "reserved for the generation that is now coming up: all of us already know something of this" (BGE 55).

Apart from this renunciatory knowledge, what other sort of knowledge does the modern free spirit seek? Nietzsche leaves us in no doubt in the chapter on "Our Virtues" that it is historical knowledge. The sense that is most profoundly developed in the free spirit of the nineteenth century is the historical sense, which Nietzsche defines here as "the capacity for quickly guessing the order of rank of the valuations according to which a people, a society, a human being has lived" (BGE 224).[25] It was precisely this historical sense that Nietzsche criticized previous philosophers for lacking at the outset of his middle works (HH 2). And in a note from the summer of 1885, when he still conceived of Beyond Good and Evil as a second edition of Human, All too Human, he continued to differentiate his own free-spirited philosophy from traditional philosophy on this basis: "What differentiates us from all Platonic and Leibnitzian ways of thinking at bottom is this: we believe in no eternal concepts, eternal values, eternal forms, eternal souls; and philosophy, insofar as it is science and not legislation, signifies only the broadest extension of the concept of history" (KSA 11:38 [14]). This note is revealing not only because it differentiates the free spirit's historical philosophizing from previous, nonhistorical philosophizing but also because it differentiates such historical philosophizing from philosophy as legislation. This is a distinction that Nietzsche goes on to develop.

Hints of this distinction are already present in the aphorism devoted to the historical sense. On the one hand, Nietzsche praises the free spirit's ability to enter into a wide variety of cultures and live through many ideals. He also acknowledges that "we men of the historical sense" possess a number of commendable virtues: "we are unpretentious, selfless, modest, courageous, full of self-overcoming, full of devotion, very grateful, very accommodating." On the other hand, he claims that the historical sense is an "*ignoble* sense" and completely lacking in good taste. In a revealing passage, he points up the crucial limitation of the historically minded free spirit:

> Let us finally own it to ourselves: what we men of "historical sense" find most difficult to grasp, to feel, to taste once more, to love once more, what at bottom finds us prejudiced and almost hostile, is precisely the perfection

and maturity of every culture and art, that which is really noble in a work or human being, the moment when their sea is smooth and they have found halcyon self-sufficiency, the golden and cold aspect of all things that have consummated themselves. (*BGE* 224)

The suggestion that the free spirit is deficient in a crucial way and preparatory to some higher and more complete manifestation of the human spirit is evident in the very first aphorism of the chapter on "Our Virtues." Initially suggesting there that the virtues of "we Europeans of the day after tomorrow, we first-born of the twentieth century—with all our dangerous curiosity, our multiplicity and art of disguises, our mellow and, as it were, sweetened cruelty in spirit and senses"—will not be the same old-fashioned virtues that our grandfathers possessed, Nietzsche goes on to argue that there is still something quintessentially moral in the way that we free spirits believe in and prides ourselves on our intellectual honesty and other virtues. We, too, seek to enjoy a "good conscience," that "venerable long pigtail of a concept that our grandfathers fastened to the back of their heads." In this respect, we are "worthy grandsons of these grandfathers, we last Europeans with a good conscience: we, too, still wear their pigtail.—Alas, if you knew how soon, very soon—all this will be different" (*BGE* 214).

The free spirit, with his "piety of the search for knowledge" (*BGE* 105), will soon be superseded by a figure who does not merely investigate the multifarious values by which peoples and human beings have lived but actually creates them. In *Zarathustra*, this creative role was assigned to the *Übermensch*; in *Beyond Good and Evil*, it is assigned to the "new philosophers." Nietzsche tells us at the end of the chapter on the free spirit that "we free spirits" are merely "the heralds and precursors" of the new philosophers. These latter figures will themselves be "free, *very* free spirits," but they will also be "something more, higher, greater, and thoroughly different" (*BGE* 44). What exactly does this "something more" consist in? Nietzsche points to the key, differentiating characteristic of the new philosophers when he baptizes them with the name "attempters" or "experimenters" (*Versucher*) (*BGE* 42; see also 210).[26] By setting goals and legislating values, the new philosophers make attempts or experiments with human beings in order to elevate or enhance them. Unlike the free spirit, who in birdlike freedom remains somewhat aloof from the "wicked game" of life, the new philosopher enters into it, feeling "the burden and the duty of a hundred attempts and temptations of life—he risks *himself* constantly, he plays the wicked game" (*BGE* 205).

Nietzsche's definitive statement of the differentia of the philosopher vis-à-vis the free spirit appears in aphorism 211. There he distinguishes between "philosophical laborers," who ascertain, investigate, and classify past valuations, and "genuine philosophers," who create new values. These latter

> are commanders and legislators: they say, "thus it shall be!" They first determine the Whither and For What of man, and in so doing have at their disposal the preliminary labor of all philosophical laborers, all who have overcome the past. With a creative hand they reach for the future, and all that is and has been becomes a means for them, an instrument, a hammer. Their "knowing" is creating, their creating is a legislation, their will to truth is—will to power.

While the focus in this passage is on the creative role of philosophers, it is important to note that their creativity is not understood to be divorced from the knowledge acquired by the free spirit: genuine philosophers "have at their disposal the preliminary labor of all philosophical laborers." In an earlier aphorism, Nietzsche mentioned that the new philosophers will be free spirits, though also something more than free spirits (BGE 44). Here he underlines that it is a precondition of the philosopher's creation of values that, like the free spirit, he "pass through the whole range of human values and value feelings and be able to see with many different eyes and consciences" (BGE 211).[27]

It should perhaps be noted that, in making the distinction between the philosopher and the free spirit in Beyond Good and Evil, Nietzsche somewhat narrows his conception of the latter figure from what it had been in the middle works. In The Gay Science in particular, the knowing activity of the free spirit was considered to be eminently experimental and in no way implied removal from the "wicked game" of life. In that work, Nietzsche celebrated the "idea that life could be an experiment [Experiment] of the seeker for knowledge" and the idea of knowledge as a "world of dangers and victories in which heroic feelings, too, find a place to dance and play" (GS 324; see also 7, 283, 319). Nor did he separate the knowing activity of the free spirit there from creation and legislation in quite the same way that he does in Beyond Good and Evil. In the crucial aphorism on "The Fancy of the Contemplatives," for example, he argued that the free-spirited knower, by imagining that he is a passive spectator of life, "overlooks that he himself is really the poet who keeps creating this life." The so-called contemplative man creates the "whole eternally growing world of valuations, colors, accents, perspectives, scales, affirmations, and negations" that is then studied by practical human beings and translated into actuality (GS 301).

We will see that in some of his later writings—the prefaces of 1886 and the fifth book of The Gay Science—Nietzsche once again attributes to the free spirit the experimentation and creativity that he reserves to the philosopher in *Beyond Good and Evil*. Nevertheless, the distinction between scientific knowing and philosophic creation that he draws in the latter work points to something fundamental in his later thought and ultimately stands behind his dangerous speculations about the *Übermensch* and the new philosophers. In the end, historical knowledge of all that has given color and value to human existence cannot provide the wholeness and harmony that Nietzsche always associated with a healthy culture and human being. This is what he hints at when he says that "we men of 'historical sense'" find it almost impossible to grasp the "perfection and maturity of every culture and art, that which is really noble in a work or human being" (*BGE* 224). A little later in *Beyond Good and Evil*, he comments that genuinely higher spirits, in contrast to mediocre scientific spirits like Darwin, Mill, and Spencer, "have more to do than merely gain knowledge—namely, to be something new, to *signify* something new, to *represent* new values. . . . Those who can do things in the grand style, the creative, may possibly be lacking in knowledge" (*BGE* 253). Nietzsche makes this fundamental point most succinctly in a note from 1884: "[O]ne should value more than truth the force that forms, simplifies, shapes, invents" (*WP* 602).

When we return to the discussion of the new philosopher in *Beyond Good and Evil*, we can see that one of the things that sharply differentiates this value-legislating figure from the free spirit is his attitude toward religion. The piety of the free spirit, Nietzsche tells us, the piety of the quest for knowledge, is offended by the "holy lie" of philosophical legislators like Plato. The free spirit's "profound lack of understanding for the church" constitutes "*his* unfreedom" (*BGE* 105). "The philosopher as legislator [and] attempter of new possibilities," on the other hand, is perfectly comfortable using religion as his means (*KSA* 11:35 [45, 47]). As Nietzsche puts it toward the end of the chapter on religion: "The philosopher as *we* understand him, we free spirits—as the man of the most comprehensive responsibility who has the conscience for the overall development of man—this philosopher will make use of religions for his project of cultivation and education" (*BGE* 61).[28]

The legislative new philosopher who creates values, then, is the ideal that hovers over *Beyond Good and Evil* in the same way that the ideal of the *Übermensch* hovers over *Zarathustra*. Like the *Übermensch*, it can be a terrifying ideal, as when Nietzsche describes the new philosophers as "Caesarian cultivator[s] and violent [men] of culture" (*BGE* 207) or, even more graphically, as "philosophical men of violence and artist-tyrants" who "sculpt at 'man' himself as artists" (*KSA* 12:2 [57]). But it is on the coming of these new philosophers, in the midst of the "degeneration and diminution of man into a perfect herd animal" in modern democratic life, that Nietzsche as free spirit[29] pins his hopes:

> Where, then must *we* reach with our hopes?—Toward *new philosophers*; there is no choice; toward spirits strong enough to provide stimuli for opposite valuations and to revalue and reverse [*umzukehren*] "eternal values"; toward forerunners, toward men of the future who in the present tie the knot . . . that forces the will of millennia upon *new* tracks. To teach man the future of man as his *will*, as dependent on human will, and to prepare great ventures and overall attempts [*Gesammte-Versuche*] of discipline and cultivation by way of putting an end to that gruesome dominion of nonsense and accident that has so far been called "history." (*BGE* 203)

No sooner does Nietzsche express these hopes, however, than he expresses his profound anxiety—"an anxiety past all comparisons"—that these philosophical leaders and commanders "might fail to appear or that they might turn out badly or degenerate" (*BGE* 203). He elaborates on this anxiety in his notebooks from the summer of 1885. In one note, he claims that the rise of the philosopher "is rendered altogether impossible" today because the instincts of the age—for comfort, equality, and the big noise of the actor and demagogue—are the "reverse" (*umgekehrt*) of what is necessary for the philosopher to flourish (*KSA* 11:37 [14]). In another, he asserts that the new philosophers, the "men of great creativity, the really great men according to my understanding, will be sought in vain today and probably for a long time to come." Once again he points to the conditions of modern democratic Europe—its "herd animal morality which is striving with all its power for a universal green pasture happiness on earth, namely for security, absence of danger, comfort," along with its doctrines of "equal rights" and "sympathy with all that suffers"—as being particularly unfavorable to the growth of the creative philosopher. And he adds that "whoever has thought profoundly about where and how the plant man has grown most vigorously must conclude that it has happened under *reverse* [*umgekehrten*] conditions": danger, hardness, inequality, and so forth (*KSA* 11:37 [8]; cf. *BGE* 44).

What is particularly interesting about the latter note is the role that it assigns to the free spirit in reversing the current conditions that are so unfavorable to the emergence of the new philosophers: "To prepare a *reversal* [*Umkehrung*] *of values* for a certain strong kind of man of the highest spirituality and strength of will and to this end slowly and cautiously to unfetter a host of instincts now kept in check and calumniated—whoever reflects on this becomes one of us, the free spirits" (*KSA* 11:37 [8]). It appears that the reversal or revaluation of values is not merely the product of the new philosophers but the presupposition of their emergence. Nietzsche makes this clear in the text of *Beyond Good and Evil* as well. In the very aphorism where he refers to the revaluation and reversal of eternal values by the new philosophers, he also speaks of the conditions that the free spirit "would have partly to create and partly to exploit" for the genesis of these new philosophers. Among these conditions, he includes "the probable ways and tests that would enable a soul to grow to such a height and force that it would feel the *compulsion*" for the creative and cultivating tasks of the new philosophers; also, "a revaluation of values under whose new pressure and hammer a conscience would be steeled, a heart turned to bronze, in order to endure the weight of such responsibility" (*BGE* 203).

As the language of this passage suggests, the revaluation of values that is prepared by the free spirits and that makes possible the new philosophers is ultimately the work of the idea of the eternal recurrence, the "great cultivating idea" and "hammer" that strengthens the strong and breaks the weak (*WP* 1053–61; also 55–56, 862). This revaluation belongs to the "great noon" that divides human history into two essential periods, the *menschlich* past and the *übermenschlich* future. All of this, of course, is developed in *Zarathustra*, which we need not revisit now. Instead, I want to conclude my analysis of *Beyond Good and Evil* by considering one final idea that pervades the work, especially the culminating chapter devoted to "What Is Noble," and brings out its peculiarly political character: the idea of the order of rank.

We have already seen that one of the chief obstacles to the emergence of the creative, legislative new philosophers is the democratic doctrine of the equality of rights. Nietzsche therefore insists that inequality of rights and even slavery are among the most important of the "reverse conditions" necessary for the growth of the plant man (*KSA* 11:37 [8]; *BGE* 44). He states this point clearly in the first aphorism of the final chapter of *Beyond Good and Evil*: "Every enhancement of the type 'man' has so far been the work of an aristocratic society—and it will be so again and again—a society that believes in a long ladder of an order of rank and differences in value between man and man, and that needs slavery in some sense or other" (*BGE* 257).[30] It is this aristocratic emphasis on the order of rank that most directly refutes the popular interpretation of Nietzsche as an exponent of radical individualism. Any individualistic philosophy that still pays homage to the liberal doctrine of the equality of rights—Mill's, for example—is anathema to Nietzsche. As he succinctly puts it in a note: "My philosophy aims at an ordering of rank: not an individualistic morality" (*WP* 287; see also 783–84).

But though Nietzsche upholds the order of rank against the leveling tendencies of democracy, he does not see the two as necessarily incompatible with one another. Echoing his earlier analysis from the *Human, All too Human* series (see especially *WS* 275), he argues that there is a way in which the democratization of Europe is inadvertently creating conditions for a new and even more refined aristocracy: "The very same new conditions that will on average lead to the leveling and mediocritization of man—to a useful, industrious, handy, multipurpose herd animal—are likely in the highest degree to give birth to exceptional human beings of the most dangerous and attractive quality." The process of democratization thus serves as a training ground for "*slavery* in the subtlest sense" and at the same time as "an involuntary arrangement for the cultivation of *tyrants*" in the "most spiritual" sense (*BGE* 242).[31]

In addition to becoming democratized, Nietzsche also sees Europe as becoming increasingly homogenized. Again echoing his analysis in *Human, All too Human*, he claims that Europeans are becoming more and more similar to one another: "*Europe wants to become one*" (*BGE* 242, 256; cf. *HH* 475). This development, too, supports the possibility of ever more "comprehensive forms of dominion" (*KSA* 12:2 [57]), or what Nietzsche now begins to call "great politics." Great politics involves rule over Europe—or the earth—by a new caste of men capable of setting long-term goals for humanity (*BGE* 208, 251). Once again, we come back to the rule of the new philosophers, who "sculpt at 'man' himself as artists" (*KSA* 12:2 [57]). In a note from the summer of 1885, Nietzsche brings together the notions of the new philosopher and great politics in this way: "The new philosopher can only arise in conjunction with a ruling caste, as its highest spiritualization. Great politics, rule over the earth, are at hand" (*KSA* 11:35 [47]). Thus the argument of *Beyond Good and Evil* culminates in a version of Plato's philosopher-king—on steroids.[32]

Nothing like this notion of great politics can be found in Nietzsche's middle works, as we have seen already. Indeed, in *Human, All too Human*— the book for which *Beyond Good and Evil* was originally intended to be a new edition—Nietzsche disparages the idea of great politics, arguing that it leads to cultural and spiritual impoverishment (*HH* 481). It is true that great politics there is identified with nationalism, against which Nietzsche speaks, for the first time, as a "good European" (*HH* 475). But the whole tenor of the book—and of *Daybreak* and *The Gay Science* as well—is antipolitical. This comes through most clearly in the critical discussion of socialism and its desire for the "Caesarian despotic state." Nietzsche sounds almost liberal when he claims that "socialism can teach, in a truly brutal and impressive fashion, what danger there lies in accumulations of state power, and to that extent implant mistrust of the state itself"(*HH* 474). The free spirit of the middle works, who lives a life of "refined heroism which disdains to offer itself to the veneration of the masses . . . and tends to go silently through the world and out of the world" (*HH* 291), is a far cry from the legislative new philosopher and Caesarian cultivator of *Beyond Good and Evil*.

But before we draw this contrast between the political outlooks of Nietzsche's middle and later periods too quickly, it is important bear in mind just how ambiguous his later conception of great politics is. In this regard, the comparison to Plato is again apposite. The specific ambiguity lies in whether Nietzsche's great politics has anything to do with politics conventionally understood. The fact that up until the end of his sane life Nietzsche remained hostile to the modern state, seeing it as the great enemy of cultural greatness, suggests that we have to take his references to ruling castes and tyrants with a grain of salt.[33] In this vein, he writes against great politics in *Twilight of the Idols*: "Culture and the state . . . are antagonists. . . . All great ages of culture are ages of political decline: what is great culturally has always been unpolitical, even *antipolitical*. . . . [W]hat matters most . . . is always culture" (*TI* Germans 4). The ambiguity lies nakedly on the surface of *Ecce Homo*, where Nietzsche maintains at one and the same time that he is the "last *antipolitical* German" (*EH* 1.3) and that it is only with him that the "earth knows *great politics*" (*EH* 4.1). I am certainly not defending Nietzsche's ambiguity here, which made his philosophy singularly easy to abuse by tyrants in the least spiritual sense.[34] But not to recognize it would be to reduce his philosophy to a grotesque caricature.

The Later Critique of Morality

In my analysis of *Beyond Good and Evil* in the previous section, I focused on the relationship between the free spirit and the new philosophers and skipped over Nietzsche's important discussion of morality in the chapter on "The Natural History of Morals" and the crucial aphorism 260 on master and slave morality. The latter aphorism, of course, leads directly to the first essay of the *Genealogy of Morals*, a work that was originally conceived of as an addendum to *Beyond Good and Evil*.[35] In this section, I want to look at Nietzsche's critique of morality in *Beyond Good and Evil* and especially the *Genealogy of Morals* in order to see how it compares with the one (or ones) found in the middle works.

We will find that there are significant differences. The most obvious of these is that the later critique contains a much more radical questioning of the *value* of morality understood in terms of unegoism, selflessness, altruism, and pity than anything found in the middle works. Whereas in *Human, All too Human* (to take the most extreme example) Nietzsche was concerned to expose the error involved in the idea of the unegoistic—to show that there was no such thing as an unegoistic action—in his later works he wants to bring out the nihilism and decadence involved in the moral values of unegoism, altruism, and pity. These values lead to the "degeneration and diminution of man into the perfect herd animal . . . the dwarf animal of equal rights and claims" (*BGE* 203), the "hopelessly mediocre and insipid man" (*GM* I 11). All of this was already articulated in Zarathustra's speech on the "last man," and it was even intimated in Nietzsche's lament in *Daybreak* that the morality of pity was "well on its way to turning mankind into sand" (*D* 174). But it is only in *Beyond Good and Evil* and the *Genealogy of Morals*—not to mention *Twilight of the Idols* and *The Antichrist*—that this lament turns into a central and almost obsessive theme.

Related to Nietzsche's more radical calling into question of the value of the moral values of altruism and pity in his post-*Zarathustra* writings is his increasing emphasis on the unnaturalness of these values, their incompatibility with the fundamental principles of life. This new emphasis obviously grows out of the doctrine of the will to power that was first articulated in *Zarathustra*. Life aims not at mere self-preservation but at growth, expansion, self-overcoming, in a word, power (*Z* 2.12). In *Beyond Good and Evil*, Nietzsche gives this doctrine one of its most succinct formulations: "A living thing seeks above all to *discharge* its strength—life itself is *will to power*; self-preservation is only one of the indirect and most frequent results" (*BGE* 13; see also 259). The morality of altruism and pity denies this essential feature of life, making self-preservation, the elimination of suffering, and comfort its supreme goals. But because it, too, is a piece of life and therefore an expression of the will to power, Nietzsche infers that it is symptomatic of a declining will to power, of weakness, degeneration, and physiological exhaustion. This is one of the most significant innovations of his later critique of morality: that morality is seen as sign-language, as symptomatic of something else and something more fundamental.

Nietzsche announces his symptomological approach to morality in one of the opening aphorisms of the chapter on "The Natural History of Morals" in *Beyond Good and Evil*. After listing a variety of purposes a morality might serve—self-justification, self-torture, revenge, self-concealment, or self-transfiguration—he comments: "In short, moralities are also merely a

194 / Chapter Four

sign-language of the affects" (*BGE* 187; see also 196). Earlier in the book, he makes essentially the same methodological point, claiming that a morality is something derivative or epiphenomenal, a symptom or interpretation of a more fundamental fact: "There are no moral phenomena at all, but only a moral interpretation of phenomena" (*BGE* 108).[36]

The most famous application of Nietzsche's symptomological method in *Beyond Good and Evil* is his analysis of master and slave moralities in aphorism 260, a draft of which appears in a note from 1883 (*KSA* 10:7 [22]).[37] In each of these two moralities, it is the degree of power a group enjoys that determines its moral values. In master morality, the ruling group considers "good" those qualities that give its members power over themselves and others: strength, courage, severity, and hardness. "Bad" is whatever lacks these "noble" qualities; it is a totally derivative term meaning essentially "ignoble" or "contemptible." In slave morality, on the other hand, it is the powerless and oppressed who moralize, and therefore they consider "evil" precisely the virtues of the powerful. "Good" are those qualities that "serve to ease existence for those who suffer: here pity, the complaisant and obliging hand, the warm heart, patience, industry, humility, and friendliness are honored" (*BGE* 260).

This aphorism inevitably recalls Nietzsche's earlier attempt, in *Human, All too Human*, to provide an account of the "twofold prehistory of good and evil." In that earlier aphorism, however, he concluded—in sharp contrast to the later perspective of *Beyond Good and Evil*—that "our present morality has grown up in the soil of the *ruling* tribes and castes." This conclusion sprang from Nietzsche's radically different concern in *Human, All too Human* to bring out the egoistic basis of all our moral sensations. The morality of the ruling castes was thoroughly egoistic insofar as it was based on requital: he who had the power to requite was considered good; he who was powerless and could not requite was considered bad. For the subjected and powerless, on the other hand, "every *other* man" was seen to be a threat and therefore considered evil. It is not difficult to see why our present morality could not be based on such a suspicious disposition. As Nietzsche points out, no community in which this disposition prevails could survive for long (*HH* 45). In *Beyond Good and Evil*, he introduces the crucial modification that the slave regards not "every other man" but only the powerful man as a threat and therefore evil. Out of *this* slavish soil our present morality *could* grow.

On the basis of the distinction between master morality and slave morality, Nietzsche constructs the schematic history that runs through almost all of his later works. It begins, of course, with the Jews, who carried out the first "slave rebellion in morals." It was the Jews who accomplished the "miraculous feat of a reversal of values, thanks to which life on earth has acquired a novel and dangerous attraction for a couple of millennia." According to this Jewish reversal of values, wealth, violence, and sensuality came to be identified with evil, and poverty became synonymous with goodness (*BGE* 195).

It was Christianity, however, that consummated what Judaism had begun, taking the self-cruelty and self-sacrifice inherent in slave morality to its highest and most sublime pitch. "Never yet and nowhere has there been," Nietzsche claims, "an equal boldness in reversal, anything as horrible, questioning, and questionable" as the Christian formula of "god on the cross." This formula "promised a revaluation of the values of antiquity" (*BGE* 46). No one exemplifies the gruesomeness and absurdity of Christian self-sacrifice and self-mutilation for Nietzsche more completely than Pascal. In a late note, he comments: "One should never forgive Christianity for having destroyed such men as Pascal. One should never cease from combating just this in Christianity: its will to break precisely the strongest and noblest souls." This is what most disturbs Nietzsche about Christianity: its success in seducing the strong to its ideal of weakness, converting "their proud assurance into unease and distress of conscience" and turning their will to power against itself so that they end up perishing "through orgies of self-contempt and self-abuse" (*WP* 252; see also *BGE* 46).[38]

It is this debilitating effect on the strong that dominates Nietzsche's final assessment of Christianity in *Beyond Good and Evil*. He acknowledges that, in providing comfort to the sick and the suffering, Christianity has "kept the type 'man' on a lower rung" and "preserved too much of *what ought to perish*." But even worse, in carrying out this task Christianity had to "stand all valuations *on their head*" and thereby "break the strong, . . . cast suspicion on the joy in beauty, bend everything haughty, manly, conquering, domineering, all the instincts characteristic of the highest and best-turned-out type of 'man,' into unsureness, agony of conscience, self-destruction." Once again, Nietzsche refers to Pascal and decries the calamitous failure of Christianity to properly sculpt or artistically form higher human beings (*BGE* 62).

The reversal of values that began in Judaism and was deepened by Christianity continues to flourish under the guise of modern democracy. The "*democratic* movement is the heir of the Christian movement" (*BGE* 202); and it completes the transformation of man into a "perfect herd animal" (*BGE* 203). Nevertheless, democracy lacks the spiritual agony and Pascalian self-torture of Christianity. For this reason, Nietzsche refers to it as "Christianity made natural." Whereas Christianity denaturalized herd-animal morality, making it more dangerous and exciting but also more dishonest and self-deceptive, democracy represents a "more natural" and "less menda-cious" form of that morality (*WP* 215). Nietzsche thus concludes the chapter on "The Natural History of Morals" with a portrait of the democratic "last man," who lacks even the elevating longing and self-contempt of Christian-ity, adding only that he looks forward to the coming of "new philosophers" who will reverse and revalue the inverted values that have hitherto reigned over European morality. Having discussed this task of revaluation on the part of the new philosophers in the previous section, we may now pass on to the most complete statement of Nietzsche's later critique of morality in the *Genealogy of Morals*.

The *Genealogy of Morals* is of particular interest from the point of view of this study because it explicitly refers back to the proto-genealogies of moral-ity found in the middle works. In the Preface, Nietzsche remarks that his "ideas on the *origin* of our moral prejudices . . . received their first, brief, and provisional expression" in *Human, All too Human* (*GM* Preface 2). He goes on to point out that his initial treatment of the genealogy of morals in *Human, All too Human* was inept because he lacked his "own language for [his] own things and with much backsliding and vacillation." He also mentions that the original impetus for his investigations into the origin of morality came from reading Paul Rée's *Origin of the Moral Sensations*; but he obscures the extent to which that book influenced his thinking in *Human, All too Human* by claiming that "I have never read anything to which I would have said to myself No, proposition by proposition, conclusion by conclusion, to the extend that I did to this book" (*GM* Preface 4).

In this comment and others in the Preface, Nietzsche tends to assimilate his earlier point of view to his later one and iron out the development we have been tracing in this study. Thus he asserts that even in *Human, All too Human* his concern was not simply with "hypothesis-mongering" about the origin of morality but with calling into question the "*value* of morality." This is what led him to reject his "great teacher Schopenhauer" in that book, which in its own way was also a "polemic":

> What was especially at stake was the value of the "unegoistic," the instincts of pity, self-abnegation, self-sacrifice, which Schopenhauer had gilded, dei-fied, and projected into a beyond for so long that at last they became for him "value-in-itself," on the basis of which he *said No* to life and to himself. But it was against precisely *these* instincts that there spoke from me an ever more fundamental mistrust, an ever more corrosive skepticism! It was pre-cisely here that I saw the *great* danger to mankind, its sublimest enticement and seduction—but to what? to nothingness—it was precisely here that I saw

the beginning of the end, the dead stop, a retrospective weariness, the will turning *against* life, the tender and sorrowful signs of the ultimate illness: I understood the ever spreading morality of pity that had seized even on philosophers and made them ill, as the most sinister symptom of a European culture that had itself become sinister, perhaps as its by-pass to a new Buddhism? to a Buddhism for Europeans? to—*nihilism*? (GM Preface 5)

I have quoted this passage at length because it graphically illustrates the degree to which Nietzsche reads his later critique of morality back into his earlier one. It is true that in *Human, All too Human* he questioned the value of morality, but his reasons for doing so were quite different from the ones adduced in this passage. It was not so much the *value* of the unegoistic that he criticized in that book as it was the *error* of the unegoistic.[39] It was the erroneousness of moral evaluation that was responsible for heightening the savage passions of the age and whetting its appetite for religious and artistic intoxication. It is only in *Daybreak* and *The Gay Science* that Nietzsche begins to question the *value* of unegoistic actions and discern the dangerousness of the morality of pity. In *Daybreak*, as we have seen, he worries that the morality of pity is "well on its way to turning mankind into *sand*" (D 174). And in *The Gay Science*, he even more unambiguously proclaims that it is the "strongest and most evil spirits," not the good and the altruistic, that "have so far done the most to advance humanity" (GS 4).

This latter statement encapsulates the radical questioning of the value of morality that is characteristic Nietzsche's later outlook and his self-proclaimed immoralism. In the Preface to the *Genealogy of Morals*, he points out that up till now it has been assumed that "the good man" is of greater value than "the evil man" and that he contributes more to the "advancement and prosperity of man in general (the future of man included)." But, Nietzsche asks, "what if the reverse were true? What if a symptom of regression were inherent in the 'good,' likewise a danger, a seduction, a poison, a narcotic, through which the present was possibly living *at the expense of the future?*" (GM Preface 6; see also EH Destiny 4). This is where utilitarian genealogists of morality like Rée and Spencer go wrong. They assume that our judgments of good and evil sum up what has been beneficial and harmful to the species: "They have no conception of the grand economy, which cannot do without evil" (WP 291; see also GS 1, 4).

Interestingly, Nietzsche opens the first essay of the *Genealogy of Morals* with a criticism of the utilitarian theories of "English psychologists" like Rée and Spencer. Rée, of course, is not English, but Nietzsche insists throughout the Preface that his Darwinian theory of the origin of morality is the epitome of the "English type" (*GM* Preface 4.7).[40] Indeed, the "English" theory that Nietzsche summarizes at the beginning of the first essay resembles no one else's more than Rée's. According to this "English" theory, unegoistic actions were originally praised and called good because they were useful to the community; "later one *forgot* how this approval originated and, simply because unegoistic actions were always *habitually* praised as good, one also felt them to be good—as if they were something good in themselves" (*GM* 1.2). Not only is this the theory that Rée defends in *The Origin of the Moral Sensations*; it is also the theory that Nietzsche himself invoked at various point in *Human, All too Human* and its sequels (see *HH* 92; *WS* 40).

Nietzsche now emphatically rejects this genealogical theory that rests on utility, habit, and forgetting. In the first place, "the judgment 'good' did *not* originate with those to whom 'goodness' was shown!" Rather, it originated with the noble and powerful who used the term to designate their own qualities and actions in contrast to those of the lowborn and plebeian. Therefore, "goodness" originally had nothing to do with unegoistic actions; it only came to have this meaning with the decline of aristocratic morality and the rise of herd morality (*GM* I 2). Second, the idea that the utility of unegoistic actions was somehow forgotten is psychologically absurd. Nothing could have been more firmly impressed on the consciousness of the herd than precisely this utility. In this regard, Nietzsche claims that Spencer's utilitarian theory, which holds that "in the judgments 'good' and 'bad' mankind has summed up and sanctioned precisely its *unforgotten* and *unforgettable* experiences" regarding what is beneficial and harmful, is far more coherent than Rée's (*GM* 1.3).

Nietzsche's remarks about the origin of "goodness" in the self-approbation of the noble class rather than in those to whom goodness was shown set up the discussion in the rest of the first essay about master morality and slave morality. Since we have already touched on this distinction in connection with *Beyond Good and Evil*, there is no need to develop it further here. I would, however, like to say something about the interesting note that Nietzsche appends to the first essay because it sheds further light on how he approaches the question of the value of morality and how he differs from the "English" or Darwin-inspired genealogists of morals.

With respect to determining the value of a morality or particular table of values, Nietzsche insists that "value *for what?*" is the fundamental question to be asked. Something that is valuable for the longest possible survival of a race may have little value in relation to the production of a stronger or higher type: "[T]he well-being of the majority and well-being of the few are opposite points of value" (*GM* 1.Note). This is a point that Nietzsche made as far back as *Daybreak*, where he argued that the definition of the goal of morality as the "preservation and enhancement of mankind" is meaningless. We need to know exactly *what* we are preserving and *to what* end. Do we seek the longest possible existence for human beings or "the greatest possible deanimalization"? Do we seek the highest happiness that an individual can attain or the greatest amount of happiness for all (*D* 106)?

This is where Nietzsche once again expresses his divergence from the Darwinian point of view. He states that "English biologists" naively assume that the long-term preservation of the average type is of more value than the production of the higher or stronger type and that the well-being of the majority is of higher value than the well-being of the few (*GM* 1.Note). In *Twilight of the Idols* and some of his later notes, he develops this critique of Darwin and his school in a slightly different way, arguing that they assume that natural selection favors the strong and the healthy when in fact the opposite is the case. The strongest and most fortunate individuals are at a disadvantage "when opposed by organized herd instincts, by the timidity of the weak, by the vast majority. . . . Strange as it may sound, one always has to defend the strong against the weak" (*WP* 685; *TI* Expeditions 14). Given the Darwinians' fundamental misunderstanding of the problem of value, Nietzsche maintains that the sciences must "from now on prepare the way for the future task of the philosophers": the "determination the *order of rank among values*" (*GM* 1.Note).

We may now pass on to the second essay of *Genealogy*, which contains the clearest echoes of the middle works, especially in its analysis of the primeval morality of custom. Referencing his earlier analysis of this morality, Nietzsche once again highlights his differences with Rée and the English Darwinians. With its positive evaluation of cruelty and suffering, the morality of custom "differs *toto caelo* from the altruistic mode of evaluation (in which Dr. Rée, like all English moral genealogists, see moral evaluation *as such*)" (*GM* Preface 4). The moral genealogies of Rée and the English Darwinians exhibit a total lack of historical sense insofar as they attempt to naturalize the current altruistic mode of evaluation by tracing it back to primitive society: unegoistic actions were originally praised in primitive society because they were considered good for the community; later the utilitarian origin of this approval was forgotten and unegoistic actions came to be considered as good in themselves (*GM* 1.2). Nietzsche, by contrast, seeks to denaturalize our current evaluations. He delights in showing how different primitive evaluations were from our own, how everything that is now considered good was originally considered evil. This is in keeping with the canon of historical method he laid down at the beginning of *Daybreak*:

"Does not every precise history of an origination impress our feelings as paradoxical and wantonly offensive? Does the good historian not, at bottom, constantly *contradict*?" (*D* 1).[41]

It would be hard to find a more radical application of this historical canon than in the opening sections of the second essay of *Genealogy*, where Nietzsche considers the painful process by which human beings became responsible beings and acquired the "right to make promises." The first step in this process involved creating a memory in human beings. As he did in the early essay on "The Uses and Disadvantages of History for Life," Nietzsche points out that forgetfulness is an essential part of living, crucial for the healthy "incorporation" of our experiences. Therefore extraordinary means were required to "burn" a memory into human beings: punishments, sacrifices, mutilations, and much blood and torture. In addition to memory, promising also presupposes that human beings are able to stick to what they have promised, to maintain their will over a long period of time in the midst of changing circumstances. If a human being "is to be able to stand security for *his own future*," he "must first of all become *calculable, regular, necessary.*" This is the fundamental labor accomplished by the morality of custom. Though it involved the most gruesome "severity, tyranny, stupidity, and idiocy," it was only through "the morality of custom and social straitjacket [that] man was actually *made* calculable" (*GM* 2.1–3; cf. *BGE* 188).

In the course of his analysis, Nietzsche refers once again to his discussion of the morality of custom in *Daybreak* (*GM* 2.2). And he concludes with a passage that recalls the famous statement in *Daybreak* that "nothing has been bought more dearly that that little bit of human reason and feeling of freedom that now constitutes our pride" (*D* 18). The passage in *Genealogy* reads: "Ah, reason, seriousness, mastery over the affects, the whole somber thing called reflection . . . how dearly they have been bought! how much blood and cruelty lie at the bottom of all 'good things'" (*GM* 2.3). Nietzsche actually quotes at length from aphorism 18 of *Daybreak* later on in *Genealogy*, when discussing the connection between philosophy and the ascetic ideal. In the era of the morality of custom, philosophy—and indeed all independent thinking—was afflicted with a bad conscience. Therefore, philosophers employed self-cruelty and "ascetic wraps and cloaks" to inspire fear in others and confidence in themselves, exemplifying the general historical rule that "every smallest step on earth has been paid for by spiritual and physical torture" (*GM* 3.9–10; see also *D* 14, 42).

Nietzsche continues his ruthless denaturalization of current moral evaluations when he takes up the central question of the origin of guilt or "bad conscience." He shows that nothing like our modern notion of guilt or the idea of personal responsibility upon which it rests existed in primitive morality. Guilt (*Schuld*) then referred to debts (*Schulden*), and punishment consisted in exacting material compensation for an injury done. What particularly offends modern moral sensibility in this primitive system of justice is that compensation generally took the form, not of money or material possessions, but of the pleasure derived from the creditor's exercise of cruelty upon the debtor, "the pleasure of being allowed to vent his power freely upon one who is powerless . . . the enjoyment of violation." Virtually quoting from *Daybreak*, Nietzsche comments that "cruelty constituted the great festival pleasure of more primitive men" (*GM* 2.4–6; *D* 18).

Clearly this purely material and external conception of morality in terms of the creditor–debtor relationship did not provide the soil out of which the more internal and spiritual notion of guilt or the "bad conscience" grew. This leads Nietzsche to put forward his own hypothesis about the origin of the "bad conscience": that it originated when human beings came to be "enclosed within the walls of society and peace." No longer able to discharge their power, aggression, and cruelty outwardly, human beings directed these instincts against themselves. This marks the beginning of the "gravest and uncanniest illness" in the history of humanity, but it also marks the moment when man ceased to be an animal and acquired what might be called a "soul." Nietzsche tries to do justice to both sides of this momentous event: "The bad conscience is an illness, there is no doubt about that, but an illness as pregnancy is an illness" (*GM* 2.16–19).

The transition to civil society was, of course, inevitable, and so, therefore, was humanity's becoming ill within its confines. What was perhaps not quite as inevitable was the way in which religion—especially Christianity—exploited this illness and developed the self-torture involved in the bad conscience "to its most gruesome pitch of severity and rigor." It is in relation to this development that Nietzsche's "polemic" becomes most polemical and he stresses the "unnaturalness" of Christianity. In the "psychical cruelty" of the latter "there resides a madness of the will that is absolutely unexampled," leading him to exclaim: "Oh this insane, pathetic beast man! What ideas he has, what unnaturalness, what paroxysms of nonsense, what *bestiality of thought* erupts as soon as he is prevented just a little from being a *beast in deed*" (*GM* 2.22).

It is in the third essay of *Genealogy*, in his treatment of the ascetic priest, that Nietzsche delivers his sharpest indictment of the antinaturalness of Christianity. That the ascetic priest denies life and all that is natural goes without saying. What Nietzsche finds more interesting is that the ascetic priest's denial of life itself springs from the desire to preserve life: "[T]he

202 / Chapter Four

ascetic ideal springs from the protective instinct of a degenerating life." As this formula suggests, it is the sick in particular that the ascetic priest helps to preserve; but this comprises no small class. As we have seen, illness inevitably accompanied entry into civil society; and Nietzsche adds that man, insofar as he is the most courageous and adventurous animal, is also *the* sick animal." At any rate, it is to the sick herd that the ascetic priest, "this strange shepherd," ministers, and he does so by providing the sick with a reason for their suffering, indeed by identifying who is to blame for their suffering, namely, themselves. The sick themselves are guilty for their suffering, which is now interpreted as punishment for their sinfulness (*GM* 3.11–15).

Here we have the invention of "sin," which Nietzsche calls "the greatest event so far in the history of the sick soul" (*GM* 3.20). In keeping with his symptomological approach to morality, he insists that "man's 'sinfulness' is not a fact, but merely the interpretation of a fact, namely of physiological suffering" (*GM* 3.16). It is an interpretation designed to alleviate this suffering by paradoxically intensifying it, producing "orgies of feeling" in which the sinner is "shattered, bowled over, crushed, enraptured, transported" (*GM* 3.20). Christianity has been particularly adept at producing such orgies of feeling; indeed, it "may be called a treasure house of ingenious means of consolation," offering a vast "collection of refreshments, palliatives, and narcotics" and showing tremendous "refinement and subtlety . . . in guessing what stimulant affects will overcome, at least for a time, the deep depression, the leaden exhaustion, the black melancholy of the physiologically inhibited" (*GM* 3.17). Nietzsche's language here is highly reminiscent of his critique of Christianity and romantic, Wagnerian art in *Human, All too Human*. And here, as there, he argues that the medicine offered to the sick by Christianity does not ultimately make them better but leaves them sicker than they were before; it constitutes "*the true calamity* in the history of European health" (*GM* 3.21).

Nietzsche's attack on the unnaturalness of Christianity, with its interpretive framework of sin, guilt, punishment, and redemption, concludes with a call for the revaluation of Christian values. Such a revaluation would involve taking the bad conscience that is currently attached to our natural inclinations and wedding it "to all of the *unnatural* inclinations." But who is strong enough to accomplish this task? Nietzsche first points to the need for free spirits: "spirits strengthened by war and victory, for whom conquest, adventure, danger, and even pain have become needs"; spirits whose heroic quest for knowledge presupposes "great health." But then he posits the need for a figure who seems to supersede the free spirit:

the *redeeming* man of great love and contempt, the creative spirit whose compelling strength will not let him rest in any aloofness or any beyond. . . . This
man of the future, who will redeem us not only from the hitherto reigning
ideal but also from that which was bound to grow out of it, the great nausea,
the will to nothingness, nihilism; this bell-stroke of noon, and of the great
decision that liberates the will again and restores its goal to the earth and his
hope to man; this Antichrist and antinihilist. (*GM* 2.24)

Earlier in the chapter, I identified the "redeeming man of great love and
contempt" spoken of here with Zarathustra. Nietzsche confirms this reading
when he comments in the section immediately following the passage just
quoted that he must silence himself lest he usurp what properly belongs
only to Zarathustra to utter (*GM* 2.25). We are back once again to the question of the relationship of the free spirit to the human type that supersedes
it: Zarathustra in the first instance, but also the *Übermensch* or new philosopher for whom Zarathustra serves as herald and midwife. It is this question
that we must now try to resolve through an analysis of the fifth book of *The
Gay Science*.

Placing the Free Spirit

Toward the end of the third essay of the *Genealogy of Morals* devoted to
the meaning of ascetic ideals, Nietzsche examines the relationship between
science and the ascetic ideal. Contrary to the belief that modern science
offers a counter-ideal to the ascetic ideal that has reigned over human history up till now, especially through religion, he argues that "science today
has absolutely *no* belief in itself, let alone an ideal above it—and where it
still inspires passion, love, ardor, and *suffering* at all, it is not the opposite
of the ascetic ideal but rather *the latest and noblest form of it*" (*GM* 3.23). It
is Nietzsche's attitude toward the latter, idealistic version of science that is
of particular interest, given that it seems to evoke his own ideal of the free
spirit. He describes modern scientific unbelievers as unconditional in "their
insistence on intellectual cleanliness"; as "hard, severe, abstinent, heroic
spirits who constitute the honor of our age"; and as the "last idealists of
knowledge in whom alone the intellectual conscience dwells and is incarnate." And yet he concludes that these scientific unbelievers "are far from
being *free* spirits: *for they still have faith in truth*" (*GM* 3.24).[42]
    Nietzsche goes on to quote from the conclusion of the aphorism in *The
Gay Science* entitled "How We, Too, Are Still Pious," an aphorism I will

analyze in depth below and one that, in its use of the first-person pronoun, raises once again the question of the relationship between the scientific ideal and the ideal of the free spirit. On the basis of this aphorism, he argues that "a *new problem arises*: that of the *value* of truth" and directs the reader to read the rest of the aphorism, "or preferably the entire fifth book of [*The Gay Science*], as well as the Preface to *Daybreak*" (*GM* 3.24). In this section, I intend to follow Nietzsche's instruction and provide an analysis of book 5 of *The Gay Science*, which was written in the fall of 1886, after *Beyond Good and Evil* and before the *Genealogy of Morals*. I will also analyze the five prefaces he wrote at this same time for the new editions of *The Birth of Tragedy, Human, All too Human, Daybreak*, and *The Gay Science*. In all of these writings, Nietzsche is concerned to "place" his free-spirit ideal and assess the quest for knowledge and will to truth that lie at the heart of it. For this reason, they provide a fitting conclusion to this study.

I will begin with the prefaces, which Nietzsche considered to be "perhaps the best prose that I have ever written" (*SB* 7:282). In the summer of 1886, he succeeded in getting the publisher E. W. Fritzsch to agree to reissue his earlier works, from *The Birth of Tragedy* through *The Gay Science*. He promptly asked Fritzsch if he could write prefaces for the new editions, explaining that he now had a distance and perspective on these works that he did not have when writing them and that this would allow him to identify what was "peculiar and imperishable" in them. He went on to write: "My writings represent a continuous development that does not merely reflect my own personal experience or fate. . . . The prefaces could make the necessity in the progress of such a development clear" (*SB* 7:225). In several places, Nietzsche repeats this point that his prefaces provide a guide to his intellectual development, "a kind of 'developmental history' [*Entwicklungsgeschichte*]" (*SB* 8:151).

What immediately strikes the reader upon reading these prefaces is how Nietzsche frames his "developmental history" in terms of the trope of health and sickness. In the Preface to the second volume of *Human, All too Human*, which in the new edition included the previously independently published supplements, *Assorted Opinions and Maxims* and *The Wanderer and His Shadow*, he describes his experience as the "history of an illness and recovery" (*HH* 2.Preface 6). This particular preface concerns itself with the break with Wagner recorded in *Human, All too Human*, characterizing it as a recovery from the illness of romanticism and the discovery of a new health. In this book, Nietzsche as both physician and patient administers the "*anti-romantic* self-treatment" and prescribes "precepts of health" (*HH* 2. Preface 2). The optimism of the book as a whole is to be understood as an antidote to the sickness of romantic pessimism, and one that "resulted in a great spiritual strengthening, an increasing joy and abundance of health" (*HH* 2.Preface 5). Nor is it Nietzsche's health alone that is at stake. He writes for a generation consisting of the "most imperiled, most spiritual, most courageous men who have to be the *conscience* of the modern soul . . . and in whom all that exists today of sickness and poison and danger comes together . . . [and] whose comfort it is to know the way to a *new* health . . . a health of tomorrow and the day after" (*HH* 2.Preface 6).

It is in this Preface to the second volume of *Human, All too Human* that we also encounter the distinction between a romantic pessimism born of sickness and weakness and a "courageous pessimism" born of strength and overflowing health, a distinction that runs through almost all of the prefaces and receives its definitive expression in aphorism 370 of *The Gay Science* (*HH* 2.Preface 4, 7). In the new Preface to *The Birth of Tragedy*, for example, Nietzsche distinguishes the pessimism that animates Greek tragedy from the modern, romantic pessimism that springs from "decline, decay, degeneration, weary and weak instincts." The pessimism of the Greeks was a "pessimism of strength" that embraced the "hard, gruesome, evil, problematic aspect of existence" and was "prompted by well-being, by overflowing health, by the *fullness* of existence." Viewed from the perspective of this pessimism, the optimism of Socrates and even of Epicurus appears to be a symptom of physiological weariness and decline (*BT* "Attempt at a Self-Criticism," 1, 4).

Not only art but philosophy, too, can be understood as springing from either weakness or strength. Nietzsche makes this point in the Preface to *The Gay Science*, as he considers the relationship between health and philosophy: "In some it is their deprivations that philosophize; in others, their riches and strengths." In the former case the philosopher seeks an escape from suffering in peace, stillness, and mildness, whereas in the latter case the philosopher will find refreshment precisely in suffering, change, and self-overcoming. Evoking the symptomological approach that runs through all of his post-Zarathustra writings, Nietzsche wonders whether philosophy hitherto "has not been merely an interpretation of the body and a *misunderstanding of the body*" (*GS* Preface 2).

Let us return to Nietzsche's specific accounts of his philosophical development in the prefaces. There are two such accounts that deserve particular attention. The first occurs in the Preface to *The Gay Science*, which begins with the statement that the book exudes overflowing gratitude, "the gratitude of a convalescent." What exactly was Nietzsche convalescing from? Not romanticism, as in *Human, All too Human*, but, rather, the harsh measures he had taken to counteract romanticism: this "stretch of desert, exhaustion, disbelief, icing up in the midst of youth, this interlude of old age at the wrong time . . . this determined self-limitation to what was bitter, harsh, and hurtful to know, prescribed by the *nausea* that had gradually developed out of an incautious and pampering spiritual diet, called romanticism" (*GS* Preface 1). It was the anti-romantic, scientific regimen of the first two works of his middle period, *Human, All too Human* and *Daybreak*, that constituted a new sickness for Nietzsche. While he is certainly not ungrateful for this sickness, for "only great pain is the ultimate liberator of the spirit, being the teacher of the *great suspicion*" (*GS* Preface 3), he nevertheless celebrates his emergence from it in *The Gay Science* and "the rejoicing of strength that is returning, of a reawakened faith in tomorrow and the day after tomorrow, of a sudden sense and anticipation of a future, of impending adventures, of seas that are open again, of goals that are permitted again, believed again" (*GS* Preface 1).

Here Nietzsche makes clear the important difference between the first two works of his middle period and the third, between the ascetic science of the former and the gay science of the latter. This difference also bears on the discussion of science and the ascetic ideal in *Genealogy*. In *The Gay Science*, Nietzsche abjures the unconditionality of the will to truth and thereby opens the door to a more profound appreciation of the role of art and appearance in life. As he puts it in the incomparable final paragraphs of the Preface:

> And as for our future, one will hardly find us again on the paths of those Egyptian youths who endanger temples by night, embrace statues, and want by all means to unveil, uncover, and put into a bright light whatever is kept concealed for good reasons. No, this bad taste, this will to truth, to "truth at any price," this youthful madness in the love of truth, has lost its charm for us: for we are too experienced, too serious, too merry, too burned, too *profound*. We no longer believe that truth remains truth when the veils are withdrawn. . . . Oh, those Greeks! They knew how to live. What is required for that is to stop courageously at the surface, the fold, the skin, to adore appearance, to believe in forms, tones, words, in the whole Olympus of appearance. Those Greeks were superficial—out of *profundity*. (*GS* Preface 4)

The second account of Nietzsche's philosophical development that commands our attention is found in the Preface to the first volume of *Human, All too Human*. This was the first of the five prefaces that Nietzsche wrote in 1886,[43] and it is of crucial importance because it contains the clearest account anywhere to be found in his works of the stages in the "history of the great liberation" of the free spirit. Three principal stages are delineated. The first—which recalls the transition from the camel to the lion in *Zarathustra*—involves breaking the sacred bonds that fetter the reverent spirit. Here the youthful soul savagely severs its connection to all that it has hitherto loved and revered. It is a painful process, and one that involves much sickness, solitude, and restless wandering in the desert (*HH* 1.Preface 3). The second stage constitutes the beginning of the free spirit's convalescence from the savage self-cruelty of the first stage; "it is characterized by a pale, subtle happiness of light and sunshine, a feeling of bird-like freedom, bird-like altitude, bird-like exuberance, and a third thing in which curiosity is united with a tender contempt. . . . One lives no longer in the fetters of love and hatred, without yes, without no" (*HH* 1.Preface 4).

Aspects of both the first and second stages in the development of the free spirit can be discerned in *Human, All too Human* and *Daybreak*.[44] The third stage, however, seems to belong to a later development. Before advancing to it, Nietzsche mentions one further step in the process of convalescence in which "the free spirit again draws near to life—slowly, to be sure, almost reluctantly, almost mistrustfully." Very much as he described the significance of *The Gay Science* in the Preface to that work, Nietzsche here remarks that this step in convalescence is marked by overwhelming gratitude. The free spirit is "grateful to his wandering, to his hardness and self-alienation, to his viewing of far distances and bird-like flights in cold heights. . . . They are the most grateful animals in the world, also the most modest, these convalescents and lizards again half-turned towards life." The long sickness constituted by the lion-willed No of the first stage of the great liberation is put behind him, and the free spirit slowly, very slowly becomes healthy (*HH* 1.Preface 5).

Now comes the third and final stage in the development of the free spirit, that of the "*mature* freedom of spirit that is equally self-mastery and discipline of the heart and permits access to many and contradictory modes of thought." Self-mastery and mastery over one's virtues lie at the heart of the "mature freedom" Nietzsche ascribes to the free spirit at this stage.[45] Also health: a "tremendous overflowing . . . health which may not dispense even with sickness as a means and fish-hook of knowledge." It is precisely the free spirit's willingness to risk himself and experiment with himself that points to his possession of "*great* health"—a term of art which we have seen Nietzsche use in *Genealogy* (*GM* 2.24), and which we will see him use again in the fifth book of *The Gay Science* (GS 382). Here he defines it as "that superfluity which grants to the free spirit the dangerous privilege of living *experimentally* [*auf den Versuch*] and of being allowed to offer itself to adventure: the master's privilege of the free spirit!" (*HH* 1.Preface 4). We are reminded that Nietzsche distinguished the new philosopher from the free spirit in *Beyond Good and Evil* by virtue of being an "attempter" or "experimenter" (*Versucher*) (*BGE* 42; see also 205, 210). Here he returns to the conception of the free spirit in the original edition of *The Gay Science* as someone who approaches life as "an experiment of the seeker after knowledge" (GS 324).

It is at this final stage in his development that the free spirit also begins to "unveil the riddle of [the] great liberation" and discern the higher goal that it serves. As a result of his adventures, experimentation, and circum-navigation "of that inner world called 'man,'" the free spirit learns "to grasp the sense of perspective in every value judgment" and the degree of injustice that inheres in every perspective. But this insight into the perspectival character of things does not lead the free spirit into an acquiescent relativism; rather, it opens the door to a new problem and a new task. For though injustice inheres in every perspective, not every perspective is unjust to the same degree. Injustice is at its greatest "where life has developed at its smallest, narrowest, neediest, most incipient"; and in order to preserve itself such a constricted perspective must take "*itself* as the goal and measure of things" and call "into question the higher, greater, richer." Insight into this aspect of perspectivism allows the free spirit to see the "problem of *order of rank*, and how power and right and spaciousness of perspectivism grow into the heights together" (*HH* 1.Preface 6–7). Nietzsche's perspectivism thus calls forth a new teaching about justice.

To what work of Nietzsche's does the "mature freedom of spirit" described here correspond? *The Gay Science*? *Beyond Good and Evil*? In the latter work, the task of determining the order of rank seemed to be given to the new philosophers. Here again we see a certain blurring of the distinction between the new philosopher and the free spirit that was drawn there. Interestingly, Nietzsche comments that the problem of the order of rank, which is *the* problem of "we free spirits," only arises at the "noon of our life" (*HH* 1.Preface 7)—noon, of course, being the critical hour of *Zarathustra*. However that may be, it is probably misguided to try to find one-to-one correspondences between the stages in the development of the free spirit and the various works Nietzsche devoted to this figure. Nevertheless, it does not seem unreasonable to assume that the fifth book of *The Gay Science*, which was written at roughly the same time as the Preface to the first volume of

Human, All too Human and which culminates in an aphorism devoted to the "great health," must embody the "mature freedom" that Nietzsche has been talking about. It is to this book that we now turn.

The fifth book of *The Gay Science* was the last of the writings under consideration in this section to be completed. In a letter to Fritzsch at the end of December 1886, Nietzsche announced its completion (*SB* 7:296).[46] The book represents the last sustained discussion of the free spirit in Nietzsche's oeuvre. Its title, "We Fearless Ones," picks up the theme of adventure, danger, and experimentation found in the description of the final stage in the development of the free spirit in the Preface to the first volume of *Human, All too Human*; and in general, it constitutes the most profound statement of what Nietzsche means by the mature free spirit—what he refers to here as the "free spirit par excellence" (*GS* 347)—that corresponds to this stage. Though the aphorisms in the book comprise a tightly interconnected whole, they have rarely been treated in this way.[47] One of purposes of my analysis is to bring out the unity of the book by viewing it in terms of the free-spirit theme.

Book 5 begins by acknowledging the defining feature of the historic predicament of late-modern European humanity that serves as the essential starting-point of Nietzsche's entire philosophy: that "'God is dead,' that the belief in the Christian god has become unbelievable." As he did so graphically in the earlier aphorism on the madman in which he originally announced the death of God , Nietzsche at first focuses on the nihilistic and cataclysmic consequences of this event. It presages the collapse of the whole of European morality, which was "built upon this faith, propped up by it, grown into it"; and it ushers in a "gloom and an eclipse of the sun whose like has probably never yet occurred on earth." But Nietzsche's real concern in this aphorism is not with the nihilistic consequences of the death of God but with the rather different effect this event has on the free spirit. He claims that we free spirits

> look forward to the approaching gloom without any real sense of involvement and above all without any worry and fear for *ourselves* . . . the consequences for *ourselves* are quite the opposite of what one might perhaps expect: they are not at all sad and gloomy but rather like a new and scarcely describable kind of light, happiness, relief, exhilaration, encouragement, dawn [*Morgenröte*]. . . . At long last the horizon appears free to us again . . . all the daring of the lover of knowledge is permitted again; the sea, *our* sea, lies open again; perhaps there has never been such an "open sea." (*GS* 343)

By highlighting the liberating effects of the death of God on the free spirit and lover of knowledge in this first aphorism, Nietzsche makes clear that his focus in book 5 will be confined to this preparatory figure. The redemption of European humanity from the world-night of nihilism belongs to Zarathustra, "the *redeeming* man of great love and contempt, the creative spirit whose compelling strength will not let him rest in any aloofness or beyond" (GM 2.24). Though added later, book 5 still belongs to *The Gay Science* and the preparatory task assigned to that book.

As he did in the aphorisms leading up to the one on the madman, Nietzsche in book 5 traces the demise of belief in the Christian god to Christianity itself: "You see what it was that really triumphed over the Christian god: Christian morality itself, the concept of truthfulness that was understood ever more rigorously, the father confessor's refinement of the Christian conscience translated and sublimated into a scientific conscience, into intellectual cleanliness at any price" (GS 357; cf. 122). This is a recurrent theme in Nietzsche's notebooks. In a famous note from 1885–86 that begins "Nihilism stands at the door," for example, he writes that the "collapse of Christianity [was] brought about by its morality," specifically by the "sense of truthfulness" cultivated by it (KSA 12:2 [127]). Incidentally, the notebook from which this note comes contains much draft-material for book 5, and we will have occasion to refer to it at several points in the analysis that follows.

The consideration that scientific truthfulness has its roots in Christian morality leads directly into the second aphorism of book 5, "How We, Too, Are Still Pious." This is the aphorism that Nietzsche quoted from extensively in his examination of the relationship between the ascetic ideal and science in the *Genealogy of Morals,* and it provides a more elaborate argument for the conclusion arrived at there. Though science at its best and as the free spirit practices it prides itself on questioning all convictions,[48] it does not succeed in being absolutely presuppositionless. The "unconditional will to truth" ultimately rests on unquestioned moral ground. This will cannot be explained simply in terms of rational prudence or utility, since in many cases untruth proves to be more useful than truth. The disutility of the will to truth is evident to anyone who has "offered and slaughtered one faith after another on this altar!" This, of course, is one of the most pervasive themes in Nietzsche's philosophy: truth is deadly; untruth and error are conditions of life. Given that this is so, the will to truth upon which science rests seems to be not only a "minor slightly mad enthusiasm" but possibly "something more serious, namely, a principle that is hostile to life and destructive . . .

a concealed will to death." Herein lies the ascetic character of science, which Nietzsche summarizes in this way:

> [T]hose who are truthful in that audacious and ultimate sense that is presupposed by the faith in science *thus affirm another world* than the world of life, nature, and history; and insofar as they affirm this "other world"—look, must they not by the same token negate its counterpart, this world, *our* world?—But you will have gathered what I am driving at, namely, that it is still a *metaphysical faith* upon which our faith in science rests—that even we seekers after knowledge today, we godless anti-metaphysicians still take our fire, too, from the flame lit by a faith that is thousands of years old, that Christian faith which was also the faith of Plato, that God is the truth, that truth is divine. But what if this should become more and more incredible, if nothing should prove to be divine anymore unless it were error, blindness, the lie—if God himself should prove to be our most enduring lie?— (*GS* 344)

As in the discussion of science and the ascetic ideal in *Genealogy*, which quotes this very passage, Nietzsche's use of the first person pronoun in this aphorism is somewhat confusing. Does he include himself among those who are still pious and who take their inspiration from the moral and metaphysical faith upon which science ultimately rests? In some sense he clearly does, since he not only uses the first person pronoun but also refers to "we seekers after knowledge today, we godless anti-metaphysicians." But insofar as he is calling attention to the ascetic and metaphysical character of the unconditional will to truth and thereby calling it into question, he is also clearly beyond it. Another way of putting the question is whether Nietzsche sees the free spirit as ultimately bound by the ascetic ideal of science. Here again his attitude seems to be more complicated. From what we have already seen in the prefaces of 1886, though there is a stage of the free spirit that corresponds to the unconditional and ascetic will to truth, there is also a mature freedom of spirit that seems to transcend it. We will see a similar development of Nietzsche's notion of the free spirit in book 5.

In the course of his reflections on the "piety" of science, Nietzsche shows that the question "Why science?" raises an even more fundamental problem: "*Why have morality at all* when life, nature, and history are 'not moral'?" (*GS* 344). Therefore, it is not surprising that in the next aphorism he takes up the topic of "Morality as a Problem." And what more than anything else strikes his attention is how little morality has been a problem for philosophers up to now. For the most part they have simply deferred to the prevalent morality and at most sought to find a rational foundation for it. No one has "ventured a *critique* of moral valuations." Even historians who have inquired into the origins of morality—"mostly Englishmen," Nietzsche comments, but he also refers obliquely to Rée—have not ventured such a critique but instead have simply accepted the common opinion that "what is characteristic of moral actions is selflessness . . . and pity" (GS 345; cf. BGE 186).

What does a critique of morality consist in? Here Nietzsche makes an important methodological point that differentiates his later critique of morality from his earlier one. He remarks that one of the mistakes historians of morality have made is in thinking that by exposing the erroneousness of the opinions people have held about morality—for example, that there are nonegoistic actions or that we possess free will—they have actually criticized morality. This is exactly the mistake Nietzsche made in *Daybreak*, where he claimed that his distinctive way of denying morality consisted in denying that "moral judgments are based on truths" (D 103). Now he claims that the *value* of a moral prescription is in no way affected by the erroneous opinions that might be held about it, in the same way that the value of a medication is in no way affected by the unscientific opinions a patient may hold about it: "Even if a morality has grown out of an error, the realization of this fact would not as much as touch the problem of its value" (GS 345).[49] Here Nietzsche encapsulates the shift in his critique of morality that we have already detected in *Beyond Good and Evil* and the *Genealogy of Morals*. In contrast to the intellectualism that still informs his critique of morality in *Daybreak*, he now focuses his critique on the *value* of moral values. This value is to be understood in relation to life, which is itself to be understood in relation to the will to power.

Nietzsche's exposure of the moral/ascetic foundations of science in aphorism 344 and his critique of those foundations in aphorism 345 lead to a reconsideration of the nature of the free spirit in the following aphorism, "Our Question Mark." Specifically, Nietzsche needs to emancipate the free spirit completely from the moral or ascetic ideal. He asks, "Who are we anyway?" Somehow the expressions "godless," "unbelievers," and even "immoralists" are not entirely adequate in that they still retain an ascetic odor: "Ours is no longer the bitterness and passion of the person who has torn himself away and still feels compelled to turn his unbelief into a new belief, a purpose, a martyrdom." For Nietzsche, modern pessimism à la Schopenhauer is the great example of a godlessness that remains entangled in asceticism and morality. The modern pessimist penetrates to the meaninglessness, purposelessness, and immorality of the world—Nietzsche refers at one point to Schopenhauer's "horrified look into a de-deified world that has become stupid, blind, mad, and questionable" (GS 357)—but because the world now no longer has the value previously accorded to it, he concludes that it is somehow worth less. Though modern pessimism evacuates the world of god and morality, it still invokes morality to pass judgment on it. This is what ultimately makes it nihilistic (GS 346; see also WP 32).[50]

That nihilism is what is ultimately at stake in this aphorism becomes clear in the paradoxical conclusion to it.[51] Having rejected Schopenhauerian pessimism for setting itself up as the "judge of the world who in the end places existence itself upon the scales and finds it wanting," Nietzsche wonders whether he and other free spirits are not guilty of carrying contempt for man and pessimism one step further by opening up a rift "between the world in which we were at home up to now with our reverences that perhaps made it possible for us to *endure* life, and another world *that consists of us.*" We are reminded of the ascetic denial of "*our* world," the world of "life, nature, and history" that Nietzsche spoke of in the aphorism on the piety of the free spirit. Here the fundamental question of our time—and, one might say, of Nietzsche's entire philosophy—has been raised. The aforementioned rift produces an

> inexorable, fundamental, and deepest suspicion about ourselves that is more and more gaining worse and worse control of us Europeans and that could easily confront coming generations with the terrifying Either/Or: 'Either abolish your reverences or—*yourselves!*' The latter would be nihilism; but would not the former also be—nihilism?—This is *our* question mark. (GS 346)

In the draft note for this passage, Nietzsche referred only to the abolition of ourselves as nihilism,[52] but the more interesting point is his questioning of the free spirit's attempt to abolish the reverences that make it possible for us to endure life. Somehow science must be deprived of its ascetic character and reconciled with life-preserving reverences, errors, and illusions. It must join with "artistic energies and the practical wisdom of life" to form a "higher organic system" (GS 113). It must, in short, become gay science.

The following aphorism, "Believers and Their Need to Believe," confirms this point and concludes Nietzsche's initial effort to emancipate the free spirit from the ascetic ideal. Once again, he attacks those modern unbelievers who still retain vestiges of faith, like the scientific positivists who are driven by the "demand for certainty," the desire that something in the world should stand firm, or the Russian nihilists who believe in unbelief "even to the point of martyrdom." It is against such incomplete and ultimately ascetic free spirits that Nietzsche defines his own ideal of the mature free spirit, what he calls the *"free spirit* par excellence,"* who has taken leave "of all faith and every wish for certainty, being practiced in maintaining himself on insubstantial ropes and possibilities and dancing even near abysses" (GS 347). In the light of passages such as this one—and of the repeated references to experimentation, adventure, risk, and ambiguity that run through book 5 of *The Gay Science*—Heidegger's tendentious attempts to associate Nietzsche with the Cartesian quest for certainty ring quite hollow.[53]

This brings to an end Nietzsche's initial attempt to define the free spirit in book 5. The first five aphorisms of the book describe a movement from the pious free spirit who still partakes of a moral/metaphysical faith to the free spirit par excellence who has taken leave of all faith. Nietzsche will return at the end of book 5 to complete his portrait of the free spirit, but before he gets there he considers a variety of human types that are opposed to and sometimes confused with the free spirit: the scholar or scientific man, the religious sage, and the artist.[54]

He begins with scholars and scientists, whose proclivity to classify, schematize, exalt logic, and interpret the world in crude mechanistic or materialistic terms betrays their origin in the lower or middle classes, the clerical or mechanical trades (GS 348). This is clearly the case with natural scientists who see self-preservation instead of the expansion of power as the fundamental instinct of life. The Darwinian emphasis on the "struggle for existence" could only emanate from scientists whose impoverished background made sheer survival the primary concern. Indeed, the "whole of English Darwinism breathes something like the musty air of English overpopulation, like the smell of distress and overcrowding of small people." It is in this context that Nietzsche refers—for the first and only time in book 5—to his doctrine of the will to power: "The struggle for existence is only an *exception*, a temporary restriction of the will to life." The fundamental struggle always revolves "around growth, expansion, around power—in accordance with the will to power, which is the will of life" (GS 349; cf. BGE 13).

A little later, Nietzsche expands on his critique of science in an aphorism entitled "'Science' as a Prejudice." The scare quotes around "science" indicate that he has a naïve, positivistic understanding of science in mind, not the radically skeptical scientific attitude of the free spirit. Once again, he points to the middle-class origins of scientists as an explanation of their crude and superficial interpretation of things. How else to explain Herbert Spencer's enthusiasm for his ideal reconciliation of egoism and altruism, a possibility that fills the rest of us with disgust? Nietzsche also sees commonness in the efforts of "materialistic natural scientists" to interpret the world in purely quantitative terms. Such an interpretation, which "permits counting, calculating, weighing, seeing, and touching, and nothing more," is capable of grasping only the "most superficial and external aspect of existence"; it is the "stupidest" interpretation of the world, and one that is "poorest in meaning." A more refined taste seeks instead not "to divest existence of its *rich ambiguity*" (*GS* 373).

These thoughts on "science" lead Nietzsche to reflect more deeply on the concept of "knowledge" presupposed by it—once again he uses scare quotes to differentiate the knowledge pursued by the positivistic scientist from the knowledge sought by the free spirit. The concept of "knowledge" that the positivistic scientist shares with the common people involves the reduction of "something strange" to "something *familiar*." And what lies behind this will to reduce "everything strange, unusual, and questionable [to] something that no longer disturbs us" is the "instinct of fear" and the desire for security. Precisely the opposite impulse governs psychology and the investigation of the elements of consciousness. These "*unnatural* sciences" seek to discern what is strange and questionable in what is most familiar to us (*GS* 355).[55] The contrast Nietzsche draws here parallels the one he drew in *Beyond Good and Evil* between the simplifying "basic will of the spirit" that seeks "to file new things in old files" and the self-cruelty of the free-spirited seeker after knowledge that thrives on complexity and ambiguity (*BGE* 230).

The kind of simplifying and abbreviating of experience that belongs to the concept of "knowledge" is a general feature of all conscious thinking, and therefore it is to the "problem of consciousness" that Nietzsche turns in the important aphorism "On the 'Genius of the Species.'" The fundamental problem of consciousness is why we need it at all, given that we could carry on all of our functions—thinking, feeling, willing, and acting—without it. Why do we need to see our lives as if in a mirror? The answer Nietzsche gives is that consciousness originally developed out of the need on the part of human beings as herd animals to communicate. Especially in primitive times, it was necessary for human beings to communicate with one another when they were in distress and needed help. But in order to communicate what they needed, human beings first had to become conscious of it. In this way, consciousness developed in relation to "herd utility"; it had nothing to do with individual existence. "Fundamentally, all our actions are altogether incomparably personal, unique, and infinitely individual." By translating them into consciousness we simplify them and make them generic. The world of which we become conscious "is only a surface and sign-world, a world that is made common and meaner," shallower and stupider (*GS* 354).[56]

Nietzsche's assault on consciousness here extends not only to conscious thinking but to conscious willing as well, a topic he takes up in the aphorism on "Two Kinds of Causes That Are Often Confounded." The two kinds of causes he refers to are, first, the dammed-up energy that causes us to act, and second, the goal or purpose that causes us to act in a certain way. And the fundamental point he wants to make is that the second of these causes is relatively insignificant as compared with the first, "a match versus a ton of powder." Goals, purposes, motives, intentions—these belong to consciousness, and in keeping with his analysis in the previous aphorism, Nietzsche argues that they are merely interpretations, rather simplistic interpretations, of a much more complex and generally unconscious process. This is a point we have seen him make in a variety of ways ever since *Daybreak*. Here he uses the vivid metaphor of a ship without a helmsman to capture the epiphenomenal character of our conscious goals and purposes:

> Is the "goal," the "purpose' not often enough a beautifying pretext, a self-deception of vanity after the event that does not want to acknowledge that the ship is *following* the current into which it has entered accidentally? That it "wills" to go that way *because it—must*? that it has a direction, to be sure, but—no helmsman at all?—We still need a critique of the concept of "purpose." (*GS* 360)[57]

From Nietzsche's critical discussion of the scholar or scientist, we were led to his more fundamental reflections on knowledge, consciousness, and volition. We must now turn to the second figure from whom he seeks to differentiate the authentic free spirit: the religious priest or sage. Like the "famous wise" of *Zarathustra*, the priest embodies the kind of serene, detached "wisdom" that is revered by the people and is worlds away from the "great *passion* of the seeker after knowledge" (*GS* 351). The religious saint or sage is the enemy of the spirit (*GS* 359), which Zarathustra once defined as "life that cuts into life," increasing knowledge through its own agony (*Z* 2.8). And the founders of religions do not so much create new values as recognize and glorify the values of the common people that are already there (*GS* 353).

A somewhat surprising feature of Nietzsche's treatment of religion in book 5 is the praise he lavishes on the Roman Catholic church, which he sees as an aristocratic institution that exhibits a profound skepticism about the common people so flattered by the priestly type. The Catholic church "rests upon a southern suspicion about the nature of man," in contrast to the more democratic and egalitarian north (*GS* 350). It embodies a "*south-*

ern freedom and enlightenment of the spirit" that was completely misunderstood by Luther, who in all respects was a "man of the common people." In short, against the Catholic church, which was "above all a structure of ruling that secure[d] the highest rank for the *more spiritual* human beings," the Protestant Reformation represents the "peasant rebellion of the spirit" (*GS* 358). Nietzsche's appreciation for religion and especially the church here is not altogether new. In *Beyond Good and Evil*, we saw him criticize the free spirit's "profound lack of understanding of the church" (*BGE* 105) and endorse the new philosopher's use of religion for his "project of cultivation and education" (*BGE* 61).

Let us now turn to the third human type that Nietzsche considers in book 5, the artist. Unlike the religious sage with his "wisdom" and the scholar with his "knowledge," both of whom can be seen as rivals to the free spirit (see *KSA* 11:35 [24]), the artist represents the complete antithesis of the free spirit, upholding falseness against the latter's truthfulness. Indeed, it was against the artist in the form of Richard Wagner that Nietzsche originally defined his free spirit in the period surrounding the first Bayreuth Festival in 1876. In his notebooks from that period, especially 1874, Nietzsche frequently referred to Wagner as an "actor" primarily concerned with producing striking effects. Reflecting on his relationship to Wagner years later, in 1885–86, he comments that he "loved and admired Richard Wagner more than anyone else" but eventually realized that "his cause was not to be confused with mine." It was then that "I came to my senses about the extraordinary problem of the actor . . . [and] discovered and recognized the actor at the root of every artist" (*KSA* 12:2 [34]). It is through the "problem of the actor" that Nietzsche now approaches the problem of the artist in book 5, arguing that both exhibit the same delight in falseness, simulation, roles, and masks (*GS* 361).

Before elaborating on this relationship between the actor and the artist, Nietzsche points to the more pervasive role of acting in modern culture in an aphorism entitled "How Things Will Become Ever More 'Artistic' in Europe." This is a striking aphorism because it condemns precisely the arbitrary creativity and experimentalism with which Nietzsche has become identified in the popular imagination.[58] As social mobility and the freedom to choose one's occupation have grown, he argues, individuals have come to think of themselves more and more as role-players. In contrast to the faith that one is predestined for a certain occupation, a faith that helped "to erect those monsters of social pyramids that distinguish the Middle Ages," a new faith has emerged, one that Nietzsche associates preeminently with America but believes has started to infiltrate Europe as well: the faith that the individual "can do just about everything and *can manage almost any role,*" so that "everyone experiments with himself, improvises, makes new experiments, enjoys his experiments; and all nature ceases and becomes art." Nietzsche acknowledges that this actor's faith produces some interesting "new human flora and fauna," but he also worries that it disadvantages another human type, the "great master builders" of the future. Sounding a little like Tocqueville,[59] he writes: "The strength to build becomes paralyzed; the courage to make plans that encompass the distant future is discouraged. . . . What is dying out is the fundamental faith . . . that man has value and meaning only insofar as he is *a stone in a great edifice*; and to that end he must be *solid* first of all, a 'stone'—and above all not an actor!" (GS 356).[60]

Of all the "actors" in modern culture, Nietzsche reserves a special contempt for the "man of letters" (*Literat*), who "plays the 'expert'" (GS 361)—today he often goes by the name of "public intellectual." So repulsed is he by these "salesmen of the spirit" that he is moved to praise scholars, who, despite their "nooks" and "hunched backs," have at least mastered a craft, possess an "unconditional probity," and do not pretend to be something that they are not (GS 366). His own strategy for opposing the actors and demagogues of the spirit—a strategy that appears in almost all of his writings—is to flee into solitude, become a hermit, practice the arts of concealment, don a mask, and cherish his incomprehensibility (GS 364–65, 371).

Nietzsche is now ready to take up the question of art proper, and he begins by making a distinction between "monologue-art" and "art before witnesses." The latter, of course, is the kind of art produced by the actor, but the fact that Nietzsche acknowledges the possibility of a different kind of art, an art that "has forgotten the world," suggests that the identification of the artist with the actor is not absolute (GS 367). In the next aphorism Nietzsche finally names Wagner, characterizing him as "essentially a man of the theater and an actor, the most enthusiastic mimomaniac of all time" (GS 368). But as is often the case with his judgments on Wagner, he does not simply leave it at that. In the very next aphorism, he describes an artist who is so absorbed in what he creates that he does not have time to reflect on what he is doing and thereby becomes capable of uttering stupidities about himself and his work (GS 369). Though Nietzsche does not explicitly refer to Wagner here, we need only look at the aphorism on "Schopenhauer's Followers" in the first edition of *The Gay Science* to see that he has him in mind. There he claims that Wagner's attempt to understand his art in terms of Schopenhauer's philosophy had nothing to do with what was true and authentic in it but was merely a bit of play-acting typical of artists (GS 99).

Schopenhauer and Wagner are both at the heart of Nietzsche's culminating aphorism on art, "What is Romanticism?" Here he returns to the
distinction between romantic pessimism and the pessimism of strength
that he made in his 1886 prefaces. The former, which he associates with
the philosophy of Schopenhauer (also of Epicurus) and the music of Wagner, springs from the experience of those who "suffer from the *impoverishment of life* and seek rest, stillness, calm seas, redemption from themselves
through art and knowledge, or intoxication, convulsions, anaesthesia, and
madness." The latter pessimism corresponds to those who "suffer from the
overfullness of life" and who "want a Dionysian art and likewise a tragic view
of life." Nietzsche claims that his great mistake in *The Birth of Tragedy* was to
interpret the former, romantic pessimism in terms of the latter, Dionysian
pessimism. However that may be, the distinction between these two types
of pessimism offers a slightly different way of judging works of art from
the previous distinction between monologue-art and actor's art. The question now to be asked of works of art is whether they spring from "hunger
or superabundance." It is the same question that Nietzsche has addressed
to philosophies, moralities, and religions in the other later works we have
considered in this chapter. Indeed, in the aphorism on romanticism, he
provides as good a short summary of the psychological and symptomological method that is so fundamental to his later outlook as is to be found in
any of his mature works: "the backward inference from the work to the
maker, from the deed to the doer, from the ideal to those who *need it*, from
every way of thinking and valuing to the commanding need behind it"
(GS 370).

Having considered the human types that are opposed to and have
sometimes been confused with the free spirit, Nietzsche returns in the final
aphorisms of book 5 to the free spirit himself to round out the portrait he
began to paint at the beginning of the book. Before diverting to consider the
scholar/scientist, the religious sage, and the artist as actor and pessimist, he
had arrived at the notion of the "free spirit par excellence" who has taken
leave "of all faith and every wish for certainty" (GS 347). It is this highest
stage of the free spirit, characterized by supreme "self mastery and discipline
of the heart" (*HH* I Preface 4), that he proceeds to elaborate in the ten aphorisms (GS 374–83) at the end of the book.

He begins with a statement of the perspectivism that underpins the adventurous and experimental quest for knowledge of the free spirit. The aphorism entitled "Our New 'Infinite'" comes immediately after the aphorism
in which Nietzsche critiques scientific positivism for its belief that there is

only one justifiable interpretation, thereby divesting "existence of its *rich ambiguity*" (*GS* 373). In a note from this period, he encapsulates his critique of scientific positivism in this way: "Against the positivism which halts at phenomena—'There are only facts'—I would say: no, facts are just what there are not, only interpretations" (*KSA* 12:7 [60]). Given the interpreted or perspectival character of existence, Nietzsche now asks how far it extends or "whether existence has any other character than this." This is ultimately a metaphysical question, and he deftly sidesteps it by saying we cannot really know whether there is some ultimate reality beyond our interpretations, or whether it is interpretation all the way down: even the "most scrupulously conscientious analysis and self-examination of the intellect . . . cannot avoid seeing itself in its own perspectives, and *only* in these. We cannot look around our own corner." Though we cannot answer the ultimate metaphysical question, Nietzsche claims that it would be "immodest" of us to think that perspectives are permitted only from our little corner. In this way "the world has become 'infinite' for us all over again, inasmuch as we cannot reject the possibility that *it may include infinite interpretations.*" But unlike the old infinite, this new "infinite" (always in quotation marks) is not to be deified, for "too many *ungodly* possibilities" are contained in it, "too much devilry, stupidity, and foolishness of interpretation" (*GS* 374).

The perspectival and infinitely interpretable character of the world inevitably makes the free spirit suspicious of all ultimate convictions, strong faiths, and unconditional Yeses and Nos. Is this mistrust to be understood as the defensive reaction of the "disappointed idealist"? Nietzsche believes there is something less ascetic, more positive and Epicurean, to this mistrust of all certainties: "the jubilant curiosity of one who formerly stood in his corner and was driven to despair by his corner, and now delights and luxuriates in the opposite of a corner, in the boundless, in what is 'free as such.'" "Boundless" (*Unbegrenzten*) is the word Nietzsche used to describe the historical sense in *Beyond Good and Evil* (*BGE* 224), where it suggested both the distinctive pleasure and the ignoble taste of this sense. To what extent he means to point to the limitations of the free spirit ideal in *The Gay Science* we will discuss in a moment. It is interesting that, as in the aphorism in *Beyond*, he here employs the metaphor of the horse and rider to evoke the free spirit's fearless quest for knowledge. But unlike in *Beyond*, he stresses the self-mastery and discipline of the free spirit. Instead of "dropping the reins before the infinite," he speaks of tightening them "as our urge for certainty races ahead, this self-control of the rider during his wildest rides; for we still ride mad and fiery horses, and when we hesitate it is least of all danger that makes us hesitate" (*GS* 375).

And what of the politics of these free-spirited riders who rein in their drive to certainty? Nietzsche addresses this subject in the aphorism entitled "We Who Are Homeless." He describes the free spirits as homeless because they live in a "fragile, broken time of transition," between the dead ideals of the past and the unborn ideals of the future. This is not the first time in book 5 that Nietzsche has characterized the present age as a time of transition (see GS 343, 356, 358). And because it is a time of transition, the free spirits will not be "conservative"—there is nothing worth conserving. But even more emphatically they will not be "liberal," because the ideas of "progress" and "equal rights" that belong to liberalism constitute a path to the "deepest leveling and *chinoiserie*." Echoing the aphorism on "Preparatory Human Beings" from the first edition of *The Gay Science* (GS 283), Nietzsche writes: "[W]e are delighted with all who love, as we do, danger, war, and adventures, who refuse to compromise, to be captured, reconciled, and castrated." Echoing the aphorism on the authentic free spirit in *Beyond Good and Evil* (BGE 44), he goes even further in his rejection of humane and egalitarian liberalism: "[W]e think about the necessity for new orders, also for a new slavery—for every strengthening and enhancement of the human type also involves a new kind of enslavement" (GS 377).

To think about the necessity for new orders and a new slavery is something different from actually instituting them. The free spirit is a preparatory human being and as such not yet the practitioner of "great politics." This is evident in Nietzsche's scathing indictment of the "nationalism and race hatred" that is infecting Europe. Though he dismisses nationalist politics as "petty politics"—in *Human, All too Human*, he criticized them under the rubric of "great politics" (HH 481)—he seems more concerned with how such politics spoil the honesty and intellectual conscience of the free spirit. For nationalist politics "we are too open-minded, too malicious . . . too 'traveled': we far prefer to live on mountains, apart, 'untimely,' in past or future centuries, merely in order to keep ourselves from experiencing the silent rage to which we know we should be condemned as eyewitnesses of politics that are desolating the German spirit." Invoking the expression he used all the way back in *Human, All too Human* (HH 475), Nietzsche describes the homeless free spirits as "good Europeans" (GS 377).[61]

The conclusion to "We Who Are Homeless" raises once again the question of the purpose or point of the free spirit's repudiation of all faith and certainty. Nietzsche reiterates that the free spirit's rejection of Christianity is itself an outgrowth of the intellectual honesty demanded by Christianity. And as earlier Christians "willingly sacrificed possessions, and position, blood and fatherland," for their faith, so we free spirits "do the same." The question of asceticism comes up again: Why do we free spirits sacrifice our most comforting illusions? "For our unbelief? For *every* kind of unbelief? No, you know better than that, friends! The hidden Yes in you is stronger than all Nos and Maybes that afflict you and your age like a disease; and when you have to embark on the sea, you emigrants, you, too, are compelled to do this by—a *faith*!" (GS 377). In a note to this passage, Kaufmann directs the reader back to aphorism 344 on the residual piety and morality in the free spirit's quest for scientific knowledge. While not wholly implausible, this interpretive claim misses the degree to which Nietzsche's "free spirit par excellence" has left behind the moral and metaphysical faith attributed to the still pious free spirit in aphorism 344. In the passage from "We Who Are Homeless," Nietzsche once again says No to turning unbelief into a "new belief, a purpose, a martyrdom" (GS 346). The "faith" he refers to is not the old ascetic faith but a faith in a future ideal for which, in this time of transition, the free spirit serves as a preparatory figure.

Before elaborating further on this future ideal, Nietzsche amplifies on the necessary homelessness of the free spirit—the aloofness from his times and other human beings that his task of acquiring knowledge requires. He warns first against misanthropy and "Timonic" hatred, which only serves to entangle and imprison the free spirit. It is better to practice "refined contempt," to be a "virtuoso of contempt," concealing the inward shudder one feels when associating with other human beings behind a mask of politeness and finding refreshment in the "artist's escape from man, or the artist's mockery of man, or the artist's mockery of himself "(GS 379). In the next aphorism, we hear from the "wanderer," the figure Nietzsche first introduced in the final aphorism of *Human, All too Human* (HH 638), who indicates that in order to assess European morality one must occupy a position outside of it. Therefore, one "has to be *very light* to drive one's will to knowledge into such distances and, as it were, beyond one's time, to create for oneself eyes to survey millennia." In a sly reference to his early writings, Nietzsche claims that the free spirit's overcoming of his time in himself also involves overcoming his hatred of this time, "his suffering from this time, his untimeliness [*Zeit-Ungemässheit*], his *romanticism*" (GS 380).

Part of the free spirit's art of evasion consists in communicating with a select audience and erecting barriers against the vulgar. In the aphorism "On the Question of Being Understandable," Nietzsche provides one of his clearest explanations of his esotericism and aphoristic style. He concentrates on two aspects of this style: liveliness and ignorance. With respect to the first, he indicates that he has always found it better to "approach deep problems like cold baths: quickly into them and quickly out of them again."

Insights generally come in flashes, not in long brooding. The other reason for brevity is that every immoralist must "take steps against corrupting innocents." And what about ignorance? Here Nietzsche returns to the theme of differentiating the free-spirited philosopher from the scholar: "We have different needs, grow differently, and also have a different digestion: we need more, we also need less." For the adventures of the free spirit, it is better "to live in freedom with little to eat than unfree and stuffed. It is not fat but the greatest possible suppleness and strength that a good dancer desires from his nourishment—and I would not know what the spirit of a philosopher might wish more to be than a good dancer" (GS 381).

The image of dancing was invoked earlier in connection with the "free spirit par excellence" (GS 347), and it pervades the final aphorism of book 5, which is given over to "gaiety" (GS 383). The climax of book 5, however, comes in the penultimate aphorism of the book, "The Great Health." Nietzsche used this image in the Preface to *Human, All too Human* to designate the highest stage of the free spirit, the stage of the mature free spirit. He now elaborates on it in what may be his most beautiful evocation of the "jubilant curiosity" of the free spirit. Such curiosity presupposes a new and overflowing health as its precondition:

> Whoever has a soul that craves to have experienced the whole range of values and desiderata to date, and to have sailed around all the coasts of this ideal "mediterranean"; whoever wants to know from the adventures of his own most authentic experience how a discoverer and conqueror of the ideal feels, and also an artist, a saint, a legislator, a sage, a scholar, a pious man, a soothsayer, and one who stands divinely apart in the old style—needs one thing above everything else: the *great health*.

The adventures of the free spirits or "argonauts of the ideal" ultimately disclose an "as yet undiscovered country whose boundaries nobody has surveyed yet, something beyond all the lands and nooks of the ideal so far, a world . . . overrich in what is beautiful, strange, questionable, terrible, and divine" (GS 382).

We have reached the pinnacle of the free spirit's intrepid quest for knowledge. And yet Nietzsche raises one more question, the question that in many ways provoked the project of *Zarathustra* with which we began this chapter. "After such vistas," he asks, "how could we still be satisfied with *present-day man*?" Indeed, how can the free spirit return from his travels and adventures without experiencing an even more profound nausea with the insipid ideal of modern democratic man. A new ideal is needed, and one that goes beyond the knowledge-seeking free spirit and points to the *Übermensch* and the legislative new philosophers of *Beyond Good and Evil.* Nietzsche describes it this way:

> Another ideal runs ahead of us, a strange, tempting [*versucherisches*], danger-ous ideal to which we should not wish to persuade anybody because we do not readily concede *the right to it* to anyone: the ideal of a spirit who plays na-ively—that is, not deliberately but from overflowing power and abundance—with all that was hitherto called holy, good, untouchable, divine . . . the ideal of a human, superhuman [*übermenschlichen*] well-being and benevolence that will often appear *inhuman*—for example, when it confronts all earthly seri-ousness so far, all solemnity in gesture, word, tone, eye, morality, and task so far, as if it were their most involuntary parody—and in spite of all this, it is perhaps only with him that *great seriousness* really begins, that the real ques-tion mark is posed for the first time, that the destiny of the soul changes, the hand moves forward, the tragedy *begins*. (GS 382)[62]

The final words of this aphorism of course recall the *Incipit Tragoedia* with which the 1882 edition of *The Gay Science* concluded and the first part of *Zarathustra* began. The aphorism makes clear that Nietzsche has not given up on the "strange, tempting, and dangerous" ideal of the latter work.[63] But even more importantly, the aphorism makes clear how that ideal grows out of the ideal of the free spirit. The later Nietzsche and the Nietzsche of the middle works here join hands.

This study began with Nietzsche's flight from Bayreuth, Wagner, and romanticism in general in 1876. In the book he began to write shortly thereafter, *Human, All too Human*, he constructed his new ideal of the free spirit, a figure who, animated by reason and the scientific spirit, rejects the comforting illusions of metaphysics, religion, and morality and lives "among men without praising, blaming, contending, gazing contentedly, as though at a spectacle, upon many things for which one formerly felt only fear" (*HH* 34). Though in the books immediately following *Human, All too Human*, Nietzsche modified his purely contemplative understanding of the free spirit—in *Daybreak* he spoke of the "passion for knowledge" (*D* 429), and in *The Gay Science* he revealed that the so-called contemplative human being is actually the "poet who keeps creating this life" and who continually fashions "something that had not been there before" (*GS* 301)—he never abandoned his commitment to the ideal of a life devoted to the quest for knowledge and the ceaseless exploration of the "whole marvelous uncertainty and rich ambiguity of existence" (*GS* 2).

The free-spirit trilogy of the middle period thus discloses the appealing image of a rational Nietzsche. A rational Nietzsche? The idea sounds almost as paradoxical as an "artistic Socrates" (*BT* 14). What about Nietzsche's post-*Zarathustra* writings and his ominous-sounding ideas of the *Übermensch*, the will to power, and the eternal recurrence? Don't these make the idea of a rational Nietzsche seem naïve and apologetic?

We are thus inevitably led to the question of the relationship between Nietzsche's middle and mature works. In the course of this study, especially in the final chapter, I have tried to show that, while there are certainly important differences between these two phases of Nietzsche's philosophical career, there are also equally important continuities. In many ways, *The Gay*

Science constitutes the crucial bridge between them. In that work, as we have seen, the skepticism and renunciatory knowledge that animate the activity of the free spirit in the middle works lead not only to the death of God and the advent of nihilism but also point the way out of this horrific predicament. The de-deification of nature and the disclosure of the inhuman necessity or chaos that underlies it do not necessarily result in desolation but can lead to open seas that permit the daring of the free-spirited knower and the creativity of the philosopher. It is this unprecedented opportunity that inspires the project of *Zarathustra* and explains the ideas of the *Übermensch*, the will to power, and the eternal recurrence. The eternal recurrence guarantees the chaos or endless becoming that serves as the basis for the radical creativity or spiritual will to power of the *Übermensch* or new philosopher.

This, of course, raises the specter of relativism. As Allan Bloom has eloquently put it: once "one ventures out into the vast spaces opened up by Nietzsche, it is hard to set limits."[1] But to argue that there are no constraints on the creativity of the *Übermensch* or new philosopher ignores the important role that knowledge and the free spirit continue to play in Nietzsche's mature philosophy. As we have seen, he insists that the free spirit is a necessary precursor and precondition for the new philosopher, and that the new philosopher is a free spirit, a very free spirit, as well as something more, higher, and greater. First, the free spirit prepares the revaluation of values and brings about the self-overcoming of morality that are the preconditions of the creativity of the new philosopher. Second, by looking at the world through many different eyes and perspectives and experiencing the "whole range of values and desiderata to date" (GS 382), the free spirit insures that the creativity of the new philosopher or *Übermensch* has depth and breadth and is not cramped or confined to a narrow nook. It is precisely this breadth and comprehensiveness of perspective that establishes the order of rank among human beings and values, an order of rank where "power and right and spaciousness of perspective grow into the heights together" (HH 1. Preface 6). All of this suggests that Nietzsche's mature philosophy is not nearly as relativistic or unconstrained as conservative critics like Bloom or postmodern defenders like Foucault or Deleuze suppose.

It does not suggest, however, that there is nothing problematic in Nietzsche's mature philosophy. This is especially true with respect to what he referred to as "great politics." I have already remarked on the ambiguity that surrounds Nietzsche's political speculations in his later works. Given his blanket dismissal of all the real-world political options of his time, from nationalism and socialism to anarchism and democracy, and given his contempt for the modern state and modern politics in general, it is never clear how Nietzsche's great politics or "aristocratic radicalism" connects even remotely with politics conventionally understood. Nor is it clear what he means when he calls for ruling castes, spiritual tyrants, and a new slavery, not to mention the "annihilation of millions of failures" (WP 964; see also 862). In his early and middle writings, Nietzsche had been principally concerned with culture over and against politics; indeed, it was in the name of culture that he initially attacked great politics. This antipolitical preoccupation with culture continues to inform Nietzsche's later outlook—"what matters most . . . is always culture" (TI Germans 4)—but he combines it with a vision of great politics that makes it extremely unclear at any given time whether he is talking about culture or politics. All of this is unsatisfactory in the extreme and leads Nietzsche to oscillate between an irresponsible denigration of politics, on the one hand, and an indulgence in dangerous political fantasies and rhetoric, on the other.

I do not think these political consequences, such as they are, follow necessarily from the enduring core of Nietzsche's philosophy. And while I do not think one should ignore them (à la Walter Kaufmann), I do not think it particularly helpful or illuminating to dwell on them either.[2] What more than anything else Nietzsche's political speculations suggest is the need for a new investigation—and one that is far more nuanced and hardheaded than anything Nietzsche has to offer—of the relationship between culture and politics, the former being concerned with the highest enhancement and richest development of human possibilities, the latter being concerned to insure that this perfectionist quest does not lead to the degradation of human beings below the level of ordinary decency.

Needless to say, I cannot hope to contribute anything very substantial to such an investigation at this late stage of my analysis. What I can affirm is that, at least with respect to the side of culture, the side that is concerned with meaning, values, self-realization, and spiritual fulfillment, Nietzsche remains an indispensable guide. In his philosophy, he unflinchingly faces up to our nihilistic predicament, but he also shows us a way out of it that does not involve relapsing into romantic nostalgia, resorting to edifying mythology, or abandoning human reason. It is, of course, the last of these features of Nietzsche's philosophy that I have stressed in my interpretation, and it is the feature that the free-spirit trilogy from the middle period, more than any of Nietzsche's other works, allows us to appreciate.

NOTES

PREFACE

1. Ruth Abbey, *Nietzsche's Middle Period* (Oxford: Oxford University Press, 2000).

2. An exhaustive listing of such scholarly examinations of Nietzsche's influences and targets must await the analysis that follows. Here I will confine myself to a representative sampling: for his engagement with the French moralists, see Brendan Donnellan, *Nietzsche and the French Moralists* (Bonn: Bouvier, 1982); for his engagement with the neo-Kantian philosopher Afrikan Spir, see Michael Steven Green, *Nietzsche and the Transcendental Tradition* (Urbana and Chicago: University of Illinois Press, 2002); and for his engagement with the Darwinian historian of morality Paul Rée, see Robin Small, *Nietzsche and Rée: A Star Friendship* (Oxford: Oxford University Press, 2005).

3. The *locus classicus* of the view that Nietzsche is an irrationalist thinker is Georg Lukàcs' chapter "Nietzsche as Founder of Irrationalism in the Imperialist Period," in *The Destruction of Reason*, trans. Peter Palmer (London: Merlin, 1980). A similar, though more sympathetic view can be found in Thomas Mann's classic 1947 essay "Nietzsche's Philosophy in the Light of Recent History," in *Last Essays*, trans. Richard and Clara Winston (New York: Knopf, 1959), 141–77, not to mention his 1947 novel *Doctor Faustus*. In a 1936 diary entry, however, Mann wrote that Nietzsche "stood for utmost 'intellectual rectitude,' for the Dionysian will to know . . . [and he] was ready to endure every suffering caused by the truth and for the sake of the truth"; quoted in Steven E. Aschheim, *The Nietzsche Legacy in Germany, 1890–1990* (Berkeley and Los Angeles: University of California Press, 1992), 319n11. Other interpretations that emphasize Nietzsche's irrationalism include Alasdair MacIntyre, *After Virtue: A Study in Moral Theory*, 2nd edition (Notre Dame, Ind.: University of Notre Dame Press, 1984), chap. 9, especially 113–15; Allan Bloom, *The Closing of the American Mind: How Higher Education Has Failed Democracy and Impoverished the Souls of Today's Students* (New York: Simon and Schuster, 1987), 194–226; and Michael Allen Gillespie, *Nihilism Before Nietzsche* (Chicago: University of Chicago Press, 1995), chaps. 6–7 and epilogue. Interestingly, Heidegger does not subscribe to this irrationalist view of Nietzsche. Against Ludwig Klages's vitalistic interpretation of Nietzsche in *Die psychologischen Errungenschaften Nietzsches* (1926), for example, he insists that "Nietzsche cannot be hailed as the opponent of the sciences, and not at all as the enemy of knowledge, provided we think him in his proper and ownmost thoughts";

see Heidegger, *Nietzsche*, vol. 3: *The Will to Power as Knowledge and as Metaphysics*, ed. David Farrell Krell (New York: Harper & Row, 1987), 93. Other interpretations that emphasize Nietzsche's rationalism and affinity with the Enlightenment include Karl Jaspers, *Nietzsche: An Introduction to the Understanding of His Philosophical Activity*, trans. C. J. Wallraff and F. J. Schmitz (Baltimore: Johns Hopkins Press, 1997), 171–228; Georg Picht, *Nietzsche* (Stuttgart: Klett Cotta, 1988), especially 24, 37, 163; Laurence Lampert, *Nietzsche and Modern Times: A Study of Bacon, Descartes, and Nietzsche* (New Haven and London: Yale University Press, 1993), part 3, esp. 360; Richard Schacht, "The Nietzsche-Spinoza Problem: Spinoza as a Precursor?" in *Making Sense of Nietzsche: Reflections Timely and Untimely* (Urbana and Chicago: University of Illinois Press, 1995), 185–86. Peter Berkowitz, in *Nietzsche: The Ethics of an Immoralist* (Cambridge, Mass.: Harvard University Press, 1995), takes an ambivalent position on the question of Nietzsche's rationalism/irrationalism. On the one hand, against postmodern interpreters, he emphasizes the role of reason, knowing, and intellectual conscience in Nietzsche's thought (see xi–xii, 14–18); in this regard, he regrets that he does not give Nietzsche's middle works the "attention they deserve" (281n41). On the other hand, he sees Nietzsche's philosophy as culminating in a doctrine of radical creativity, "exaltation of the will," and "untrammeled and absolute freedom or autonomy" (19–20, 149–50, 174, 263–68). Similarly, Stanley Rosen sees Nietzsche as a "figure of the Enlightenment, but of an Enlightenment that has turned on itself"; Nietzsche draws the final, nihilistic consequences of the Enlightenment, revealing its "inner darkness"; see *The Mask of Enlightenment: Nietzsche's Zarathustra* (Cambridge: Cambridge University Press, 1995), xv, 1–4, 7, 245–46; *The Ancients and the Moderns: Rethinking Modernity* (New Haven and London: Yale University Press, 1989), 198–99, 207–8; and *The Limits of Analysis* (New York: Basic Books, 1980), 190.

4. See, for example, Maudemarie Clark, *Nietzsche on Truth and Philosophy* (Cambridge: Cambridge University Press, 1990) and Brian Leiter, *Nietzsche on Morality* (London: Routledge, 2002).

5. Examples of interpretations that view the middle works as anomalous with respect to the rest of Nietzsche's oeuvre include Bruce Detwiler, *Nietzsche and the Politics of Aristocratic Radicalism* (Chicago: University of Chicago Press, 1990), especially chap. 8; Julian Young, *Nietzsche's Philosophy of Religion* (Cambridge: Cambridge University Press, 2006), esp. 60–61.

6. See Abbey, *Nietzsche's Middle Period*, xiv, 156.

7. Sarah Kofman, *Nietzsche and Metaphor*, trans. Duncan Large (Stanford: Stanford University Press, 1993), 116. For similar arguments against "totalistic" readings of Nietzsche's texts, see Gilles Deleuze, *Nietzsche and Philosophy*, trans. Hugh Tomlinson (New York: Columbia University Press, 1983); Deleuze, "Nomad Thought," in *The New Nietzsche*, ed. David Allison (Cambridge, Mass.: MIT Press, 1985), 142–49; Jacques Derrida, *Spurs/Éperons*, trans. Barbara Harlow (Chicago: University of Chicago Press, 1979); Eric Blondel, *Nietzsche: The Body and Culture: Philosophy as a Philological Genealogy*, trans. Seán Hand (Stanford: Stanford University Press, 1991). For a balanced account of the French Nietzsche, see Alan Schrift, *Nietzsche and the Question of Interpretation: Between Hermeneutics and Deconstruction* (London: Routledge, 1990), chaps. 3–4. For a less balanced but nonetheless cogent account, see Richard Wolin, "Zarathustra Goes to Hollywood: On the Postmodern Reception of Nietzsche," in *The Seduction of Unreason: The Intellectual Romance with Fascism from Nietzsche to Postmodernism* (Princeton: Princeton University Press, 2004), 27–62.

8. Derrida, *Spurs/Éperons*, 133. Derrida uses this seemingly random notebook entry

from the fall of 1881 (*KSA* 9:12 [62]) to illustrate the radical indeterminacy of Nietzsche's texts.

9.   Abbey shows an awareness of this point, commenting that "while the works of the middle period are often referred to as if they were a single entity, it is important to remain sensitive to the differences among them" (*Nietzsche's Middle Period*, xii). In practice, though, she tends to lump the middle works together and often fails to register crucial differences between them.

PROLOGUE

1.   Nietzsche writes about this turning point in his philosophical development in several places: see his letter to Mathilde Maier of 15 July 1878 (*SB* 337–38); *WP* 1005; and *EH* 3, on *HH* 2–4. Good biographical treatments of it include R. J. Hollingdale, *Nietzsche: The Man and His Philosophy*, rev. ed. (Cambridge: Cambridge University Press, 1999), chaps. 6–7; Ronald Hayman, *Nietzsche: A Critical Life* (New York: Oxford University Press, 1980), chap. 7; Rüdiger Safranski, *Nietzsche: A Philosophical Biography*, trans. Shelley Frisch (New York: W. W. Norton, 2002), chaps. 6–8; and Curtis Cate, *Friedrich Nietzsche* (Woodstock, N.Y.: Overlook Press, 2005), chap. 21.

2.   The literature on the Nietzsche-Wagner relationship is vast and contentious. Much of the contention arises from the partisan allegiance of individual interpreters to either Nietzsche or Wagner. Elisabeth Nietzsche's account of the relationship in *The Life of Nietzsche*, trans. Anthony M. Ludovici and Paul V. Cohn (New York: Sturgis and Walton Co., 1912) is obviously slanted in favor of her brother, while Ernest Newman's account in *The Life of Wagner* (New York: Knopf, 1946) errs in the opposite direction. Bryan Magee's chapter on the Nietzsche–Wagner relationship in *The Tristan Chord: Wagner and Philosophy* (New York: Metropolitan Books, 2001) ultimately comes down on the side of Wagner, claiming that "in Wagner [Nietzsche] encountered someone whose calibre he knew in his heart to be greater" (341). Joachim Köhler, on the other hand, in his *Nietzsche and Wagner: A Lesson in Subjugation*, trans. Ronald Taylor (New Haven and London: Yale University Press, 1998), gives a left-handed defense of Nietzsche by showing him to be the dupe of the egotistical machinations of the Wagners. More balanced discussions of this relationship can be found in Mazzino Montinari, "Nietzsche and Wagner One Hundred Years Ago," in *Reading Nietzsche*, trans. Greg Whitlock (Urbana and Chicago: University of Illinois Press, 2003), and Dieter Borchmeyer, "Wagner and Nietzsche," in *Wagner Handbook*, ed. Ulrich Müller and Peter Wapnewksi, trans. John Deathridge (Cambridge, Mass.: Harvard University Press, 1992).

3.   Richard Wagner, *Religion and Art*, trans. William Ashton Ellis (1897; Lincoln: University of Nebraska Press, 1994), 213. See George S. Williamson, *The Longing for Myth in Germany: Religion and Aesthetic Culture from Romanticism and Nietzsche* (Chicago: University of Chicago Press, 2004), chap. 5, on the religious function of Wagner's music dramas. This book also contains a fine chapter on Nietzsche's complex relationship to the discourse on myth and religion in nineteenth-century Germany.

4.   Arthur Schopenhauer, *The World as Will and Representation*, trans. E. F. J. Payne (New York: Dover, 1969), vol. 1, secs. 33–38.

5.   Ibid., vol. 1, secs. 51–52.

6.   Ibid., vol. 1, sec. 68.

7.   Ibid., vol. 2, sec. 17.

8.   A number of commentators point out that Nietzsche's rejection of Schopenhauer in *Human, All too Human* and the writings that follow is not as sweeping as he often

portrays it; see the essays by Janaway, Clark, Soll, and Cartwright in *Willing and Nothingness: Schopenhauer as Nietzsche's Educator*, ed. Christopher Janaway (Oxford: Clarendon Press, 1998); also Julian Young, *Nietzsche's Philosophy of Art* (Cambridge: Cambridge University Press, 1992), 3, 148–52; Gillespie, *Nihilism Before Nietzsche*, 181–202 (see preface, n. 3); Ruth Abbey, *Nietzsche's Middle Period*, 142, 199n7 (see preface, n. 1). In his most recent book, *Nietzsche's Philosophy of Religion*, 58–59, 196 (see preface, n. 5), Julian Young maintains that not only Schopenhauer but also Wagner continued to exercise an important influence on Nietzsche throughout his career. Without denying the validity of some of these qualifications of Nietzsche's rejection of Schopenhauer and Wagner, the crucial point remains that *Human, All too Human* marks a radical break with Schopenhauer and Wagner on fundamental issues, and this break only becomes deeper in the works that follow.

9. In *Nietzsche's Philosophy of Religion*, chap. 3, Young argues that religion remains essential to Nietzsche's vision of cultural unity during the period of the *Untimely Meditations*. Nietzsche's unpublished notes, however, tell a different story.

10. Many of the unpublished notes from this period can be found in Friedrich Nietzsche, *Philosophy and Truth: Selections from Nietzsche's Notebooks of the Early 1870s*, ed. and trans. Daniel Breazeale (New Jersey: Humanities Press, 1979). Contrary to what the editor suggests in his introduction, these notes are largely consistent with the outlook on culture articulated in *The Birth of Tragedy* and the first two *Untimely Meditations* and quite different from the one articulated in *Human, All too Human*.

11. Nietzsche makes a similar comment in his letter to Cosima Wagner of 19 December 1876 (*SB* 5:210). In his 1886 Preface to the second volume of *Human, All too Human*, he repeats the point: "When, in the third *Untimely Meditation*, I then went on to give expression to my reverence for my first and only educator, the *great* Arthur Schopenhauer . . . I was, so far as my own development was concerned, already deep in the midst of moral skepticism and destructive analysis . . . and already 'believed in nothing any more' . . . not even in Schopenhauer" (*HH* 2.Preface, 1). Already in his unpublished 1868 essay "On Schopenhauer," Nietzsche expressed serious misgivings about Schopenhauer's metaphysics, specifically his identification of the unknowable thing in itself with the will and his assigning of determinate predicates to it; see *Writings from the Early Notebooks*, ed. Raymond Geuss and Alexander Nehamas (Cambridge: Cambridge University Press, 2009), 1–8.

12. See Wagner's letter to Nietzsche of 13 July 1876, where he writes: "Your book is tremendous! Wherever did you get to know so much about me?" in *Selected Letters of Richard Wagner*, ed. and trans. Stewart Spencer and Barry Millington (London and New York: W. W. Norton & Co., 1987), 857.

13. *Cosima Wagner's Diaries: An Abridgement*, ed. Geoffrey Skelton (New Haven and London: Yale University Press, 1994), 269–70; Elisabeth Förster Nietzsche, *Life of Nietzsche*, vol. 2, 11–13.

CHAPTER ONE

1. As with almost everything else in his philosophy, much has been written on Nietzsche's aphoristic style. Karl Löwith provides a good early discussion, emphasizing the nonfragmentary, systematic character of Nietzsche's aphorisms, in *Nietzsche's Philosophy of the Eternal Recurrence of the Same*, trans. J. Harvey Lomax (Berkeley and Los Angeles: University of California Press, 1997), 11–20. See also Jaspers, *Nietzsche*, 3–5, 400–401 (see preface, n. 3); Walter Kaufmann, *Nietzsche: Philosopher, Psychologist, Antichrist*, 4th ed. (Princeton: Princeton University Press, 1974), 72–95; Georg Picht,

Nietzsche, xxi–xii, xxix, 20–21, 33–45, 56–61 (see preface, n. 3); Gilles Deleuze, "No-mad Thought," 144–49 (see preface, n. 7); Kofman, *Nietzsche and Metaphor*, 114–19 (see preface, n. 7); Alexander Nehamas, *Nietzsche: Life as Literature* (Cambridge, Mass.: Harvard University Press, 1985), 13–23; Brendan Donnellan, *Nietzsche and the French Moralists*, 120–65 (see preface, n. 2); Jill Marsden, "Nietzsche and the Art of the Aphorism," in *A Companion to Nietzsche*, ed. Keith Ansell-Pearson (Oxford: Oxford University Press, 2006): 22–37; Robin Small, *Nietzsche and Rée*, 57–61 (see preface, n. 2).

2. On Nietzsche's reading of and engagement with the French moralists, see W. D. Wil-liams, *Nietzsche and the French: A Study of the Influence of Nietzsche's French Reading on His Thought and Writing* (Oxford: Blackwell, 1952); Donnellan, *Nietzsche and the French Moralists*; David Molnar, "The Influence of Montaigne on Nietzsche: A Raison d'Être in the Sun," *Nietzsche-Studien* 22 (1993): 80–93; Vivetta Vivarelli, "Montaigne und der 'Freie Geist,'" *Nietzsche-Studien* 23 (1994): 79–99; Jessica N. Berry, "The Pyr-rhonian Revival in Montaigne and Nietzsche," *Journal of the History of Ideas* 65 (2004): 497–514; Picht, *Nietzsche*, xxii, 36–38, 44–52. In his recent *Nietzsche, Psychology, and First Philosophy* (Chicago: University of Chicago Press, 2010), Robert Pippin has made Nietzsche's relationship to the French moralists, especially Montaigne, the linchpin of his interpretation. He writes in one place: "Nietzsche is much better understood not as a great German metaphysician, or as the last metaphysician of the West, or as the destroyer or culminator of metaphysics, or as very interested in meta-physics or a new theory of nature at all, but as one of the great 'French moralists'" (9).

3. Georg Picht writes: "For Nietzsche the encounter with the nimble and biting skep-ticism of the French moralists was the great cure through which he emancipated himself from the romantic pessimism of Schopenhauer and the narcotizing spell of Wagnerian music" (*Nietzsche*, 37).

4. In a note from 1885, Nietzsche emphasizes the esoteric character of his aphorisms: "In aphorism-books like mine, between and behind short aphorisms stand more au-dible long forbidden things and chains of thought [*Gedanken-Kette*]; and underneath many, that which may be questionable enough for Oedipus and his Sphinx. I don't write treatises: they are for asses and newspaper-readers" (*KSA* 11:37 [5]).

5. Once again, Kofman, *Nietzsche and Metaphor*, 114–19 (especially 116), epitomizes the antisystematic, deconstructive reading of Nietzsche. Along the same lines, De-leuze writes in "Nomad Thought," 145: "An aphorism means nothing, signifies noth-ing, and is no more a signifier than a signified." See also Derrida's discussion of the note "I have forgotten my umbrella" in *Spurs/Éperons*, 122–35 (see preface, n. 7). Löwith provides a good corrective to these deconstructive readings of Nietzsche's aphoristic style in the first chapter of *Nietzsche's Philosophy of the Eternal Recurrence of the Same*, where he writes: "Nietzsche's philosophy is neither a unified, closed system nor a variety of disintegrating aphorisms, but rather a system in aphorisms" (11). He goes on to quote from Nietzsche's letter to Georg Brandes of 8 January 1888 to show that "Nietzsche himself stressed the *unity* of his aphoristic production" (18): "It is a question here [Nietzsche is specifically referring to *Beyond Good and Evil*] of the long logic of a very specific philosophical sensibility and not a mishmash of a hundred arbitrary paradoxes and heterodoxies" (*SB* 8:228).

6. Kaufmann, *Nietzsche: Philosopher, Psychologist, Antichrist*, 72–95.

7. Ibid., 184.

8. Nietzsche repeatedly refers to *Assorted Opinions and Maxims* and *The Wanderer and His Shadow* in his letters as "appendices" or "supplements" (*Anhänge* or *Nachträge*)

234 / Notes to Pages 15–18

to *Human, All too Human* and clearly thought of the three books as belonging to a single work; see *SB* 5:365, 443, 453, 471. In 1886, he gathered the three books together and published them as a single two-volume work under the title *Human, All too Human*, with the original 1878 book comprising volume 1 and the two later books volume 2. In the preface to volume 2, he once again refers to *Assorted Opinions and Maxims* and *The Wanderer and His Shadow* as "continuations and appendices" of the original *Human, All too Human*. See William H. Schaberg, *The Nietzsche Canon: A Publication History and Bibliography* (Chicago: University of Chicago Press, 1995), 55–76, 126–34, for a complete publication history of *Human, All too Human*.

9. From his notebooks, it appears that some of the chapters of *Human, All too Human* were originally conceived of as independent essays for the *Untimely Meditations*; see *KSA* 8:16 [10].

10. See, for example, Iain Morrisson, "Nietzsche's Genealogy of Morality in the *Human, All too Human* Series," *British Journal for the History of Philosophy* 11 (2003): 657–72. Robin Small's discussion of *Human, All too Human* in *Nietzsche and Rée* necessarily focuses on morality, since this was the theme on which their philosophical interests converged; the same goes for Brendan Donnellan, "Friedrich Nietzsche and Paul Rée: Cooperation and Conflict," *Journal of the History of Ideas* 43 (1982): 595–612. The first four chapters of Ruth Abbey's book on *Nietzsche's Middle Period* (see preface, n. 1) focus on morality and moral psychology.

11. For this argument about the centrality of the theme of culture to *Human, All too Human*, I draw heavily on my article "Nietzsche's *Human, All too Human* and the Problem of Culture," *The Review of Politics* 69 (2007): 215–43. Ruth Abbey takes issue with my focus on this theme in her "Bricks and Stones: A Reply to Paul Franco," *The Review of Politics* 70 (2008): 272–77; see also my response, "Nooks and Hunched Backs: A Reply to Ruth Abbey" in the same issue, 278–83. It is significant that there is no entry for "culture" in the index of Abbey's book on *Nietzsche's Middle Period*. The one commentator who does grasp the centrality of this theme to *Human, All too Human* is Safranski; see chaps 6–8 of his *Nietzsche: A Philosophical Biography* (see prologue, n. 1). See also Blondel, *The Body and Culture* (see preface, n. 7), especially his comment that the "problem of culture in Nietzsche has been underestimated, and yet if forms the origin and centre of his thought" (51; see also 42).

12. In *Nietzsche's Philosophy of Religion*, Young maintains that Nietzsche never abandoned the "religious communitarianism" that characterized his early thinking in *The Birth of Tragedy*. He dismisses Nietzsche's apparent reversal of this outlook in *Human, All too Human* as "entirely ungrounded" and suggests that "Nietzsche has simply decided to try the *Zeitgeist* on for size" (60–61). I am sympathetic to Young's effort to see Nietzsche as not merely a radical individualist but as someone with a profound concern with cultural unity and wholeness. But this concern does not require the romanticism, religiosity, and "Volkishness" that Young ascribes to Nietzsche. Indeed, what makes *Human, All too Human* and the middle works in general so interesting is the way in which Nietzsche tries to ground cultural wholeness in the modern scientific spirit instead of religion.

13. Maudemarie Clark, *Nietzsche on Truth and Philosophy*, 173–75 (see preface, n. 4), maintains that there is an important difference between the respective accounts of metaphysical philosophy's "faith in opposites" in *HH* 1 and *BGE* 2, but I do not really see it.

14. See Walter Bagehot, *Physics and Politics* (Chicago: Ivan R. Dee, 1999), 40: "In historic times there has been little progress; in prehistoric times there must have been

much." On Nietzsche's relationship to Bagehot, see David Thatcher, "Nietzsche, Bagehot and the Morality of Custom," *Victorian Newsletter*, no. 62 (Fall 1982): 7–32; also Small, *Nietzsche and Rée*, 121–25.

15. In a note from 1888, for example, he writes: "It is not the victory of science that distinguishes our nineteenth century, but the victory of scientific method over science" (*WP* 466). And in another note from the same period: "The most valuable insights are arrived at last; but the most important insights are *methods*" (*WP* 469). Finally, in *The Antichrist*, he writes of the Greeks and Romans: "All the preconditions for a scholarly culture, all the scientific *methods* were already there . . . methods, one must say it ten times over, *are* the essential as well as the most difficult things; also that which has habit and laziness against it for the longest time" (*A* 59). Jaspers devotes some good pages to Nietzsche's conception of science in his *Nietzsche*, 171–84.

16. The motto comes from part 3 of the *Discourse*, where Descartes relates his decision "to employ my entire life in cultivating my reason and to advance myself as far as I could in the knowledge of the truth, following the Method that I had prescribed to myself. I had felt such deep contentment since having begun to use this Method that I did not believe that anyone could obtain anything sweeter or more innocent in this life." On this motto, see Robert Rethy, "The Descartes Motto to the First Edition of *Menschliches Allzumenschliches*," *Nietzsche-Studien* 5 (1976): 289–97.

17. Nietzsche defined science in opposition to conviction throughout his career. In the 1887 book 5 of *The Gay Science*, for example, he writes: "In science convictions have no rights of citizenship. . . . Would it not be the first step in the discipline of the scientific spirit that one would not permit oneself any more convictions?" (*GS* 344; see also 375).

18. Nietzsche alludes to this remark in *The Antichrist* (see *A* 55).

19. Schopenhauer, *The World as Will and Representation*, vol. 2, sec. 17 (see prologue, n. 4).

20. In a notebook entry from 1876, Nietzsche writes: "The so-called metaphysical need proves nothing about a reality corresponding to this need" (*KSA* 8:19 [85]).

21. On Afrikan Spir's influence on Nietzsche, see especially Green, *Nietzsche and the Transcendental Tradition* (see preface, n. 2); also Small, *Nietzsche and Rée*, 67–70; Small, *Nietzsche in Context* (Aldershot: Ashgate, 2001), chap. 1; Nadeem J. Z. Hussain, "Nietzsche's Positivism," *European Journal of Philosophy* 12 (2004): 333, 341–43.

22. Clark assigns Nietzsche's position on the metaphysical world in *Human, All too Human* to the fourth stage of his account of "How the 'True World' Became a Fable" in *Twilight of the Idols* (*Nietzsche on Truth and Philosophy*, 112). In general, I think it is misleading to establish one-to-one correspondences between the stages in the development of Nietzsche's thinking and the stages of his account in *Twilight*. But if one opts to play this game, it seems to me that Nietzsche's position in *Human, All too Human* could just as easily be equated with the fifth stage as with the fourth.

23. Philosophically sophisticated attempts to come to grips with Nietzsche's "error theory" include Clark, *Nietzsche on Truth and Philosophy*; Green, *Nietzsche and the Transcendental Tradition*; R. Lanier Anderson, "Overcoming Charity: The Case of Maudemarie Clark's *Nietzsche on Truth and Philosophy*," *Nietzsche-Studien* 25 (1996): 307–39; Anderson, "Nietzsche on Truth, Illusion, and Redemption," *European Journal of Philosophy* 13 (2005): 185–225; and Hussain, "Nietzsche's Positivism," 326–68. Clark argues that Nietzsche held the error theory in his early and middle works, but that he abandoned it sometime between *Beyond Good and Evil* and *Genealogy of Morals*. Apart from introducing an artificial distinction between Nietzsche's philosophical

outlooks in *Beyond Good and Evil*, book 5 of *The Gay Science*, and *Genealogy of Morals*, Clark's interpretation fails to account for Nietzsche's continued defense of the error theory all the way through his final works (see, e.g., *TI* "Reason" 2, 5). I agree with Green, 28–35, Hussain, 327–40, and Anderson, "Overcoming Charity," 316–22, that Nietzsche seems to have held the error theory throughout his philosophical career.

24. Nietzsche refers to Lubbock in *HH* 111. In 1875 he acquired the German translation of Sir John Lubbock's *The Origin of Civilization and the Primitive Condition of Man: Mental and Social Condition of Savages* (1870; repr. ed. Peter Rivière (Chicago: University of Chicago Press, 1978). On Lubbock's influence on Nietzsche, see David S. Thatcher, "Nietzsche's Debt to Lubbock," *Journal of the History of Ideas* 44 (1983): 293–309.

25. This argument about the way language creates a world of meaning goes all the way back to Nietzsche's unpublished 1873 essay "On Truth and Lies in a Nonmoral Sense."

26. Clark doesn't appreciate this point when she claims that "Nietzsche's major project in [*Human, All too Human*] . . . seems designed to remove the world's remaining colour, its appearance of value"; Clark, "On Knowledge, Truth, and Value: Nietzsche's Debt to Schopenhauer and the Development of Empiricism," in *Willing and Nothingness: Schopenhauer as Nietzsche's Educator*, ed. Christopher Janaway (Oxford: Clarendon Press, 1998), 55.

27. See Alexis de Tocqueville, *Democracy in America*, trans. Harvey C. Mansfield and Delba Winthrop (Chicago: University of Chicago Press, 2000), vol. 2, pt. 2, chap. 17.

28. Here I agree with Clark's comment that in this passage Nietzsche "follows the model of Schopenhauer's aesthetic contemplator and finds value not in the objects of the contemplative gaze, but rather in the gazing" ("On Knowledge, Truth, and Value," 56). Compare with Nietzsche's letter to von Gersdorff of 13 December 1875 (*SB* 5:128–29).

29. Arthur Schopenhauer, *On the Basis of Morality*, trans. E. F. J. Payne (Indianapolis: Hackett, 1995), sec. 16. By basing morality on the foundation of compassion, Schopenhauer follows Rousseau, who, he says "was undoubtedly the greatest moralist of modern times" (sec. 19).

30. Schopenhauer makes this argument in *The World as Will and Representation*, 1:63–66; *On the Basis of Morality*, sec. 22.

31. On the distinction between the empirical and intelligible characters, see Schopenhauer, *On The Basis of Morality*, secs. 10, 20; also Schopenhauer, *Prize Essay on the Freedom of the Will*, ed. Günter Zöller (Cambridge: Cambridge University Press, 1999), chap. 5.

32. On the relationship between Nietzsche and Rée, see Small's very useful *Nietzsche and Rée*; also Donnellan, "Friedrich Nietzsche and Paul Rée: Cooperation and Conflict."

33. Paul Rée, *The Origin of the Moral Sensations*, in *Basic Writings*, ed. and trans. Robin Small (Urbana and Chicago: University of Illinois Press, 2003), 87.

34. See Rée, *Origin of Moral Sensations*, especially chap. 1. On the relationship between Rée's naturalistic account of morality and Darwin's, see Small's helpful discussion in his introduction to Rée's *Basic Writings*. Despite some differences, Darwin, like Rée, traces morality back to the social instincts of human beings, which are selected because of their contribution to social utility and reinforced by social approbation and habituation; see Charles Darwin, *The Descent of Man, and Selection in Relation to Sex*, ed. James Moore and Adrian Desmond (London: Penguin, 2004), chaps. 4–5.

35. In this regard, I think Nietzsche is telling the truth when he writes to his friend Er-

win Rohde on 16 June 1878, shortly after the publication of *Human, All too Human*: "Parenthetically: always seek only me in my book and not friend Rée. I am proud to have discovered the splendid qualities and goal of this man, but on the conception of my *philosophia in nuce* he has not had the slightest influence. This was ready and in good part committed to paper when I made his closer acquaintance in the fall of 1876" (*SB* 5:333).

36. Here I disagree with Clark and Leiter's claim that *Human, All too Human* is not concerned with questioning the *value* of morality understood in terms of nonegoistic action and motivation, though I agree that it does not do so in exactly the same way that the *Genealogy of Morals* does; see their introduction to Nietzsche's *Daybreak*, trans. R. J. Hollingdale (Cambridge: Cambridge University Press, 1997), xxiv–xxv.

37. Nietzsche seems to have borrowed the idea for this aphorism from Rée; see the latter's *Psychological Observations*, in *Basic Writings*, 22.

38. In his letter to Gersdorff of 13 December 1875, Nietzsche describes his friend as possessing the "glorious power of sharing joy [*Mitfreude*]," which is "even more rare and noble than the power of sharing someone's suffering [*Mitleid*]" (*SB* 5:129).

39. Kaufmann, *Nietzsche: Philosopher, Psychologist, Antichrist*, 184–86.

40. For a comparison of Nietzsche's and La Rochefoucauld's moral critiques, see Donnellan, *Nietzsche and the French Moralists*, 65–93. For a good discussion of Nietzsche in relation to psychological egoism, see Bernard Reginster, "Nietzsche on Selflessness and the Value of Altruism," *History of Philosophy Quarterly* 17 (2000): 178–83. My analysis of Nietzsche's psychological egoism in this paragraph disagrees with that of Clark and Leiter in their introduction to *Daybreak*, xxiv–xxv.

41. In a note from the time of *Human, All too Human*, Nietzsche observes how "philosophy in the manner of La Rochefoucauld" reinforces the Christian tendency by which "all human actions are slandered and poisoned, and the trust in men disturbed" (*KSA* 8:23 [152]).

42. This aphorism from *The Wanderer and His Shadow*, which distinguishes between two different kinds of moralists, should be compared with the oft-cited aphorism 103 from *Daybreak*, which distinguishes between two different kinds of deniers of morality: namely, those, like La Rochefoucauld, who "deny that the moral motives which men *claim* have inspired their actions really have done so," and those, like Nietzsche, who admit that these motives "really are motives of action" but deny that the moral judgments that impel men to moral actions "are based on truths." In their introduction to *Daybreak*, Clark and Leiter adduce this aphorism as evidence that *Daybreak* marks a complete repudiation of the La Rochefoucauldian psychological egoism of *Human, All too Human* (xxiv–xxv), but the aphorism from *The Wanderer and His Shadow* suggests that Nietzsche was never a psychological egoist in the sense that La Rochefoucauld was.

43. Rée, *Origin of the Moral Sensations*, chap. 4.

44. Bagehot, *Physics and Politics*, chap. 1.

45. Letter from Rée to Nietzsche of 22 March 1879; see Nietzsche, *Briefwechsel: Kritische Gesamtausgabe*, ed. Giorgio Colli and Mazzino Montinari (Berlin: de Gruyter, 1975–), 2.6/2:1058. See also Small, *Nietzsche and Rée*, 112.

46. Bagehot, *Physics and Politics*, chap. 5.

47. In a note from 1876–77, Nietzsche writes: "One praises the nonegoistic originally because it is useful and blames the egoistic because it is harmful. But what if that were an error! What if the egoistic in many higher cases was more useful than the nonegoistic!" (*KSA* 8:23 [54]).

48. Rée, *Origin of the Moral Sensations*, chap. 3.

49. When he was writing *Human, All too Human*, Nietzsche had yet to discover Spinoza as his "precursor," though there are two favorable references to him in the book (*HH* 475 and *AOM* 408). In the oft-cited letter to Overbeck of 30 July 1881 in which he announces his discovery of Spinoza (*SB* 6:111), Nietzsche highlights his agreement with the latter's denial of freedom of the will, of the unegoistic, and of evil, all three of which he had already rejected (as we have seen) in *Human, All too Human*.

50. George J. Stack, "Nietzsche's Earliest Essays: Translation and Commentary on 'Fate and History' and 'Freedom of Will and Fate,'" *Philosophy Today* 37 (1993): 156, 158.

51. Ralph Waldo Emerson, "Fate," in *Essays and Lectures* (New York: Library of America, 1983), 953.

52. Schopenhauer, *The World as Will and Representation*, 1:55; see also *On the Basis of Morality*, sec. 10, 20; *Prize Essay on the Freedom of the Will*, chap. 5.

53. On the unaccountability of criminals, see also *HH* 70, 105 and *WS* 23–24, 28.

54. See note 49 above.

55. Abbey, *Nietzsche's Middle Period*, 52–53; Detwiler, *Nietzsche and the Politics of Aristocratic Radicalism*, 178 (see preface, n. 4). For Abbey, the praise of moderation in the middle works points to their superiority over the later works, whereas for Detwiler it suggests that those works are less reliable indicators of Nietzsche authentic view, which he tends to associate with "advocacy of new ruling castes or master races," "conscious breeding experiments," "domination of the earth," and "annihilation of millions of failures" (177).

56. See *Der Gottesdienst der Griechen*, in Nietzsche, *Werke: Kritische Gesamtausgabe*, ed. Giorgio Colli and Mazzino Montinari (Berlin: de Gruyter, 1967–), 2.5:355–520. Nietzsche offered this lecture course twice, once in the Winter Semester of 1875–76, and again in the Winter Semester of 1877–78. See Williamson, *The Longing for Myth in Germany*, 259–66 on these lectures (see prologue, n. 3).

57. Schaberg, *The Nietzsche Canon*, 58–60; Small, *Nietzsche and Rée*, 29–30.

58. Quoted in Hollingdale, *Nietzsche: The Man and His Philosophy*, 111 (see prologue, n. 1).

59. Again, see Wagner, "Religion and Art," 213.

60. For Hegel's famous pronouncement on the "end of art," see *Aesthetics: Lectures on Fine Art*, trans. T. M. Knox (Oxford: Clarendon Press, 1975), 1:11.

61. Robert W. Gutman, *Richard Wagner: The Man, His Mind, and His Music* (New York: Harcourt, 1990), 279–80. In his famous Preface to the *Philosophy of Right*, Hegel condemns this murder as the logical outcome of the flawed ethics of subjective conviction.

62. In *Nietzsche's Philosophy of Art* (Cambridge: Cambridge University Press, 1992), Julian Young rightly points out that Nietzsche ascribes a new function to art in this aphorism that is not found in the original, 1878 volume of *Human, All too Human*. But he is wrong to argue that Nietzsche's equation of this "signposting" function with "classical" or Goethean art is problematic or incoherent (see 74–82). The confusion here stems from Young's attribution to Nietzsche of an exaggerated view of art as value-creating or value-legislating that is simply not in the text. The ideal that poetry signposts (but does not create) is that of the higher culture based on knowledge that Nietzsche elaborates in the following chapter of *Human, All too Human*.

63. In a fascinating essay, J. P. Stern shows how Stifter's *Der Nachsommer* (*Indian Summer*) perfectly embodies the serenity and harmoniousness that Nietzsche exalts in *AOM* 99, though he doubts whether in Stifter's case this serenity is achieved "without any withdrawal from" the modern world; see *Reinterpretations: Seven Studies in*

Nineteenth-Century German Literature (Cambridge: Cambridge University Press, 1964), chap. 6. See also Carl Schorske's illuminating discussion of Stifter's ideal of *Bildung* in *Der Nachsommer* in Schorske, *Fin-de-Siècle Vienna: Politics and Culture* (New York: Vintage, 1981), 281–95.

64. Compare *BGE* 204, where Nietzsche criticizes Schopenhauer for his lack of historical sense and his "unintelligent wrath against Hegel."

65. Nietzsche's notes from the summer of 1876 repeatedly refer to repose as an essential condition of culture: "I want to restore to men the repose without which no culture develops or endures. Likewise the simplicity" (*KSA* 8:17 [22]; see also [26, 43, 46, and 53]).

66. This is one place where Heidegger's controversial interpretation of Nietzsche as the consummation of the Cartesian project to make human beings the "masters and possessors of nature" and establish their "absolute dominion over the earth" finds some justification; see Heidegger, *Nietzsche*, vol. 3: *The Will to Power as Knowledge and Metaphysics*, 216–34 (see preface, n. 3); *Nietzsche*, vol. 4: *Nihilism*, trans. David Krell (New York: Harper & Row, 1982), 28–29, 116–17, 134–35. Even here, though, there is much exaggeration and distortion. In one place, for example, Heidegger uses the aphorism "The Machine as Teacher" (*WS* 218) to argue that Nietzsche advocates the total "mechanization" of things (*Nietzsche*, 3:230), the "machine-based reckoning of all activity and planning" (*Nietzsche*, 4:116–17). But Nietzsche makes clear a few aphorisms later that he is no fan of "machine culture" (see *WS* 220, 288).

67. Nietzsche's anti-Darwinian emphasis on the fundamental importance of weakness and corruption for cultural progress goes all the way back to 1875. In a note entitled "On Darwinism," Nietzsche states emphatically that "the struggle for existence is not the important principle" and dismisses Darwinism as "a philosophy for butcher-boys [*Fleischerburschen*]." The two German Darwinians he mentions are Ernst Häckel and David Strauss (*KSA* 8:12 [22]). It should be pointed out that amongst German Darwinians the "struggle for existence" (*Kampf ums Dasein*) loomed larger than the more authentically Darwinian principle of natural selection; see Andrew Kelly, *The Descent of Darwin: The Popularization of Darwinism in Germany, 1860–1914* (Chapel Hill: University of North Carolina Press, 1981), 30.

68. Compare Nietzsche's discussion of "inverse cripples" in *Z* 2.20.

69. See Friedrich Hölderlin, *Hyperion*, ed. Eric Santner (New York: Continuum, 1990), 23–24; Jacob Burckhardt, "Culture Determined by the State," *Reflections on History*, trans. M. D. Hottinger (Indianapolis: Liberty Press, 1979), 123–39. Nietzsche attended Burkhardt's lectures on which this book was based in 1870.

70. See, for example, Detwiler, *Nietzsche and the Politics of Aristocratic Radicalism*, chap. 8.

71. In the same work, he also claims that it "is only with me that the earth knows *great politics*" (*EH* 4.1). Clearly "great politics" here means something different from what it means in *Human, All too Human*, where it is associated with the nationalistic and bellicose policies of Bismarck. On Nietzsche's antipolitical stance with respect to the German politics of his time, see Peter Bergmann, *Nietzsche, the "Last Antipolitical German"* (Bloomington: Indiana University Press, 1987).

72. In *Nietzsche and the Politics of Aristocratic Radicalism*, Detwiler argues that Nietzsche's more favorable attitude toward democracy in the middle period, especially in *The Wanderer and His Shadow*, is anomalous with respect to both his early and later writings (see especially 171–78). But he overstates just how favorable Nietzsche's attitude toward democracy is in the middle writings, and he underestimates the persistent aristocratic elements in them. Keith Ansell-Pearson, in *An Introduction to Nietzsche as*

Political Thinker (Cambridge: Cambridge University Press, 1994), rejects the idea that the political views expressed in the middle works constitute a sharp break with the views of either the early or later writings.

73. Nietzsche's analysis of religion and government in this aphorism bears comparison with Tocqueville's more famous analysis in *Democracy in America*. On the point about the necessary gulf between governors and governed, however, Tocqueville diverges from Nietzsche by democratizing the utilitarian and hypocritical outlook on religion of the aristocratic governing classes. For a probing discussion of the difficulties with Tocqueville's position, see Pierre Manent, *Tocqueville and the Nature of Democracy*, trans. John Waggoner (Lanham, Md.: Rowman & Littlefield, 1996), 89–96.

74. Ansell-Pearson argues that this passage "shows that the widely held view of [Nietzsche] as an extreme individualist, or an existentialist, solely preoccupied with the nature of an asocial, isolated individual, is profoundly misleading. . . . Like the political thinking of Rousseau and Hegel, Nietzsche's political thought is characterized from beginning to end by the desire to transcend the atomistic basis of modern societies" (*An Introduction to Nietzsche as Political Thinker*, 87).

75. For Nietzsche's conservative defense of gradual evolution over violent revolution, see also *HH* 450, 452, 454, 464.

76. Graeme Garrard, "Nietzsche For and Against the Enlightenment," *The Review of Politics* 70 (2008): 595–608, documents how Nietzsche reversed his view on the discontinuity between the Enlightenment and the French Revolution in his later works. The evidence from the *Nachlass* (see *WP* 94–123), however, is more ambiguous than Garrard suggests (see, e.g., *WP* 96, 98), and Nietzsche continues to oppose the aristocratic and conservative Voltaire to the plebeian and revolutionary Rousseau (*WP* 94, 100, 123). Garrard's conclusion, that Nietzsche's view of the Enlightenment "was not really anchored in a detailed knowledge of the period or its leading writers" and that he "would be judged a signal failure as an intellectual historian" by contemporary standards (608), does not do justice to the philosophical issues at stake.

CHAPTER TWO

1. Maudemarie Clark and Brian Leiter, Introduction to *Daybreak*, xx–xxvi, xxxiv (see chap. 1, n. 36). See also Maudemarie Clark, "Introduction: Nietzsche's Path to the End of the Twentieth Century," in Friedrich Nietzsche, *On the Genealogy of Morality*, trans. Maudemarie Clark and Alan Swenson (Indianapolis: Hackett, 1998), xvii; Brian Leiter, *Nietzsche on Morality*, 188 (see preface, n. 4).

2. The quote comes from Spencer's 1863 letter to John Stuart Mill, which is cited in *The Data of Ethics*, in Herbert Spencer, *The Principles of Ethics* (Indianapolis: Liberty Classics, 1978), 157. Darwin quotes approvingly from this letter of "our great philosopher" in *The Descent of Man*, 148 (see chap. 1, n. 34).

3. See also *KSA* 9:1 [123], 8 [103], 11 [40, 73]. On Nietzsche's relationship to Spencer, see Gregory Moore's illuminating article, "Nietzsche, Spencer, and the Ethics of Evolution," *Journal of Nietzsche Studies* 23 (2002): 1–20.

4. Marco Brusotti, "Erkenntnis als Passion: Nietzsches Denkweg zwischen *Morgenröthe* und der *Fröhliche Wissenschaft*," *Nietzsche-Studien* 26 (1997): 204–12.

5. Arthur Danto, "Nietzsche's *Daybreak: Thoughts on the Prejudices of Morality*," in *Reading Nietzsche*, ed. Robert Solomon and Kathleen Higgins (Oxford: Oxford University Press, 1988), 187. That Nietzsche thought of *Daybreak* as a whole and not as a miscellaneous collection of aphorisms is clear from his letter to Köselitz of 23 June 1881: "When the copy of *Daybreak* gets into your hands, then do me one more favor: take

it to the Lido for a day, read it as a whole, and try to make a whole of it for your-self—i.e., a passionate state" (*SB* 6:95).

6. A good example of Nietzsche's intellectualism appears in a note from this period: "Moral prescriptions stem from a time in which one knew less about nature, peoples, and men than one knows now. Ignorance and false presuppositions have been disseminated through the solemn inviolability in which morality lives" (*KSA* 9:3 [93]).

7. On this anthropological background of Nietzsche's thought, see Thatcher, "Nietzsche, Bagehot and the Morality of Custom" (see chap. 1, n. 14)); and "Nietzsche's Debt to Lubbock" (see chap. 1, note 24).

8. Bagehot, *Physics and Politics*, 93–94, 122–26 (see chap. 1, n. 14). In a note from the period of *Daybreak*, Nietzsche comments that it is only when the fear of the enemy recedes that the individual, "the uncustomary [*das Unsittliche*]," comes into the foreground (*KSA* 9: 4 [16]).

9. Sir John Lubbock, *Origin of Civilization*, 152–55 (see chap. 1, note 14).

10. Ibid., 304. See also Bagehot, *Physics and Politics*, 113–18.

11. Here Nietzsche does not seem to get his anthropological information from Lubbock. Edward Tylor mentions the Kamshadales' prohibition on sticking a burning coal with a knife in his *Researches into the Early History of Mankind and the Development of Civilization* (New York: Henry Holt, 1878 [1865]), 277; and he references G. W. Steller, *Beschreibung von dem Lande Kamtschatka* (Frankfurt, 1774), where a number of strange Kamchatkan superstitions are listed, including the prohibition on scraping snow from shoes with a knife; see the English translation, *Steller's History of Kamchatka* (Fairbanks: University of Alaska Press, 2003), 207.

12. Bagehot, *Physics and Politics*, 25.

13. Beginning with *KSA* 9:4 [170] and running through *KSA* 9:4 [259], there are numerous references to the feeling of power; see also *KSA* 9:4 [284, 299, 301, 314, 322]. In *KSA* 9:4 [239] there is a reference to the will to power (*Wille zur Macht*).

14. See Lubbock, *Origin of Civilization*, chap. 5; Edward Tylor, *Primitive Culture* (London: John Murray, 1871).

15. On whether Nietzsche commits the genetic fallacy in his genealogical analyses of morality, see Alexander Nehamas, *Nietzsche: Life as Literature*, 110 (see chap. 1, n. 1); Brian Leiter, *Nietzsche on Morality*, 173–80; Paul Loeb, "Is There a Genetic Fallacy in Nietzsche's Genealogy of Morals?" *International Studies in Philosophy* 27 (1995): 125–41.

16. Nietzsche's dissolution of the unified ego and conception of the self as a multiplicity of affects and drives burst into prominence in his notes from the fall of 1880; see *KSA* 9:6.

17. Again, contra Clark and Leiter, this is *not* the way of *Human, All too Human*. Nietzsche's purpose in *Human, All too Human* is not to criticize the virtuous for being hypocritically egoistic but to show that there is no action that is not egoistic: everyone is not guilty but innocent.

18. Again see Clark and Leiter, Introduction to *Daybreak*, xxv–xxvi. Nehamas, *Nietzsche: Life as Literature*, 202–4, sees no difference between the denial of morality defended in *D* 103 and Nietzsche's later immoralism. He argues that the latter, like the former, is more concerned with reinterpreting morality than attacking it. This, however, seriously neuters Nietzsche's later immoralism, which does attack and discourage actions and especially instincts that have hitherto been considered the heart of morality.

19. A note from the summer of 1880 is relevant here: "We act so often for the wills of others, almost always, that the actions in which we think only of ourselves are exceptions: the egoists are the great exceptions!" (*KSA* 9:4 [51]).

20. This passage suggests that the formula Peter Berkowitz uses to understand Nietzsche's ethics—"right making [is] based upon right knowing"—may be oversimplified; see Berkowitz, *Nietzsche: The Ethics of an Immoralist*, 14–15, 42, 98 (see preface, n. 3).

21. Stanley Rosen offers a detailed reading of this aphorism in his essay "Poetic Reason in Nietzsche: *Die dichtende Vernunft*," in *The Ancients and the Moderns*, especially 227–30 (see preface, n. 3).

22. The references to infinite time and the "dice-box of chance" in *D* 130 begin to anticipate Nietzsche's imminent doctrine of the eternal recurrence; cf. *WP* 1066 on infinite time and the "great dice game of existence."

23. That Nietzsche has Spencer in mind here is evident from a parallel passage in the notebooks: "An adaptation such as Spencer had in view is thinkable, so that each individual becomes a useful instrument, a means, a part. . . . This remolding is possible, indeed perhaps history is moving that way. But then will the individual become ever weaker—it is the history of the going under [*Untergang*] of humanity" (*KSA* 9:10 [60]).

24. Again versus Nehamas, *Nietzsche: Life as Literature*, 202–4.

25. Christopher Janaway, *Beyond Selflessness: Reading Nietzsche's Genealogy* (Oxford: Oxford University Press, 2007), stresses the importance of changing feelings, not just beliefs, in Nietzsche's project of revaluation.

26. Again, Berkowitz's simple formula that "right making [is] based upon right knowing" does not seem to do justice to the complexity of Nietzsche's views on theory and practice and his divergence from the intellectualism of Socrates and Plato. On the inability of science or knowledge to provide goals, see also *KSA* 9:8 [2, 98]).

27. Nehamas, *Nietzsche: Life as Literature*, 182. Nehamas makes the notion of the aesthetic self—along with perspectivism—the centerpiece of his interpretation of Nietzsche's thought; see especially chaps. 5 and 6.

28. In "Schopenhauer as Educator," Nietzsche already hints at this idea of the self as something achieved, not found. The things you have revered in the past, he writes there, "constitute a stepladder upon which you have clambered up to yourself as you are now; for your true nature lies, not concealed deep within you but immeasurably high above you" (SE 1).

29. Michael Tanner spends a good deal of his introduction to *Daybreak* analyzing this aphorism and its implications for Nietzsche's attitude toward Wagner's art; see Friedrich Nietzsche, *Daybreak: Thoughts on the Prejudices of Morality*, trans. R. J. Hollingdale (Cambridge: Cambridge University Press, 1982), xi–xvii.

30. One is reminded of the advice Kierkegaard gave to his emotionally distressed niece: "Above all, do not lose your desire to walk: every day I walk myself into a state of well-being and walk away from every illness; I have walked myself into my best thoughts, and I know of no thought so burdensome that one can not walk away from it" (Letter to Henriette [Jette] Kierkegaard from 1847, in Sören Kierkegaard, *Letters and Documents*, trans. Henrik Rosenmeier [Princeton: Princeton University Press, 1978], 214).

31. Kaufmann cites *D* 360, in which Nietzsche remarks that the Greeks "valued the feeling of power more highly than any kind of utility or good name," as a key example of Nietzsche's more positive assessment of the feeling of power in *Daybreak*: "The will

to power is thus not only the devil who diverts man from achieving culture, or a psychological urge that helps to explain diverse and complex types of human behavior: it is also envisaged as the basis of Greek culture, which Nietzsche then considered the acme of humanity" (*Nietzsche: Philosophy, Psychologist, Antichrist*, 192). Nietzsche's attitude toward the Greeks in *Daybreak*, however, is more equivocal than Kaufmann suggests, as is his attitude toward the feeling of power in the aphorism Kaufmann cites. In another aphorism, Nietzsche claims that the Greeks are to be considered less noble than the feudal aristocracy of Europe insofar as they valued fame and the feeling of power more highly than a good name or honor (*D* 199).

32. See Abbey, *Nietzsche's Middle Period*, 32–33 (see preface, n. 1); see 24–33 in general for a good discussion of the issue of free will in Nietzsche's middle works.

33. Schopenhauer, *The World as Will and Representation*, 1:55 (see prologue, n. 4). See Leiter, *Nietzsche on Morality*, 58–63; Leiter, "The Paradox of Fatalism and Self-Creation in Nietzsche," in *Willing and Nothingness*, ed. Janaway, 248–51 (see chap. 1, n. 26).

34. In a note from 1880, Nietzsche explicitly contrasts Wagner to the moderation of Apollo (*KSA* 9:7 [214]).

35. On the role of social classes in the transmission of culture, see T. S. Eliot, *Notes Towards the Definition of Culture*, in *Christianity and Culture* (New York: Harvest, 1948), chap. 2.

36. Leo Strauss, "Why We Remain Jews," in *Jewish Philosophy and the Crisis of Modernity*, ed. Kenneth Hart Green (Albany: SUNY Press, 1997), 325.

37. See also *HH* 475 and *BGE* 250–51.

38. See *HH* 43, 66, 70; *WS* 23, 24, 28.

39. See Brusotti, "Erkenntnis als Passion," on this development in Nietzsche's understanding of the free-spirited quest for knowledge, though again I think he overlooks the persistence of certain aspects of the contemplative ideal from *HH*.

40. In *Zarathustra*, Nietzsche also refers to honesty as the "youngest of the virtues" (*Z* 1.3). See Alan White's analysis of *Redlichkeit* in "The Youngest Virtue," in *Nietzsche's Postmoralism: Essays on Nietzsche's Prelude to Philosophy's Future*, ed. Richard Schacht (Cambridge: Cambridge University Press, 2001), 63–78.

41. In *Human, All too Human*, see especially the aphorisms devoted to conviction (*HH* 483, 511, 629–38). On honesty as the quintessential virtue of the free spirit in the later works, see especially *BGE* 227.

42. This echoes Stendhal's famous definition of beauty as "une promesse de bonheur," which Nietzsche cites in *GM* 3.6 in contradistinction to Kant's definition of beauty as "pleasure without interest."

43. Here I follow Anderson's discussion of Nietzsche's falsificationist thesis in "Nietzsche on Truth, Illusion, and Redemption," 187–92 (see chap. 1, n. 23).

44. Janaway, *Beyond Selflessness*, chap. 12 contains a good discussion of this passage from *GM* in connection with the role of the affects in enabling and enhancing knowledge.

45. Brusotti, "Erkenntnis als Passion," 208, cites the prominence of the *Gefühl der Macht* in *Daybreak* as evidence of Nietzsche's abandonment of his earlier ideal of repose of soul and moderation in the life of the free spirit, but he fails to notice that the *Gefühl der Macht* is almost completely absent in Nietzsche's analysis of the free spirit's quest for knowledge in book 5.

46. With respect to *Human, All too Human*, again see the aphorisms devoted to conviction (*HH* 483, 511, 629–38).

CHAPTER THREE

1. An English translation of this important notebook entry can be found in *The Nietzsche Reader*, ed. Keith Ansell-Pearson and Duncan Large (Oxford: Blackwell, 2006), 238–39.

2. The problem of the "incorporation" of knowledge goes all the way back to "On the Uses and Disadvantages of History for Life," where Nietzsche describes modern man with his overdeveloped historical consciousness as dragging around with him a "huge quantity of indigestible stones of knowledge" (UDH 4). Heidegger underlines the importance of "incorporation" in the plan from August 1881 in *Nietzsche*, vol. 2: *The Eternal Recurrence of the Same*, trans. David Krell (New York: Harper & Row, 1984), 75–76. On the idea of "incorporation" in *The Gay Science* and Nietzsche's thought in general, see Robert Pippin, "Gay Science and Corporeal Knowledge," *Nietzsche-Studien* 29 (2000): 136–52; Keith Ansell-Pearson, "The Incorporation of Truth: Towards the Overhuman," in *A Companion to Nietzsche*, ed. Keith Ansell-Pearson (Oxford: Blackwell, 2006), 230–49; Ansell-Pearson, "Incorporation and Individuation: On Nietzsche's Use of Phenomenology for Life," *Journal of the British Society for Phenomenology* 38 (2007): 61–89.

3. The phrase "alleviation of life" (*Erleichterung des Lebens*) also appears in WS 350 in connection with the free spirit's emancipation from the "heavy and pregnant errors contained in the conceptions of morality, religion, and metaphysics."

4. As Ansell-Pearson points out in "The Incorporation of Truth," 232–33, Nietzsche speaks in WS 16 of the need to cultivate indifference toward the metaphysical certainties about first and last things that have hitherto imposed such a "calamitous weightiness" on human existence. In the notebooks, there are several references to indifference (see, e.g., *KSA* 9:11 [1, 110]).

5. This idea of the "self-overcoming [*Selbstüberwindung*] of morality" or the "self-cancellation [*Selbstaufhebung*] of morality" becomes very prominent in Nietzsche's mature writings (see BGE 32; D Preface 4; EH 4.3). Nietzsche also speaks of the "suicide of morality," the destruction of morality as a result of the moral demands of truth and honesty, in his notes from the fall of 1881 (see *KSA* 9:15 [15]). In the notes from July and August 1882 referred to in the text, Nietzsche puts forward a plan for a complete edition of his free-spirit writings under the title "The Plowshare: A Tool for the Liberation of the Spirit" (*KSA* 10:1 [14]), once again suggesting the end of a chapter in his philosophical development.

6. In his letter to Köselitz of 20 August 1882, Nietzsche writes that he has changed several things in the final corrections to GS, including "the conclusions to the 2nd and 3rd books (*SB* 6:238).

7. Jörg Salaquarda, "Die *Fröhliche Wissenschaft*: Zwischen Freigeisterei und Neuer 'Lehre,'" *Nietzsche-Studien* 26 (1997): 183.

8. In "Nietzsche's *Gay Science*, Or How to Naturalize Cheerfully," in *Reading Nietzsche*, ed. Robert C. Solomon and Kathleen M. Higgins (Oxford: Oxford University Press, 1998), 68, Richard Schacht confirms that *The Gay Science* "goes well beyond the other volumes in this [free-spirit] series, in both coherence and content."

9. See also WP 291. This new, "immoralistic" emphasis on the positive role of evil appears for the first time in a note written in the winter of 1880–81, just as Nietzsche was finishing *Daybreak*: "Gradually the insight grows and slips from one's hand: to advance human culture and direct it one must do much evil. NB. NB" (*KSA* 9:8 [11]).

10. In a notebook entry entitled "Main Idea," Nietzsche contrasts the narrow perspective of the "imaginary individual" with the more capacious perspective of the "true 'life-

system'" and urges that we go beyond the former to achieve *"experience on a cosmic level"* (*KSA* 9:11 [7]).

11. Robert Pippin makes desire and eros central to his understanding of the meaning of "gay science"; see *Nietzsche, Psychology, and First Philosophy*, 32–44 (see chap. 1, n. 2).

12. Nehamas accords *BGE* 24 considerable importance in his discussion of Nietzsche's perspectivism in *Nietzsche: Life as Literature*, chap. 2 (see chap. 1, n. 1).

13. It is difficult to see this aphorism, as Clark does, as a repudiation of the error theory of knowledge; see *Nietzsche on Truth and Philosophy*, 100–102 (see preface, n. 4).

14. In general, there is a much greater emphasis on experimentation in *The Gay Science* than in the other middle works (though see *D* 432, 453). We have already seen Nietzsche claim that the ultimate question as to the degree to which truth can endure incorporation can only be settled "by experiment [*Experiment*]" (*GS* 110). And in the momentous note in which he relates his discovery of the eternal recurrence, he refers to the "individual as experiment [*Experiment*]" as a key feature of the stage corresponding to *The Gay Science* (*KSA* 9:11 [141]).

15. Somewhat strangely, in the chapter devoted to *The Gay Science* in his book on *Nietzsche's Philosophy of Art* (see chap. 1, n. 62), Julian Young does very little with this second book, referring only briefly to aphorisms 78 and 107. Young's general interpretation of *The Gay Science* in this chapter as not very gay and reflective of "Nietzsche's anguished demand for consolation over the death of God," a demand in which "the old pain and the old yearning for 'metaphysical comfort' has returned" (95), is not very convincing.

16. Nietzsche calls attention to the connection of *The Gay Science* to *la gaya scienza* of the troubadours in the subtitle of the 1887 edition of the book and in *EH* 3.*GS* (see also *GS* 377). But even at the time of the writing of the original edition, Nietzsche evinces an awareness of this connection; see *KSA* 9:11 [337] and his letter to Rohde of December 1882 (*SB* 6:292).

17. See *BGE* 231–39. Interestingly, these aphorisms on women from *Beyond Good and Evil* appear in the chapter devoted to intellectual honesty and the scientific spirit—as a contrast. Already in *Human, All too Human* Nietzsche considered women unsuitable for science: "For what could be rarer than a woman who knew what science is?" (*HH* 416). His identification of science with men in *HH* is also clear when he speaks of the "manliness" of the scientific spirit (*HH* 3) and the "progressive *masculinization* of man" in the Enlightenment (*HH* 147).

18. See RWB 4–5, 8; *AOM* 169–70; *WS* 170.

19. Nietzsche does not mention Wagner by name in this aphorism, but that he has Wagner in mind is made clear by the fact that he included a slightly revised version of this aphorism in *Nietzsche Contra Wagner*.

20. Apropos of this aphorism, Nietzsche writes to Köselitz on 20 August 1882: "[A]bout Schopenhauer I have explicitly spoken (to him and Wagner I may never again come back, but now I must establish my relationship to my earlier opinions—for in the last analysis I am a teacher and have an obligation to say wherein I remain the same and wherein I have become something different)" (*SB* 6:238).

21. Again see Nietzsche's letter to Köselitz of 20 August 1882, in which he indicates that he has revised the conclusions to books 2 and 3 in the final corrections to *GS* (*SB* 6:238).

22. As we have seen, the idea of the eternal recurrence appears for the first time in *KSA* 9:11 [141]. The first draft note for "The Madman" appears in the immediately following notebook, from the fall of 1881 (*KSA* 9:12 [77]; see also 9:12 [9, 157] and 9:14 [25–26]).

23. Stanley Rosen makes this conception of the world as chaos central to his interpretation of Nietzsche; see Rosen, *The Limits of Analysis*, 190–215 (see preface, n. 3); *The Quarrel Between Philosophy and Poetry: Studies in Ancient Thought* (New York and London: Routledge, 1988), 191–97, 202; *The Ancients and the Moderns*, 197–202, 219–21 (see preface, n. 3); and *The Mask of Enlightenment*, xi–xii, 15, 32, 47, 60, 190–91, 245–46 (see preface, n. 3).

24. On the relationship between eternal recurrence and the character of the world as necessitous chaos, see Heidegger, *Nietzsche*, vol. 2: *The Eternal Recurrence of the Same*, 90–96.

25. For a good discussion of these notes, see Safranski, *Nietzsche: A Philosophical Biography*, 225–30 (see prologue, n. 1); also Heidegger, *Nietzsche*, 2:84–85.

26. Rosen, *The Mask of Enlightenment*, 17–19, assumes that this note is a sketch for *Zarathustra*, even though there is no mention of Zarathustra in it. Nietzsche does mention Zarathustra for the first time in the notes immediately preceding this one (*KSA* 9:11 [195–95]). Nevertheless, some of the entries in the sketch seem more relevant to *The Gay Science*: not only the reference to the "dehumanization of nature," but also the reference to the "incorporation of experiences."

27. Thomas Brobjer, the indefatigable researcher of Nietzsche's reading, indicates that Nietzsche never actually read Spinoza but came to know him second hand through other scholars' accounts, especially Kuno Fischer's *Geschichte der neuern Philosophie*; see Brobjer, *Nietzsche's Philosophical Context: An Intellectual Biography* (Urbana and Chicago: University of Illinois Press, 2008).

28. On the relationship between Spinoza and Nietzsche, see Yirmiyahu Yovel, *Spinoza and Other Heretics: The Adventures of Immanence* (Princeton: Princeton University Press, 1989), chap. 5; Richard Schacht, "The Nietzsche–Spinoza Problem: Spinoza as a Precursor?" in *Making Sense of Nietzsche*, 167–86 (see preface, n. 3); and Michael della Rocca, *Spinoza* (London: Routledge, 2008), 292–303. Schacht's essay usefully stresses not only Spinoza as a precursor to Nietzsche but Nietzsche as a worthy successor of Spinoza, embodying the latter's love of truth and knowledge (see especially 85–86).

29. In a letter to Nietzsche of 31 January 1881, Köselitz comments on GS 112 and suggests that our "sense for causality" is somehow hardwired into our nervous system: see Nietzsche, *Briefwechsel: Kritische Gesamtausgabe*, ed. Colli and Montinari, 2:217–19 (see chap. 1, n. 45). Nietzsche responds on 5 February 1881 that he does not see the "sense for causality" as a permanent fact of our biology but as a contingent product of history. He then asks, "Where does the unconditional belief in the all-validity and all-utility of that sense for causality come from? People like Spencer believe that it is an inference based on countless experiences repeated through many generations. . . . I think this belief [in causality] is a residue of older, much narrower beliefs. Yet why? I am not permitted to write about such a thing, my dear friend, and must point you to the 9th book of *Daybreak* [book 4 of *GS*], where you will see that I at the very least deviate from the thoughts which your letter attributes to me" (*SB* 6:166–67).

30. References to "herd" morality begin to appear in the notebook from 1881 in which Nietzsche announces his discovery of the eternal recurrence (see *KSA* 9:11 [130, 209, 226, 343]).

31. Robert Pippin makes a similar point in his very insightful article, "Nietzsche and the Melancholy of Modernity," *Social Research* 66 (1999): 495–520. He argues there that the madman's guilt-obsessed response to the death of God not only does not corre-

spond to Nietzsche's own attitude but constitutes a psychological portrait of a certain melancholic pathology that is characteristic of modernity. My only reservation about Pippin's argument is that it may go too far in distancing Nietzsche's point of view from that of the madman, at least as far as the latter's (largely correct) diagnosis of the nihilistic implications of the death of God is concerned.

32. Interestingly, in one of the draft notes for this passage, Nietzsche writes that we must become the "mightiest and holiest poet[s]" instead of gods (KSA 9:12 [77]).

33. See BGE 61 for a more complete catalogue of religious utilities.

34. On the "Oriental" element in Judaism and Christianity, see also GS 141 (cf. GS 136, 140).

35. From the very first aphorism of The Gay Science, Nietzsche identifies tragedy with morality and religion: "For the present, we still live in the age of tragedy, the age of moralities and religions" (GS 1).

36. Again see Nietzsche's letter to Köselitz of 20 August 1882 (SB 6:238).

37. Safranski may even overstate the case when he comments: "Even though the idea of recurrence is not placed squarely in the foreground [of The Gay Science], it is still omnipresent behind the scenes" (Nietzsche: A Philosophical Biography, 235).

38. In Ecce Homo, Nietzsche says his "gaya scienza belongs in the interval" between the vision of the eternal recurrence in August 1881 and the completion of part 1 of Zarathustra in February 1883: it "contains a hundred signs of the proximity of something incomparable; in the end it even offers the beginning of Zarathustra, and in the penultimate section of the fourth book the basic idea of Zarathustra" (EH 3.Z.1).

39. On the link between chaos and creativity in Nietzsche's thought, see Rosen (see note 23 above). The problem with Rosen's interpretation is that it pictures this link too melodramatically, implying that the radical chaos and flux of the world licenses unfettered and arbitrary creativity, a "merely willful will to power," as Laurence Lampert puts it (see Nietzsche and Modern Times, 346n17) (see preface, n. 3). Pippin's emphasis on desire and eros instead of arbitrary will and spontaneous creativity serves as a good corrective to Rosen's hyper-voluntarist interpretation (see Nietzsche, Psychology, and First Philosophy, 64, 69, 124).

40. See Nietzsche's 1862 essays "Fate and History" and "Freedom of Will and Fate," translated by George Stack in "Nietzsche's Earliest Essays" (see chap. 1, n. 50).

41. Emerson's original wording in "History" is: "To the poet, to the philosopher, to the saint, all things are friendly and sacred, all events profitable, all days holy, all men divine" (Emerson, Essays and Lectures, 242) (see chap. 1, n. 51).

42. In another entry from this notebook, Nietzsche writes of Emerson: "the author of this century who has been richest in thoughts up till now has been an American (unfortunately clouded by German philosophy—milky glass)" (KSA 9:12 [151]). Walter Kaufmann devotes considerable space to the relationship between Nietzsche and Emerson in the introduction to his translation of The Gay Science (7–13). For a book-length discussion of this relationship that somewhat exaggerates Emerson's influence on Nietzsche, see George J. Stack, Nietzsche and Emerson: An Elective Affinity (Athens: Ohio University Press, 1992).

43. Pippin, Nietzsche, Psychology, and First Philosophy, 63–64, emphasizes this aphorism in connection with his claim about the centrality of desire and eros in Nietzsche's response to nihilism. See also Picht, Nietzsche, 221–28 (see preface, n. 3).

44. This contrasts with Nietzsche's claim in his letter to Overbeck that Spinoza agrees with him that "knowledge [is] the most powerful affect" (SB 6:11).

45. Picht uses this crucial aphorism on "The Fancy [*Wahn*] of the Contemplatives" to bring out the similarities between Nietzsche and Plato on the artistic and legislative character of philosophy (*Nietzsche*, 228–38).

46. Richard Schacht interprets "physics" too literally when he identifies it with natural science in contradistinction to social science, history, and Nietzsche's later notion of "genealogy"; see "Of Morals and Menschen," in *Nietzsche, Genealogy, Morality: Essays on Nietzsche's "On the Genealogy of Morals,"* ed. Richard Schacht (Berkeley and Los Angeles: University of California Press, 1994), 427. There is nothing in GS 335—or *The Gay Science* as a whole—to suggest that Nietzsche identifies the intellectual conscience or knowledge of "everything lawful and necessary in world" with natural science. As Kaufmann points out in his editorial note, Nietzsche seems to be using "physics" in an extended sense, comparable to how he used "chemistry" in *HH* 1. Bagehot used "physics" in just such an extended sense in his *Physics and Politics*, a book with which Nietzsche was very familiar.

47. Berkowitz, *Nietzsche: Ethics of an Immoralist*, 17–18 (see preface, n. 3).

48. Aristotle, *The Politics*, trans. Carnes Lord (Chicago: University of Chicago Press, 1985), 1.5.

49. In the notebook containing excerpts from Emerson's *Essays*, Nietzsche jotted down the following: "I want to live through all of history in my own person and make all power and force my own" (*KSA* 9:17 [4]). This is a rough rendering of a passage from Emerson's essay on "History": "There is no age or state of society or mode of action in history, to which there is not somewhat corresponding in [each man's] life. Every thing tends in a wonderful manner to abbreviate itself and yield its own virtue to him. He should see that he can live all history in his own person" (Emerson, *Essays and Lectures*, 239). In GS 337 this becomes: "Anyone who manages to experience the history of humanity as a whole as *his own history* . . ."

50. Kaufmann's translation of *Menschlichkeit* as "humaneness" has the unfortunate connotation of pity or compassion (especially in the light of the very next aphorism), and "humanity" (which is also used to translate *Mensch* and *Menschheit*) does not quite capture Nietzsche's specific meaning.

51. This opposing of *Mitfreude* to *Mitleid* goes all the way back to Nietzsche's letter to Gersdorff of 13 December 1875 (*SB* 5:129). See also *HH* 499; *AOM* 62.

52. Laurence Lampert, *Nietzsche's Teaching: An Interpretation of "Thus Spoke Zarathustra"* (New Haven and London: Yale University Press, 1986), 168, 198–99, emphasizes that the idea of the eternal recurrence is ultimately directed against the spirit of Socratic rationalism.

53. The analytic breakdown of Nietzsche's idea of the eternal recurrence into a cosmological theory, on the one hand, and an ethical imperative, on the other, goes all the way back to Karl Löwith's 1935 *Nietzsche's Philosophy of the Eternal Recurrence of the Same* (see chap. 1, n. 1); see also *Meaning in History: The Theological Implications of the Philosophy of History* (Chicago: University of Chicago Press, 1957), 214–22. Löwith famously—and, I think, erroneously—saw these two meanings of the eternal recurrence as contradictory to one another. For the rejection of the so-called cosmological interpretation of the eternal recurrence, see Ivan Soll, "Reflections on Recurrence: Nietzsche's Doctrine, *Die Ewige Wiederkehr des Gleichen*," in *Nietzsche: A Collection of Critical Essays*, ed. Robert Solomon (New York: Anchor, 1973): 322–42; Bernd Magnus, *Nietzsche's Existential Imperative* (Bloomington: Indiana University Press, 1978); Nehamas, *Nietzsche: Life as Literature*, chap. 5 (see chap. 1, n. 1); Lampert,

Nietzsche's Teaching, 165–67, 258–60; Clark, *Nietzsche on Truth and Philosophy*, chap. 8; Bernard Reginster, *The Affirmation of Life: Nietzsche on Overcoming Nihilism* (Cambridge, Mass.: Harvard University Press, 2006), chap. 5; Bernard Williams, Introduction to *The Gay Science*, ed. Bernard Williams (Cambridge: Cambridge University Press, 2001), xv–xvii. All of these commentators acknowledge that Nietzsche attempts to provide a scientific demonstration of the eternal recurrence in his unpublished notes, but they find it significant that he did not provide such a scientific demonstration in his published writings (e.g., GS 341). This distinction between unpublished notes and published writings is somewhat artificial, however, given that the scientific proofs of the eternal recurrence in the notes are found side by side with Nietzsche's reflections on the nonanthropomorphic, nonteleological, necessary, mechanistic, and chaotic character of the universe, which in turn find their way into the published text of *The Gay Science*, most importantly in GS 109. In the end, I tend to agree with Heidegger that the unpublished notes are indispensable to understanding Nietzsche's cryptic published communications of the doctrine of the eternal recurrence (see *Nietzsche*, vol. 2: *The Eternal Recurrence of the Same*, 15).

54. On the connection between the total character of the world as chaos and the eternal recurrence, see GS 109.

55. On nihilism as weightlessness and loss of gravity, see Löwith, *Nietzsche's Philosophy of the Eternal Recurrence of the Same*, 36–55; Heidegger, *Nietzsche*, 2:23–24.

56. See also "Schopenhauer as Educator," where Nietzsche speaks of the "turmoil of secularization" in which the educated classes "grow daily more restless, thoughtless, and loveless" (SE 4).

57. Magnus, *Nietzsche's Existential Imperative*, 57, argues that this passage reflects "Nietzsche's uneasy merger of normative imperative and cyclical cosmology," but in fact it clearly discloses just how he understands the relationship between them: because everything we do recurs eternally, it is of the utmost importance that we strive to do whatever gives us the "highest feeling." In Löwith, *Nietzsche's Philosophy of the Eternal Recurrence of the Same*, this "uneasy merger" becomes an outright contradiction.

58. Heidegger, *Nietzsche*, vol. 2: *The Eternal Recurrence of the Same*, 132.

59. Ibid., 135–36. Heidegger's interpretation here contrasts with Löwith's fatalistic interpretation of the eternal recurrence as a "repetition" or "revival" of the ancient doctrine of the eternal cycle of nature; see *Nietzsche's Philosophy of the Eternal Recurrence of the Same*, especially chap. 4; *Meaning in History*, 220–22. It is only on the basis of this fatalistic interpretation of the eternal recurrence that Löwith can argue that Nietzsche's interpretation of the idea as an ethical imperative as well is self-contradictory.

60. Emerson, "Fate," in *Essays and Lectures*, 953. See also Nietzsche's early essays, "Fate and History" and "Freedom of Will and Fate," both written in 1862.

61. Reginster, *The Affirmation of Life*, 224–27, is particularly good on the connection between the idea of the eternal recurrence and the revaluation of values.

62. See Georg Simmel, *Schopenhauer and Nietzsche*, trans. H. Loiskandle, D. Weinstein, and M. Weinstein (Amherst: University of Massachusetts Press, 1986), 172–73; Arthur Danto, *Nietzsche as Philosopher*, expanded ed. (New York: Columbia University Press, 2005), 185–91; and Magnus, *Nietzsche's Existential Imperative*, chap. 4.

63. Soll makes much of this note in "Reflections on Recurrence," 324–26.

64. Magnus, Clark, and Nehamas (see note 53 above), among many other commentators, offer this sort of existential, pragmatic interpretation of the eternal recurrence.

CHAPTER FOUR

1. Ruth Abbey offers nothing so crude as this when she discusses the relationship between Nietzsche's middle and later works in her book on *Nietzsche's Middle Period* (see preface, n. 1). Nevertheless, she, too, seriously underestimates the strengths of the later works when she argues that they represent a narrowing and dogmatic hardening of Nietzsche's philosophical outlook and are far inferior to the middle works in psychological complexity and nuance (see xiv, 156). For a more balanced assessment of the relationship between the middle and later works, see Laurence Lampert, *Nietzsche and Modern Times*, 300–301 (see preface, n. 3).

2. In a note from the winter of 1882–83, Nietzsche characterizes the difference between the pre- and post-*Zarathustra* perspectives in this way: "The *Freigeisterei* itself was moral activity: 1) as honesty; 2) as bravery; 3) as justice; 4) as love. I have left over for myself value-assessment" (*KSA* 10:6 [1]).

3. See note 3 in the preface.

4. In *Nietzsche's Teaching* (see chap. 3, n. 52), his indispensable commentary on *Zarathustra*, Laurence Lampert argues that Nietzsche's teaching on the *Übermensch* is provisional and "rendered obsolete by the clearly definitive teaching on eternal return." He cites the absence of any "call for a superman in the books following *Zarathustra*" as evidence of this (258; see also 80–82, 171). The latter claim strikes me as dubious (see, e.g., *GS* 382), and in general the idea of the eternal recurrence does not seem so much to replace the *Übermensch* ideal as to render it possible. For a different but no more plausible criticism of the *Übermensch* ideal, see Clark, *Nietzsche on Truth and Philosophy*, 270–77 (see preface, n. 4).

5. In the Preface to *HH* 1, Nietzsche makes clear that this stage of reverent submission is not at all an ignoble one. Prior to the "great liberation," the spirit must be fettered. "What fetters the fastest? What bonds are all but unbreakable? In the case of men of a high and select kind they will be their duties: that reverence proper to youth, that reserve and delicacy before all that is honored and revered from of old" (*HH* 1.Preface 3).

6. In his notebooks, Nietzsche evokes the cruelty of the free spirit in terms of the imagery of the lion and the child: "And he didn't know how to overcome his virtue. The lion in him tore to pieces the child in him: and finally the lion ate himself. Cruel was this hero and wild—see, I teach you the love of the *Übermensch* (*KSA* 10:4 [218]).

7. The two most comprehensive commentaries on *Zarathustra* in English seem to take opposite positions on this question; see Lampert, *Nietzsche's Teaching*, 80–84, 157–58, 170–71, 204, 263; Rosen, *The Mask of Enlightenment*, 20 (see preface, n. 3); see also Rosen, *Limits of Analysis*, 214 (see preface, n. 3).

8. See *KSA* 9:11 [141].

9. This, of course, touches on another one of the standard debates that runs through the secondary literature on Nietzsche. Heidegger famously interprets the will to power as a metaphysical doctrine throughout his *Nietzsche* volumes. Lampert agrees, though he sharply rejects Heidegger's claims about Nietzsche as the consummation of modern subjectivity and technological thinking (see *Nietzsche's Teaching*, 111–20, 245–63). On the other hand, Kaufmann, drawing heavily on Nietzsche's middle works, rejects Heidegger's metaphysical interpretation of the will to power and claims that it is "first and foremost the key concept of a psychological hypothesis" (see *Nietzsche: Philosopher, Psychologist, Antichrist*, chap. 6) (see chap. 1, n. 1). Pippin also has reservations about Heidegger's metaphysical interpretation, and this forms the background of his statement that Nietzsche is best understood, not as the "last metaphysician

of the West," but as "one of the great 'French moralists'" (see *Nietzsche, Psychology, and First Philosophy,* 4–9) (see chap. 1, n. 2). Jaspers has a very balanced view of the relationship between Nietzsche's psychological observations about the feeling of power in the middle works and his later doctrine of the will to power: "Nietzsche's conception of the 'will to power' is by no means identical with his conception of the drives that aim to provide a feeling of power. The one relates to genuine being that has become extra-empirical; the other to observable psychological experience. . . . But the psychological is nevertheless an experiential point of departure that provides clarity as well as contrast whenever the will to power is spoken of" (*Nietzsche,* 303) (see preface, n. 3).

10. Compare *GS* 382 on the "ideal of a human, superhuman [*übermenschlichen*] well-being and benevolence that will often appear *inhuman*—for example, when it confronts all earthly seriousness so far, all solemnity in gesture, word, tone, eye, morality, and task so far, as if it were their most incarnate and involuntary parody."

11. On this, see Heidegger's analysis in *Nietzsche,* vol. 2: *The Eternal Recurrence of the Same,* chap. 8 (see chap. 3, n. 2).

12. Schopenhauer, *The World as Will and Representation,* 1:29, 38 (see chap. 1, n. 4).

13. See also the slightly different formulations of this nihilistic doctrine in *Z* 3.12:16 and 3.13.

14. Heidegger sees the relationship between the will to power and the idea of the eternal recurrence differently, arguing that the former grows out of the latter (see *Nietzsche,* vol. 2: *The Eternal Recurrence of the Same,* 153–56; also *Nietzsche,* vol. 3: *The Will to Power as Knowledge and Metaphysics,* 10) (see preface, n. 3). I find Lampert, *Nietzsche's Teaching,* 149–50, more convincing on the relationship between these two doctrines.

15. See *KSA* 9:11 [175–76]; 10:1 [83]; 10:4 [39, 94]; 11:25 [323]; 11:26 [466]; 11:34 [78, 145, 191]; 11:35 [39–41]; and 12:2 [71, 72, 75]).

16. One of the more intriguing references to the "great noon" appears in *Ecce Homo,* where Nietzsche associates it with what Bayreuth used to signify for him: the decisive moment when the "most elect consecrate themselves for the greatest of all tasks" (*EH* 3.BT.4).

17. On Nietzsche's original intention to write a new edition of *Human, All too Human,* see his letters to Elisabeth of 15 August 1885 (*SB* 7:81); to Köselitz of 22 September 1885 (*SB* 7: 94); to Schmeitzner of 20 October 1885 (*SB* 7:103); to Overbeck at the beginning of December 1885 (*SB* 7:117–18); and again to Köselitz of 6 December 1885 (*SB* 7:119–20). On the publication history of *Beyond Good and Evil,* see Schaberg, *The Nietzsche Canon,* 120–28 (see chap. 1, n. 8).

18. See Nietzsche's letters to Credner of mid-January 1886 (*SB* 7:140); to his mother of 30 January 1886 (*SB* 7:144–45); and to Overbeck of 25 March 1886 (*SB* 7:163).

19. See also letters to Credner of 27 March 1886 (*SB* 7:163–64) and the end of March (*SB* 7:168). The title "Beyond Good and Evil" first appears in Nietzsche's notes from the fall of 1882 (*KSA* 10:3 [1]). The title pops up again in his notes from the summer-fall of 1884 (*KSA* 11:26 [139, 221, 241, 297, 325, 467), among other projected titles like "The New Rank Order: Preface to the Philosophy of the Eternal Recurrence" (*KSA* 11:26 [243]), "Philosophy of the Eternal Recurrence: An Attempt at the Revaluation of All Values" (*KSA* 11:26 [259]), "The New Enlightenment: A Preparation for the 'Philosophy of the Eternal Recurrence'" (*KSA* 11:26 [293, 298]), "The Philosophers of the Future" (*KSA* 11:26 [426]), "Noon and Eternity: A Philosophy of the Eternal Recurrence" (*KSA* 11:26 [465]), and "What is Noble? Thoughts on the Order of Rank of Man and Man" (*KSA* 11:26 [468]).

20. Laurence Lampert, *Nietzsche's Task: An Interpretation of "Beyond Good and Evil"* (New Haven and London: Yale University Press, 2001), 3. Lampert's commentary stands out as one of the few sustained attempts to bring out this political (in the broadest possible sense) dimension of *Beyond Good and Evil*. In general, though, I am not as enthusiastic about Nietzsche's "politics" as Lampert seems to be; see especially his *Nietzsche and Modern Times*, 279, where he says of Nietzsche's political philosophy that it "grounds a deep ecology and a new sense of the edifying for the human species."

21. Lampert, *Nietzsche's Task*, 6; see also 61.

22. On Nietzsche's critical attitude toward Jesuitism, see ibid., 14–16, 186–87.

23. Here I differ from Lampert, who denies that Nietzsche questions the value of truth at all in *Beyond Good and Evil*: "The opening question [of *Beyond Good and Evil*] does not remain an open question. Facing up to the deadly question of the value of truth leads ultimately to the affirmation of truth as wholly compatible with the affirmation of life and humanity" (*Nietzsche's Task*, 24).

24. Berkowitz misreads *BGE* 24 when he claims that Nietzsche is expressing disapproval of "the will to knowledge that drives science because it produces pleasing lies" (*Nietzsche: The Ethics of an Immoralist*, 238) (see preface, n. 3). Nietzsche is not criticizing the will to knowledge of the free spirit in this aphorism but merely reminding us that this will never escapes from the apparent world to some sort of error- or perspective-free "real" world.

25. I do not find very convincing Lampert's claim that, when Nietzsche speaks of the historical sense as "our great virtue" in this aphorism, the "our" refers to "we modern humans" rather than "we free spirits" (*Nietzsche's Task*, 216).

26. Picht, *Nietzsche*, 31–131 (see preface, n. 3), makes this notion of the philosopher as *Versucher* central to his interpretation of Nietzsche, using it to counteract Heidegger's metaphysical reading. *Versuch* can also mean "essay," and so the German translations of two of Nietzsche's favorite authors, Montaigne and Emerson, were titled *Versuche*.

27. It is interesting to note that in drafts for this aphorism Nietzsche distinguished, not between "genuine philosophers" and "philosophical laborers," but between "two distinct types of philosophers" (*KSA* 11:26 [407] and 38 [13]). Depending on which sense one is using the term, free spirits can be understood as philosophers or not (see also *KSA* 11:38 [14]).

28. Reflective of this more sympathetic attitude toward religion, especially as a means of shaping human beings, Nietzsche speaks in a note of a "new understanding of religion" and his "sympathy with the pious" (*KSA* 11:27 [79]; see also 34 [176], 37 [8]).

29. Throughout *Beyond Good and Evil*, Nietzsche uses the expression "we free spirits." In a note from the summer of 1885, however, he refers to "we new philosophers" (*KSA* 11:36 [17]).

30. The phrase "slavery in some sense or other" points to Nietzsche's rather broad understanding of this concept. It will be remembered that in *Human, All too Human* he classified as a slave anyone "who does not have two-thirds of his day to himself" (*HH* 283). And in a note from the spring of 1884, he responds to the "radical question" whether "there must be slavery" by claiming that "in truth, there is always slavery, whether you want it or not: for example, the Prussian civil servant, the scholar, the monk" (*KSA* 11:25 [225]).

31. The dialectical relationship between "democratic dwarfing" and aristocratic enhancement is a prominent theme in Nietzsche's later notes (see *WP* 864, 866, 888–901, 954, 956).

32. Lampert captures this Platonic aspect of *Beyond Good and Evil* nicely: "This book of anti-Platonism . . . ends on a Platonic theme, the best social order and the philosopher who rules it. The whole second division of the book, chapters 5–8, has prepared this culmination" (*Nietzsche's Task*, 262). Contrast this with Berkowitz's claim that in the final three-and-a-half chapters of *Beyond Good and Evil* Nietzsche "initiates a visible though unheralded retreat from the idea of that the philosopher is a commander and legislator" (*Nietzsche: The Ethics of an Immoralist*, 247, 248). This latter claim is very hard to square with the emphasis on the order of rank in "What is Noble" and the references to "spiritual tyrants" and "ruling castes" in "Peoples and Fatherlands."

33. Ansell-Pearson interprets Nietzsche's conception of great politics too literally in his *Introduction to Nietzsche as Political Thinker* (see chap. 1, n. 72) and as a result draws the contrast between the political outlooks of the middle and later periods too starkly: "In his mature political thinking Nietzsche accepts a machiavellism which in the thought of his middle period he associates with the despotism of socialism and clearly rejects because of its reliance on force and deception" (96–97). Ansell-Pearson finds this later "machiavellian-inspired immoral politics" not only in *Beyond Good and Evil* but, even more puzzlingly, in the fifth book of *The Gay Science* (148).

34. A number of writers have drawn attention to Nietzsche's rhetorical irresponsibility in this regard; see Leo Strauss, *An Introduction to Political Philosophy: Ten Essays by Leo Strauss*, ed. Hilail Gildin (Detroit: Wayne State University Press, 1989), 56–57, 98; Werner Dannhauser, "Friedrich Nietzsche," in *History of Political Philosophy*, 3rd edition, ed. Leo Strauss and Joseph Cropsey (Chicago: University of Chicago Press, 1987), 849; Rosen, *The Ancients and the Moderns*, 190, 206 (see preface, n. 3).

35. Schaberg, *The Nietzsche Canon*, 149. The original title page of *Genealogy* bore the following notice: "An addition to the last published *Beyond Good and Evil* which is meant as a supplement and clarification."

36. In his notebooks, Nietzsche calls this his "chief proposition" (*WP* 258). In the same note, he also refers to his "attempt to understand moral judgments as symptoms and sign languages which betray the processes of physiological prosperity or failure" (see also *TI* Improvers 1). One of the earliest examples of Nietzsche's symptomological approach to religion and morality appears in the section "On the Afterworldly" in part 1 of *Zarathustra*. There Nietzsche speaks of suffering, incapacity, and weariness as the source of all afterworlds: "It was the sick and decaying who despised body and earth and invented the heavenly realm and the redemptive drops of blood" (*Z* 1.3).

37. In the same notebook in which this note on master and slave moralities appears, we also find Nietzsche's first formulation that morality is "a sign-language of the affects" (see *KSA* 10:7 [47, 60]).

38. In another late note, Nietzsche writes: "It should be added that the seductive force of the Christian ideal works most strongly perhaps upon such natures as love danger, adventure, and opposition—as love all that involves risking themselves while at the same time engendering a *non plus ultra* of the feeling of power" (*WP* 216; cf. *BGE* 51 on the profound effect the ascetic saint had on powerful individuals).

39. See Reginster, "Nietzsche on Selflessness and the Value of Altruism," 184–85 (see chap. 1, n. 40), on the shift in Nietzsche's later works away from the question of the *possibility* of altruism to the question of its *value*.

40. In *Beyond Selflessness*, Janaway argues that Rée is the prime referent in Nietzsche's discussion of the "English psychologists" in *GM* 1.1–3: "The theory under discussion in *GM*, I, 1–3 is Rée's pure and simple" (78–82) (see chap. 2, n. 25). See also Clark

and Swenson's note in their edition of *On the Genealogy of Morality* (Indianapolis: Hackett, 1998), 129. Nietzsche read Rée's book on *The Origin of Conscience* in 1885 and found it quite disappointing, though well written; see his letters to von Stein of 15 October 1885 and Overbeck of 17 October 1885 and the beginning of December 1885 (*SB* 7:99, 102, 118).

41. In one of his notes, Nietzsche underlines how his analysis of the morality of custom illustrates this crucial canon of historical or genealogical method: "There is lacking a knowledge and consciousness of the revolutions that have already occurred in moral judgments, and of how fundamentally 'evil' has several times been renamed 'good.' I indicated one of these displacements with the term 'morality of custom'" (*WP* 265).

42. Anderson, "Overcoming Charity," 328–33, has a good discussion of Nietzsche's identification of the will to truth with the ascetic ideal in *GM* 23–27 (see chap. 1, n. 23). He maintains that Nietzsche's argument in these sections poses serious problems for Clark's attempt to free Nietzsche of the falsification thesis in her *Nietzsche on Truth and Philosophy* (see chap. 1, n. 13).

43. The Preface is dated Spring 1886. In a letter to Fritzsch of 16 August 1886, Nietzsche writes that he composed the Preface during the final month of his stay in Nice—which would have been April 1886—and that he has made a couple of improvements to it over the summer in Sils. He adds that the Preface "is an essential contribution to the understanding of my books and of the hard to understand self-development lying at their foundation" (*SB* 7:228).

44. At the end of the Preface, Nietzsche states that "no psychologist or reader of signs will have a moment's difficulty in recognizing to what stage in the evolution just described the present book belongs (or has been *placed*)" (*HH* 1.Preface 8). As indicated above, I would argue that *Human, All too Human* contains elements of both the first and second stages.

45. Amy Mullin, in her illuminating article "Nietzsche's Free Spirit," *Journal of the History of Philosophy* 38 (2000): 383–405, puts special emphasis on the free spirit's mastery over his virtues.

46. Nietzsche writes in this letter: "So I am finished, still before the end of the year, with everything that I planned to do for the good of my earlier writings. The last—which has reached you as a manuscript along with this letter—is the final (fifth) part of *The Gay Science*, which was always planned but never completed because of unfortunate health problems at the time" (*SB* 7:296).

47. An exception is Laurence Lampert in *Nietzsche and Modern Times*, chaps. 12–14. In keeping with the larger theme of his book, which focuses on Bacon, Descartes, and Nietzsche as philosophical legislators, Lampert treats book 5 of *The Gay Science* largely in terms of Nietzsche's "great politics." My focus on the theme of the non-legislative free spirit leads in the opposite direction.

48. See *HH* 483, 629–36.

49. In this aphorism, Nietzsche shows an awareness of the genetic fallacy, the fallacy of confusing questions of origin with questions of value or validity. In the same notebook that contains a draft of *GS* 345 (see *KSA* 12:2 [163]), Nietzsche penned a note that clearly repudiates the genetic fallacy: "The inquiry into the *origin of our evaluations* and tables of good is in absolutely no way identical with a critique of them, as is so often believed: even though the insight into some *pudenda origo* certainly brings with it *a feeling* of a diminution in value of the thing that originated thus and pre-

pares the way to a critical mood and attitude toward it" (*KSA* 12:2 [189]). Again in the same notebook, he writes: "*Origin* and *critique* of moral valuations. These two do *not* coincide, as is too easily believed" (*KSA* 12:2 [131]).

50. See *KSA* 12:2 [197] for the draft version of this argument.

51. Nihilism emerges as an important theme in the notebook of Fall 1885–Fall 1886 (see *KSA* 12:2 [127, 131]).

52. "The opposition is dawning between the world we revere and the world which we live, which we—are. It remains for us to abolish either our reverences or ourselves. The latter would be nihilism" (*KSA* 12:2 [131]).

53. See Heidegger, *Nietzsche*, vol. 3: *The Will to Power as Knowledge and Metaphysics*, 178–80, 216–34; *Nietzsche*, vol. 4: *Nihilism*, 28–29, 86 (see chap. 1, n. 66).

54. In a note from 1885, after describing the genuinely wise man as the free-spirited philosopher who has "tried out life personally in a hundred ways," Nietzsche comments that the "wise man has for too long been confused with the scholar, and even longer with the religious enthusiast" (*KSA* 11:35 [24]).

55. Nietzsche's draft note for this aphorism makes clear the connection between the concept of "knowledge" under discussion and "science": "*Fear of the unpredictable* as the *hidden instinct* of science" (*KSA* 12:5 [10]; see also 5 [14, 16]).

56. Nietzsche's concern with the problem of consciousness was evident in the original edition of *The Gay Science* (see, e.g., *GS* 11, 333). And in a letter to Lou Salomé written shortly after finishing *The Gay Science* (in September 1882), he proudly announced his discovery of the relationship between his notion of the "herd" and the origin of language: "The greatest confirmation of my herd-instinct theory came to me most recently in reflection on the origin of language" (*SB* 6:252).

57. In a draft note for this aphorism, Nietzsche makes the connection between the critique of "purpose" and the critique of will: "But with this [critique of purpose], we have subjected the *will itself* to critique: is it not an illusion to take as a cause what appears in consciousness as an act of will? Are all the phenomena of consciousness not merely final phenomena . . . ?" (*KSA* 12:7 [1]; see also 1 [20], 2 [83]).

58. Lampert is very good on distinguishing Nietzsche from "mere existentialism"; see *Nietzsche's Task*, 198–99; *Nietzsche and Modern Times*, 353.

59. See the chapter on "Why in Ages of Equality and Skepticism It is Important to Set Distant Goals," in Tocqueville, *Democracy in America*, vol. 2, pt. 2, chap. 17 (see chap. 1, n. 27).

60. Though there is not space to develop it, *GS* 362–63 on Napoleon and the different opinions the sexes have about love, serve as counterpoints to the actor's mentality described here. Napoleon is said to have "brought back again a whole slab of antiquity, perhaps even the decisive piece, the piece of granite" (*GS* 362). And the different ideas about love that men and women hold point to natural limits on the malleability of roles (*GS* 363). Lampert considers the latter aphorism to be both numerologically and philosophically the central aphorism of book 5 (see *Nietzsche and Modern Times*, 368–87).

61. Ansell-Pearson, *An Introduction to Nietzsche as Political Thinker*, 148–50, cites this aphorism as emblematic of Nietzsche's later, "machiavellian-inspired immoral politics," but it is far more emblematic of the antipolitics of his middle period. Ansell-Pearson draws particular attention to Nietzsche's reference to a "new kind of enslavement," but as I have pointed out before, Nietzsche has a rather broad and unconventional understanding of this notion (see note 27 above).

62. Nietzsche quotes this entire aphorism in *EH* 3.Z.2. Interestingly, he comments that the great health is the physiological presupposition of Zarathustra as a type. Does this suggest that Zarathustra is the highest type of free spirit and not the *Übermensch*?

63. Again, contra Lampert (see note 4 in this chapter).

EPILOGUE

1. Bloom, *Closing of the American Mind*, 214 (see preface, n. 3).

2. Detwiler, I think, is guilty of this in his *Nietzsche and the Politics of Aristocratic Radicalism* (see preface, n. 4). Dannhauser, who otherwise has many acute things to say about Nietzsche's politics, also seems to overstate the case when he attributes to Nietzsche the desire for a "eugenics program"; see "Friedrich Nietzsche," 848 (see chap. 4, n. 34).

INDEX

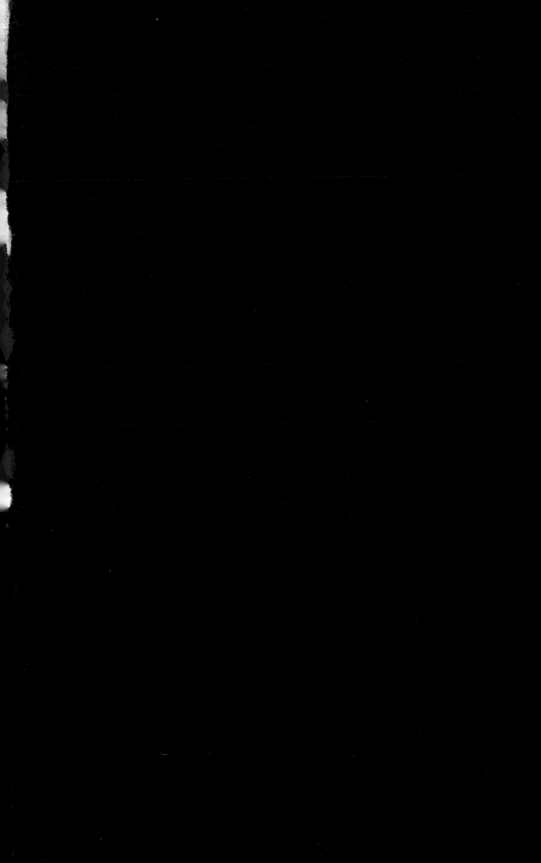